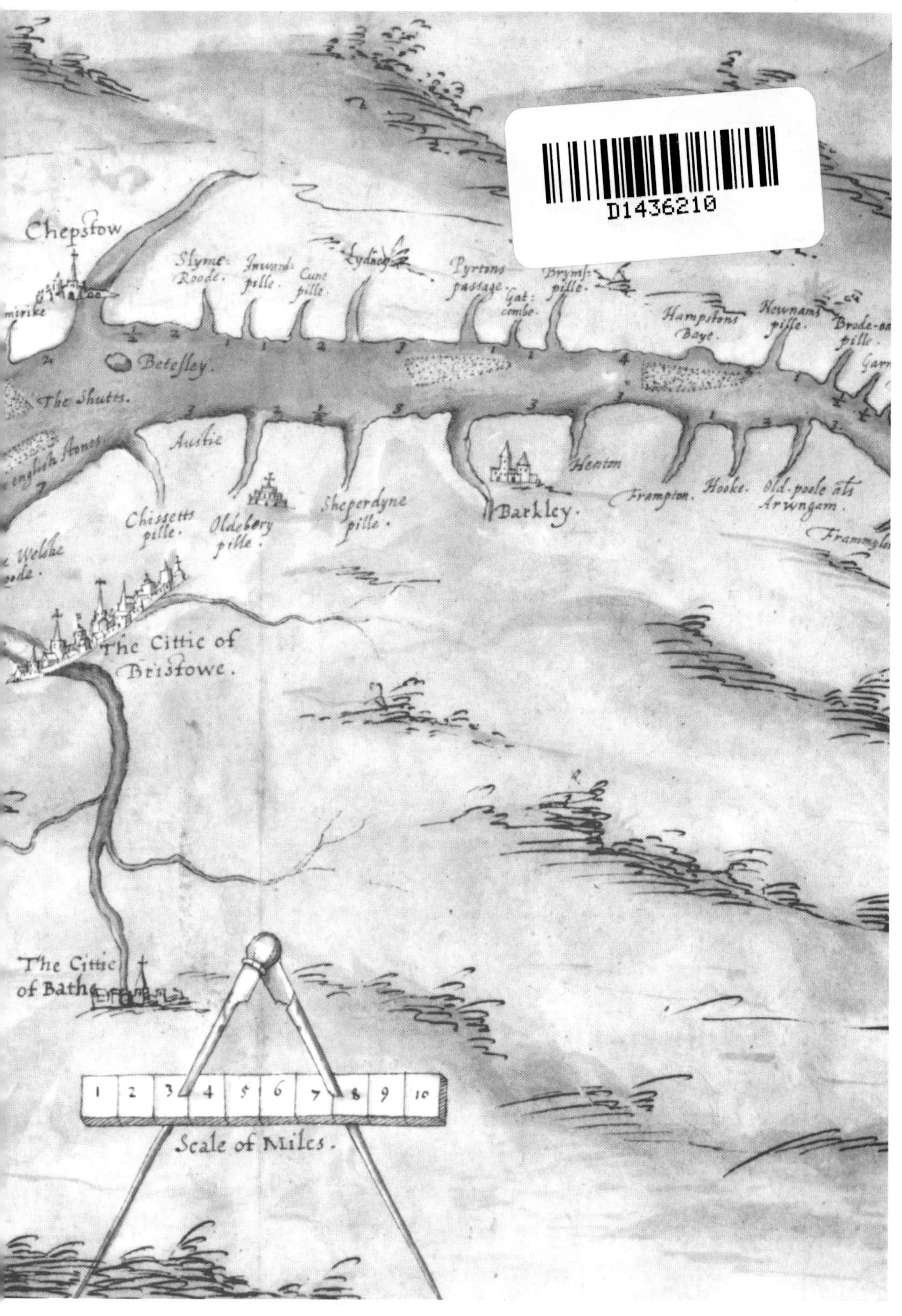
D1436210
Chepstow
Slyme Roode.
Inward pille.
Cune pille.
Lydney
Pyrtons passage.
Gat combe.
Bryms pille.
Hampstons Baye.
Newnams pille.
Betesley.
The Shutts.
Austie
Henton
Barkley.
Frampton.
Hooke.
Old-poole als Arwngam.
Chissetts pille.
Oldebery pille.
Sheperdyne pille.
The Cittie of Bristowe.
The Cittie of Bathe
1 2 3 4 5 6 7 8 9 10
Scale of Miles.

Publications of the South Wales Record Society
No 14

THE LETTER-BOOK OF JOHN BYRD

The Letter-book of John Byrd: Part of Letter 95 to Michael Sansom, dated Caerleon 26 January 1649 [i.e. 1650]

The Letter-Book of
JOHN BYRD
Customs Collector in South-East Wales
1648-80

Edited by

Stephen K. Roberts

With best wishes
Stephen K. Roberts

Cardiff:
South Wales Record Society
1999

Published by the South Wales Record Society
12 The Green, Radyr, Cardiff CF15 8BR

First Published 1999

ISBN 0 9525961 4 8

Printed by Brynymor Press

CONTENTS

	page
ILLUSTRATIONS	vi
ACKNOWLEDGEMENTS	vii
ABBREVIATIONS	ix
INTRODUCTION	
I: The Life and Career of John Byrd	xi
II: Customs Administration in the time of John Byrd	xvi
III: The Bristol Channel and its Trade in the Mid-seventeenth Century	xxi
IV: Customs Administration in South Wales	xxii
V: The Public Service Ethos of John Byrd	xxviii
VI: John Byrd and Politics	xxxviii
VII: Conclusion	xliii
VIII: A Note on the Letter-Book and this Edition	xlv
THE LETTER-BOOK	1
NOTES ON THE TEXT	202
JOHN BYRD'S CORRESPONDENTS: BIOGRAPHICAL NOTES	225
GLOSSARY OF WORDS AND PHRASES	243
GLOSSARY OF PLACES	259
INDEX OF PERSONAL NAMES AND PLACES	263
INDEX OF SUBJECTS	276

ILLUSTRATIONS

Late Elizabethan map of the River Severn and Bristol Channel, Gloucester to Cardiff. British Library, MS Cotton Augustus I ii 17. By permission of the British Library. Endpapers

The Letter-Book of John Byrd, By permission of the Glamorgan Archivist. Frontispiece

'Plan de Cardiff', c. 1650. A French plan after John Speed, 1610. British Library, Add. 11564 fos. 6v-7. By permission of the British Library. 36

The Bristol custom house in the time of John Byrd. From James Millerd, *An Exact Delineation of the Famous Cittie of Bristol* (Bristol, 1671). By permission of Bristol Museums and Art Gallery. 54

The London custom house in the time of John Byrd. Engraved by Bartholmew Howlett from a print dated 1663. By permission of Guildhall Library, London. 96

Impression of the customer's cocket seal for tonnage and poundage, creek of Chepstow, port of Cardiff, c. 1605. D.H. Williams, *Catalogue of the Seals in the National Museum of Wales* i (Cardiff, 1993), W231. By permission of the National Museums and Galleries of Wales. 130

Impression of the controller's cocket seal, creek of Swansea, port of Cardiff, c. 1649. D.H. Williams, *Catalogue of the Seals in the National Museum of Wales* i (Cardiff, 1993), W274. By permission of the National Museums and Galleries of Wales. 130

The Families of Byrd and Seys Endpiece

ACKNOWLEDGEMENTS

I am grateful to the committees of the Glamorgan County History Trust and the Marc Fitch Fund for their generous awards, which helped me undertake the research necessary to prepare this edition.

Brian Ll. James has been a supportive and understanding General Editor at every stage of the process by which John Byrd's manuscript has been made a book. He and Hilary M. Thomas checked my transcript for errors; their labours have ensured that the final text is as exactly near Byrd's original as is practicable. Philip Riden first suggested the manuscript as a South Wales Record Society text, and helped arrange the photocopies from which this edition was prepared. Dr Gerald Aylmer encouraged me to pursue the idea of an edition of Byrd's letters, and shared with me his unrivalled knowledge of government personnel in the 1650s.

In pursuit of the often elusive John Byrd, I have had to range widely, and have incurred many debts to individuals and institutions.

The following individual people have kindly answered queries or helped with materials and in other ways: Ms Jayne Armstrong, Miss J. F. Bischoff, Dr Colin Brooks, Mr Michael Byrd; Mr M. R. Cadogan, Ms Susan Campbell, Revd Dr G.A. Hodge, Prof John Miller, Revd Dr G. F. Nuttall, Dr Stephen Porter, Mr R. Gwyn Thomas, Mr Robert Yorke. Mr Ian McMillan deserves thanks for doing so much to make coastal cruising on sea routes known to John Byrd still possible for the general public.

I am grateful to the staff and representatives of the following institutions and bodies for their help: Birmingham Central Libraries; Bodleian Library; Bristol Record Office; British Library Depts. of Manuscripts and Printed Books; Brogdale Horticultural Trust; Cardiff City Library; Cheshire Record Office; College of Arms; Dublin City Archives; East Sussex Archives; The Archivist, Eton College Library; Faringdon Local History Society; Flintshire Record Office; Glamorgan Archive Service; Gloucestershire Record Office; Guildhall Library, London; Gwent Record Office; HM Customs and Excise Library Services and Records Management Services; History of Parliament Trust; House of Lords Record Office; John Rylands University Library, Manchester; Merseyside Maritime Museum; National Library of Wales; National Museum and Gallery of Wales; Newport Library; Oxford English Dictionary, Oxford University Press; Oxfordshire Record Office; Public Record Office; Royal Commission on Historical Manuscripts; Royal Commission on Historical Monuments of England; Royal Commission on Historical Monuments of Wales; Society of Genealogists, London; University of Birmingham Library; University of London Institute of Historical Research; University of London Library; The

Worshipful Company of Skinners, London.

The members of seminars at The Centre for Advanced Welsh and Celtic Studies, Aberystwyth, University of Wales, Cardiff and members of the Seventeenth Century British History seminar at the Institute of Historical Research patiently listened to material now incorporated into this book, and I am grateful for their comments and advice.

All this help and advice notwithstanding, I alone am responsible for any errors and misinterpretations which may be found in this book.

The final obligations I should like to note are more personal ones. Carolyn, Tom, Ellie and Huw have prevented me from adopting the identity of John Byrd. My parents have helped in more ways than they can realise. Part of the pleasure in working on John Byrd has been in mentally and physically travelling the landscape of Glamorgan and Monmouthshire where I grew up and where I first became fascinated by history. Much of that fascination was fostered by my four grandparents, to whose memory I dedicate this book. The legend once guarded by the cats at Ewenni evokes their example and their values: *gwell crefft na golud.*

Stephen K. Roberts

The Editor and the South Wales Record Society record their thanks to the Glamorgan Archivist for so readily granting permission to publish the text of the Letter-book of John Byrd.

ABBREVIATIONS

Throughout this book, the place of publication of works is London, except where otherwise specified; and JB stands for John Byrd.

Abbott, *Writings and Speeches*	W.C. Abbott, *Writings and Speeches of Oliver Cromwell* (4 vols., Cambridge, Mass., 1937-47)
Aylmer, List	G.E. Aylmer, 'List of Central Officeholders, 1640-1660', typescript, Institute of Historical Research, London
Aylmer, *SS*	G.E. Aylmer, *The State's Servants* (1973)
BBCS	*Bulletin of the Board of Celtic Studies*
BL	British Library
Beaven, *Aldermen*	A.B. Beaven, *The Aldermen of the City of London* (2 vols., 1908)
Beaven, *Bristol Lists*	A.B. Beaven, *Bristol Lists* (Bristol, 1900)
Besse, *Sufferings*	J. Besse, *A Collection of the Sufferings of the People called Quakers* (2 vols., 1753)
Bodl.	Bodleian Library, Oxford
Boyd's Inhabitants of London	Numbered typescript notes in Society of Genealogists, London
Bradney	J.A. Bradney, *A History of Monmouthshire* (4 vols., 1904-33; vol. 5, ed. M. Gray, National Library of Wales and South Wales Record Society Publications no. 8, Aberystwyth and Cardiff, 1993).
BRO	Bristol Record Office
Capp	B. Capp, *Cromwell's Navy* (Oxford, 1989)
CCC	M.A.E. Green (ed.), *Calendar of the Committee for Compounding with Delinquents* (5 vols., 1889-92)
Chandaman	C.D. Chandaman, *The English Public Revenue, 1660-1688* (Oxford, 1975)
CJ	*Journals of the House of Commons*
CSPD	*Calendar of State Papers Domestic*
CSPI	*Calendar of State Papers, Ireland*
CTB	*Calendar of Treasury Books*
Dale, *Inhabitants of London*	T.C. Dale, *The Inhabitants of London in 1638* (1931)
Deposition Books of Bristol	H. E. Nott (ed.), *The Deposition Books of Bristol vol. i: 1643-1647* (Bristol Record Society Publications, 1935); H.E. Nott and E. Ralph (eds.), *vol. ii: 1650-54* (Bristol Record Society Publications, 1948).
Diary of Walter Powell	J.A. Bradney (ed.), *The Diary of Walter Powell of Llantilio Crossenny* (Bristol, 1907)
Dircks	H. Dircks, *The Life, Times and Scientific Labours of the Second Marquis of Worcester* (1865)
DNB	*Dictionary of National Biography*
Dodd, *Studies*	A.H. Dodd, *Studies in Stuart Wales* (2nd ed., Cardiff, 1971)
DWB	*Dictionary of Welsh Biography*
F&R	C.H. Firth, R.S. Rait (eds.), *Acts and Ordinances of the Interregnum* (3 vols. 1911)
Firth and Davies, *Reg. Hist.*	C.H. Firth, G. Davies, *The Regimental History of Cromwell's Army* (2 vols., Oxford, 1940)
Glam. Co. Hist.	G. Williams (ed.), *Glamorgan County History vol. iv* (Cardiff, 1974)
Glamorgan Hearth Tax	E. Parkinson (ed.), *The Glamorgan Hearth Tax of 1670* (Publications of the South Wales Record Society, x, 1994)

GRO	Glamorgan Record Office (Glamorgan Archive Service)
Gweithiau Morgan Llwyd	*Gweithiau Morgan Llwyd* i (ed. T.E. Ellis, Bangor, 1899); ii (ed. J. H. Davies, Bangor, 1908); iii (ed. J.G. Jones, G. W. Owen, Cardiff, 1994)
Herbert Correspondence	W.J. Smith (ed.), *Herbert Correspondence* (Cardiff, 1968)
HLRO	House of Lords Record Office
HMC	*Historical Manuscripts Commission*
House of Commons 1660-1690	B.D. Henning (ed.), *The History of Parliament. The House of Commons, 1660-1690* (3 vols., 1983)
Huygens	Lodewijck Huygens, *The English Journal 1651-1652,* ed. A.G.H. Bachrach, R.G. Collmer (Leiden, Brill, 1982)
Latimer	J. Latimer, *The Annals of Bristol in the Seventeenth Century* (Bristol, 1900)
Leech, *Topography*	R.H. Leech, *The Topography of Medieval and Early Modern Bristol* (Publications of the British Record Society xlviii, 1997)
Limbus Patrum	G.T.Clark, *Limbus Patrum Morganiae et Glamorganiae* (1886)
List of Sheriffs	*List of Sheriffs* (Public Record Office, List and Index ix)
Merchant Venturers	P. McGrath (ed.), *Records relating to the Society of Merchant Venturers of the City of Bristol in the Seventeenth Century* (Publications of the Bristol Record Society, 1952)
Merchants and Merchandise	P. McGrath (ed.), *Merchants and Merchandise in Seventeenth Century Bristol* (Publications of the Bristol Record Society, 1955)
NLW	National Library of Wales
OED	*Oxford English Dictionary*
Orridge, *Citizens of London*	B. B. Orridge, *Some Account of the Citizens of London* (1867)
Pepys	R.C. Latham, W. Matthews (eds.), *The Diary of Samuel Pepys* (11 vols., 1970-83)
Pepys, *Companion*	Latham and Matthews (eds.), *Diary of Samuel Pepys vol. x: Companion* (1983)
Phillips, *Civil War*	J. R. Phillips, *Memoirs of the Civil War in Wales and the Marches* (2 vols., 1874)
Phillips, *Justices*	J.R.S. Phillips, *Justices of the Peace in Wales and Monmouthshire, 1558-1714* (Cardiff, 1975)
PR	Parish Register
PRO	Public Record Office
RCAHMW	Royal Commission on Ancient and Historical Monuments in Wales
Richards, 'Eglwys Llanfaches'	T. Richards, 'Eglwys Llanfaches', *Transactions of the Hon. Society of Cymmrodorion* , 1941
Richards, *Puritan Movement*	T. Richards, *History of the Puritan Movement in Wales, 1639-53* (1920)
RO	Record Office
Sea Officers	D. Syrett, R.L. DiNardo (eds.), *The Commissioned Sea Officers of the Royal Navy, 1660-1815* (Occasional Publications of the Navy Record Society, i, Aldershot, 1994)
South Wales and Mon. Rec. Soc.	South Wales and Monmouthshire Record Society
Thurloe State Papers	*State Papers of John Thurloe* (7 vols., ed. T. Birch, 1742)
Visitations in Wales	M.P. Siddons (ed.), *Visitations by the Heralds in Wales* (Harleian Soc., 1996)
Wadmore, *Skinners*	J.F. Wadmore, *Some Account of the Worshipful Company of Skinners of London* (1902)
Williams, *Parliamentary History*	W.R. Williams, *The Parliamentary History of the Principality of Wales...1541-1895* (Brecon, 1895)

INTRODUCTION

I: The Life and Career of John Byrd

The letter-book of John Byrd leaves us few insights into the early life of its author, and in seeking his identity there are many of his name in the public records of seventeenth-century England and Wales from whom to choose.[1] We know that he was well enough acquainted with forms of law to offer informed judgments on quasi-legal matters; we know that he was of sufficient standing to make a credible match with the Monmouthshire branch of the Seys family; and he tells us that he was not Welsh by birth [**310**]. His letters speak of his kinship ties with the Hands, Hann or Hamme family, and of course with the family of Pennant, and his brother William. From this meagre background, the search for the origins of John Byrd can at least be narrowed, and the balance of probability is tilted heavily in favour of Bristol as the place of his birth. With a large measure of confidence, we can pin down his date of birth to May 1594, as he was baptised in the ancient city parish of St Werburgh on the 20th of that month.[2] He was the third son (brother William being the eldest) of William Byrd gentleman and his wife Mary, whose maiden name was Langford. William and Mary had married in 1591 in the same parish[3], and both families were of substance and standing in Bristol. John Byrd's grandfather had undoubtedly been the most distinguished of his name in the city, and was the first William Byrd to settle there. The Byrds had come originally from Huntley, near Gloucester, but William became a very successful Bristol woollen-draper, with property in the parishes of St Werburgh and St Ewen's. He became sheriff of Bristol in 1573, and mayor in 1590. When he died later that year, he left a large bequest for a hospital in Bristol, a pet scheme of his which became Queen Elizabeth's hospital, made further careful arrangements to benefit the poor of Bristol, Huntley and Newent, and showered his numerous family with thoughtful legacies. He is commemorated in an impressive tomb in the Mayor's Chapel on College Green. [4]

John Byrd's father, William, was the youngest son of the eminent woollen-draper, and although he therefore did not inherit the bulk of his father's estate, he was certainly comfortable, enjoying the title 'gentleman' and achieving parish office in St Werburgh, where he took over the family's leases of parish property.

[1]For a misidentification of JB with the family which provided stewards to the earls of Bute in a later period, P. Jenkins, '"The Old Leaven": The Welsh Roundheads after 1660', *Historical Journal* xxiv (1981), 823.

[2]BRO FCP/St W/R 1(a)1.

[3]FCP/St W/R 1(a)3.

[4]PRO PROB 11/76/71; Betty R. Masters, Elizabeth Ralph (eds.), *The Church Book of St Ewen's, Bristol 1454-1584* (Pubs. of the Bristol and Gloucestershire Archaeological Society vi, 1967), many refs. inc. 180, 199, 213, 221, 250; W.R. Barker, 'On the Later Monuments etc. in the Mayor's Chapel, Bristol', *Trans. Bristol and Glos. Arch. Soc.* xv (1890-1), 79; A. E. Hudd, 'Two Bristol Calendars', ibid., xix (1894-5), 135-6; T.P. Wadley, *Notes or Abstracts of the Wills Contained ... in the Great Orphans Book ... Bristol* (Bristol, 1886), 256-7.

His marriage to Mary Langford in 1591 and the property deals in which he was involved in the early 1590s with leading Bristol citizens such as Hierom Ham, the city clerk, suggested that he was poised to repeat the pattern set by his father, and that the six children born to him would enjoy a secure status in their native city.[5] Such expressions of confidence would come less easily to people of the seventeenth century than to those of the twentieth; in the event William Byrd was dead by January 1598, leaving his family with an uncertain future.[6]

As the third son of a youngest son, John Byrd would have needed to make his way in the world, but the death of his father when he was only three made his position even more precarious. It is not known where he was educated, but it was likely to have been at the grammar school in Bristol. What he did subsequently is also unknown, although by 1614 he may have been the John Byrd paying duties in St Werburgh, where his mother remained.[7] His situation was transformed by the marriage of his widowed mother, some time soon after 1599, to John Dowell or Dowle, a merchant of comparable status to that of her late husband. John Dowell and Mary Langford had many children of their own, and relations between the stepchildren were strained enough to lead later to a chancery case in 1641, when two of John Byrd's brothers took to court a claim against their half-brother Robert Dowell.[8] But even in this poisoned atmosphere John Dowell was accounted a loving stepfather, and he helped John Byrd in two particular ways. First he introduced him to the Middle Temple, a London inn of court, a place which was for many gentry merely a finishing-school, but which provided Byrd with a legal training he could use. Byrd went to the Middle Temple in June 1616, at the age of twenty-one: late, for most gentlemen, but not exceptionally so.[9] It was probably during this period in London that Byrd first met Thomas Pennant, scrivener and member of the London company of skinners, who was serving his apprenticeship when Byrd was at the inn. There is no evidence to support or refute the point, but it is at least possible that during this period Byrd may have married for the first time.[10] With no estate or patrimony to rely upon, Byrd needed employment, and stepfather Dowell here assisted him in a second crucial way. Dowell was customer, or senior customs official, in the port

[5]BRO P/St. W/chw/3 (a) fos. 62v, 63r, 65r, 66r, 67r, 68r; city deeds 26166/273; 00349(2).

[6]PROB 11/91/2.

[7]P/St W/chw/3(a) fos. 91v, 93r, v.

[8]PRO C 2/CHAS I/B136/63.

[9] H.A.C. Sturgess, *Register of Admissions to the Honourable Society of the Middle Temple* (1949), 105.

[10]This might account for the relationship of brother-in-law he held with Thomas Pennant, which it has not yet proved possible to clarify; alternatively, given the looseness with which the term 'brother' could be used, to refer to the in-laws of a spouse, the link could be an as yet untraced one with one of the Seys family.

of Bristol, and it was at least partly by this means that Byrd would have come to the attention of the farmers of the customs, his future employers.

What Byrd was doing in the 1620s remains a mystery, and it is not yet known exactly in what circumstances John Byrd met Margery Seys and found employment in the customs service. It is clear, however, that he was in post as comptroller of customs in the port of Cardiff by December 1629.[11] No record of his appointment has yet been traced, but evidence from after 1660 suggests that he held his office by a patent at the pleasure of the king, as did most officers in the customs service.[12] It seems likely that he acquired the office either through contacts he had made in the London custom house while in London or through the good offices of John Dowell. It is also certain that he had married Margery Seys by May 1632: she was born around 1615, and was thus some twenty-one years younger than her husband.[13] In February 1633 he bought a substantial property in Caerleon which it has been suggested was Millbrook House, on Mill Street.[14] He was the overseer of the will of his father-in-law, Alexander Seys, in 1632, when Seys bestowed the bulk of his property on his youngest son, another Alexander, who died unmarried in 1642, making Byrd and his wife his principal heirs.[15]

The Seys family were long-established in South Wales. Roger Seys of Lincoln's Inn had in 1579 been appointed steward of the Glamorgan and Monmouthshire manors of the earl of Pembroke, and the earl's eventual petition against him for oppressing the tenantry of Vale of Glamorgan manors did nothing to inhibit the upward social mobility of the family.[16] After the death of Roger the family divided into the Glamorgan branch, headed by his eldest son, Richard, who had ten children - settled in the Vale of Glamorgan, Swansea, Neath and Gower - and the cadet Monmouthshire branch, founded by John Byrd's father-in-law, Alexander, the second son of Roger Seys.[17] The family connections with the earls of Pembroke remained strong two generations after Roger Seys. Evan Seys, the prominent judge and MP and an ally of John Byrd after the restoration, inherited Boverton Place, a mansion house in the demesne of Boverton and Llantwit manor, property of the earl of Pembroke, while Alexander, and subsequently John Byrd himself, was free tenant of many Pembroke holdings in

[11]PRO E 190/1274/18.

[12]PRO SP 29/53/68.

[13]PROB 11/162/107; Gwent RO MAN B/15/0007.

[14]GRO D/DF Deeds 2919; Eija Kennerley, MS History of Caerleon, Newport Reference Library.

[15]PROB 11/189/56.

[16]GRO D/DF M/395; NLW Bute M5/392. RCAHMW, *Glamorgan Vol. IV, Pt. I,* 126.

[17]Clark, *Limbus Patrum*, 218-21; Bradney ii (pt.i), 94-5. *Limbus Patrum* is the fuller pedigree, but both are to be approached with caution. Both, for example, give JB's wife as 'Margaret' not Margery.

and around Caerleon. Boverton and Llantwit in Glamorgan, and Caerleon in Monmouthshire, shared similar manorial customs. Both Pembroke manors were largely composed of lands held by custom of the court roll, where lands could be alienated with few restrictions, where exchanges and purchases were relatively simple, and where customary land was thus as attractive a proposition for investors as freehold land.[18] In these circumstances both branches of the Seys family flourished.

By the terms of Alexander Seys's will of 1642, Byrd inherited lands in St Woollos, Llanhennock and Christchurch and three houses in Newport.[19] In Caerleon itself, Byrd held four tenements or properties in Jany Crane Street, another four in the street from the cross to the water mills, with lands at Hendre in the parish of Christchurch. Part of his inheritance from the Seys family were the two water mills in Caerleon, the associated 40 acres of pasture called the marches or marshes, a fulling mill and a further unspecified area of pasture bordering the sea or the river, called, in local parlance, wharfs or warths. These mills and lands were enjoyed by Byrd by lease from the earl of Pembroke, confirmed in 1648, and were the cause of a certain amount of anxiety on Byrd's part when he was negotiating for the name of his son, Matthias, to be inserted in the lease, duly renewed in 1669.[20] By 1668 he was paying chief rents to the earl of Pembroke on 15 burgages in the town, and in 1677 headed the jury of survey as the principal tenant of the earl.[21] Only a little to the south of Caerleon were the lordships of Liswerry and Lebenyth, crown lands, in which he held a little over 70 acres as a customary tenant, in Lebenyth second to Edward Herbert of the Grange and the lords Herbert of Cherbury, and in Liswerry to Herbert of Cherbury alone.[22] When the confiscated lands came up for sale during the interregnum, Byrd was naturally interested, but seems not to have risked anything by a purchase [**173**]. Instead, he acquired the interest of customary tenants as their holdings came up for surrender. Byrd took over the small parcels of three men between 1651 and 1653, and was to acquire another four acres in this way only a short time before his death.[23] One of those whose lands passed to him in Liswerry was John Morgan of Pentrebach, a sequestered royalist whose rehabilitation Byrd was keen to assist, probably for these material reasons [**204, 205**]. Tredunnock and Llanfrechfa were two other nearby places in which he held messuages.[24] To complete his landholdings, he was a customary tenant at Coldra

[18]RCAHMW, *Glamorgan Vol. IV, Pt. II*, 479-80.
[19]PROB 11/189/56.
[20]Gwent RO MAN/B/15/007; MAN/B/16/0002; Williams and Tweedy MS 1111.
[21]MAN/B/16/0001, 0002.
[22]Bradney, iv (pt.II), 286-93.
[23]NLW Tredegar Park 107/24, 27, 74, 124.
[24]Bradney iii (pt.II), 116-7.

manor, whose owners were the master and fellows of Eton College, but which the college leased to Sir John Trevor of Trefalun in 1646.[25] The mills leased from the earls of Pembroke were of value for their lands not for their own productive capacity: they are described in surveys as 'decayed'. Byrd did take an active interest in milling, however, and in 1656 took a lease from the Morgan family of Llantarnam of Sôr mills, set in the fields a little away from Caerleon, although the lease turned out to be unprofitable [**395, 398**].

Byrd's estates were a mixture of scattered holdings in the country and burgages in the town of Caerleon, held freehold and copyhold, but the total is witness to his steady climb to prominence in his adopted town. Just as Alexander Seys the elder had been the leading subsidy-payer in Caerleon in the 1620s, so John Byrd paid the most tax in the 1661 subsidy, even though he retained the title 'gentleman' while Thomas Williams, who paid less, was described as 'esquire'.[26] Between 1629 and the 1660s John Byrd transformed his standing: once an unencumbered newcomer to Wales, he was by dint of marriage, inheritance and presumably by prudence in business an established gentleman in Caerleon, with a good estate and access to the oldest Glamorgan and Monmouthshire families. He and Margery Byrd are known to have had four sons who reached manhood. Andrew, probably the eldest, by the mid-1660s lived in his own three-hearthed house in Caerleon.[27] and died in April 1673 [**424**]. William became an attorney and for a while helped his father with contacts in his customs work; Edward, perhaps in reaction against his father's sober ways, sowed wild oats in London before he died violently in a coaching inn brawl in Berkshire [**307, 315**]. Only Matthias, after an adventurous naval career traceable in many of his father's letters, made the kind of marriage into Monmouthshire gentry society which had established John Byrd [**438**]: to Margaret, the daughter of Edward Morgan of Pencrug. It was in the next generation that the Byrd family acquired the unambiguous title and reputation of gentry. When Matthias's son William died in 1707 he was buried inside the church at Caerleon: his will and his marble memorial inscription described him as 'esquire'.[28]

Although John Byrd prized his customs position and clung on to it with tenacity, he could never be described as anything like a full-time, professional administrator. His letters bear manifest evidence to his legalistic turn of mind and phrase, and his spell at the inn of court stood him in very good stead. But the

[25]Flintshire RO D/G/648, 649; Eton College MSS, vol. 42 nos. 15,16, 19.

[26]PRO E 179/148/80; 148/91.

[27]E 179/148/97

[28]NLW LL/1708/114; Bradney iii (pt. II), 212. Wills of two other sons of Matthias - John and Edward - are NLW LL/1718/61, LL/1718/60.

extent of his land holdings is proof that agriculture was his main source of income, and the letter-book contains examples of his lively interest in horse breeding [**289**] and in propagating fruit trees [**370, 371, 372**]. As a customary tenant of the earls of Pembroke, Byrd had each year to attend the audit at Cardiff Castle of all the tenants [**136, 409**]: an event which must have been as much a part of the South Wales calendar as meetings of quarter sessions, great sessions or assizes.[29] Another custom, enshrined in the culture of the manors of Llantwit and Boverton, and of Caerleon, was that of inheritance by the custom of Borough English, in which customary lands were inherited by the youngest son. This custom had governed the terms of the will of Alexander Seys in 1632, by which his youngest son was his principal heir, and when after 1660 the Pembroke political power bloc had declined, the old manorial customs still prevailed. John Byrd ensured that it was the younger of his two surviving sons, Matthias, whose name was inserted in the lease of the mills and marches in 1669 [**391, 401, 402, 403**].

II: Customs Administration in the Time of John Byrd

John Byrd began his customs service under the 'great farm' of the customs, an arrangement which lasted from December 1604 to 25 May 1641.[30] Under the early Stuart kings, the farming of taxes and duties on commodities offered an attractive option for the crown, which was guaranteed a fixed sum for a lease of the revenues, which were then collected by the lessee. The government would get immediate funds, and the lessee would aim to recover more than his investment when he collected from the duty- or tax-payers. The great farm of the customs, which covered a wide range of duties but not all of them, was a means of rationalising what under Elizabeth had been an anarchic system of sub-divided branches of customs administration, in which potential revenues were being lost on a massive scale. The great farms were let to a succession of syndicates of London business tycoons. From December 1628 to December 1632, the start of Byrd's involvement, the farmers were Paul Pindar, John Wolstenholme, John Jacob and Abraham Dawes. Later in the 1630s, the farmers were George Lord Goring, Nicholas Crispe, Jacob, Dawes, Job Harby and John Mills. On the eve of the civil war, when Charles I was desperate for funds from city financiers, a new farm, based on all the customs and not just on a certain range of duties, was leased by a bigger syndicate, with Goring, Crispe and their associates being joined by Pindar and Sir John Harrison.

[29] For evidence of procedures at the audit, NLW Bute M 44/20; M 61/29, 30.
[30] For what follows, see F. C. Dietz, *English Public Finance, 1558-1641* (1932), 328-61; M. Ashley, *Financial and Commercial Policy under the Cromwellian Protectorate* (2nd ed., 1962), 49-61; H. Atton, H.H. Holland, *The King's Customs* (1908); E.E. Hoon, *Organisation of the English Customs System* (New York, 1938); H. Hall, *History of the Custom-revenue in England* (2 vols. 1885).

The most important duties outside the terms of the great farm were those on wines, currants, seacoal (coal brought by sea to London and elsewhere from the collieries of Tyneside) and tobacco. From 1632, duties on wines and currants were amalgamated under a single 'petty farm' and by the late 1630s the petty farm and the separate farm of tobacco was concentrated in the hands of the same syndicates who controlled the great farm. It was during the separate farm of tobacco under John Nulls in the late 1630s that John Byrd's difficulties with the Spencer family of Aberthaw began, when he was instructed to impound their cargoes imported from St Christopher (St Kitts) in the West Indies [**152, 154, 155, 157, 163** and notes]. The tendency through the 1630s had been for the farming of customs to become more centralised. As some of the customs duties belonged to the king, and were not subject to parliamentary approval, it was comparatively easy for the government to develop the potential of the revenues in defiance of those who opposed the personal rule of Charles I. It was equally easy, when Parliament met in November 1640, for its leaders to identify the principal agents in this defiance, to remove them and continue the centralising process of customs administration under its own nominated commissioners.

The return to the direct collection of customs by commissioners - among them James Russell [**35, 64, 77**] - under the terms of the parliamentary ordinance of May 1643 was not the break with the past that some historians have implied it was. At local level, and in the London customs house, the headquarters of the service, there was much continuity of personnel, as there was in other branches of government. Furthermore, the king continued to collect customs in ports where royalist rule prevailed during the civil war. This was certainly not true of London, where it has been estimated that three-quarters of foreign trade took place,[31] but it was the case that in Bristol between July 1643 and September 1645, the customs were paid to the king's exchequer.[32] In places where the customs were contested were the most extensive changes in local personnel. During the 1640s and 50s Parliament changed the commissioners as often as the king had re-let the farms: a new set, including Samuel Avery [**3, 36, 54, 64**] was appointed in February 1645, and in 1649 the commissioners included Edmund Harvey [**116, 118, 228**].

Whether the customs were in farm or under the direct control of commissioners, their administration was accountable to the King and, after 1642 to Parliament. Officers had made their accounts directly to the court of exchequer, but by 1648 they were paying in to the separate treasury at the London customs house, which was the headquarters of the system, before the accounts were audited and relayed to the higher body. In Byrd's period of service, the

[31]Ashley, *Financial and Commercial Policy,* 51.
[32]Bodl. MS Clarendon 27 fo. 107.

London custom house was located in the parish of All Hallows, Barking, on the river and near the Tower of London. It had been built in 1559, and stood until 1666, when it was completely destroyed in the Great Fire, and subsequently rebuilt.[33] From here were sent the port books on which officials entered details of coastal cargoes in what were called the 'out-ports', all ports other than that of London. If London perspectives seem to have dominated terminology in the service, it was because the volume of sea-borne trade in the capital was massively dominant. Clerks at the London custom house maintained records from the out-ports (destroyed with the building in the Great Fire), and made returns to the court of exchequer, to that branch known as the exchequer of audit or upper exchequer, to provide the government with accurate figures on revenue.

Accounting procedures governed the customs whether they were in farm or under the control of commissioners: neither system involved a loss of control by the government. There was no consistency in the way posts in the customs were granted, however. Some offices were bestowed by the Crown under the great seal: the searchers in the port of London held theirs for life in this way in 1642.[34] Others had been granted by the Crown as sinecures to favoured courtiers: Endymion Porter held collectorships at Chester and in Ireland in this way.[35] Some were held in reversion: that is, they were given to one person, with the succession of another or others to the post stipulated in the grant: the 1638 grant to William Toomes of the surveyor-generalship named reversionary holders. Toomes and one of the collectors of subsidy in London, William Thornbury, were 'patent officers': details of the grants they enjoyed were entered on the chancery patent rolls.[36] John Byrd, too, was a patent officer, and most patents, like his, were granted at the pleasure of the king, rather than for life, and could be revoked at any time. Some posts were bought. During the later 1640s and in the 1650s successive governments were tending to replace the variety of tenures by a simplified structure of salaried appointments. When in April 1649 the committee for the navy and customs reported to the Rump Parliament, it set the establishment for the port of London, including its outlying sub-ports, at 204 salaried appointments, naming posts from 'cheques' and the solicitor and accountant-general at the top, to oarsmen at the bottom of the pyramid.[37] Of these 204 posts, only 37 were still held by patent.[38]

In its size and political importance, London was, of course, exceptional. Officers there were in the public eye and under the gaze of politicians to an extent

[33] *Survey of London xv, All-Hallows, Barking-by-the-Tower* (1934), 36-9.
[34] HLRO Main Papers, 15 February 1642.
[35] *CSPI 1625-32*, 255, 377, 439; *CSPD 1635*, 78.
[36] T. Rymer (ed.), *Foedera* (20 vols., 1727-35), ix, pt. ii, 206; viii pt iii, 278.
[37] *CJ* vi, 193-4.
[38] PRO E 122/236/19.

not usually sustained elsewhere. In February 1642, for example, the searchers for the port of London complained to Parliament - doubtless opportunistically - of the interference their work of seizing popish books and relics had suffered under Archbishop Laud.[39] Posts there, and in the out-ports, were always subject to placements by gentry and aristocratic patronage, but this does not explain the majority of appointments. What is striking as a common factor among customs officials in London, especially in Byrd's heyday during the 1650s, is their membership of the London guilds. Most of the tidesmen - junior officials servicing the ships - claimed in 1659 to be members of city companies.[40] Of Byrd's contacts in the London custom house, Henry Kersley, clerk of bonds and certificates for coast business, was a member of the bowyers' company, George Langham was a merchant taylor, and Edmund Harvey was a draper. They did not practise these trades: membership of the companies gave them primarily status and access to a preferential system of credit among members. His membership of, and position in, the skinners' company was what made Thomas Pennant [**Letter-book,** passim] so useful to Byrd, even though he had no position in the customs service at all.[41] In the absence of banks, credit in the form of bills of exchange were drawn on members of the business community, and those with the greatest capacity for credit facilities and the movement of capital were the members of the London companies. Byrd's contacts were, of course, offering him in microcosm what the merchant princes - the customs farmers and commissioners - were providing on a large scale for the Crown and the republican governments. The whole customs structure in London was in this sense operated by the business community, and as those who paid duties were also businessmen, the enterprise could be described as partly an exercise in self-regulation: there was little to choose between the *curriculum vitae* of the merchant Henry Futter and those of officials like Edmund Harvey and George Langham.

Certainly there was no concept of a professional customs service, in which salaries would have been completely independent of the duties collected. Salaries in the service were very modest, not because public service was thought to carry its own reward, but because remuneration was partly composed of fees. There was certainly a relationship between size of salary and volume of normal business - and here Byrd lost out, as he presided over Cardiff, a port with a lamentably small turnover - but fees and perquisites were always additional. Each transaction and administrative action bore a fee. At Milford Haven in 1660,

[39]HLRO Main Papers, 15 February 1642.
[40]BL Add. 15858 fo. 232.
[41]See biographical notes below for sources.

the shipper of every cargo recorded out of the port paid 3s. to the customer, 16d. to the comptroller and 12d. to the searcher; there were surcharges payable by foreigners. Every bond, every pass, every returning cargo filed and every warrant seen, triggered a fee, and sent the merchant or ship's master fumbling in his purse. Unlike salaries, the fees at ports bore no relation to their relative importance: busy Great Yarmouth was more modest in its exactions than Milford.[42] Only the most lowly of officers were unable to benefit by taking fees.

The burden of fees on the merchant was as nothing compared with the customs duties themselves, of course. Duties were paid on cargoes into the port ('inward') and those leaving the port by sea ('outward'). In a major port like London, there would be separate officers supervising these import and export divisions of the work. Inward and outward duties were paid on cargoes going overseas, and lesser imposts on those moving from port to port within the country 'coastwise'. Higher duties were paid by foreign merchants. There were many separate leases of the customs on specific commodities, such as the 'great farm' and the 'petty farm', but the main type of duty paid when John Byrd began his customs work, was called 'subsidy of tunnage and poundage', known usually as 'subsidy'. This duty, introduced in 1559, was paid on casks ('tuns') of wine and on a range of commodities by weight and size. Subsidy was payable on the widest range of commodities imaginable, and was regulated by the published Books of Rates. The principle of the Book of Rates was that the customs officer would consult it to establish the value of the commodity before him, instead of calculating duty on a market value, fluctuating and difficult to establish as that would be.[43] Typical rates in 1642, for example, were 5s. per Barbary hide, 10s. per barrel of one hundredweight of Irish butter, and 16s. 8d. per hundredweight of tallow.[44] These were not duties paid, but values on which calculations of duties were based, using a percentage. Books of Rates were revised regularly throughout Byrd's period of service, and were common to all governments of the seventeenth century. Additional duties, or 'impositions', levied and recorded by Byrd were Algier duty and the new impost on coal [e.g. **197, 202**]. Algier duty was a tax of one quarter of one per cent of customs duties payable by the book of rates, used to fund attempts by the navy to retrieve English captives of Turkish and other pirates operating off north Africa. From 1651 the 'new impost' on coal became the third strand of Byrd's exactions from the merchants [**169** and note]. A customary rebate of 15 per cent to merchants was withheld from 1650 and was accounted for as an additional levy [**135** and note, **139, 213**].

[42]BL Add. 34601 fos. 156, 159.

[43]N. S. B. Gras, *The Early English Customs System* (Cambridge, Mass. 1918), 122.

[44]*The Rates of Merchandizes* (1642) in *Subsidie Concerning Tonnage and Poundage* (Birmingham Reference Library 336.26/094/1642/3). Other Books of Rates for the interregnum survive, and may be traced through the following Wing, *Short-Title Catalogue* numbers: E920, E920B, E921, E922.

III: The Bristol Channel and its Trade in the Mid-seventeenth Century

In John Byrd's day, trade was more plentiful, and navigation easier, on the English, rather than the Welsh side of the Channel.[45] Master mariners were advised to sail up-channel along the Devon and Somerset coast, avoiding the Welsh coast, 'foule and shoaly ... with many banks, sands and riffs that lye off'. The best course was to steer between the islands of Flat Holm and Steep Holm, and to take care near the English and Welsh Grounds, continually taking soundings with the lead. Sandbanks and the extreme tidal range, which could catch out even those with local knowledge [**71**], called for careful navigation : 'The Welsh side you must shun and take very good heed of it, because it is very uneven and full of steep banks that are very sharp, which at many places do fall dry at low water'. Large ships bound for Bristol anchored in King-Road, at the mouth of the Avon, awaiting pilots to take them via Hung-Road, where they could safely careen at low tide. Smaller ships could proceed up the river. Whether they stayed in Hung-Road or made with the tide up-river to Bristol, their coming was heralded by the 'warner', who took news of new arrivals up the Avon Gorge to the city.[46] Vessels making for the Severn or to Chepstow were also advised to take a pilot; Cardiff by contrast was a 'tide-haven', a place to make for in all weathers. The master of the Eagle evidently acted on that belief [**91, 92, 95**].

The ships plying across the Channel were relatively small. The least substantial, but most serviceable in the upper reaches, were carriers of shallow draught and thirty tons burthen called trows. The most recent research suggests that there were relatively few of these operating the full navigable length of the Severn, and that those boats trading from towns on the lower reaches of the river were more likely to venture further down-channel.[47] Vessels trading from ports further west in the Channel were not necessarily of greater size. Swansea, Burry and Neath ships - usually called barques - in 1630 were around thirty tons.[48] The few ships mentioned by Byrd ranged from 15 tons to 80 tons. In contrast to these, the Aberthaw ships of Thomas Spencer trading with St Kitts, *Long Thomas* of 200 tons, and *Great Thomas*, of 100 tons, were indeed leviathans.[49] *Great Thomas* had a complement of 19 men and boys; the coastal barques and trows had crews of no more than half a dozen.[50]

[45]For what follows, J. Seller, 'A Chart of the Chanell of Bristoll, from Silly to St. Davids head in Wales', in *The English Pilot* (1671); G. Collins, *Great Britain's Coasting Pilot* (1779 ed.), 9.

[46]J. Rich, *The Bristol Pilots* (Pill, North Somerset, 1996), 39-40.

[47]M.D.G. Wanklyn, 'The Severn Navigation in the Seventeenth Century: Long-Distance Trade of Shrewsbury Boats', *Midland History* xiii (1988), 34-58.

[48]T.S. Willan, *The English Coasting Trade 1600-1750* (Manchester, 1938), 12.

[49]E 134/ 22, 23 Charles I/ Hil. 2.

[50]M.I. Williams, 'Aberthaw: the Port of the Vale', in S. Williams (ed.), *Saints and Sailing Ships* (Cowbridge, 1962), 16; Willan, *English Coasting Trade,* 16.

The ocean-going tobacco ships were exceptional in the cargo they carried, as well as in their size. Most of the Bristol Channel trade was of the miscellaneous cargoes typical of coasting. Cargoes outward from Aberthaw included wool, butter, grain, stockings, gloves, raw and tanned hides and livestock; coming in were cloth, brandy and wine, perfume, oils, pottery, salt, soap and iron implements of various kinds. Other ports at the eastern end of the Channel were similar. The strikingly different trade was further west, where coal dominated.[51] Small ships, lightly manned, with diverse cargoes: the picture is of a seemingly adaptable trade, with relatively modest capital investment. In this respect again, the Spencers' involvement in the high-risk, long-distance, politically-sensitive tobacco trade seems exceptional. As T.S. Willan long ago pointed out, the merchant mariners were flexible. Sometimes the port books record them as merchants and masters on coastal journeys, and sometimes masters carrying goods for another. Sometimes they shipped commodities in boats not their own.[52] The coastal trade, unlike the administration of the customs duties levied on it, was marked by a protean quality: no wonder that Thomas Spencer, in a less adaptable, more capital-intensive branch of commerce, felt oppressed by the government's agents.

IV: Customs Administration in South Wales

The first recorded customs appointment of a permanent kind in the port of Cardiff was that of a searcher in 1559: a customer was appointed in 1563. For a brief period, customs due at Cardiff were collected by Bristol officers.[53] In the Elizabethan and early Stuart period, the service seems to have been attended by perpetual instability, with frequent cases of dismissal, and allegations of misconduct that came regularly to court, especially the exchequer court.[54] During the sixteenth century, there was an evolution of the administrative structure of the customs with which John Byrd was familiar. In customs parlance, the term 'port' or head port, meant the principal place where the custom house was located, the place where most business was transacted. Each port had sub-ports or 'creeks' as they were known; Byrd provides a list of these, which for the port of Cardiff extended beyond Swansea [**49**]. Dr. Thomas Phaer, who might be described as a pioneer of the customs service in South Wales, reported around 1553 that the ports of Chepstow and Magor in the east, and Swansea and Gower harbours and

[51] Williams, 'Aberthaw', 17-19, Willan, English Coasting Trade, 176-8.
[52] Willan, *English Coasting Trade,* 53; Wanklyn, 'Severn Navigation in the Seventeenth Century', 38-9 shows how the terms 'merchant' and 'master' in port books refer specifically to roles on the particular journeys entered in them.
[53] W. R. B. Robinson, 'The Establishment of Royal Customs in Glamorgan and Monmouthshire under Elizabeth I', *BBCS* xxii (1968-70), 347-96; G. Williams, 'The Economic Life of Glamorgan, 1536-1642' in *Glam. Co. Hist.* iv, 60-62.
[54] T. I. Jeffreys Jones, *Exchequer Proceedings Concerning Wales in tempore James I* (Cardiff, 1955), 214, 218, 253; G. Williams, 'Economic Life of Glamorgan', 62.

quays in the west belonged to the earl of Worcester, while ports in between - Cardiff and Neath, for example - were under the sway of the earl of Pembroke. These baronial rights derived from ownership of lordships, and gave their proprietors control of local dues, which were being levied without challenge in 1586.[55] The rival houses of Worcester and Pembroke could not hold sway over the crown right to collect the subsidy of tunnage and poundage, but they remained a century after Phaer's report an important ingredient in the make-up of impositions on merchants in South Wales ports. The earl of Worcester was involved in several exchequer cases during the reign of James I when he claimed his right to wrecks in the Severn and Wye, and throughout Wales to the duty called 'prisewines' on wine imports.[56] The fact that members of the Somerset family were so frequently instigators of exchequer suits over the dues suggests, of course, that their collection was attended by increasing resistance and evasion. More routinely, there were further purely local tolls and duties, where as in the case of Aberthaw, the gentry family of Stradling insisted on its rights.[57] In other places, residual baronial influence could be detected. The creek of Newton Nottage, for example, in a parish where there were three manors with three different proprietors, was in the Herbert manor. The controlling Herbert family of Swansea were clients of the earl of Pembroke's interest in Glamorgan parliamentary elections; by the mid-seventeenth century it was in this sense of being part of a network of patronage that ports, creeks and harbours played a part in the politics of the élite.[58]

John Byrd's place in the sphere of influence of the earls of Pembroke is visible in various aspects of his life and career. He married into a client family of theirs; he lived in a town described by the rival earls of Worcester as belonging to Pembroke;[59] he was a tenant on various Pembroke manors and lordships. In his customs work all of these connections were background; although he commented on Col. Thomas Harrison's movement of the earl of Pembroke's rents in November 1649 and thought him a likely carrier of his customs revenues [**81**], he certainly saw himself as an officer of the state, and was no retainer of a baron. Before 1642, his loyalties were to the crown as a patent officer, and unlike the customer at Aberthaw in the late sixteenth century, who virtually sought permission from Sir Edward Stradling of St Donats to act in the interests of the crown, he did not have to clear his actions with gentry or aristocracy.[60]

[55]Robinson, 'Royal Customs', 349-50; BL Lansdowne 46, fo. 102.

[56]Jeffreys Jones, *Exchequer Proceedings*, 11, 253.

[57]J. M. Traherne, *Stradling Correspondence* (1840), 122-3.

[58]L. S. Higgins, *Newton Nottage and Porthcawl* (Llandysul, 1968), 36-7.

[59]Dircks, 60.

[60]*Stradling Correspondence* , 324-6.

The power of the barons might ensure that allegiances in manors and ports would be predictable in times of political stress, but of greater import to merchants were the local duties themselves, part of the fabric of commercial life. At Newton, cargoes of salt, grain, apples or pears entering the harbour paid duty of one bushel to the lord, with 2d. 'pillage' on any ship touching ground there. In Penarth in 1659, visiting ships paid 'killage', 'houseage' and 'bockage', local tolls enjoyed by Sir Thomas Lewis of Penmark, who assigned his lease to Thomas Morgan of Machen and Thomas Young of Newport, mercer, a probable collaborator of John Byrd's [**204**].[61] On cargoes originating from the Usk ports, 'murrage' and 'keelage' were payable at Bristol.[62] At Cardiff, merchants from outside the town paid duties on corn and salt, and a bushel was kept in the castle for the purpose.[63] It was an unco-ordinated pattern of local tolls and privileges, but the effect was to inhibit trade and produce many disputes, such as that arising from the claims of Bristol merchants over butter [**68, 118, 120**].

As collectors, comptrollers, customers and searchers were mostly appointed by patent at the king's pleasure, and because many patents were granted as reversions, it was commonly the case that offices stayed in families. Thomas Williams, searcher at Cardiff in 1618, was succeeded by his brother, Philip, who was working with Byrd from 1638 at the latest until 1651.[64] William Thornbury, a regular correspondent of Byrd's, and Isaac Thornbury enjoyed the more privileged office for life of the collectorship of customs on wool, hides and other commodities in the port of London.[65] Byrd seems not to have inherited his post, nor was he able to pass it on to a relative or client.

The structure of the customs service in the port of Cardiff and elsewhere in Wales in Byrd's day was outlined long ago by E.A. Lewis. The job of the customer as the chief financial officer was to record shipments, collect the customs and issue receipts. He had authority to make compositions with merchants, by which they paid a sum in settlement on large or complex cargoes, and he kept the cocket seal, by which means he could issue sealed receipts or cockets to merchants to show that import or export duties had been paid.[66] John Byrd was, as comptroller, evidently jointly responsible with the customer for making cockets [**65**], and distinguished between port cockets for cargoes to or from overseas, and coast cockets or certificates [**66, 100, 124, 234**]. Before the civil war the posts of comptroller and the customer were intended as a check on

[61]Higgins, *Newton Nottage*, 36-7; NLW Tredegar Park 56/177.

[62]J. W. Dawson, *Commerce and Customs. A History of the Ports of Newport and Caerleon* (Newport, 1932), 20-1.

[63]NLW Bute M7/60.

[64]Williams, 'Economic Life of Glamorgan', 62; Jeffreys Jones, *Exchequer Proceedings*, 214; E134/ 22, 23 Charles I/ Hil. 2.

[65]Birmingham City Archives, Coventry mss, DV 896/ 210; T. Rymer, *Foedera* ix, pt. ii, 206.

[66]E.A. Lewis, *The Welsh Port Books (1550-1603)* (1927), ix; Jeffreys Jones, *Exchequer Proceedings*, 218.

each other, and indeed, when in July 1649 the post of customer at Cardiff was abolished by the Rump Parliament, it introduced a new office, held by Francis Mallory, with the title of 'check' to maintain the principle of that system [**66, 68, 77, 100**]. Byrd seems to have held that title himself at some previous point [**118**]. By the mid-eighteenth century, the searcher confined his activities to supervising the export business at a port.[67] In the port of Cardiff in the mid-1650s we find him, true to his name, boarding ships to investigate holds and their contents on the state's behalf [**56**]. The searcher held with the customer and comptroller an office which by statute the lord treasurer allocated by a warrant to the lord chancellor or lord keeper.[68] The medieval origins of these offices and their basis in statute helps explain how independently the holders of the posts operated in the same port. There was no hierarchy. When Byrd and his two colleagues boarded and seized the ships of Thomas Spencer and their cargoes of St Kitts tobacco in the late 1630s, they each independently employed a waiter to act as a guard.[69]

The structure of the customs service in the late 1640s and 1650s was often under review. During the civil war a pattern of naval administration by Parliament had developed which saw the service managed by various bodies with overlapping functions. The navy committee of Parliament, whose members were all MPs, extended their authority over all customs matters too. There was a parallel admiralty committee which primarily addressed matters of naval policy. Accountable to the navy committee, or committee for navy and customs as it was otherwise known, were two sets of commissioners, one body supervising day-to-day matters of the navy, another fulfilling the same function over customs affairs. Before 1649 Parliament's navy committee intervened in appointments [**1, 2**]. From January 1649 yet another body was appointed, the 'committee of merchants' or 'regulators', given the brief of assessing the suitability of officeholders in both customs and navy [**35**].[70] By 1648, Byrd was described as 'collector', as well as comptroller [**5, 49**].[71] He worked opposite Edward Herbert of Magor, later to become MP for Monmouthshire in 1656, who held the parallel post of customer. The offices of collector and comptroller carried separate salaries [**49**].[72] Another important, in Byrd's view necessarily peripatetic officer [**68, 101**] was the surveyor of customs, who identified ships and cargoes throughout the port and who the Rump wished to use as a countersigning official on all salary payments [**129**]. Before the reforms of the summer of 1649, it was

[67]Hoon, *Organisation of English Customs*, 11.

[68]BL Add. 36081 fo. 13v.

[69]E134/ 22, 23 Charles I/ Hil. 2.

[70]Aylmer, *SS*, 16.

[71]E 351/68.

[72]For a description of these offices in more settled times, Lewis, *Welsh Port Books*, ix-x.

a structure which encouraged these officials to view themselves as semi-autonomous. Customer, collector and searcher each appointed eight or nine deputies in the ports and sub-ports [**49**]. After 1649, the model was more pyramidal and more skeletal: the commissioners seemed to prefer a clearer hierarchy of authority and queried the need for so many deputies. The post of customer disappeared, as its incumbent moved into more overtly political activity, as did the position of comptroller, which seems to have been conceived as integrally attached to the customership. Byrd was left as collector only, as were his colleagues in other ports of the Bristol Channel. The position of collector was not granted by the King's patent, as the post of comptroller had been: the abolition may have owed much to the desire by the Rump to circumvent possible problems of authority. From January 1653, the establishment was changed again, with separate port status being given by the navy committee to Swansea to recognise the greater volume of trade there than up-channel [**210**]. But however often the navy committee or the 'regulators' altered the structure, in his day-to-day work, Byrd had to account to the commissioners of the customs.

The ports under John Byrd's supervision in the 1650s saw relatively little business activity, especially in the area of overseas trade [**20**]. Customs officers dealt separately with the coasting trade and commerce with foreign countries. The principal customs duties were not payable on cargoes shipping coastwise, except for the duty of 2s. per chaldron on coal imposed by parliamentary ordinance. The purpose of the customs procedures governing them was not so much to collect duty but to prevent the evasion which would occur if cargoes certified as travelling between home ports were instead carried abroad [**124**]. A merchant applied to the custom house where the cargo was put aboard ship for a cocket or coquet, a sealed certificate describing his cargo and stating its coastal destination. Usually he was at the same time asked to give bond, to name two sureties who would pay a stated sum if he defaulted and did not present his cargo to the receiving custom house by a specified time. When the ship reached the named port, the cocket was presented by the merchant to the receiving custom house, whose officers then issued a certificate, which when presented to the original custom house cancelled the bond.[73] The certificate and cocket were the merchant's indemnity against double taxation, but it was a rigid system which could not cope well with changes of plan or error [**252**]. Byrd's correspondence shows that there were variations in practice between custom houses [**99**]. In 1649

[73]Willan, *English Coasting Trade,* 1-9; Lewis, *Welsh Port Books*, 25-7; Hoon, *Organisation of English Customs,* 264-9. Wanklyn, 'Severn Navigation in the Seventeenth Century', 36 is in error in asserting that money was deposited as security. Money would be forfeited if a bondsman defaulted, but the officers would have to resort to law to recover it.

he reckoned that there were in his area about 800 of these transactions a year [**86**]. They generated various series of record books, collectively known as port books, and Byrd sometimes queried changes in record-keeping [**147**]. One set of books - 'entry books' - recorded cargoes arriving from other ports. The other set - 'port cocket books' - recorded cockets issued and bonds cancelled when shipments were finally discharged. Entries in the latter books naturally took longer to complete [**153**]. Although in 1730 no cockets were required on cargoes travelling between Cardiff and Bristol, and sometimes goods were in the 1650s allowed to travel 'on sufferance'[74] or by 'letpass' [**174**], under the rule of the Rump Parliament Byrd and his colleagues were evidently not allowed to exempt this trade [**65, 70**].

Overseas trade was much less busy at Cardiff, partly because goods shipped coastwise in the Bristol Channel were more likely to be exported abroad from the major port of Bristol [**234**], where an imposing custom house on the Back bore the legend *Quae Caesaris sunt Caesari*.[75] Byrd had to report that in his greatly inferior port for whole weeks at a time no duties were collected on imports and exports [**214**]. Some idea of the different volume of trade between Bristol and Cardiff may be given by sample figures from the exchequer accounts: in 1648, £4811 was received at Bristol, £1886 at Cardiff. In the accounts for the year 1657 Bristol yielded £12,424 against the lamentably low £36 recorded for Cardiff.[76] (In comparison, however, in three months in 1650 when Bristol took £200 in duties, London received £5505.)[77] Coal was the major commodity sent 'for beyond sea' [**246**], but only from the western ports in Byrd's care. Cardiff at this time exported no coal. Caerleon seems surprisingly to have been a busy port at this time [**81, 100**], and Byrd implies that it was the leading export port for choicer commodities [**210**]. His verdict is confirmed by data on the volume of coasting business in the up-channel ports, measured in cargoes entered at the Cardiff custom house from December 1653 to December 1654:

Entries, Dec. 1653-Dec. 1654[78]

	Inward	Outward
Cardiff	78	69
Newport	68	55
Caerleon	83	64
Chepstow	63	210

Swansea was quite busy as a coal port, and most of this production was carried to destinations within the Bristol Channel area. Even so, when in the later 1650s

[74] Willan, *English Coasting Trade*, 2.

[75] The Bristol custom house is depicted on Millerd's 1673 map of the city.

[76] E 351/ 648, 658.

[77] SP 18/ 10.

[78] E 122/ 232/ 20.

it was run as a separate head port it could send over £800 per annum in export duties to the London customs house.[79] When the Rump Parliament brought in an ordinance imposing a new duty on coal, Byrd wrote to query whether it applied in circumstances of local shipments [**178**]. In other areas of trade, the customs officials' work in the Channel was slack, and Byrd attributed not a little of this slump to the advent of the excise tax [**10**], evidently settled in South Wales for the first time in 1648, which deterred mercantile activity of all kinds because duty had to be paid on such a wide range of imports at ports of entry. Excise officers worked alongside customs officials and countersigned bills of entry.[80]

Despite the modest volume of trade in the area, there were evidently nevertheless sufficient difficult cases to exercise Byrd and his colleagues. A number involved compositions by merchants.[81] Composition was often an alleged malpractice of customs officers, but this was when the procedure was unauthorised or at collusive rates.[82] Byrd made compositions when cargoes were seized [**131, 183**] or was driven to it when there were irregularities in the processing of the cargo [**151**]. Directions were given by the solicitor to the customs commissioners to officers on how to arrive at compositions: local officials themselves received a fee from the compounding merchant [**146, 151**].

The customs commissioners in London noted that the cost of maintaining the customs operation based at Cardiff was high in relation to receipts of revenue. Byrd in response pointed out the huge territory he had to cover, from Chepstow in the east to Burry Port in the west, and advanced as a defence against the prospect of job and salary cuts the argument that the existing establishment was a necessary bulwark against fraud by merchants. There needed to be one officer in each sub-port, and if the merchants learned of staff reductions, there would be an increase in evasion of duties [**100**].

V: The Public Service Ethos of John Byrd

Byrd maintained a proprietorial attitude to his territory, and a willingness to represent the views of his subordinates to the commissioners. Apart from threats to the size of his staff, a further recurrent issue was that of the shift in the service from fees to salaries. In a region where trading activity was sluggish, and where therefore the number of transactions which would attract fees was limited, it might have been thought in Byrd's interests to support this change. In fact Byrd

[79] E 351/ 658.

[80] For ordinances establishing how excise was paid in this period, F&R i, 202-14, 346-7, 466-8, 501-2, 806-9, 863-5, 1004-7; ii, 213-35, 368-9.

[81] Hoon, *Organisation of English Customs,* 94-5 for a discussion of the practice.

[82] In 1622, Edmund Morgan, customer at Cardiff, alleged that his deputy in Swansea made compositions with merchants in alehouses, and was inclined to 'wynke' at the shipping of leather custom-free: Jeffreys Jones, *Exchequer Proceedings*, 218.

opposed the move, realising that the level of salary would depend on the volume of business before an individual officer [**35, 49**]. When news of this change broke, Byrd hastily consulted his opposite number in the local customs hierarchy, Edward Herbert, the customer, and declared himself willing to travel to London to try to secure a reversal [**35**]. By October 1649, Byrd had been greatly disappointed at the attitude of the commissioners, who had declined to increase his salary beyond the £30 he received as collector and took away the £10 he had received when comptroller: in his view the travel and need to be in constant attendance justified a salary of £100 [**49, 86**]. In February 1650 he was afraid he would be out of pocket if the commissioners refused to pick up the bill for the salaries of his deputies at his sub-ports [**97**]. In January 1653, after four years of what Byrd felt was a lack of recognition for his efforts in far-flung, difficult territory, the commissioners delivered what he may have felt like taking as the final insult: they appointed the godly Griffith Bowen, associate of Col. Philip Jones, as collector at Swansea, in recognition of the importance of trade at that port compared with the sister port of Cardiff. Taking the meaning of the commissioners to be that he should confine his operations to Cardiff, Newport and Chepstow only, Byrd asked them to instruct Thomas Shewell, the Bristol collector, to look after the revenue in those ports, 'soe smale that it will not clear salaryes' [**210**]. It was as near as he ever came to writing a letter of resignation, but a few weeks later he was writing to ask for further guidance from the commissioners 'if anything else bee expected from mee herein' [**214**].

The frustration Byrd felt in his work for the commissioners was not confined to matters of remuneration. He had to ask repeatedly for instructions on various aspects of the service [**102, 118, 185**], sometimes seeking clarification on difficult cases before him, sometimes chasing up requests for receipts or 'acquittances' for accounts and financial statements. He needed a good supply of blank bonds for completion when entering details of merchants' cargoes: on one occasion he got the bonds but they were the wrong sort, with not enough space to fill in the details of transactions. As Byrd kept repeating, his post was concerned with security: of trade and of revenue. He seemed inadequately supported even though his work had implications locally for the security of the state. The role of customs officers as local intelligence-gatherers or monitors on the state's behalf is well-attested.[83] Byrd conveyed information to his superiors on the movement of navy shipping in the Bristol Channel [**56, 57**] and was the means by which ships bound for Virginia and Barbados would be detained [**120, 125**]. The information he supplied Sir John Trevor on Thomas Lewis of St Pierre shows his usefulness as a man with local knowledge [**9**], and this quality alone

[83]Most recently, M. Questier, 'Practical Antipapistry during the Reign of Elizabeth I', *Journal of British Studies* xxxvi (1997), 371-96.

may have justified the continuation of a separate customs operation based at Cardiff when judged purely on its revenue potential it could have been transferred to Bristol. But Byrd was one of many local agents of the state in South Wales; the Cardiff, Swansea and Llangybi garrisons (totalling 550 troops in 1649) and the two ships the navy kept in the Bristol Channel (140 men, 38 guns), rather undermined any claim he might have made for himself as a first line of defence.[84] The story of the *Eagle* [**91, 92, 95**], an Irish ship driven ashore in 1649, shows how different branches of the security service could be rivals. In this respect, and in what he perceived as a lack of support, Byrd's experience mirrored that of local committees in the 1640s and Cromwell's major-generals and other servants of the state in the 1650s: we cannot assume that breakdowns of communication and failures of bureaucracy represent conscious or unconscious lack of interest by central government.[85]

It is instructive to look at the contacts Byrd used to perform his official duties effectively and to ward off threats to his position. Taking only the official record of exchequer declared accounts, port books and state papers into account, a simple model could be described of communications back and forth between the custom house in London and Byrd in South Wales. This would be to miss a much more complex set of relationships which Byrd was able to trigger in ordinary circumstances and times of crisis. Without doubt, as Byrd himself on many occasions confessed, the most crucial of his contacts was his brother-in-law Thomas Pennant, a Flintshire man by birth, but long settled in London; one who had worked up though parish office in the city of London and practised the solid, respectable and unremarkable profession of scrivener. More importantly, however, Pennant was a freeman of the company of skinners and by 1640 had become the company's clerk. By virtue of this office, Pennant had the ear of many leading London merchant princes, some of whom were farmers and subsequently commissioners of the customs. On occasion Byrd asked Pennant to pull strings for him with the commissioners [**58, 87**], and routinely used Pennant as his agent with letters and messages: Byrd thought only good could come of Pennant's interventions. Furthermore, Pennant had at his disposal a capacity Byrd completely lacked in South Wales: access to financial credit. Byrd often lamented the paucity of the financial mechanisms open to him: it was dangerous to move specie up to London from Wales [**21**] and 'good bills' - sound bills of exchange - were hard to find even in south-east Wales, by far the most prosperous region of the principality, partly incorporated as it was into the economy of

[84]Clarke MSS (microfilm, ed. G.E. Aylmer, Harvester Press, 1978) 1/5 (lxii); BL Stowe 322 fo. 73v.

[85]Cf. S.K. Roberts, *Recovery and Restoration in an English County: Devon Local Administration 1646-1670* (Exeter, 1985), 51-2; A.J. Fletcher, *Reform in the Provinces* (1986). The fullest study of Welsh committees remains that by A. H. Dodd in *Studies in Stuart Wales* (Cardiff, 2nd ed. 1971), 110-76.

Bristol [**105**]. Pennant provided the banking service whereby Byrd was able to clear his accounts at the London custom house and subsequently the exchequer. Periodically he took the risk of travelling up to London himself to settle things with his brother-in-law [**26, 53, 75, 98**], and in between times he could despatch one of his prodigious 65 lb. pies [**310**] in gratitude. It seems scarcely credible that someone in his position could have functioned effectively without such metropolitan contacts.

Byrd took care to acknowledge the help of Pennant, his principal agent, but he also kept sweet in a less spectacular way a range of middle-ranking officers at the custom house in London, such as the surveyor of the outports and the clerk to the solicitor of the customs, with small sums of money, delivered by Pennant, for them to buy drinks or the occasional breakfast [**69, 185, 209**]. There was a carefully-recognised etiquette in this oiling of wheels: Byrd was happy to give such tips to back-room officials, to whom he considered himself equal, but refrained from ever becoming over-familiar with a man like Michael Sansome, secretary to the customs commissioners. Byrd often wrote to try to bend Sansome's ear, but never patronised him with a gift.

Only one man ever approached Pennant's importance in assisting Byrd's public activities: his wife's first cousin, Evan Seys. Seys's estate lay mainly in the Vale of Glamorgan, centred on Boverton Place, but more importantly he, too, was well-connected in London. Seys was a barrister and from 1649 serjeant-at-law, who retained his post of attorney-general at the courts of great sessions in south-east Wales from the 1630s to 1668. Beyond asking for occasional legal advice from him, Byrd generally left Seys alone in the 1640s and 50s. In 1660 it looked for a while as if Seys's career was finished, but he retained his serjeantcy and was re-elected to Parliament, where he sat for Gloucester from 1661 to 1681. Seys was no use to Byrd in his work as a customs officer, and could not help Byrd save his post after 1662. Nevertheless, as someone with political influence Seys could at least help him with other, sometimes domestic, problems, and Byrd forged close links with the lawyer MP, looking after his horses [**289**] and supplying him with saplings from his nursery [**370, 371, 372**].

It was not only after the Restoration that Byrd feared for his customs post. In February 1648 he was threatened when one Christopher Rogers of Swansea persuaded Luke Hodges, a member of Parliament's committee for the navy, to settle him in a customs job at Swansea, on the pretext that Byrd's deputy there was dead. Rogers obtained an order from Lord General Sir Thomas Fairfax to this effect. Byrd's swift and determined response was to get Pennant to show the navy committee a certificate of Byrd's loyalty to Parliament, and to write to Sir John Trevor of Trefalun to ask him to intervene personally with the committee [**1, 2**]. Trevor was a very powerful politician. His Welshness was incidental;

crucially he was on many important committees of Parliament, and was Byrd's landlord in that from 1646 he had taken a lease of Coldra lordship, near Caerleon, from Eton College. Byrd held some customary tenements there. The connection proved a fortunate one. Trevor saved Byrd's job, and in return asked his tenant to suggest someone for an unnamed local position, or perhaps even assess his suitability for a marriage alliance. Byrd was happy to oblige, though the pay-back nearly turned sour when weeks later his favoured candidate was implicated in the second civil war in South Wales [**9, 11**].[86] In turning to Trevor, Byrd was importuning the most powerful man with whom he could claim acquaintance. Byrd was able to reassure Edward Herbert, the customer, that the committee for the navy and customs did not after all intend to 'clear [them] from employments' [**6**].

The strategy of turning to men with powerful local influence was one adopted by Byrd on other occasions when he ran into trouble with his customs work: he seems never to have expected much from his employers. In February 1651, one of the sons of Thomas Spencer, a master mariner of Aberthaw, declined to pay customs duties on some horses he was importing from Ireland. Byrd refused to back down, and commenced legal proceedings. Spencer senior retaliated by producing a warrant from six years previously, by which Byrd was supposed to have delivered some money to Spencer on the service of Parliament. The intention was to land Byrd in trouble by showing that Byrd had never paid the £400 involved. Again Byrd acted swiftly, and went some way to organising a meeting of four Monmouthshire gentry who could vindicate him. Spencer backed down [**151, 152, 154, 155, 157, 162, 163, 168**]. The final occasion on which Byrd mobilised local gentry support - this time unsuccessfully - was in May 1662, when he was fighting hard to keep his job. He organised a petition signed by thirteen Monmouthshire gentry, all serving in the commission of the peace, and most of them new to the bench of magistrates in 1660, to attest to his loyalty to the king, putting the best spin on the facts that he could. He was not at the battle of Worcester; never a sequestrator, had never 'wronged any person' and - and here Byrd's capacity for stretching the truth was at its most inventive - had been sequestered from his office of comptroller by Parliament [**262**]. He produced a similar certificate from the constable of the castle, and the bailiffs, justices and aldermen of Cardiff [**263**]. The tactic failed on this occasion, not because of the poor credentials of his referees - they could hardly have been bettered - but because he was on collision course with a former royalist soldier, Richard Dutton, an associate of Lord Gerard and Roger Whitley, inveterate plotters on

[86]Despite the emphasis in these two letters on personal qualities, no marriage between the Trevors and the Lewises ever ensued: Bradney iv pt 1, 76-77.

behalf of Charles Stuart in the 1650s, and determined to lever what rewards they could from the new king.

By 1662 Byrd's political skills had been exhausted, neither Seys, Trevor nor Pennant was able to save him, and he left his customs post for ever. At the end he was attempting to portray himself as one ever loyal to the monarchy, and could of course point to his twelve or thirteen years' service in the customs under Charles I. More convincingly, however, and more subtly, his letters evinced his perceptions of the working of the public sphere in the 1640s and 50s which indicate how he perceived his work. 'The state' as a term figures half a dozen times in Byrd's letters, the first time on 31 January 1649, the last in February 1651, with most usages in 1649 [**35, 40, 54, 65, 91, 153**]. Thereafter it does not figure in Byrd's 400 or more letters. He had a spatial view of the workings of authority. Orders came from 'above' [**75, 98, 158, 180, 229, 241**], and he implemented them 'below' [**180**]. He had a lively sense of 'private' behaviour, of which he disapproved: smuggling was landing goods privately [**68, 72**]. In the case of the Irish ship *Eagle*, driven ashore at Cardiff in January 1650, he acted in what he saw as the interests of the state when he asserted a claim to customs on the forfeit cargo [**91, 92, 95**]. The officers of the Cardiff garrison, led by Colonel Philip Jones and Sheriff John Herbert, encouraged by the commissioners for prize goods and James Powell, an officer in the Bristol garrison, were intent on claiming their 'full interest' in the prize.[87] The story made the 'national press':

> There came in a little Irish frigot to Milford, which had two prizes, and shot off a gun for a pylot, and there came six in a boat to them, and they took one and went away; the same came into this channell, and cast anchor against Cardiffe in Wales, and the most of the chiefe in the frigot went ashore to Cardiffe to fetch in provisions, and the governor having some suspition of them, secured them and sent a party in small boates, and took the frigot. It is thought it came from Lymerick in Ireland, it is very richly laden with plate and other rich commodities.[88]

Byrd's version of the story is less heroic. He mentioned darkly that the soldiers carried matters 'somme things privatly and somme things by power' [**92**]: an early verdict on the career of Col. Philip Jones, viewed by contemporaries and by historians as a man of questionable moral probity in public dealings.[89]

Byrd's participation in public affairs was not confined to the customs service. His work for the customs effectively exempted him from a range of local offices to which he might have otherwise been called. He was indignant that he had to turn up for possible service on juries at quarter sessions and assizes, writing in

[87]GRO D/DF F/37.

[88]*A Perfect Diurnall of Some Passages no.* 5 (7 Jan. - 14 Jan. 1650) (BL E533.37), 44.

[89]*DNB*; *DWB*; A. G. Veysey, 'Colonel Philip Jones', *Trans. Hon. Soc. Cymmrodorion* (1966), 316-40.

1651 to Robert Blackborne, solicitor to the customs commissioners, that he needed from him a letter of exemption [**176**]. In 1661 he tried to get exemption from jury service by means of the influence of his lawyer son, William, in London. The strategy failed, and Byrd was fined for non-attendance, to his chagrin [**241**]. This blot on his copybook was quickly expunged; he was too dependable to pass over, and he served again quickly enough.[90] He served in 1662 as a commissioner for sewers, dealing with water-courses and sea-walls in Monmouthshire,[91] and from the early 1670s acted as an assessment commissioner, rating those in his part of Monmouthshire for taxes.[92] His involvement in this service outlived his customs activities. Even more locally, in 1663 he served as churchwarden at Caerleon [**298**]. In November 1663 he was thrown into a panic by a rumour that he was on the shortlist from whom the sheriff of the county would be chosen [**307**], and asked Evan Seys to get him off. Unlikely as it seems that someone of Byrd's modest standing would achieve this prominence, it was certainly the case that he kept a watch on developments in the shrievalty, and in 1667 again contacted Seys when he feared an unsuitable ('evil' in his words) appointment might be made [**365**]. After he had been removed from his customs post, he thus settled into the conventional public career of a minor gentleman, proof that he never became *persona non grata* to the restored monarchy.

These unpaid local offices were for him at best a duty, at worst an irksome imposition. During the 1650s there was the prospect that more lucrative assignments could come his way. Even though he had reported that the establishment of the excise in South Wales had virtually killed trade stone dead [**10**], Byrd was interested in September 1650 in becoming an excise farmer for South Wales. He had seen or heard of the act permitting farming, and wrote to his nephew in London that he might take a farm of Glamorgan and Monmouthshire should the current sub-commissioners no longer be interested [**130**]. Byrd calculated that his putative farm would only be worthwhile to the Commonwealth if the whole English excise were farmed, to prevent re-routing of commodities via English Bristol Channel ports. He moved cautiously, anxious not to prejudice the livelihoods of the sub-commissioners, with whom he evidently got along well: 'it is not lawfull to take another mans house over his head' [**138**]. In the event nothing came of the possibility. An easier, though no more certain way of making money was to 'double' on public faith bills [**173**]. Byrd had evidently lent money to the state against the security of confiscated land. He sought to advance twice the original amount ('doubling') and hoped that

[90] PRO ASSI 5/2, Mon. grand jury list, 1 Aug. 1665.
[91] PRO C 187/7 p. 132.
[92] *Statutes of the Realm* v, 765, 817.

nearby lands in the former crown lordships of Liswerry and Lebenyth would provide the security. If he went ahead, it was not a long-term investment, since by December 1652 he was trying to find an agent who would sell his bills [**205**].

Attention has already been drawn to Byrd's belief that the role of the customs officials in the Bristol Channel ports was more to prevent fraud than to collect revenue [**100**]. His views on the probity of the mercantile community may well have evolved partly if not entirely as a response to what he saw as a threat to his income with the shift from fees to salaries. Whatever their genesis, his opinion of merchants was less than flattering to them. After a spat with Bristol and Cardiff merchants about duties payable or not on butter, Byrd concluded to his colleague in Bristol, Thomas Shewell, that 'wee may not put any confidence in what any of them saye, if theyr owne advantage bee concerned therein' [**119**].

There were of course limits to Byrd's concept of the public sphere, as one would expect. The need to mobilise personal connections to retain a post is sufficient evidence that private interests necessarily underpinned public ones. Byrd was pleased to do business favours whenever he could for his associates: in March 1649 he was able to help Samuel Avery, customs commissioner for the outports, the man at the very apex of power in customs matters, by trying to act as a debt collector at the Monmouth assizes on Avery's behalf. Evidently he saw nothing inappropriate in this [**36**]. His dabbling in public faith bills and in the possibilities of excise farming showed that for him private profit and state service could dovetail as neatly as for any modern free-marketeer.

What kind of people did Byrd consider were the most suitable for public service? On a number of occasions he recommended men to his superior officers. In 1651 an individual he recommended was 'honest' (a recurrent adjective of approval of his), 'ever faithful to the Parliament' and had 'suffered ... by the cavileeres' [**164**]. On other occasions he described his deputies as 'able' and 'faithful' [**49**]. In the small port of Newton Nottage, Byrd employed as deputy Jenkin Arnold, 'one of the ablest men in that place' [**81**]. The customer's deputy at Newport, John Plumley, was defended against a possible reprimand as 'ever ... faithfull to the Parliament ... [he] forsooke his estate and suffred much for their sakes' [**66**]. Speaking of himself, Byrd wrote: 'I formerlie lost my employment and all my personall estate and was most dangerously wounded, and all for my faithfullnes to the Parliament and I am still both willinge and ready to doe any service which may bee in my power for the commonwealth of England' [**96**]. In these recommendations and expressions of confidence in his men, Byrd stressed their ability above that of their fellow citizens. His men were dedicated to the reputation of the service: 'the creditt of the service is more to them then the proffitt' [**133**]. We might consider that this emphasis was natural and unexceptional, but it is noticeable that Byrd did not select social status as a qualification. A number of his deputies were in fact aldermen - Patrick Jones of Swansea, Arthur Roberts of Cardiff, Plumley of Newport - but he never stressed their civic standing or reputation to justify their appointments. The one occasion when social rank did figure in his calculations was when he recommended Thomas Lewis of St Pierre near Chepstow to Sir John Trevor for unidentified service. The three qualities he stressed to Trevor were, in the order in which Byrd mentions them, his lack of addiction to drink, the size and value of his estate and the eminence of his ancestry [**9**]. In January 1662 he wrote in very different circumstances to recommend Moses Nicholas of Newport for the post of customs waiter: he had, he assured the commissioners, 'suffred for his late majesty's sake ... in whose service hee lost the benefitt of one of his hands' [**254**]. When it came a few months later to mounting his defence against his dismissal, Byrd justified himself in terms of negatives: he had not been at the battle of Worcester in 1651, had never been a sequestrator, had never 'wronged any person' and had been sequestered from his office of comptroller by Parliament. This last point was something of a technicality. He meant that his patent post had been removed in 1649: but he had continued as collector on a better salary. Francis Malory had perhaps been described as comptroller or 'check', but Byrd was always the principal officer. 'Suffering' had to come into the defence somewhere, it seems [**262**].

Whatever the inconsistencies and ambiguities, therefore, Byrd showed a lively awareness of private and public behaviour and placed a premium on empirical examples of the latter. The public sphere and the private could not be separated in daily practice, even if the intellectual distinction between them could be sustained. The best illustration of this is the necessary recourse to private mercantile credit in order to make the entire customs operation work, a limitation which had caused even greater problems for Charles I than for John Byrd at Cardiff. It was, however, typical of Byrd's outlook that this aspect of his work nourished his jealous regard for his own reputation. Like Cassio in *Othello*, Byrd knew the value of his good name. 'Credit' was a word Byrd frequently used, and his repeated expression 'upon my credit' was no mere catchphrase. When things were going wrong in his public affairs, Byrd was often worried that his credit would be 'in question' or 'at stake' [**30, 67, 68, 97, 99, 111**]. The practical consequences of diminished moral standing were of course very real: men might not accept his bonds, he might have difficulty with bills of exchange. The financial and moral senses of 'credit' were inseparable.

In the light of Byrd's emphasis on the virtuous public life, and the climate of belief he lived through, it would seem natural to inquire into his religious outlook - and his views on the family, often viewed as the private realm, the antithesis of the public arena. What is immediately striking about the 400-odd letters of John

Byrd is the comparative absence of God. It is true that Byrd commends family members to God in times of bereavement or other trouble [**138, 199, 231, 441**], and he offered praise to God for the good health of himself and his family [e.g. **379, 392, 394, 405, 415, 425**]. He had a lively sense of the providence of God, which of course he shared with so many of his contemporaries: 'God willing' was a qualification he appended to many of his declared intentions. There is, however, nothing of the Puritan about him. Unlike Col. Robert Bennett, for example, whose letters on public business dripped with religious allusion, or the regicide Cols. John Jones of Maesygarnedd and Edmund Ludlow, whose every verbal or written utterance on political matters was conditioned by scriptural imagery, the tone of Byrd's letters was resolutely secular. He did not change his style when he corresponded with known religious radicals like Robert Blackborne. Byrd's views on public service or business ethics did not appear to evolve from any strong religious persuasion.

Family ties played a much more distinctive part in the shaping of Byrd's life. His letters suggest that relations with a wide variety of relatives by blood and by marriage mattered greatly to him. They do not support the judgment of historians who have relegated kinship as a factor in the family life of the period.[93] On the other hand, Byrd did not maintain relationships with all his relatives indiscriminately. He selected strands of his kinship network for active management, and ignored others. He cultivated one brother-in-law assiduously, tolerated one brother [**373**], ignored other brothers and brothers-in-law completely. He latched on to Evan Seys, one of his wife's first cousins, and seems to have had nothing to do with other less important ones. Generally speaking, he related better to his wife's family than to his own Bristol-born kin. Byrd developed what we might describe as 'factitious kinship', selecting a kinship circle from the range of possibilities.[94] One of the important ends of his choice of relatives with whom to correspond was evidently the more effective operation of his customs work. His sons, his nephew, his brother-in-law and the brother with whom he got on only moderately well were all useful to him in different ways and in different periods. Byrd's customs post was something of a family business, and had he been allowed to retain it, he would surely have wished to bequeath it in the same way as his mills and other properties. This intermingling of arenas often viewed by historians as separate compartments of life, the public and the private, may be among the distinctive features of the customs service as compared with other agencies of the state in the localities. One cannot imagine a justice of the peace or a civic official of the period, holding unremunerated office,

[93]A. Macfarlane, *The Family Life of Ralph Josselin* (Cambridge, 1970), 139, 149; K. Wrightson, D. Levine, *Poverty and Piety in an English Village: Terling 1525-1700* (London, 1979), 85, 86.

[94]The evidence of Byrd's behaviour towards his kinship circle corroborates the findings of David Cressy, who notes that 'kinship involved a range of possibilities, rather than a set of concrete obligations'. D. Cressy, 'Kinship and Kin Interaction in Early Modern England', *Past and Present* cxiii (1986), 38-69.

behaving in this way. The career and private life of John Byrd both fed into, and shaped, each other. Nevertheless, his commitment to his 'nuclear' family was never compromised. He followed the careers of his sons with devoted interest, and the frequency with which he associated his wife, Margery Byrd, with his thoughts and wishes is evidence that he discussed with her the widest range of matters: other than customs business, so far as one can tell.

VI: John Byrd and Politics

Politics is the working out of conflict, and Byrd's career was one of increasing conflict from the 1630s to the 1660s. The glimpses we have of him in the period before the civil war suggest that when aggrieved merchants alleged that he persecuted them, he was able to shrug off their complaints and plead higher orders.[95] This sense of enjoying protection was not open to him in the 1640s. It is not known what happened to him in 1642. As a customs officer at Cardiff, which on the outbreak of war was garrisoned for the king by Sir Anthony Mansel of Margam, as a tenant of the earl of Pembroke, whose rents were seized by the royalists, and as a resident of Caerleon, where the magazine was seized for the earl of Worcester, Byrd would have swum against the tide had he shown himself for parliament.[96] He accounted for a couple of cargoes of coal from Swansea between September and Christmas 1642, his last known reckoning before the conflict began to bite.[97] It is likely that the breakdown of security and the collapse of trade brought by the war would have put paid to his customs work regardless of his own political allegiances. We know that in the later stages of the war he suffered harassment by the royalists, during the short-lived but brutal intervention in South Wales by Charles Gerard.[98] In October 1644 Byrd was arrested, forced against his will to enter a bond to pay the royalist soldier, Roger Whitley, and was made to ride with him to Worcester [**283, 284**]. In February 1645 his house was plundered and his cattle stolen by John Morgan [**8**], captain of foot in Monmouthshire.[99] Whether these were the experiences which pushed him into open allegiance, or whether he was already known by his tormentors to be hostile or unsympathetic to them, at some time in 1646 Byrd was involved in arms supply for parliament [**154**], although there is no evidence he held a military commission.

It seems likely that Byrd began to keep the letter-book as a response to his sense of uncertainty as he resumed his customs work. Threats to his position were not removed by the decisive victory of parliament [**1, 2**], but he was able to

[95] E 134/ 22, 23 Charles I/ Hil. 2.

[96] C. M. Thomas, 'The Civil Wars in Glamorgan' in *Glam. Co. Hist.* iv, 260-1; Dircks, 60.

[97] HLRO Main Papers, n.d. 1642.

[98] Thomas, 'Civil Wars in Glamorgan', 265-66.

[99] BL Add 33590 fo. 73.

mobilise some support locally and more importantly in London to fend off attacks. Through the 1650s he seems to have been more concerned to maintain his connections at the London custom house than to keep in with the local gentry. He seems to have known how to play his hand when given some opportunities to name local men of influence to unpaid positions. He chose the godly in matters of probate [**180**] and members of the merchant community in cases of cargo seizures [**79**].

The same tactics were not good enough in 1662 to ensure his continued tenure. Byrd survived the restoration itself well enough, and was in London in August 1660, probably to secure his position, and collect the patent granted him of his old post of comptroller [**285**].[100] An even earlier appointment, however, on 2 August, was that of Edmund Wogan, who had disappeared from the customs service at the outbreak of civil war, but who was now reinstated as customer; and a month later, Philip Mansel was made searcher, thus completing the triumvirate of patent officers in the port.[101] Richard Dutton's petition for his post took Byrd by surprise. As well as having been a determined plotter in the interest of Charles Stuart, Dutton was owed reward by Charles's government for having arrested Col. Daniel Axtell, the regicide - by leading him into a trap by deception.[102] Dutton was an associate of Whitley's in the royalist army and after 1660 in the law courts [**280, 283** and notes] and may have become acquainted with Byrd and his office when the latter was kidnapped by Whitley. When Dutton's petition against Byrd reached the privy council, Secretary Nicholas endorsed it on 23 April 1662 with a note that the king was inclined to grant the request for Byrd's post. The Lord Treasurer was asked to confirm the truth of the allegations against him. On being shown the petition, the customs commissioners could only confirm that Byrd's patent was at the pleasure of the king, not for life, thus making him easier to dismiss. They could not comment on any allegation against him, except that they noted it was supported by three MPs. (In fact, only two of those named sat in the House of Commons). On 24 May Lord Treasurer Southampton noted that all he could do was return to the king the petition of Dutton and a counter-certificate asserting Byrd's loyalty. The investigation proceeded no further, and Byrd's fate was sealed.[103] He was later able to demonstrate to his own satisfaction that Dutton had manufactured the support he had alleged from Laugharne, Stradling and Thomas [**326**], but by that time no-one was listening.

The evidence suggests that Byrd had had the misfortune to be targetted by an

[100] *CTB* i, 16.
[101] *Ibid.*, 10, 56.
[102] PRO SP 29/53/68; Edmund Ludlow, *A Voyce From the Watchtower* ed. A.B. Worden (Camden Soc. 4th ser. xxi, 1978), 179.
[103] SP 29/53/68; SP 44/7 p. 95.

unscrupulous and fanatical cavalier. Even so, he was left to look rather out of place after the round of customs appointments in 1660. He had a poor relationship with Wogan, and was unable to bring himself to name the customer when describing their tussle over the arms in the custom house in October 1661 [**234**]. The restored Wogan and the new men were minor representatives of important royalist families. Wogan was probably connected by marriage with the Mansels, governors of Cardiff for the king and against the earl of Pembroke in 1642. Philip Mansel, the searcher, must surely have come from the same family; and in 1661, William Paulett, scion of an aristocratic family associated with the royal court, was granted an interest in the customer's post.[104] The Pembroke interest, by contrast, was not revived at the restoration, except as a rent-collecting machine [**409**]; and Byrd seemed increasingly an isolated relic of a bygone age. This was less the result of a political conspiracy than of an inclination by the government to see posts in the revenue as part of the spoils of patronage. After Byrd's dismissal, the share-out process continued. Mansel Stradling, whose name was an obvious indication of his Glamorgan gentry family ties, was made searcher at Cardiff in 1665.[105]

The pattern of politics in Monmouthshire showed more of a focussed political direction. The political influence of the Pembrokes may not have been restored after 1660, but that of the marquis of Worcester was, however: with a vengeance. Although Raglan castle was allowed to remain in ruins while Badminton in Gloucestershire was developed as the family seat, Monmouthshire politics remained important to the Somersets, particularly to Henry Somerset, Lord Herbert of Raglan, MP for Monmouthshire in the Convention and Cavalier Parliaments. His estates were recovered from interregnum buyers; new lands were bought and secured by strict marriage settlements; a marriage was clinched with the Seymours, another powerful dynastic noble family. By these means, and by continuing the pre-civil war pattern of drawing gentry families into the Worcester influence, Somerset, who succeeded to the title Marquis of Worcester from 3 April 1667 on the death of the second marquis,[106] regained a personal ascendancy quite forgone by the Pembrokes.[107] Among the Monmouthshire families patronised by the marquis were the Morgans of Llantarnam, Sir George Probert and Herbert Evans. Byrd was a tenant of the Llantarnam Morgans at Sôr mill [**290**] but otherwise he seems to have had little to do with that powerful family. Probert was willing to swear to Byrd's innocence in his struggle against

[104]W. De Gray Birch (ed.), *Descriptive Catalogue of the Penrice and Margam MSS* (2nd ser.,1894), 105, 111, 114; CTB i, 248, 730.

[105]*CTB* i, 736.

[106]GEC, *Complete Peerage* (new edn., 14 vols. 1910-59), xii, part 2.

[107]Molly A. McClain, '"I Scorn to Change or Fear": Henry Somerset, First Duke of Beaufort, and the Survival of the Nobility Following the English Civil War' (Yale University PhD thesis, 1994), 65, 86-90.

Dutton [**262, 329**], but that was as far as their relationship went. Nevertheless as late as October 1666, Byrd was happy to mediate on behalf of the Jones family of Llanarth [**343**], a Catholic family whose sons were before the civil war educated at Raglan.[108]

It was a feature of Monmouthshire society that there was a high incidence of Roman Catholicism in particular parts of the county, notably the deanery of Abergavenny, the country between Abergavenny and Monmouth. Newport deanery, the area where Byrd lived, was, by contrast the part of the county where Catholics were fewest in number.[109] As the 1660s and 70s wore on, political tensions rose between those who were seen as Catholic and crypto-catholic clients of the Marquis and those gentry who saw themselves as standing for Protestant moderation.[110] Among these latter gentry were Sir Trevor Williams of Llangybi, the Morgans of Tredegar and - crucially for Byrd - the Seys family, whose most powerful member was Evan, a serjeant-at-law whose sponsors at his admission to that order in 1656 were John Disbrowe and Col. Philip Jones, both leading Cromwellians.[111] Byrd had not cultivated Seys assiduously during the 1650s, if the letter-book is reliable testimony, but in the 1660s he saw his wife's cousin as crucial first in the recovery of his customs post [**284**] (here, wrongly, as it turned out) and then in helping the career and prospects of his son Mathias [**382, 391**]. Later still he was calling on the serjeant to appear in legal cases for his friends [**414**]. Some of this developing relationship may be accounted for by Byrd's close links with London customs house figures in the 1650s, for whom a decade later Seys was substituting; some by Seys's own steady rise to eminence, and some by Byrd's anxieties about Monmouthshire politics. He was so upset about the prospect of being named to the office of sheriff in 1663 that he listed it before the sudden death of his son as a personal trouble [**307**]. Three years later, in October, the time the king 'pricked' sheriffs, Byrd was on to Seys again about it [**344**], and when the sheriff, Christopher Perkins, died in office in the summer of 1667 Byrd wrote once more for Seys's intervention in his interest [**365**]. The causes of Byrd's anxiety on this occasion were greater than the mere threat of personal inconvenience. The old marquis of Worcester was dead; a parliamentary by-election was in the offing, and the sheriff was in charge of the election. The Perkins family had provided deputy stewards for the earl of Pembroke's Monmouthshire properties.[112] Which was the worse 'evell' worrying him: that he himself might be chosen or that a client of the new, aggressive marquis would be successful in taking the shrievalty? A month after Byrd wrote to Seys, the

[108]McClain thesis, 32.

[109]P. Jenkins, 'Anti-popery in the Welsh Marches', *Historical Journal* xxiii (1980), 277.

[110]Jenkins, 'Anti-popery', 281; McClain thesis, 94-8.

[111]Jenkins, 'Anti-popery', 282-3, J.H. Baker, *The Order of Serjeant-at-Law* (1984), 442.

[112]NLW Badminton Deeds and Documents, 804.

marquis complained to his wife of the 'open defiance' of the Monmouthshire gentry toward him.[113] Whether or not Seys was effective in this case, the by-election, held on 7 November, was a victory for the anti-Worcester gentry, whose candidate, Sir Trevor Williams, was successful in the teeth of the eight files of musketeers sent by the marquis to overawe the electors.[114] From this point, Byrd may have become more open about naming the marquis as an opponent [**414**], and in 1671 wrote to remind Seys about the annual choice of sheriff, thanking him at the same time for intervening in a case at Chepstow, a town in the heartlands of the marquis's influence [**410**]. There is also the suggestion of his good opinion of Henry Walter, leader of the nonconformists in his locality, and brother of Byrd's fellow-sufferer in the civil war, even though Byrd himself stayed within the established church [**298, 414**]. Opposition to the marquis may have drawn in other shadowy figures like Byrd, who had no appetite for active politics, so far as we can tell.

The political history of Monmouthshire cannot be written from the perspective of one participant, and Byrd was in any case on the margins of politics, but various aspects of his life were touched by this developing conflict. In 1678 Byrd arranged a marriage match between the house of another cousin of his, Richard Seys of the Rhydding, Neath, and the Williamses of Caerleon; he wrote warmly to Seys, thanking him for a gift of pickled oysters [**445**]. Soon afterwards Seys was dismissed from the commission of the peace at the instigation of the marquis of Worcester, allegedly for being 'against the king', for perverting the course of justice and interfering with the work of local excise officers.[115] It was a clear case of political revenge against Seys, whose family was coming to represent the opposition to the marquis. Byrd must have been distressed to see his old adversary, Dutton, in the same year raise with the marquis a regiment in Bristol of 100 militia volunteers.[116] However independently Dutton had launched himself into South Wales society at the restoration, he was by the end of Byrd's life a confirmed ally of the revived Raglan interest, the antithesis of all Byrd's links and associations. Despite Byrd's prediction that his enemy would sell the comptrollership [**326**], Dutton still held the post in 1672.[117] It was none the less but a stepping stone for Dutton's more glittering career in the army and eventually to the governorship of Barbados from 1680 to 1685, for behind the marquis lay an even more powerful patron, the Duke of York, the future James II.[118] As part of the building up of this Worcester-Stuart interest, not only did the

[113] McClain thesis, 94.

[114] *House of Commons* 1660-1690 i, 317-8; McClain thesis, 171.

[115] McClain thesis, 165-6.

[116] *CSPD 1667*, 234; McClain thesis, 139-40; Jenkins, 'Anti-popery', 283, 285n.

[117] BL Add. 6133 fo. 41.

[118] [Morgan], *Memorials of the Duttons of Dutton in Cheshire* (Chester, 1901), xxv; S.S. Webb, *The Governors-General* (Chapel Hill, North Carolina, 1979), 470-1.

marquis of Worcester by the late 1670s control customs appointments at Cardiff through Dutton; another client of his, John Dutton Colt, claimed to uncover corruption at the Bristol custom house after having played a significant role in the Popish Plot in 1679.[119] The plot was the culmination of well over a decade of conflict within Monmouthshire, but by then Byrd was in his dotage. The history of the Cardiff customs posts in his lifetime is surprising. Despite the upheavals of the 1640s and 50s Byrd had been left largely untouched by political changes, even when the Rump Parliament 'new modelled' the customs. The greatest change in those years was the hiving-off of Swansea as a separate port, a change seemingly made for operational reasons. The comptrollership became much more politically sensitive after 1660, when it became first a trophy in the cavalier rewards share-out, and subsequently a tool in the build-up of power and influence by the marquis of Worcester. On a longer view, the posts at the Cardiff custom house may have been less subject to specifically local pressures during the Interregnum than at any other time in the sixteenth and seventeenth centuries.

VII: Conclusion

What we can discern of Byrd's outlook from his correspondence suggests that in this relatively unimportant provincial port, a customs officer could develop quite sophisticated and self-aware approaches to his duties, and evince sturdy self-esteem in public service, even in troubled times and even when the post-holder was no particular partisan of the political regime. If John Byrd was so principled, the final obvious question to ask about him was why in 1660 he clung on to his post so tenaciously instead of departing with good grace. The label turncoat seems so inappropriate for a man of his stamp, so what clues are there in his career to explain this piece of seemingly unprincipled behaviour? Byrd had begun work in the customs service in 1629, and so it could be argued that he had begun a king's servant, and saw no wrong in wanting to end as one. Following this logic it could be argued that what was odd was his commitment to Parliament: that the obvious thing for him to have done in 1642 would have been to side with the king, his employer. Here, however, *force majeur* plays a part: as a landowner and tenant in a town known to be territory of the earl of Pembroke, and not land of the marquis of Worcester, Byrd's allegiance in the civil war could be said to have been pre-determined. He may have felt he had no choice. His determination to fight off challenges to his position suggests he needed the money, and a very limited and superficial preliminary inquiry suggests that the customs service was staffed by many like Byrd, younger sons of the gentry, or men of ambiguous status. Henry Newbury, for example, surveyor of customs in

[119]Jenkins, 'Anti-popery', 275; G. Smith, *Smuggling in the Bristol Channel* (Newbury, 1989), 71; *Memorials of the Duttons*, xxv.

the port of London after 1660, was the son of a minor Worcestershire gentleman and the grandson of a dean of Worcester. He married the daughter of a high court judge, who described their marriage as 'unfortunate'. Like Byrd, there was something *déclassé* or *déraciné* about Newbury.[120] The structure of customs administration doubtless played a major part in Byrd's sense of loyalty and allegiance. He was consistent in regarding his 'masters' as those ultimately responsible to the king or to parliament for the efficient collection of the revenue. In the 1630s these were the customs farmers, during the 1640s and 50s the commissioners. Both these types of appointment were subject to relatively frequent change. New leases were made to new farmers; whole sets of commissioners were replaced at a time. In his thirty-odd years in the service, Byrd had ten different sets of masters. The changes in 1642 came after a decade of four separate farms of the customs. Byrd might be forgiven for adopting the attitude of *plus ça change...*

John Byrd died a respected citizen in 1683. Had he lived a few months longer he would have received a visit from a Herald of the College of Arms, who had intended compiling his pedigree.[121] The inventory of his property was modest enough: the £94 he left in valued goods, with livestock his single most valuable asset, concealed his worldly success, measured in reputation.[122] He had overcome a number of factors of birth, upbringing and circumstance which might have confined him to oblivion. He was a younger son of a younger son, made fatherless at an early age, married into a family more prestigious and more wealthy than his own, was an Englishman in what was still a distinctly Welsh region. He thought of himself as living in a poor place, which afforded 'no preferment or profit' and discouraged people from moving there to make money [**195, 209, 387**]. He never completely emancipated himself from social and economic circumstance, obviously. He managed a customs port in which overseas trade, the most lucrative for revenue, was never really buoyant. The whole economy of south-east Wales was in thrall to Bristol, which affected his capacity to appear to his masters as particularly successful. Even the manorial customs of his area - the custom of inheritance to the younger son -worked against his building up a consolidated freehold estate that he could bequeath to his family. But his letters make it evident that he was a loving husband and father, a good neighbour and a conscientious public servant: a good enough epitaph, one might consider, for anyone.

[120]*Visitation of Worcestershire*, 1682-3, 74; PRO PROB 11/ 342 fo. 366. For a discussion of customs postings in the 1650s and 1660s, in Devon: Roberts, *Recovery and Restoration,* 141-46.
[121]*Visitations in Wales*, 228.
[122]NLW LL 1683/64.

VIII: A Note on the Letter-Book and this Edition

The letter-book of John Byrd is now in the custody of the Glamorgan Archive Service at County Hall, Cathays Park, Cardiff, where its reference is CL/MS 4.266. In 1925 it was acquired by Cardiff Central Library, where its callmark was MS 49.25, having been purchased from D. Creighton Jones as part of a collection of ten manuscripts. The sum of £3 5s. 0d. was paid for the Byrd MS, and it appears that the vendor was trading in manuscripts.[123] What happened to the book between Byrd's death and 1925 is unknown. The pages of the book are of paper, and it was seemingly once bound in a parchment cover. The suggestion of J.W. Dawson that it was a blank port book may be true of the binding. Port books were normally entirely of parchment, however, so this is unlikely to be a complete explanation. The book is now in a modern binding, with the original parchment covers sewn in at the front. Byrd wrote on both sides of each leaf, and the whole volume, measuring 19.5 cms. by 30.5 cms., is paginated. Earlier printed references to the letter-book appear to be confined to J.W. Dawson's study of Newport and Caerleon as ports;[124] and to a highly informative summary by Hilary Thomas in a recent Annual Report of the Glamorgan Archive Service,[125] whose very few minor inaccuracies do not undermine its usefulness.

The volume is a record of letters written by John Byrd, with a few copies of miscellanea, between 22 February 1648 and 9 July 1651; between 8 November 1652 and 14 September 1653; and between 18 October 1661 and 14 October 1680. There is no longer any evidence to be gleaned from the physical condition of the volume as to whether the omissions are the result of excisions from a larger original. It is quite clear, however, that they do not represent periods of loss of office by Byrd. He was in post from the late 1620s right through until the last of the three periods covered by the volume. He may have begun keeping the book as a measure of security against interception of letters during the troubles of the 1640s. When he had finally departed from office in the customs service he continued to make entries in it, perhaps as a way of recording his more important correspondence or perhaps even out of force of habit. We do not know whether there were other companion letter-books or indeed any other collections of papers of Byrd's to survive his death.

The habitual abbreviations and flowing, if cramped, hand of the scribe indicate that Byrd was a practised writer, and what we know of his background bears out the impression given by his literary style that he was a man with some grounding in the law. His writing is often formulaic, and even if many of his letters were summaries and repetitions of originals which had 'miscarried', to use his term,

[123] I owe these details to the kindness of Brian Ll. James.

[124] J. W. Dawson, *Commerce and Customs. A History of the Ports of Newport and Caerleon* (Newport, 1932).

[125] *Annual Report of the Glamorgan Archivist 1990.*

which thus justified re-using the same phraseology, Byrd comes across to us as not a man to coin a new phrase when an old one would do. Closer study of John Byrd's English usage must be left to those more competent to undertake it, but it is worth noting in passing his phrase 'nailed and mailed' [**209, 259**], not known to current revisers of the Oxford English Dictionary; his use of the modern-sounding 'for love nor money' (actually current in 1590)[126] [**331**] and the related phrase 'in love or by law' [**206**]; his word 'scrawlings' for scions for fruit tree grafting [**370, 371**]. His was the English of a Bristolian who had spent time in London, and it is fruitless to search the text for any Welsh influences upon his literary style. It is nevertheless improbable that he knew nothing of the language commonly spoken in south-east Wales, and dominant in the western parts of his customs territory: none of his letters mentions any difficulties or embarrassments caused by problems of language.[127]

The letter-book of John Byrd was kept as a private record of correspondence, and so was not intended to preserve fair copies of letters. It was rather a working book, and the writer probably worked quickly when using it. As far as can be known, it seems that Byrd recorded letters in their entirety, but in the interests of speed and economy used extensive abbreviations and formulaic representations for frequently-repeated words and phrases. This requires any modern editor to decide how to reproduce the text. The intention here is to reproduce Byrd's text in an accessible form true to the original, but without imposing on the reader the more intrusive obstacles of Byrd's cursive style. The following are thus the main principles by which the text has been edited:

Each letter has been given a number and given a heading where in the original there are none. Page references have been inserted in the text at the points where new pages occur in the manuscript.

The original spelling has been retained throughout, but modern patterns of punctuation have been imposed to create what to a modern eye are grammatical sentences of modest length, instead of the sometimes tortuous periods employed by Byrd. Modern paragraphing has also been imposed. Letter formations are given in modern format: u/v and i/j have been standardised, the long s and 'thorn' replaced. Superior letters have been lowered, and the ampersand replaced by 'and'.

In an age of compulsive abbreviation Byrd was a master of the art, and the examples which occur on every line of the original text have been silently expanded. The phrase 'etc.' occurs very frequently, often on line-ends, and these have been silently removed. Otherwise the whole text has been provided, with no omissions.

[126] E. Partridge, *A Dictionary of Clichés* (5th ed., 1978), 83.

[127] G. H. Jenkins (ed.), *The Social History of the Welsh Language. The Welsh Language before the Industrial Revolution* (Cardiff, 1997), 45-62.

There are occasional Latinisms in the text, which, in the interests of reaching the widest modern readership, have been rendered into English. This has been done silently when the Latin is merely literary style; where it relates to matters pertaining to the customs, a footnote to the original has been provided.

Sums of money have been consistently rendered in a single format.

The use of square brackets in the text indicate damage, illegibility, insertion of material to elucidate Byrd's meaning or to indicate doubt as to his meaning.

In the original there is no consistent use of capitalisation, so lower case has been used rather ruthlessly throughout.

Italics have been reserved for editorial glosses.

Dates are Old Style, with years given in modern reckoning silently as beginning on 1 January, not 25 March, both in the rendering of Byrd's text and the editorial apparatus.

Place-names have been rendered as Byrd spells them, but in the notes and other editorial apparatus the form adopted has been that used in modern Ordnance Survey maps. Welsh spelling forms have generally been adopted, but Ordnance Survey versions have been preferred to 'correct' Welsh ones which are not current or would not be used in English texts. Thus, 'Llanelli' not 'Llanelly'; but 'Llanhennock' has won the day over 'Llanhenwg'.

1. TO SIR JOHN TREVOR

[*Marginated*] Swansea 22 February 1648

To Sir John Trevor I make boulde to acquainte you that I ha[ve received a] lettre from Mr Christopher Rogers whoe writeth unto mee that Mr Hodges one of the honourable co[mmittee] for the navy and customes hath promist to settle him in my place at Swansey, pretendinge that place to bee vacant, for that one Richard Symons (a man whome I employed to offitiatt for mee in my absence) is dead. Nowe my humble suite to you is that you will be pleased once more to acquainte the honourable committee of my suffringe for my affecion to the Parliament (my certifficatt thereof nowe remayneth with Mr Kellam) allsoe I desier you will bee pleased to acquainte the committee that Swansey is a member of Cardiff and that Richard Symons was only employed by mee to offitiatt for mee in my absence.

2. TO THOMAS PENNANT

[*Marginated*] Swansea 22 February 1648

Brother Pennant

I lately received ii letters from you, both impartinge Mr Sansom's love and care concerning the £30 15s. 7d. for which I thanke you both. On the 18th instant, I made bould to write to you, and in my letter sent you the copie of a letter written to mee by one Christopher Rogers, by which it seemeth hee hath by meanes of the generall Sir Thomas Fairefax obteyned a graunte from the committee of the navy for an office in the custome house at Swansey in stead of Richard Symons lately dead, whoe was noe officer, but only was employed by mee when service in other parts commanded mee to bee absent from that place. This man writeth that Mr Hodges, one of the committee of the navy and customs promised to settle him in it, conceavinge the place to be vacant on the death of Richard Symons, which is noe such thinge, for the place is myne. I earnestly pray you to acquainte Mr Kellam of the truth herein and desier that hee will be pleased to shewe my certifficatt to the committee, if he sees cause. Good brother, spare noe charge to prevent this evill; pray reade, seale and deliver the inclosed to Sir John whose help I assure my selfe I shall not want. I have sent this bearer on purpose herewith and with my severall accounts. Pray write mee word by him, what you finde in this busines.

3. TO HENRY FUTTER

[*Marginated*] Cardiff 24 February [1648]

Wrote to Mr Henry Futter to procure a discharge or paie £31 10s. due from him by bond to shereiffe Averye for his sonne Mr Dudly and inclosed a letter from Robert Futter to his unkle.

4. TO THOMAS PENNANT

[*Marginated*] Caerleon 11 March 1648

Brother Pennant

Yours by Morgan Griffith I received for which I thank you. Here inclosed is Mr Herbert's acquittance and myne 20s. the which I pray please send to Mr William Thornebury and take of him 18s. The other is Mr Herbert's and I desier him to accept of it to buy him a paire of gloves. Wee desier you to remember our loving respects to Mr Thornebury; allsoe I praye (when you shall see Mr Sansom, Mr Bulkeley and Mr Gerrard Foxe or any of them) please to present my service to them and give them harty thankes for their loving letters to mee, which I nowe received by Morgan Griffith; pray present my respects to my brother William his family, whose welfare I shall be right glad to heare of. J.B.

5. RECEIPT OF THOMAS ABBERLEY

[*Marginated*] Certifficatt per my quarter booke for March 6, 1648

Received the 6th of March 1648 of Mr Thomas Aberley, sequestrator of the estate of Sir Thomas and Mr John Dawes, surveyors of the outports, the summe of 10s. for one quarter's bookes, due at Christmas last as comptroller of Cardiffe. I say received by me JB comptroller.

6. TO EDWARD HERBERT

[*Marginated*] Caerleon 11 March 1648

Mr Edward Herbert

Yours by Morgan Griffith I received, by which I perceave the committee for the navy and customes doe not thinke fitt to make an order to cleare us from employments here, whereof I formerlie wrought unto you, but that they thinke fitt to make a request to that purpose, the which I pray forbeare to procure, for some pressinge reason to the contrary, whereof I shall acquainte you at our next meeteinge, but if a power to command may bee easily had I pray procure it. Allsoe I earnestly desier the contynuance of your love towards mee in takeing notice howe the busness proceeds concerning mee, and to prevent (whatsoever it will cost) any evill that you finde likely to fall on him that is yours faithfully to serve you, JB.

7. TO WILLIAM POWELL

[*Marginated*] Caerleon 25 March 1648

Honourable Sir, I make boulde to send this bearer unto you, prayinge that if you have founde the recognizance concerning Robert Thomas (the man that wounded mee), you will be pleased to sende it to mee by this bearer or cause it to bee sent to Cardiff to the clearke of the assizes, whereby I may bee in some measure righted for the great wrongs and crueltyes which I suffred by him. Worthy justice, I presume you are soe fully satisfied of the great wrong donne unto mee that I neede not any further expression herein, but that I am your lordshipp's faithfully to serve you, JB.

For his much honoured freinde, justice William Powell, theis, Bolston.

8. TO WALTER MORGAN

[*Marginated*] 27 March 1648

Mr Walter Morgan

Yours of the 6th instant I received with what was inclosed therein, for which I thanke you. Sir, if Mr John Morgan and Margaret Rosser or other of them shall appeare, I pray declare against them for that they about the 8th daye of February 1645 tooke out of my grounde (in the parish of St Woolloes) 6 oxen, 6 kyne and 1 bull worth at least £52 and allsoe the said John Morgan and others with him (and under his commande for being then a captain against the Parliament) tooke out of my house in St Woolloes aforesaid severall sootes of [clothes] and provisions to the valew at least of £50 for all which I pray proceede against them in my name as you shall bee best advized. JB.

Page 2

9. TO SIR JOHN TREVOR

[*Marginated*] To Sir John Trevor, Caerleon, 28 April 1648

Right worshipfull, my humble [...] to you with your good lady and deere children remembered, with humble and harty thankes for the contynuance of your favors towards mee, which I find by yours of the 17th instant. Sir John Trevor, I have beene often in the company of the gent of whome you wrote and allwayes observed him to bee free from drinke and I cannot finde or heare that he is inclyned to that or any other vice. I have enquired after his estate of which some affirme £1000 per annum, some saye more, but the least report is £800 per annum. Hee hath faire houseings, great parts of his estate lyeth rounde about it, being very good grounde and very well woodded, with other convenyences. Indeede sir it is a princely seat, and I cannot heare of any debts on this gent or on his estate, and I am informed that his sister and his ii brothers are provided for by redy money left them by theyr parents. Part of this gent's estate lyeth about Porbery in Somersettshire and parte in the forest of Dene, but St Peere his principall seate lyeth neare Chepstowe in this county of Monmoth. And the gent is descended from ii auntient and worthy families. If you please to have mee make any further progresse into this busines, please to send mee your further order, the which shall be carefully observed by your worship's humble servante, JB.

10. TO THOMAS PENNANT

[*Marginated*] Cardiff 28 April 1648

Brother Pennant

Yours of the 17th instant I received and according to your order have paid Captain Hampton £5, the which was kindly accepted and I hartily thanke you, for I beeleeve it came by your meanes. Pray present my loving respects to Col. Hampton, whoe hath donne a charitable dede in this. Sir, about 4 moneths since, the commissioners for the excise came to Swansey and Cardiffe to settle the excise, since which tyme noe trade came into our ports, neyther will come soe long as they are in these partes, wherefore I desier that my bills of store may be allowed mee in London, wherein I pray Mr Sansom's assistance, to whome I pray remember my love and service. I pray present 10s. for Mr Sansom, Mr Parsons, Mr Streley and honest Thomas Swynmoue to drinke a morneings drafte, the which I pray charge to my account. I pray cause the letters which come herewith to bee sent by your porter according to theyr directions and please to write one word of the receipt hereof. My wife desireth to bee remembered hartily to you and yours. I pray call to Mr Thornebury for 18s. uppon deliverye of his letter to him. JB.

11. TO SIR JOHN TREVOR

[*Marginated*] Caerleon 9 June 1648

Sir John Trevor

Yours of the 17th of April last I received and wrote you an answer thereto on the 26th of the same. What I then wrote is true, only for the estate it is above £1000 per annum, but since that tyme the partie hath beene soe unhappy as to be enticed to adhere to that wicked business of Chepstowe, where hee was taken prisoner, and I understand that hee is to bee removed from Chepstowe to the head quarters nere (1) Pembroke. Nowe I am confident that if you will bee pleased to procure an order to bring him up to London and there assiste for his composicion you will doe the office of a noble freinde to him and obliege very worthy men to serve you. Sir John, I humbly pray you not to slight this my playne writeinge. If you will not bee pleased to take notice of this busines, I knowe there is another gent which will doe his endevour therein, but I hope to waite on you and yours in these partes which shall bee the harty prayers of your worship's faithfull servant, JB.

1. 'Chepstow' deleted.

12. TO JOHN LOCK

[*Marginated*] Caerleon 14 July 1648

Mr Lock

In April last I ordered £20 to bee sent you from Swansey but by the way the barke in which the money was did (by some mischance) put into the county of Glamorgan nere Lantwitt where the country people plundered the barke and the money I could not recover till nowe. Here inclosed is a note for it to Mr William Knight. I pray let your man call for it, and please to write one word of the receipt therof to JB.

13. TO WALTER MORGAN

[*Marginated*] 25 July [1648]

Wrote to Mr Walter Morgan for a note of the charge betweene my mother-in-lawe and hir sonne Andrew and sent him a particular of such things as Mr John Morgan and others with him tooke from mee. JB.

14. TO THOMAS BULKELEY

[*Marginated*] Caerleon 25 July 1648

Mr Bulkeley

Here inclosed is my quarter booke to Midsommer last, with the officers' acquittance. The money remayneinge for cleareinge this account I have ordered to bee paide to Alderman John Lock. Pray present the remembrance of my loving service to Mr Sansom; and I desier both you and him to bee soe much my freinds as to procure my discharge from my noble masters the commissioners for the 3 last quarters' accounts.

15. TO WILLIAM THORNBURY AND GERRARD FOXE

[*25 July 1648*]

Wrote the same daye to Mr William Thornebury and to Mr Gerrard Foxe and sent them the customer's quarter bookes and myne to Midsommer last, with account of port cocketts to Mr Toomes, in the ½ yeare from Christmas to Midsomer last.

Page 3

16. TO THOMAS PENNANT

[*Marginated*] Caerleon 12 August 1648

Brother Pennant

Sir I make boulde to send herewith my severall quar[ter boo]kes, the which I pray cause your porter to deliver according to these severall directions. I have written to Mr Thornebury to paie you 18s., uppon certificate whereof I pray deliver the inclosed receipts for 20s., allsoe pray present Mr Strely with 10s. from mee as a token of thankefullnes for his paynes in procureinge the allowance of my bill of store. Pray presente my service to Mr Sansom, with my love to Mr Parsons, Mr Swynmoure, the messenger Mr Hadson and Mr Strely on whom I pray opportunely to bestowe a breakefast on my account. Pray deliver the inclosed to Mr George Charnock at his house in Beare Lane or at the custome house, after you have read or sealed the same and please to paie him £12 5s. and desier him to order mee to paie the other £14, which is due from mee for Algier duty at sight here, or in Bristoll at 6 dayes sight, which (God permittinge) shall bee punctually performed by JB.

17. TO GEORGE CHARNOCK

[*Marginated*] Cardiff 16 August 1648

Mr George Charnock

Yours of the 25th of July last I received accordinge to your orders therein. You shall receive here inclosed the account of the Algier duty receaved by mee since Michaelmas last beinge £26 5s., £12 5s. whereof you shall receive by this bearer, my worthy freinde and brother Mr Thomas Pennant. The other £14 I desier you please to order me to paie it here at sight or to Alderman John Lock in Bristoll (where the commissioners of the customes have beene pleased to order mee to paie the customes) at 6 dayes sight, for the dangers are soe great that I cannott tell howe to send it to London. Sir I understande somethinge is allowed for collection of this money which, if it bee, I desier to knowe what it is, that I may deducte it the next quarter, but if nothinge bee allowed, noe man shall doe the service more freely then JB.

18. TO JOHN LOCK

[*Marginated*] Caerleon 24 August 1648

Mr John Lock

About a moneth since I wrote to you requestinge that you would be pleased to lett your man call to Mr William Knight for £20 according to a note which was inclosed in that my letter unto you, and this last weeke a freinde promised to paie £29 16s. 11d. for mee to you, and to receave the like summe here of mee. Sir I pray please to write mee word whether you have receaved the said summes or eyther of them or not, that I may take order therein accordinglie; thus pray one word hereof from you to JB.

19. TO JOHN LOCK

[*Marginated*] Cardiff [*no date*]

Wrote to Alderman Lock by Mr Michael Deyos and sent Mr Thomas Taynton's note to him to receive £29 16s. 11d. of Mr George Helliar.

20. TO MICHAEL SANSOM

[*Marginated*] Newport 20 September 1648

Mr Sansom

I pray please to take notice that yours of the 15th instant came safe to my hands concerning safe tradeing to London by sea, and I have sent copies thereof to the ports within my charge according to commande layde on mee therein. I pray please to present my remembrance of my humble duty and service unto my masters the commissioners and acquainte them that wee have but little trade at present in our ports, lately ii tobaccoe shipps of Bristoll beinge homewards bound stayd in Pennarth and Ely and discharged parte of theyr ladeings at Cardiffe and Newport. Sir, I pray please to acquainte them that if any thinge happen within my charge fitt to trouble them withall, I will not spare writeinge unto them. Thus etc. JB.

21. TO THOMAS PENNANT

[*Marginated*] Caerleon 25 September 1648

Brother Pennant

Yours with my certifficatt and orders I received and doe hartily thanke you for them, as alsoe for paieinge the money to Mr Charnock. Good brother, procure order from him that I may paie the £14 remayneinge in my hande, and what other money I shall receive for Algier, eyther in these partes or in Bristoll, for the sendeinge money to London is soe dangerous that I dare not adventure it. Our customer Mr Edward Herbert will shortly bee in London, whoe I have desired to call to you for this order; if it cannott bee had before the bearer hereof shall come downe I pray deliver it to Mr Herbert, whoe will convey it to mee. Pray present the inclosed to Mr Sansom, with remembrance of my humble service to him and please to bestowe a breakefast or dynner on him with Mr Streley, Mr Parsons, Mr Swynnowe and the messenger at the custom house when you have opportunety, and charge it to the account of JB.

22. TO THOMAS BULKELEY

[*Marginated*] Swansea 27 October 1648

Mr Bulkeley and true friend

Yours of the 17th instant I received by which I finde the contynnuance of your love, for which I hartily thanke you. Sir I here inclosed send you my quarter booke to Michaelmas last, with my bill of fees and charge with the officers' acquittance and I have sent parte of the money remayninge on this account to Mr Lock, and have taken course for payment of the remainder to him, which will shortly bee performed, after performance whereof I desier both goe to my worthy freinde Mr Sansom (to whome I pray present the remembrance of my service) to procure a generall discharge for mee for the yeare ended at Michaelmas last from my masters the commissioners, for which kindnes (God willinge) I will appeare really thankefull, both to you and him, and will soe rest, JB.

23. TO WILLIAM THORNBURY

[*No date*]

Mr Thornebury

You shall receive here inclosed the customer's quarter bookes and myne, to Michaelmas last. Pray please to paie 18s. to my worthy freinde and brother Mr Thomas Pennant, of whome you shall receive and acquitt for 20s. W[herefore] pray accept of the other 2s. to drinke our healthe. Thus in hast resteth JB. [*Memorandum*] Sent our quarter bookes the same tyme to Mr Gerrard Foxe and wrote my letter to him with our bookes. JB.

Page 4

24. TO THOMAS PENNANT

[*Marginated*] Swansea 27 October [1648]

Brother Pennant

True freinde, yours with Mr Sansoms and Mr Bulkeleys of the 17th instant I received, by which I finde the contynuance of your love towards mee, for which I kindly and hartily thanke you. Sir I pray please to employ your porter to deliver my severall letters which come herewith. Here inclosed are the customer's acquittances and myne for 20s. I pray uppon receipt of 18s. to deliver them to Mr Thornebury. I pray write mee word of the receipt hereof by the first conveyance and if any answers may bee had to the letters I herewith sende, I pray sende them downe with yours. Allsoe if Mr Charnock's order may be had for payment of the Algier duty, eyther in these partes, or at Bristol, I shall (God willinge) performe it, for I dare not runne the adventure of that money to London. Good brother, pardon my beinge contynually troublesome unto you, if God shall enable, or graunte opportunity, I will appear thankefull to you and yours; pray present the remembrance of my wifes true love and myne to my sister and all yours. I have written to Mr Sansom to procure my discharge from the commissioners for my receipts, in the year ended at Michaelmas last. Pray when you have opportunety please to put him in mynde thereof. Thus rest J B.

25. TO THE COMMISSIONERS OF THE CUSTOMS

[*Marginated*] For the commissioners of the customs. Swansea 27 October 1648

Right worshipful

Pray please to take notice that I have sent my quarter booke with my bill of charge and disbursements in the quarter ended at Michaelmas last to Mr Thomas Bulkeley, your accomptant, and I have sent parte of the money due by my account to Alderman Lock, and the remainder in full of my account I have ordered to bee paide him which will shortly bee performed, after performance whereof, I humbly pray that you will be pleased to give mee your discharge for my receipts in the yeare ended at Michaelmas last. Here is lately 300 rowles of tobaccoe landed out of a barque that came from the Barbathoes. I have taken securety for payment of the custome due thereon, at St Pauls tyde next, to Alderman Lock. This tobaccoe beinge a very bad parcell, wee thought fitt to give tyme for payment of the custome, rather then to deteyne it in our custody, least it should in little tyme become quite rotten. The Rebecca of Bristol lately arryved at Cardiffe laden with fresh salt, and 109 rowles of tobaccoe was landed there out of the Lylly of Bristol. The revoltinge of Silly and the Irish friggotts have spoyled our trade, but one Brittayne which came hyther since midsummer last escaped: all the rest were pillaged by those friggotts. Thus etc.

26. TO MICHAEL SANSOM

[*Marginated*] Swansea 27 October 1648

Mr Sansom

Please to take notice that yours of the 17th instant I received and accordinge to your friendly advice I have here inclosed written to my worthy masters the commissioners the state of affaires here at present, after my money shal bee all paide to Alderman Lock, which I have allready left to be retorned to him. I humbly pray your love in procureinge a discharge for mee, for my receipts in the yeare ended at Michaelmas last, as you did for mee when I was last at London, and please to deliver it to my brother Pennant and hee will conveygh it to mee. Charety remembers hir humble service to you, with Mrs Sansom and her maid Burrows.(1)

1. 'Burros' in MS.

27. TO JOHN LOCK

[*Marginated*] Caerleon 27 November 1648

Mr Lock

About a moneth since Mr Patrick Jones sent you by Mathew Williams £50 on my account from Swansea, the which I hope you have received. I alsoe left in the hands of Mr Thomas Rymbron and Mr Samuel Sicklemore in Cardiffe £76 which I hope Mr Rymbron promised to make good to you the last(1) weeke and Mr Thomas Taynter promised to pay you for my accompt this weeke(2) £56 19s. 9d., which is in all £182 19s. 9d. it beinge for my worthy freinds and masters the commissioners for the customs of England. I pray please to acquainte them hereof, with remembrance of my humble duty and service to them; alsoe I desier you please to write mee one word of the receipt of the particulars abovesaid(3) as allsoe one(4) word wheither you have received £29 16s. 11d. of Mr George Hellier for my account or not; I sent you order for it by Mr Michaell Dayos long since. I shall receave by this bearer £25 6s. 10½d. beinge Algier duty in my hands, the which I pray sende to Mr George Charnock with the inclosed letter; allsoe I pray please to write mee word what allowance is made for collectinge the Algier duty wherein you will much obliege J B.

1. 'last' interlined.
2. 'and Mr Thomas Tayntor.....this weeke' interlined over 'and nowe I sende

you by this bearer Mr Thomas Young', struck through.

3. Followed by 'wherein you will much obliege JB', struck through.

4. 'As allsoe one' interlined.

28. TO GEORGE CHARNOCK

[*Marginated*] Cardiff 22 November 1648

Mr George Charnock

Please to take notice that the customs inwards and outwards received in our port of Cardiff and members amounteth to £226 17 3¼d. in the quarter to Michaelmas 1648, the Algier duty due thereon beinge £11 6s. 10½d. with £14 formerlie in my hands I have sent to Alderman John Lock in Bristol whoe (I understande by Mr Edward Herbert our customer) hath ordered through you to receave the same. I desier you please to write mee word of the receipt hereof, with your order to contynnew this course for the future, which God permittinge shallbee carefully performed by J B.

£174 14s. 2½d.	customs inwards in the quarter to Michaelmas 1648
£052 03s. 0 ¾d.	customs outwards in the same quarter
£226 17s. 0¼d.	
£11 6s. 10½d.	Algier duty on this custom
£14 0s. 0d.	formerlie in my hande
£25 6s. 10½d.	which I sent to Alderman Lock by William Meredith

Page 5

29. TO JOHN LOCK

[*Headed*] Caerleon 6 December 1648

[*Marginated*] For Alderman John Lock

Yours of the 27th November last I received, for which I hartily thanke you. I understande by yours that 5s. is wantinge in the £50 from Swansea, which it seemes was mistaken in tellinge thereof. I here inclosed sende 5s. to make that up £50; alsoe here inclosed is a bill of exchange for Mr Thomas Taynton on Mr Edward Bovey, ironmonger, for the £56 19s. 9d. which Mr Taynton formerlie promised to paie you on my account. Pray please to call to Mr Bovey for it. Mr Thomas Rymbron and his wife are or will bee in Bristoll this weeke and I assure my selfe hee will make good the £76 to you for my account. I pray when you heare of his beinge in Bristoll, please to sende to him for this money; your love herein will much obliege mee to contynnewe, sir, yours faithfully to serve you, J B.

30. TO JAMES PARRY

[*Marginated*] Caerleon 14 December 1648

Mr James Parry

My aunte Hulls hath sent hir sonne herewith to put you in mynde of hir humble suite to Col. Herbert for restoreinge of hir oxe, beinge a beast which shee bought since my unkle Hulls dyed, and on Friday last was taken from hir for a heriott conceaved to bee due at the death of hir husbande, whose house wherein hee lyved and dyed is free houlde, and whether it bee in the lordshipp of Coldrey or not, shee cannot tell; at whose death it is generally conceaved nothing was due to the lord; for hee held his farme from Mr Kemeys only duringe pleasure. Howsoever, if you or Col. Herbert doe beeleeve in your consciences that this heriott is due, then my aunt's humble request is that the honourable colonel will bee soe favourable unto hir as to deliver the oxe to this bearer, and if it shall appeare to you and us whoe are tenants at a generall courte to bee helde in that lordship that a heriott is due, then shee will paie what hee thinkes fitt in reason in leiu thereof, which I will undertake shee shall performe. I pray present the remembrance of my humble service to the honourable colonell and I earnestly entreate him to looke upon the base condicion wherein the tenants of Coldrey are all ready. Uppon my creditt, if I did beeleeve it were due, noe more should bee more ready to finde and present it, then J B.

31. TO JOHN LOCK

[*Marginated*] Caerleon 1 January 1649

For Alderman John Lock

Worthy sir, yours of the 28th of December last I received, by which I finde the unjust dealinge of Mr Rymbron. I intende (if God permitt) to ryde to Cardiffe to morowe about this busines, and afterwards shall give you a farther account herein. I here inclosed sende you a bonde on Mathewe Franklyn of Swansey merchant of £100 dated 25th daye of October last, with condicion to paye you for my account £50 on the 28th daye of January next, the which I am confident will bee performed accordinglie. Pray please to take notice that this money is for my masters the commissioners for the customs of England, soe that when you have received it, please to charge it to that account. Pray please to write mee one word of the receipt hereof, wherein you will marke, and more obliege him that is, sir, J B.

32. TO JOHN LOCK

[*Marginated*] Caerleon 15 January 1649

For Alderman John Lock

Worthy sir, Yours of the 4th present I have received, for which and all other your favours I hartily thanke you. Sir, here inclosed I sende you a bond date 27th of December last (on Mr Mathew Francklyn of Swansey merchant and Francis Payton of your citty cooper) of £60 with condicion for the payment of £30 to mee or my assignes at your house in Bristol on the 25th day of this moneth. I have conferred with Mr Franclyn herein whoe tells mee that Mr Payton will make this good to you on the daye, to which purpose I write to him here inclosed. Also I here inclosed sende you a bill of exchange for Mr Rymbron dated 13th instant for £100 to bee paide you by Mr William Yeomans of Bristol merchant, at 5 dayes sight, with a letter of advice to him for Mr Rymbron to that purpose. Pray please to sende one of your servants to demaunde the severall summes abovesaid and to deliver the letters whereby those moneys may bee paide. Out of the £100 Mr Rymbron hath ordered you £5 14s. according to your demaunde, the rest thereof and the £30 abovesaid is for my worthy masters the commissioners for the customes of England by my account. I pray please to write mee one word by this bearer of the receipt hereof and what answers are given for payment of these moneyes, that I may order the cleare of my account accordinglie. Your wonted love herein will obliege mee to cotynnewe yours to be commanded J B.

Page 6

33. TO WALTER MORGAN

[*Marginated*] Caerleon

[*Headed*] 30 January 1649

Wrote to Mr Walter Morgan, desireinge him and Mr Thomas Powell to take advice of my cousin Mr Evan Seys, and soe to proceede for mee against Mr John Morgan.

34. TO EVAN SEYS AND OTHERS

[Marginated] 31 [January 1649]

Wrote to my cousin Seys to advize and direct as abovesaid.
Wrote to brother Pennant desireinge to here from him.
Wrote to cousin William Byrd desireinge an account concerneinge the acte for regulatinge the officers of the navy and customes.

35. TO EDWARD HERBERT

[*Marginated*] Caerleon 31 January 1649

Mr Herbert and true freinde

I have seene an acte of parliament touchinge the regulateinge the officers of the navy and customes, for which are ordained and appointed commissioners Alderman Thomas Andrewes, Mr William Barkeley, Mr Maurice Thompson, Mr Richard Shute, Col. William Willoughby, Mr William Pennoyer, Mr Samuel Penoyer, Mr Stephen Estwick, Mr John Hollande, Mr John Langley, Mr Richard Hill, Major Robert Thompson, Mr James Russell, Mr Samuel Moyer, Mr Jonathan Andrewes and Mr Richard Hutchinson, who together with the commissioners of the navy for the tyme beinge, sittinge in Mincinge Lane London, or any 5 or more of them (except such of them as are disinabled by this acte) are hereby declared commissioners. Sir by this acte the officers of the customes may not after this daye receave any fee for cockett, bill or certifficatt of any merchant, but shall have theyre sallaryes augmented according to the paynes to bee taken in theyre severall places. I am confident that twice the customes which shall hereafter bee receaved in Wales will not paie the officers and theyre deputyes sallaries, which of necessity must bee employed in the service of the customes, for the extente of the Welch ports, beinge soe large and the number of the members and creekes (where wee have deputies) soe many and the excise (upon the matter) nowe settled in all our ports, our receipts will bee[1] very little, yet the charge very great and if the fees which merchants did usually paie bee taken away, the charge must needes fal on the state. Last night I sawe this acte and this daye would have sent a message to all the ports within our charge to stopp the receipt of fees from the merchants, but our freinds advize the contrary till I should heare from you. Wherefore I desier you to conferre with the commissioners to knowe what must bee donne herein, and if they please or that you finde it convenient for mee to come up to London I pray write mee word, and I will hasten away. Allsoe pray write mee at large what must bee donne in the premises and that with the first post, or other convenyent messenger, the which shalbe carefully put in execucion by J B.

1. Followed by 'bee' in MS.

36. TO SAMUEL AVERY

[*Marginated*] Caerleon 13 March 1649

Right worshipful

After my humble duty and services remembered unto you with humble and harty thankes for all your loving favours towards mee, I rode yesterdaie to Monmoth assizes where I delivered your letter to Mr Ed[mund] Morgan and demanded your money of him according to your letter to mee; but hee beinge unprovided in that place could not performe your demaunde. Allsoe hee sayth that his sonne acquainted him that £30 of what money you demaunde was paide you by a clothier whose name hee did not remember at present, but wrote you his name formerlie, and if you please to allowe that £30, hee will paie the remainder to mee (or to whoe else you please to order him) in May next, and for his sons entertaynement whilest hee was with you, if you conceave hee did not deserve it, Mr Morgan reserveth it wholly to you and what you please to order hee will paie you. Truly worthy master, I finde Mr Morgan very willinge to satisfie you to your owne contente. If you please to write mee your pleasure herein, with what else you please to commande mee, it shal bee carefully and faithfully observed in soe much as may bee in the power of your worships humble servant J B. To the right worshipful Alderman Averye.

37. TO GEORGE CHARNOCK

[*Marginated*] Caerleon 15 March 1649

Mr George Charnock

Yours of the 20th of February last I received on the 10th instant, and according to the same you shall receive herewith the generall account and particular entryes by which the Algier duty hath beene received in the port of Cardiffe and members thereof, by which remayneth in my hands 20s. 8d. which I will paie uppon your letter at Bristoll or here, to whome you please to order. Pray please to write one word of the receipt hereof to him that is yours assuredly to serve you J B.

Page 7

38. MEMORANDUM

[*No date*]

2 letters of one tenor with copies of an order for certifieinge what shipps or other vessells in the states service arryve or stay in harbours with the reason thereof; 1 to Cardiffe and the other to Swansey; as followeth, namely:

39. TO OFFICERS OF THE CUSTOMS AT CARDIFF AND SWANSEA

[*Marginated*] Caerleon 9 April 1649

Gent[lemen]

My faithfull respects to you remembered; I pray please to write mee word by the first opportunety of the receipt of the inclosed, and if any such vessells as are therein expressed are nowe or have lately beene nere you, I pray a word what tyme they arryved and when departed and the reason of theyr stay and whoe commanded them. This I pray performe from tyme to tyme by messengers expresse, if you have not other opportuneties, with what trade or other newes in your partes, whereby I may discharge commaunde which is layde on your faithfull freinde to serve you. J B.

40. TO THE COMMISSIONERS OF THE CUSTOMS

[*Marginated*] For the Commissioners of the Customes. Cardiff 13 April 1649

Right worshipful

Pray please to take notice that according to yours of the 30th of March last, I here inclosed send you my quarter booke and bill of fees and charges in the quarter ended the 25th of March, and shall soe soone as possibly I canne paie in the moneyes to Alderman Lock. I received ii letters for Milforde, the which I sent away by a messenger expresse. An answer thereto (from Mr Buckridge) is here inclosed. I formerlie received 2 letters from you; one importinge that noe provisions etc. should bee exported to Irelande and the other requireinge an account of what shipps or other vessells employed in the service of the state should stay in any harbour within my charge, copies of which ii letters I have sent to all ports within my charge. Thus not haveinge else to trouble you with at present, I humbly take leave and rest. J B.

41. TO GERRARD FOXE

13 April 1649

Sent my quarter booke to Mr Foxe, 13 April 1649, and allsoe the customer's quarter booke.

42. TO THOMAS BULKELEY

[*No date*]

Wrote to Mr Thomas Bulkeley desireinge him to call to the commissioners for my quarter booke and bill of charge above written that it might by him audited.

43. TO NEPHEW WILLIAM BYRD

[*Marginated*] By Caerleon

Wrote to cozen William Byrd and enclosed my quarter booke and acquittance for 10s. to Mr Thornebury orderinge him to receive 9s. and take it for his paynes.

44. TO THOMAS PENNANT

[*No date*]

Enclosed the quarters letters and bookes last above written in a letter to brother Pennant, desireinge him to sende them by the porter as they are directed, and desired him to call for £10 at the custome house which was my second bill of store, and to keepe it till I should dispose thereof.

45. TO EDWARD CRESWICK

[*No date*]

Sent the packet abovesaid to Mr Edward Creswick in Bristoll, to bee sent up and sent him 28s. for a Cheddar cheese weight 56lbs. and ½ desireinge him to keep it till I should dispose thereof.

46. TO MICHAEL DEYOS

[*No date*]

Wrote to Mr Michael Deyos desireinge him to conferre with Mr Francis Yeomans about Francis Paytons bonde of £60 for payment of £30; which if paide in, to deliver the same to Alderman Lock for the commissioners of the customes.

47. TO MICHAEL SANSOM

[*Marginated*] Cardiff 3 May 1649

Mr Sansom

On the 13th of April I wrote to my masters the commissioners and sent them my account and bill of fees and charges in a packett inclosed to my brother Pennant at skynners hall. Allsoe I sent therewith a letter which came from Mr Buckridge by Pembroke but Mr Barker beinge nowe come from London tells me he heard nothing of my bokes, soe that I humbly desire you to write me one word whether they are come to hand or not. If not I will spedily sende up my booke and bill againe; but for Mr Buckridge he wrote to me to paie the messenger which went with letters to him, for that hee had noe money of the states in his hand.

48. TO JOHN LOCK

[*Marginated*] Caerleon 3 May 1649

Alderman Lock

Mr Francis Yeomans wrote to mee that he had receaved the £30 by Mr Payton, and that he would paie it to you on my account for the commissioners of the customs above a weeke since which if he hath not donne I pray doe me the favour to send to him for it. Allsoe I pray sende the inclosed to Mr Sansom by the first post. Thus prayinge one word in answer hereof I take leave and rest.

49. TO THE COMMISSIONERS OF THE CUSTOMS

[*No date*]

[*Marginated*] For the commissioners of the customs

Right worshipful

Pray please to take notice that yours of the 11th instant I received and according to your comande doe here inclosed sende you the account and extente of the port of Cardiff and members with the places where officers doe attende, as allsoe the sallaryes which were paide to the head officers whose deputies were heretofore paide by theyr care and paynes by the fees which were received from the merchants; but since those fees have beene taken of[f], both the head officers and our deputyes doe humbly depende on(1) your worships to consider of(2) such sallaryes as you shall thinke fitt for each of us. And(3) I humbly conceave it would bee proper (with your approbation and commande) that I did conferre with the severall deputyes employed in our ports to knowe what sallary each man may expect; for the service is farre greater in one place then in another; our generall trade beinge most the port to port and very little customs received in any of the ports within my charge but only in Swansey Cardiffe and Newport; and at this present noe trade in any of them but only one poore Norman arryved in Swansey to lade coles, whoe was taken by an Irish frigott by the way and robbed of all the poore men had.

I(4) am confident that all those whoe are employed in customs causes in our port and members are both honest and able men, which if I knowe the contrary shall hereafter finde any man to bee otherwise, I shall use all care, whereby such which shall bee founde unfaithfull may bee removed; for our chiefest care in this tyme of danger is to employ honest and faithfull men in each place. Thus herein desireinge to knowe your further command which shall bee [*Page 8*] faithfully performed by your worshipps humble servant J B.

The extente of the port of Cardiff and members

Imprimis Horse Pill miles

From thence to Chepstowe	3
To Matherne	2
To Redwick Pill	4
To Gouldclift Pill	2
To Newport	4
To Peeterstone Pill	4
To Cardiffe	4
To Sylly	6
To Barry	2
To Aberthawe	4
To Newton	6
To Neath	10
To Swansey	6 and to Porteynon by Swansea 8 miles
To Burry	6

The names of the officers of Cardiffe and theyr sallaryes per annum

Edward Herbert customer	£16 6s. 8d.
John Byrd collector	£30 and rydeinge charges
John Byrd comptroller	£10
Philip Williams searcher	£10
Robert Barker surveyor	£40 and rydeing charges

The customers deputyes are namely in Chepstowe Mr William Jones; in Newport Mr John Plumley; in Cardiff Mr Jenkin Williams; in Newton Mr Watkin Lyson; in Neath Mr William Morgan; in Swansey Mr John Thomas; in Bury Mr Robert Williams; in Porteynon Mr David Bennett.

The comptroller and collector his deputyes are namely in Chepstowe Mr William Huggett; in Newport Mr John Plumley; in Cardiffe Mr Arthur Roberts; in Newton Mr Jenkin Arnold; in Neath Mr John Griffith; in Swansey Mr Patrick Jones; in Aberthaw Mr Robert Williams; in Burry Mr Robert Baznett; in Porteynon Mr John Price.

The searchers deputies are in Newport John Rosser; in Cardiffe Rees Griffith; in Swansey Mr Morgan Jones; in Burry William Thomas; in Neath Hopkin Lyson; in Newton Jenkin Arnold; in Sully Thomas Tanner; In Barry Christopher Williams; in Aberthawe hee offitiateth himselfe.

1. 'Depende on' interlined over illegible words struck out.
2. 'Consider of' interlined over 'appointe' struck out.
3. This sentence appears as a postscript on p. 8, indicated by a pointing hand in margin.
4. 'I' preceded by 'And' struck out.

50. TO NEPHEW WILLIAM BYRD AND THOMAS PENNANT

[*Marginated*] Caerleon 19 May 1649

I wrote to cozen William Byrd and sent a letter to brother Pennant to bee delivered by W B and I wrote brother Pennant to deliver 40s. to William Byrd juniour: one 20s. by himselfe, the other by his mother; allsoe sent the letter and account to William Byrd to bee delivered to the commissioners and desired both brother Pennant[1]

1. Sentence incomplete.

51. TO WALTER MORGAN

[*Marginated*] Caerleon 30 May 1649

Mr Walter[1] Morgan

I wrote to you the last terme, the which my letter I understande you received, but I have not received any answer thereto; by which and by the former neglectinge of my sutes, I conceave your own employments to bee soe great that you have noe tyme spare to prosecute my poore affaires; wherefore I have desired my unkle Mr Ed[ward] Morgan to proceede in my suites for mee; wherefore I desier you to forbeare to doe any thinge in my sutes hereafter; for by your negligence I am like to suffer very much. Thus resteth, yours J B.

1. 'Water' in MS.

Page 9

52. TO EDWARD MORGAN

[*Headed*] Caerleon 4 June 1649

Unkle Morgan

Sir I understande not what a speciall impl[ead]ance meaneth. Wherefore I pray consider whether it will be best for mee to goe to tryall next assizes or not. I conceave it proper to have an answer eyther of confession or deniall that an yssue may bee had to goe to tryall on; howsoever pray proceed for mee herein as you would doe for your selfe in the like case: my witnesses are hereunder named. Sir you shall receive here inclosed the coppie of Thomas Tates bond, and a coppie of cousin Edwards declaracion, allsoe a letter to Mr Walter Morgan to surcease doeinge any thinge for me in my suite if hee hath renewed the writt at attachment and rebellyon against Tate as I wrote to him retornable in Michaelmas terme. I pray bringe that downe with you for I conceave it will doe well to proceede against him with that; howsoever I leave all to your love and care for J B.

Witnesses John Bevan, John Rosser Jones, Alice Thomas, Mary Thomas,

Margarett [*blank*]; Andrew Morgan and Elinor his wife. Pray leave blankes for more witnesses J B.

53. TO THE COMMISSIONERS OF THE CUSTOMS

[*Marginated*] Caerleon 23 June 1649

Right worshipful

Pray please to take notice that yours of the 6th present I received on the 21st. There remayned due for mee before the 25th daye of March last £247 15s. 0¾d. as by my accounts to that tyme with Mr Thomas Bulkeley appeareth; £88 whereof I have paid to Alderman Lock since that tyme and at my last being in London I left with Mr Wa[l]ter Sankey a bond on Mr Henry Futter for £31 10s. 0d. which hee hoped to bee allowed by the honourable committee for the navy and customes, by reason his tobaccoe was spoyled and exported out of England for which this money is due; but if hee cannott gett it allowed, I assure myselfe hee wil paie it in whensoever you please to commaunde it. This beinge performed there will remayne in my hands for the clearinge of my accounts to the 25th of March last £128 5s. 0¾d. which shalbe paide (when required) according to your order. About a moneth since I was over all our ports at which tyme there was not any trade in any of them but only a fewe smale Brittons at Swansey for coales, but on Mondaie next (if God permitt) I intende to ryde to all ports within my charge, that I may give you a perfect account of what this quarter produceth, which I conceave will bee very little. Thus not haveinge else to trouble you with at present, I humbly take leave and rest.

54. TO MICHAEL SANSOM

[*Marginated*] Caerleon 23 June 1649

Mr Sansom

Sir here inclosed is a letter from me to my master Alderman Avery and hisparteners in answer to theyrs of the 6th instant, which came not to my hands till the 27th. I understande by this bearer (to whome I send theis to be delivered to you), my nephew William Byrd, that myne of the 19th of May was long in goinge up yet at last delivered to your hands by the commissioners, from whome I have not heard anything since. I desier you please to write mee one word what is theyr further pleasure concerninge that busines; for the officers and deputies doe much herken after sallaryes, which I wish were settled, that they might bee encouraged to goe on freely and faithfully in the service of the state. I assure you I do encourage them what I may to act really which they doe cherefully; but I beleve it is in hope to be rewarded, and indede I have assured them that they shall not loose theyr labours. Good sir, if neyther the commissioners (to whome I pray please to present the remembrance of my humble duty and service) nor your selfe canne conveniently write to me pray please to lay your commaund on this bearer, my nephewe William Byrd, whoe will bee carefull to give mee an account of what you shal bee pleased to command herein; thus desireinge the contynnuance of your wonted love I rest your faithfull servant at commande J B.

55. TO NEPHEW WILLIAM BYRD

[*No date*]

Cozen William

I conceave I have received all your letters which you have formerlie written to mee; and nowe yours of the 18th present, with your tokens, by Mr Edward Herbert I received; for which my wife and selfe thanke you kindly. If occasion shal be to use my certifficat and the other papers at the commissioners in Mynceinge Lane, then you wil finde you have bene to rash in deliveringe to Mr Sansom that to which Mr Palmers hand is; but by a letter which I received from the newe commissioners at the custome house it seemeth those in Mynceinge Lane have given over the busines of the customs and that they at the custom house only have the management of that busines. I pray enquier of our friends at the custome house and write me the truth hereof by the first; howsoever I have sent you herewith copies of both the papers which I left with you according to your desier; allsoe I sende you herewith Mr Herberts quarter booke which should have bene sent up with myne but that it was myslayd but nowe you are desired to remember Mr Herbert and me to Mr William Thornebury and deliver him this quarter booke and receive of him 9s.; uppon receipt wherof deliver the inclosed receipt to him. I have written herewith to Mr Sansom: I pray deliver the letter to him and desier to knowe of him what he please to commande you to me and write me a word therof. I desier you not to be over importunate, neyther with Mr Sansom nor with Mr Palmer, only opportunely present my service to them and desier to knowe theyr commands. Languadge to any other sence wil not be wel taken by eyther of them from one of your name: you knowe what I meane, wherefore I pray carry yourselfe very carefully in what concerneth J B. Pray remember me very hartily to my brother Pennant and all his, and be sure to take his advice in my busines. Allso I desier to be remembered to father, mother, sister, and the ould people; so doth your aunte.

Page 10

56. TO THE COMMITTEE FOR THE NAVY

[*Headed*] Cardiff 14 July 1649. For the right honourable the committee for the regulacion of the affaires of the admiralty and navy sittinge at Darby House theis, London.

Right honourable

After my humble duty and service remembered unto you, I hereby make bould to acquainte you that about 3 dayes since, arryved in Pennarth rode 3 vessells belonginge to the Parliament namely the Charles and the Reason, ii shipps of London, and the Hunter, friggott of Bristoll. The searcher hath beene abord the Charles to knowe what shipps they are, and the cause of theyr staye, whoe answer they staye for fresh victualls and to carry forces for Irelande. Thus not haveinge else to enlarge I humbly take care and remayne your honours humble servant J B.

57. TO MICHAEL SANSOM

[*Marginated*] Cardiff 20 July 1649

Mr Sansom

Yours of the 7th of June I received on the 2nd of this moneth; a freinde by chance sawe it in the post house at Bristol where it seemes it stayed soe long. What letters shall hereafter bee directed to mee, I desier they may bee directed to bee left with Joseph Evans cuttler in Bristoll, whoe will take care to sende them eyther by an express or opportunely to mee, and they shalbe directed. The last letter which I received from the commissioners was long ere it came to my hands. Here inclosed is my quarter booke and bill of fees and disbursements in the quarter to the 24th of June last; the money due by this account and what remayned in my hand formerlie amounteth unto the summe of £203 8s. 8d. which I have ready in cash and shal bee paide when demanded, according to the commissioners last letter to mee. I would have sent this booke sooner, but I dayly expectinge a bill of exchange by this money to have sent up with my account, caused mee to forbeare. The Charles and the Reason, ii London ships, and the Hunter, friggot of Bristoll, have beene in Penarth rode about a weeke. I have written to the honourable committee at Derby House concerninge them; they stay for fresh victualls and to carry forces for Irelande, as they abord the Charles declare. I heare Colonel Deane is in Bristoll and if he calleth for the moneyes in my hands I shall paie it on demaund and send up his bill of exchange for the same. Pray remember my humble duty and service to all my masters the commissioners and please to acquainte them of the contents hereof and I humbly desire you to write mee one word of the receipt therof and of what else may concerne him that is yours faithfully to serve you J B.

58. TO THOMAS PENNANT

[*Marginated*] Cardiff 20 July 1649

Brother Pennant

I desier still to give you occasion to visitt our freinds at the custome house, to which end I sende the inclosed, desireinge (if you may with conveniency) to deliver it to Mr Sansom with your own hande and please to enquire howe my employments stande; and I desier you likewise to move your freinde (of whom you wrote) concerneinge mee. In the inclosed is my quarter booke and cleare of my accounts to the 29th of June last. I pray procure a word concerning the receipt thereof. My cozen William Byrd is very willinge to take paynes in any thinge which concerneth mee. I have written to him to bee advized by you especially what concerneth mee, and he hath promised to trouble you accordinglie. Wherefore good brother afforde him your best counsell and advice. Hee is very active yet may as well goe to fast as to softly in this vale of misery; pray please to direct your letters to bee left with Joseph Evans, a cuttler in Bristoll, to bee sent mee and I desier a word or twoe by the first post to him that is J B.

59. MEMORANDUM

[*No date; ?Cardiff 20 July 1649*]

Wrote to Mr Gerrard Foxe and sent him Mr Edward Herberts and my quarter booke to the 29th of June last; J B.

60. TO NEPHEW WILLIAM BYRD

[*Marginated*] Cardiff 20 July 1649

Cozen William

Yours of the 3rd and 14th instant I received for which I thanke you. Mr Lloyd desired to bee remembered to you and requested mee to give you thankes for your cyvyllyties towards him. I thanke you for your respects to Mr Palmer, I pray contynewe it and remember me kindly to him. Pray deliver the inclosed to Mr Foxe and desier a word in answer from him if my brother Pennant shall happen to bee out of towne (beinge vacacion) and will not come home in very little tyme, then I desier you to open his letter and deliver the inclosed to Mr Sansom, and desier a word from him, but if my brother Pennant be at home then pray deliver the letter to him and as I formerlie wrote to you, soe I still desier you to aske his advice in things materiall; and I assure my selfe you shall not want his best counsell. Pray remember mee kindly to Mr Thornebury and aske him whether he is to receive the customer's quarter bookes and myne as formerlie or not; which if hee is wee will sende them up; if not wee will spare that labour. I heard nothinge from Mr Sansom this 6 weekes; Mr Lloyd tould mee there is an acte to come forth concerning the excise which when it is out pray sende mee one; allsoe what other acts shall come forth I pray faile not to sende mee them if they concern custome or excise or any other generall thinge which all men ought to take notice of. My wife and selfe desier to bee remembred to father, mother, sister and the ould people, not forgettinge you. J B.

Page 11

61. TO MICHAEL SANSOM

[*Headed*] Newport 23 July 1649

Mr Sansom and faithfull freinde

I thanke you hartily for all loving favours towards mee. Sir on Saturdaie last I sent my quarter booke inclosed in myne of the 20th instant to you, since which tyme I have received yours of the 10th present by which I finde the course which was appointed for payment of the money which is in my hands is directed; and the commissioners' commaunde is that I retorne them up by good bills unto them, which is impossible to bee donne from hence, and I doubt hardly from Bristoll. Wherefore I humbly desier you to present the remembrance of my humble duty and service to my worthy masters the commissioners and desier that they wil bee pleased to graunte me theyr order for payment of my receipts to Alderman Lock as formerlie, or to whome else they please in Bristoll, which shal bee punttually performed by him that is etc J B.

62. TO THE COMMISSIONERS OF THE CUSTOMS

[*Marginated*] For Mr Harvy etc commissioners of the customes Cardiff 10 August 1649

Right worshipfull

After my humble duty remembered unto you pray please to take notice that yours of the 30th July last I have received and according to your command doe here inclosed sende my quarter booke to the 24th of June last with account currant at the ende of the booke. I came from Swansey the last week where was a French barke discharging salt and was to take in coles and at present here is not any other forraine trade in all our ports. Thus not haveinge else to enlarge I take leave and remayne your worships humble servant J B.

63. TO HENRY FUTTER

[*Marginated*] Cardiff 10 August 1649

Mr Henry Futter

I received a letter whereby I am required to give power to put your bond in suite, which I thought and hoped had beene long since cleared according to your desire and myne, but if it will not be cleared by allowance, then I pray please to paie in the money that neyther you nor I may bee questioned. I left your bond with Mr Sanky, solicitor to the commissioners, and if you please to paie the money (being £31 10s.) eyther to him or to Alderman Averye or Alderman Bateman, uppon payment thereof, you shall receive your bonde. JB.

64. TO NEPHEW WILLIAM BYRD

[*Marginated*] Caerleon 19 August 1649

Cozen William

Your severall letters with Mr Sansoms, brother Pennants, the 5 acts and all things expressed in yours I have received for which I hartily thanke you. I pray please to call to Mr Foxe for the quarter bookes which I sent him by your last; and I desier that you please to deliver my quarter book to Mr James Russell at the signe of the Golden Fleece in Wattling Streete nere Antholyns church and take a receipt for it, and I thinke hee will paie the fee which Mr Thornebury was woont to paie. Enquier after it: Mr Foxe or Mr Thornebury will tell you whether Mr Russell is to paie our fee or not. Keepe the customer's quarter booke by you till you heare further from mee. Pray remember mee hartily to my brother Pennant and all his, as allsoe to father, mother, sister and the ould people. I thanke you for your respects to Mr Swynnowe and Mr Palmer. I pray contynewe that course towards all our friends. I here inclosed write to Mr Futter: pray deliver it and procure a word in answer from him; alsoe pray remember mee kindly to Mr Sankey and acquainte him that I have written to Mr Futter to paie the money to him or to Alderman Averye or Alderman Bateman, which if hee will not doe then I will sende power to put his bond in sute but I hope Mr Futter will not put us to that trouble. Allsoe pray deliver the other letter which cometh herewith to Mr Sansom with remembrance of my faithfull love and service to him; pray remember my true love to Mr Foxe and Mr Thornebury and allsoe to honest Mr Hugh Lloyd.

65. TO THOMAS SHEWELL

[*Marginated*] Cardiff 25 August 1649

Mr Shuall

Yours with the packett I formerlie received and wrote to you word thereof by Mr Merrick, a Bristol merchant whoe went from hence on Thursdaie last in a trowe of Tewxbury which tooke goods out of the Aly[ce], which by oath made here was consigned to Bristol. I tooke security and gave cockett for landinge and clearinge the same with you. I allsoe wrote another letter to you to the same effect by lande. Sir this day I received yours of the 22nd instant, and for your true love to mee and your faithfullnes to the state therein expressed, I most hartily thanke you and I hereby assure you there shall not bee wantinge any care nor paynes to discharge my duty and performance of trust reposed in him that is yours faithfully to love, honour and serve you, J B.

66. TO THE COMMISSIONERS OF THE CUSTOMS

[*Marginated on page 12*] To the commissioners of the customs Cardiff 25 August 1649

Right worshipfull

After my humble duty and service remembered unto you with humble and harty thankes for your favours towards mee, pray please to take notice that your ii letters of the 13th instant with the acts of parliament and the orders of the honourable committee for the navy I have received, the which I have communicated to all the officers within my charge. Allsoe I have received a modell of officers and theyr sallaryes; in which noe mencion is made neyther of Swansey (where the chiefe of forraine trade is within my charge) nor of Bury, where is much trade for coles to England, nor of Newton, where is some trade for England, neyther of Aberthawe, where is constant trade for Mynhead and Bristoll and sometymes for beyond seas. Aberavon which is in the lyst is a place where noe shippinge cometh into, nor neere it; for that I conceave Aberthawe is intended and not Aberavon.

The customer's place beinge nowe layde aside I conceave that service is to be performed by the collector, which beinge soe then of necessitie I must have a deputy in each port to write bonds, cocketts and certifficats for goods from port to port, which is the generall trade of all the ports within my charge which service cannott be performed without a farre greater sallary then is allotted mee, for my deputye in Swansey and Neath will not undertake this service under £10 per peece and my deputy at Cardiffe £6 per annum. Chepstowe, Newport and Bury the like; one officer in Newton I conceave will bee convenyent to prevent harme, which I humbly pray may bee considered, for my constant course hath beene to spend my tyme where shippinge hapneth to arryve and not constantly in any one port.

Mr Philip Williams the former searcher did (on the 16th daye of this moneth) seaze on [*Page 12*] xiii sacks of wooll laden without warrant at Aberthawe in the Thomas of Aberthawe, Thomas Graunte master pretended for Mynhead, and in regard hee could not take it out of the barque he demised it into the hands of Morgan Jenkin and hath taken securety by bond, that the valewe of the said wooll shall bee made good if recovered by lawe. I humbly desire direccion from you what shall bee donn therein. I here inclosed sende back the certifficatt which I received in your last, the which is defective and was made without my knowledge, I beinge in Swansey when it was made, but I was at Newport when this tobaccoe was landed and did suspect it to bee French; and Mr Herbert the customer with Mr Plumley and my selfe did examyne the merchants, whoe affirmed it to bee Barbadoes tobaccoe made up in smale rowles, only for the better sale thereof.

I humbly acquainte you that Mr Plumley hath ever beene faithfull to the Parliament and forsooke his estate and suffred much for theyr sakes and is generally conceaved to bee an honest man and if you wil bee soe noble as to pardon this his error, I conceave him to bee a very fitt man to bee employed; yet hee shall not acte any thinge in customs causes till your pleasure bee knowne herein and if you will not bee pleased that hee bee employed, then I conceave Mr John Warde wil bee the fittest man in Newport, for that I knowe his honesty and fidellity to the Parliament to bee right and for the other places in the modell which are not supplyed I hereunder [have] written (according to your commaunde) be name men which I am confident will acte faithfully. God permittinge, a stricte care shalbe taken both by my selfe and all others within our charge to prevent the Parliaments deceipt according to your rule and commaunde. I further humbly acquainte you that Pennarth is noe place to lade or unlade goods except in smale cock botes and that there are adjacent and nere to Pennarth, Ely, Sully and Barry, places where vessells usually come in and out soe that I conceave the wayter for the place ought to bee authorized for the 4 places, beinge nere together. The consideracion of the premisses I humbly referre to your wisdomes, desireinge your further commaund, which shal bee faithfully performed by your worships humble servant J B.

The shipp Al[ice] of Bristoll is arryved in this ryver from the Barbathoes with sugar, cotton, tobaccoe, fustick wood and a little ginger, parte whereof is discharged into a trowe for Bristoll by port cockett and bonde given here to lande and cleare it in Bristol, beinge consigned thither as by the oath of the merchant and purser appeareth and moreover wee had not any meanes to weygh it aborde.

The remainder shal bee carefully looked unto according to the duty of your worship's humble servant J B.

Neath: Mr William Morgan; Aberthawe: Mr Philip Williams; Pennarth, Ely, Sully and Barry: Mr John Tanner; Newport, if your worships thinke fitt, Mr John Plumley, or else Mr John Warde; Chepstowe: Mr William Huggett.

67. TO PHILIP WILLIAMS

[*Marginated*] Caerleon 9 September 1649

Mr Philip Williams

I have received a letter from the commissioners by which they well approve of your care in seazeinge the wooll but doe not commende you for lettinge it goe out of your hands. They have commaunded mee to sende unto you forthwith for a true account of the weight and vallewe of the wooll with the tyme when you seazed it and into whose hands you demised it and what securety you have taken to answer the valewe thereof. This must be fairely written with your hande to it and must be soe as you may punctually prove what you write and the commissioners will employ Mr Sankey theyr solicitor to prosecute the busines. Pray gett a good cleark to write the premisses for what I received formerlie from you was defective. You may not suffer eyther butter or any other goods to bee laden or landed without warrant, which if you finde you must seaze thereon. A bote of Sulley or Barry goeinge up to Bristoll with butter without warrant was seazed on by which meanes Mr Tanners care and my creditt is in question. I pray advize him to seaze on all goods which hee shall finde eyther laden or landed without warrant, which if hee be not willinge to do I desier a word from him that I may appointe another in his roome which will acte faithfully for the common wealth; for my creditt lyeth at stake for all such officers as I have named to the commissioners. Wherefore I earnestly desier your care in the premisses for J B.

Sir I have received an acte of parliament prohibitinge the bringing in French wynes and all manufactures of wooll and silke made in the French kings domynions uppon [pain of] forfaiture shipp and goods and £200 fine. I pray your care herein in your partes: you may see the acte in the custome house of Cardiffe. I pray sende to Jenkin Arnolde to Newton to seaze all goods laden or landed there without warrant and to sende mee the bonds which I formerlie wrote to him for.

68. TO MICHAEL SANSOM

[*Marginated on page 13*] Newport 17 September 1649

Mr Sansom

Yours of the 28th past and 4th present I have received, by which I finde some informacions are presented to the commissioners against mee: i that much butter is transported from our ports beyond seas; upon my creditt wee have not permitted any butter to bee laden for beyond seas in any place within my charge this yeare, but only in June last 50 kilterkins, at which tyme butter was at a reasonable rate; great quanteties have beene passed out of our portes to Bristoll by bonde and (as the merchants do protest) is there entred for beyond sea and for coales none is shipped within our ports for Englande without bond for landeinge the same, unlesse some very smale botes which wee knowe doe constantly trade for England whoe usually goe by lettpas; whereas the merchants of the Abraham of Bristol which stayed nere Cardiffe doe give out that I cleare theyr goods by contents and not by weight.

It is a most false report, for we have not cleared any goods of that shipp but by a right weit and computacion, neyther have I cleared any parcell of that goods without the ayde and assistance of Mr Malory the checquer, Rees Griffith the searcher, twoe waiters and 2 subcommissioners for the excise in every particular herein. I pray please to present the remembrance of my humble duty and service to my worthy lords the commissioners [*Page 13*] whose worthiness I most humbly acknowledge in that they will not easily bee enduced to beleave these false informacions against mee. I wrote to Mr Philip Williams for the account of the wooll seazed by him, whoe writeth it weigheth about 1800 lbs. and cost about 100 markes the first penny; 3 baggs thereof are Edward Nicholls which were landed and are in Mr Williams his custodie, the waves rose soe high that hee could not lande the rest, wherfore hee demised it into the hands of Morgan Jenkins, whoe gave bond to answer the goods or the full valewe thereof if recovered by lawe.

The 7th of this moneth I seazed on 34 great rolls and 14 hand rolls of Barbathoes tobaccoe which was privately landed at Redwick, since which tyme one Thomas Northerne, one of the marriners from the shipp Elizabeth and Anne of Bristol, hath beene with mee about this tobaccoe by whome I finde it belongs to some poore marryners whoe (as hee protesteth) are quite undone if they loose this goods. If I had not made seazure I would have delivered it to the owners, they paieinge customs and excise for the same but beinge I have seazed it, I dare not release it without order from the commissioners, whereof I pray please to acquainte them and if they will bee pleased to give way I will deliver this tobaccoe without gaineinge one penny to my selfe for my cheife ayme is to preserve the customs in theyr right course and not seekeinge eyther by or selfe ends.

If the commissioners will not permitt the releasinge these goods, payinge custome and excise then I desier theyr speedy order for sale thereof for it will perishe if kept. The charge of a sute in the exchequer wil bee more then the tobaccoe will yeelde; besides customs and excise it wil not yeelde above 1d. per lb. cleare of all charge. All our officers expect I should paie them theyr sallaryes which if the commissioners please I shall doe; then I humbly desier theyr order for doeinge thereof or else theyr pleasure therein; allsoe those whoe have offitiated since 1st February expect satisfaccion for the service donne by them before the newe officers came downe and call on mee for payment for that I did promise they should bee satisfied for theyr care and paynes. I earnestly pray you to move the commissioners herein that some allowance may bee made therein. Mr Tench our surveyor hath bene over all our ports and went from hence on Fridaie last by whome I understande there is no foraine trade within any port in our charge at present. I humbly desier you to procure the commissioners answer to this and to my last, wherein you will much obliege yours assuredly to serve you, J B.

69. TO NEPHEW WILLIAM BYRD

[*No date*]

Approved true freinde your true love to mee will never bee requited nor deserved yet I hereby promise it shall never bee forgotton by him that will stryve to appeare to bee your faitfully than kefull servant J B.

Inclosed the letter above to William Byrd with order to present Mr Sansom, Mr Parsons, Mr Swynmour, Mr Sankey and Mr Strelly with a cupp of wyne or a breakefast and not to bee spareinge therein and allsoe to bee advized by my brother Pennant.

70. MEMORANDUM

20 September 1649

Received orders [from] the commissioners of the customes with 4 ordinances of Parliament that noe person whatsoever should lade or lande goods for or from beyond sea till custome were paid nor that any person should lade goods by port to port before bonde given and cockett taken for the same; the 27th of September I wrote to Mr William Huggett in Chepstowe, Mr Arthur Roberts in Cardiffe, Mr William Morgan in Neath and to the officers of the customes in Swansey and sent each of them one of the ordinances desireinge them to cause them to bee proclaymed that after publicacion noe man might pleade ignorance if his goods were taken without warrant or bonde according to the same ordinance.

71. MEMORANDUM

[*No date*]

Mr Philip Williams searcher did (on the 20th of August 1649) seaze on 11 sacks of Welch wooll weight about 1800 lbs which cost about 100 markes; 8 of which sacks was the goods of Morgan Jenkin, the other 3 sacks was the goods of Edward Nicholls which saide woolls was laden aboarde the Thomas of Aberthawe, burden 20 tons, Thomas Graunte master, without warrant or bonde given for landinge thereof. The 3 sacks which were Edward Nicholls Mr Williams gott on shore and hath it in custodie; the barque then rydeinge in the rode at Aberthawe the seas rose soe high that hee could not lande the other 8 sacks of wooll wherefore hee demised it into the hands of the said Morgan Jenkin and tooke securety by bonde per answeringe the valewe of the saide wooll when it should bee recovered by lawe.

This is the account of the seazure made by Mr Philip Williams abovesaid as hee declared it to mee J B.

72. MEMORANDUM

7 September 1649

John Byrd collector of the customes in the port of Cardiffe and members did seaze (at Redwick a creek under the said port) on 34 great and 14 hand rowles of Barbathoes tobaccoe weight about 2000 lbs. which was the goods of Thomas Northerne, Samuel Roche, William Tuckey and others, the which was landed privatly at Redwick abovesaid with an intent to defraude the state of custome and excise. They are Bristoll men which were owners of the tobaccoe. John Byrd collector.

Page 14

73. TO MICHAEL SANSOM

[*Headed*] Caerleon 9 October 1649

Mr Sansom

Yours of the 25th of September last I received and accordinge to the commissioners desier I here inclosed sende you the state of Mr Philip Williams wooll seazure whoe humbly desireth the commissioners will bee pleased that Mr Sankey theyr soliciter may prosecute the same in the exchequer and to direct me therein. Alsoe I sende here inclosed the state of my tobaccoe seazure which I desier Mr Sanky to entre for mee and to sende downe a writt of appraisement with all speede that it may bee disposed of before it bee spoyled for this sort of tabaccoe will not last long. Allsoe I desier some direccion howe to proceede here, when the writt cometh downe, for I am ignorant in this course. I thinke commissioners are to be named in the writt of appraisement which if soe then pray lett the names underwritten bee put in. Pray present the remembrance of my humble duty and service to my worthy masters the commissioners and please to acquainte them herewith; thus humble desireinge to heare one word from you by the first conveniency concerning the premises, I take leave and rest J B.

Philip Williams John Rosser Lewis Rees	gentlemen, commissioners names

74. TO THOMAS PENNANT

[*No date, but probably from Caerleon 9 October 1649*]

Brother Pennant

Sir I have received severall letters from my nephewe William Byrd by which I finde the contynuance of your love towards mee and the encrease of your love towards him for which I hartily thanke you. The last great sessions helde for this county I recovered from one that tooke my cattell and plundred my dayry house in the moore £102 but hee beinge a papist in armes his estate is sequestred soe that our committee cannott relieve mee as by a coppie of my peticion to them and theyr answer thereto (which I have sent my nephewe William to trouble you with) appeareth. I pray advize and assiste mee and my nephew for mee herein; I am toulde that the committee of sequestracions will upon peticion order reliefe herein, out of the estate of the plunderer, which if you finde to be soe I pray assiste William Byrd in preferringe a peticion in my name. I have written to my nephew William to buy mee some commendation and to doe some businesses for mee and to enable him to performe I pray please to deliver him £3 on my account. Brother I forbeare to write any more at present but that if you conceave I may serve you or yours pray freely commande him that will stryve to appear to bee your faithfull Welch brother J B.

75. TO NEPHEW WILLIAM BYRD

[*No date but probably from Caerleon 9 October 1649*]

Cozen William

Yours of the 25th last and 2nd present I have received by which I finde the contynuance of your care for which I thanke you kindely. Here inclosed is a blancke bond; if such may bee had, pray bestowe 5s. therein. Here is allsoe a note of the seazure of tobaccoe: I have sent the like herewith to Mr Sansom desireinge that Mr Sanky soliciter to the commissioners may enter the seazure and prosecute it in the exchequer for me. Pray remember me kindly to Mr Sanky and pray him proceede therein with as much speede as may bee, for feare it will rott before it be disposed of.

If you finde Mr Sanky may not doe this then desier him to direct you what to doe herein, which I pray observe and make use of some honest clarke in the exchequer; Mr Robert Whip (if lyveinge) you shall finde in chequer office whoe is both able and honest. Here inclosed is a coppie of a peticion; I pray shewe it to my brother Pennant and, if you might have opportunety, to Mr Sansom allsoe, and pray them to advize you where I may peticion above for reliefe; some say to the committee for sequestracions. I pray enquier exactly and advize mee. I write herewith to my brother Pennant to deliver you £3 to cleare scores and the remainder to be in banke with you.

Mr Futter wrote that his affaires since my beinge in London had beene such that he could not have tyme to take course about his bonde, but nowe would try to gett it allowed him, which indeede in equity and conscience hee ought to have for the tobaccoe for which this money is due was rotten and was exported out of the realme. Pray remember mee kindely to him and pray him to gett mee cleared for it or for the securety you write of. I knowe not whoe to name at present but when I come up I doubt not but to give the commissioners satisfacion therein. Captain John Morgan sent to acquainte mee hee would give mee lande for my money, if I canne procure order from above that hee might sell mee soe much as comes to my £102. Pray acquainte my brother Pennant thereof for his letter was sealed before I had this notice, and I pray you both to sende mee a speedy answer what you finde will bee done herein. Allsoe pray you to sende mee a full answer to all the premises with speede.

Page 15

76. TO THOMAS SHEWELL

[*Marginated*] Caerleon 17 October 1649

Mr Shuell and true freinde

Yours of the 15th instant I received about 11 a clock this daie whereby you advertize [me] of some fraude suspected by you to bee intended by one Henry Coolishe in ii Aberthawe vesseles and accordinge to your advice, care shal bee taken herein. As for the Marygould I was 3 dayes at Cardiffe supposinge it would bee discharged there, but Mr Hilman shewed mee an order from Collonell Tyson for to bringe the shipp up to Bristoll. I left i man abord and i at Pennarth and one at Cardiffe to attende hir. Noe presentment nor entry was intended to bee made with us; if any thinge shalbe donne herein or in any thing else wherein I am intrusted for the commonwealth noe care shalbe wantinge to performe the duty of him that is yours at command J B.

77. TO JAMES RUSSELL

[*Marginated*] Caerleon 12 November 1649

Worshipful

After my humble service remembered unto you, please to take notice that according to the order of the honourable the committee for the navy and customs dated the 28th July last and your direccion therein dated the 6th of August last I sent up a quarter booke to the 24th of June last, but by yours sent to Mr Malory our checquer I finde it came not to your hands. Wherefore I here inclosed sende you that and allsoe the account for the 24th of June to the 24th of August last, at which tyme Mr Malory entred on the employment. I desier you please to write one word of the receipt hereof to your worships humble servant J B.

For the worshipful James Russell esquire at the signe of the Golden Fleece nere Antholyns church these London.

78. TO THE COMMISSIONERS OF THE CUSTOMS

[*Marginated*] Caerleon 12 November 1649. For the commissioners of the customs

Right worshipful

After my humble duty and service remembered unto you with humble and harty thankes for all your favors towards mee, I here inclosed sende you my quarter booke with my bill of fees and disbursements this last quarter, which is somethinge large, yet the necessity of the service requireth it to bee soe. The trade of port cocketts and certifficats encreaseth exceedinglie in all places within my charge soe that unlesse I may have a deputy in each port the service cannott bee performed which I humbly pray may bee taken into consideracion. Allsoe I humbly pray that some allowance may bee made whereby to satisfie those whoe acted in custome causes from 1st February till this last quarter, whoe call on mee for payment because they acted by my encouragement and persuasion; and indeede I did promise they should have satisfaccion. Thus humbly prayinge your love in the premises, with one word of receipt hereof I humbly take leave and rest your worships humble servant J B.

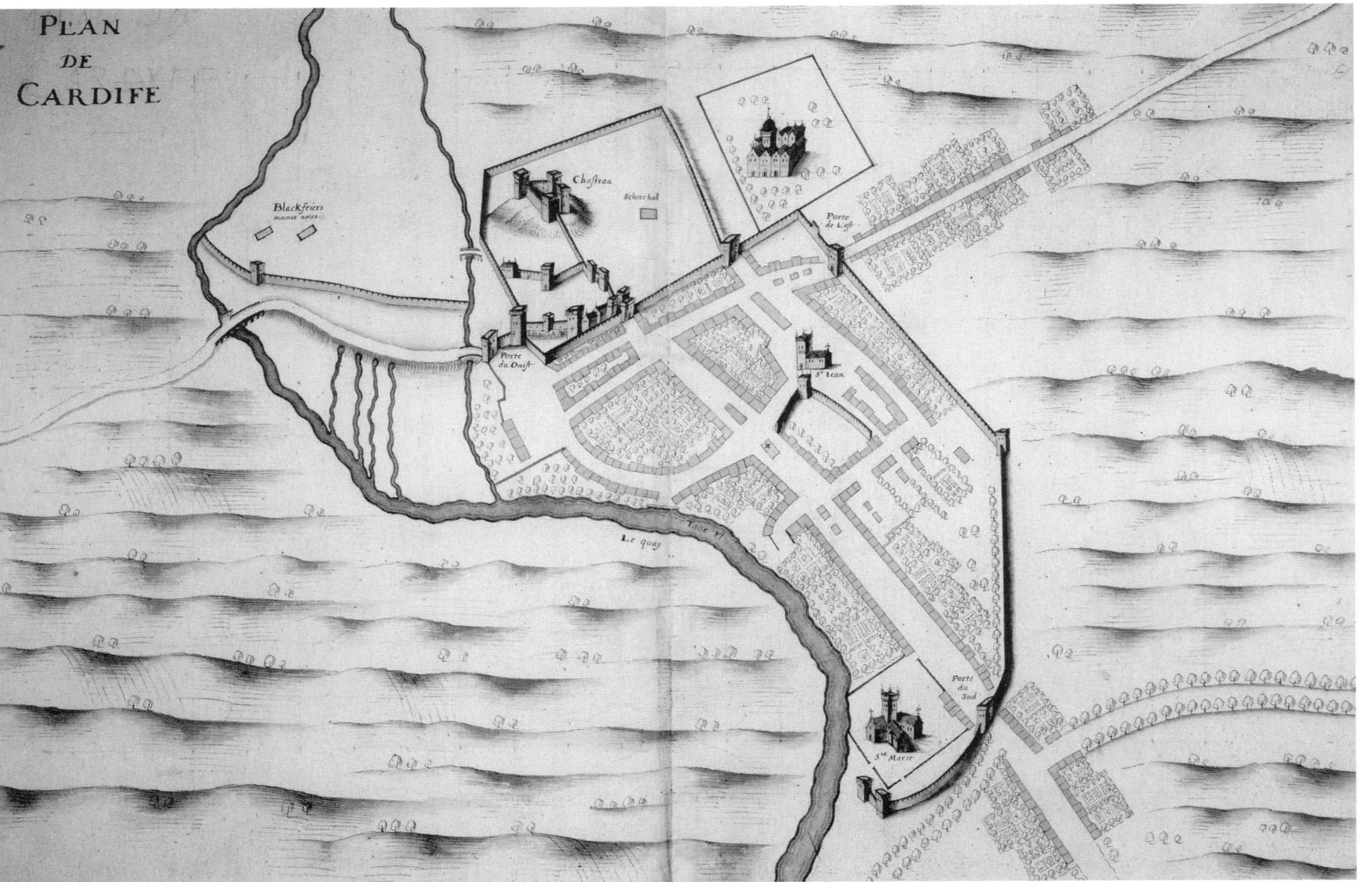

'Plan de Cardiff', c.1650. A French plan after John Speed, 1610.

79. TO WALTER SANKEY

[*Marginated*] Caerleon 12 November 1649

Mr Sankey and loving freinde

Yours with the writts I received but the names of the commissioners are mistaken, as the tobacco which I seazed was and is in the county of Monmoth and the wooll seazed by Mr Philip Williams is in the county of Glamorgan, soe that I have sent you here inclosed the ii writts, desireinge you to gett them renewed and sent downe with all speede. I pray please to name John Rosser, Philip Williams, Lewis Rees and Rees Gwynn: all of Carlion in the county of Monmoth to bee commissioners in the writt for the tobaccoe which I seazed in the county of Monmoth; alsoe pray please to name Robert Corrock, Thomas Spencer, Arthur Spencer and James Gibbon gent for commissioners in the writt for the wooll seazed by Mr Philip Williams in the county of Glamorgan. I sent the subpoena to Mr Williams to serve Morgan Jenkin but I understande hee is gon towards London, which if hee bee I assure my selfe hee will see you and advize with you about the wooll. Pray sende mee a copie of an indenture which is to bee made in this case for it is somethinge strange to mee. Pray please to present my humble and faithfull service to Mr Sansom, my loving respects to Mr Streley, Mr Parsons, Mr Swynmoue, Mr Hudson and all the rest of our true freinds with you; with my true love to your selfe I rest J B.

80. TO NEPHEW WILLIAM BYRD

[*Marginated*] Caerleon 12 November 1649

Cozen William

I have received ii letters from you dated in October last, and i of this moneth, with the acts and bookes and all things sent by you, but [lacking] only the bonds which you write you sent mee ½ a reame, which I heare not of. I doubt they are lost. I received a letter from Mr Sankey with the writts, but my writt was mistaken, for the tobaccoe was seazed and is still in the county of Monmoth and the commissioners are Monmothshere men and 1 of theyr names is likewise mistaken. I sende it here inclosed, desireinge you to deliver it to Mr Sankey and pray him to get another writt in stead thereof and name commissioners therein John Rosser, Philip Williams, Lewis Rees and Rees Gwyn, all of Carlion in the county of Monmoth, gentlemen. There is another writ of appraisment but 2 commissioners names whereof one is likewise mistaken. I have sent to Mr Philip Williams for commissioners names and at the retorne of the messenger I will sende up that writt to bee renewed, for that busines of the wooll is in Glamorganshire. I have this daie taken securety of Captain John Morgan for payment of £100, soe that I pray proceede noe further concerninge him. I hartily thanke you for your [numerous] paynes in my occasions and if the Lord will enable mee I will requite you: as for sureties you write of, I cannott tell whoe to trouble therein. I have one bonde already with the last commissioners which I hope to have up before I seale another. I received one letter from Mr Sansom of the 23rd of October for which pray give him thankes on my behalfe. I have writt herewith to Mr Sankey, please to reade, seale and deliver it to him and procure him to performe any request. If you write mee by whome the blanke bonds were sent to Bristol, I will send to enquire after them. Pray remember me to brother etc.

Page 16

81. TO MICHAEL SANSOM

[*Marginated*] Caerleon 26 November 1649

Mr Sansom

Pray please to take notice that yours of the 20th instant I received yesterdaie, wherby it seemes I have mistaken in writeinge the entry of sugars. If I have writte that ½ the sugars in the first entry at Cardiffe wer exported, I have then much mistaken, for all those sugars were exported and not one 1d. paid for customs or any other thinge with us but what is charged on my account; and whereas I should have charged the entry with the whole custom and then have added the one halfe thereof amongest my disbursements, I was quite ignorant therein; for never any such thinge happened within my charge in my tyme.

I have here inclosed sent you the particular acquittances for moneys paid by me to the officers, wherein is wantinge Mr John Tanners the waiter at Pennarth and Mr John Griffiths of Neath for 50s. per piece, for I missinge to see eyther of them in my last journey through the ports have not paid them as yet; as for my petty charge in my bill sent up and the custome houses rents both of Cardiffe and of Swansey, I have paid [£]20, and the 14s. 6d. for portage of letters and other commands downe, and my retornes up, I paid it to Mr Joseph Evans of Bristoll, for all which I have noe acquittances. Only this day, Morgan Griffith gave mee his acquittance for what I paid him, which I sende up herewith, for all the rest must of necessity be put of[f] till the next quarter, against which tyme I will get acquittances for all these particulars and then charge it in my next account. In the meane tyme I desier you to procure orders from my masters the commissioners to paie my moneyes to Colonell Harrisons souldiers here, or to Mr Shuell, collector in Bristol. Colonell Harrison is at present at the signe of the Childe and Cote in Black Friars and I beleve he will retorne up these moneyes for he lately retorned up the Lord of Pembrokes rents.

Sir my habitacion is at Carlion a port on the ryver of Uske betwene which place and Bristoll is very great trade for most things in generall, and if I did not lyve here then of necessity other officers must be setled here. Newton, a place where little or noe trade was use to be, haveinge beene for a little tyme neglected and noe certayne officers in that place, trade began to encrease there, and for prevencion of fraude I did agree with Mr Jenkin Arnold, one of the ablest men in that place, to take care that noe goods be there laden or landed without warrant, for which I have promised to paie him quarterly. I earnestly pray you to present my humble duty and service to my worthy masters the commissioners, who I humbly pray will be pleased to give allowance to my deputyes whereby the service may be the better performed. I shall take care hereafter not to paie any money without an acquittance for the same, which for petty charge and disbursements I neaver did before. Thus desireinge to heare from you herein, I humbly take leave and rest your humble servant J B. Pray please to sende downe my other bill of charge.

82. TO WALTER SANKEY

[*26 November 1649*]

Wrote to Mr Walter Sankey the same daie and sent him up a writt of appraisement of tobaccoe, with an indenture of the appraiseinge therof, desireinge him to sende mee order for disposall therof with speede; sent him alsoe in the same letter a subpoena on Morgan Jenkin, which I received from Mr Philip Williams to bee renewed, about woolls by him seazed.

83. TO NEPHEW WILLIAM BYRD

[*26 November 1649*]

Sent the ii letters abovesaid to cozen William Byrd to bee delivered, and desired him to keep a perfect account of the charge of what hee receaveth from the commissioners of the customes to be sent mee, and likewise of what charge is or shall bee on what shall be sent from me to them, and to sende mee his receipt quarterly for what hee disburseth herein.

84. TO WALTER SANKEY

[*Marginated*] Caerleon 29 November 1649

Wrote to Mr Sankey and sent him a writt of appraisement to bee renewed with 4 commissioners names to bee put in it which I received from Mr Philip Williams concerninge woolls; and both this and for the subpoena abovesaid to bee retorned the first daie of the next terme.

85. TO THOMAS SHEWELL

[*Subscribed*] Caerleon 1 October 1649

Mr Shuell

After my due respects remembered, pray please to take notice that yours of the 28th November last I received, and for answer therto you may please to take notice that the goods laden with you abord the Thomas and William of Aberthawe, William Tanner master, was landed at Aberthawe for the shopkeepers of Cowbridge and others. The vessell was hyred for transportinge one Mr Thomas Danne for Munster with his family and househould stuffe, for which hee had lycence, otherwise the vessell should not have departed from us without good securety to have gon to those whoe are faithfull freinds to the commonwealth [*Page 17*] of Englande. As for the other thinge you write of (if any such thinge happen hereafter[1] I will give you a speedy account thereof and will ever rest yours assuredly to serve you J B.

1. Followed by several words expunged.

86. TO MICHAEL SANSOM

[*Marginated*] Caerleon 8 October 1649

Worthy sir

After my service and best respects to you and yours remembered with harty thankes for all curtesies, pray please to take notice that yours of the 1st instant I received by which I finde noe allowance will bee made mee for John Griffith my deputy at Neath, nor for any other of my deputies. When I charged my account with what I paid and am to paie I made noe question but that it would have beene allowed mee, but seeinge it wil not bee, I must beare that charge my selfe and if the service bee donne in everie port as it ought and in my simple judgement must bee, the charge of my deputies will bee at least £30 per annum, for there wil bee about 800 bonds, as many cocketts and nere as many certifficatts to be made in the ports within my charge per annum; which since the customers place was layde aside the makeinge thereof is fallen on mee and my deputies. Allsoe I keepe a mare and a couple of geldings that I may bee ready at all tymes to ryde where any occasion of service requireth, soe that unlesse my sallary bee augmented or else allowance [be made] for my deputyes I shall not bee able to performe this service. Truly Mr Sansom, I was confident that at least £100 per annum would have beene settled for the collector in these ports, the travell and charge beinge farre greater then it seemes is beeleeved to bee.

I formerlie wrote to my masters that noe shippinge cometh at any tyme to Aberavon but that I conceaved Aberthawe was intended and I finde thay have beene pleased to contynewe Mr Philip Williams in the lyst for Aberthawe, which in my judgement is right. I have formerlie prevayled with Mr William Jones and Mr William Huggett to acte at Chepstowe for the sallary allowed there, as by theyr acquittance which I sent up appeareth, yet they hope to bee better rewarded hereafter. At Neath is at least 4 tymes the trade which is at Chepstowe and the service will not bee performed there under twice the sallary allowed for that place. If noe custome house shall bee kept at Neath, then I nede noe deputy in that place, for all men tradeinge there must goe to Swansey for theyr warrants, which is 6 miles from thence. I pray a word of that in your next. Sir if I may have any cheerefull encouragement I will make my residence in Cardiffe as is expected, for I am both willinge and ready to doe any service for the commonwealth which shall lye in my power.

I have forborne to seale the bond you sent mee for the present, hopeinge to receave some better encouragement then I have had; yet for what money is or shall bee received, eyther by my self or my deputyes, I will make it good uppon demaunde. I am confident all the moneyes that will bee received in all our ports hereafter will not discharge the sallaryes and other charges, for that the excise is nowe fully settled in our ports. I desier you please to sende mee one of my bills of charge with what will not be allowed in the other, that I may perfect my account accordinglie. Good Mr Sansom, please to present the remembrance of my humble duty and service to my worthy masters the commissioners, whoe I desier will bee pleased to take the premisses into theyr consideracion, hopeinge they will afforde mee such encouragement as will enable mee to goe on cheerefully in the service. Thus prayinge one word in answer hereto, I take leave and rest yours assuredly at comaunde J B.

For the worshipful Michael Sansome esquire, secretary to the right worshipful the commissioners for the customs of England at the custom house, London, these.

87. TO THOMAS PENNANT

[*No date*]

Brother Pennant

I have forborne to trouble you with my ordinary occasions and have imposed them upon my cozen William, but nowe havinge a business of consequence as by this inclosed you may perceave, I make boulde hereby to desier you to reade and afterwards seale and deliver the inclosed with your owne hande and if it may bee with your conveniency eyther at his house or, after the commissioners are gone, at[(1)] the custome house, for that I desier you would take some occasion to conferre with Mr Sansom about mee. My sallary is but £40 per annum: a man cannott write what is to bee written in our ports for soe much money, besides travell charge and losse of my own occasions. You wrote mee one of the commissioners was your good freinde; if you thinke fitt to move him in my behalfe perhaps you may procure him to doe mee some good. If tyme or your occasions will not permitt, or that you are not willinge to appear for mee herein, then I pray direct my cozen William Byrd what you thinke best and cause him to deliver my letter as aforesaid.

1. 'From' in MS.

88. TO NEPHEW WILLIAM BYRD

[*No date*]

Enclosed the letters above to cozen William Byrd and wrote him I have received his severall letters, beinge 4 since my last to him; and ordered him if brother Pennant were not at home to open his letter and performe with all care what I desired brother Pennant to doe for mee. Allsoe desired him to take notice what was saide, that I did not seale the bond which was sent mee, and to give me account therof.

89. TO THE COMMISSIONERS OF THE CUSTOMS

[*Marginated on page 18*] Cardiff 24 December 1649

Right worshipful

After my humble duty and service remembred unto you, pray please to take notice that yours of the 26th of November last came not to my hands till the 15 instant with the Engagement and direccions which I have putt in execucion accordinglie, and here inclosed sende you ii roles of parchment with the Engagement, which is subscribed by all the officers and deputyes relateinge to the customes in the port of Cardiffe and members. Only Mr James Dennis, our searcher and waiter, beinge at present in Englande, hath not subscribed but assuredlie if hee had beene in these partes he would have subscribed it. I allsoe received yours of the [*Page 18*] 24th instant, concerninge scandalous books, which I have likewise communicated to all the officers within my charge. Allsoe I received one of the 4th instant, with one enclosed to Mr Tench, surveyor, which I have delivered him; and as neare as may bee, things shall be donne according to your commande. Thus not haveinge else to trouble you with at present I humbly take leave and rest your worships humble servant J B.

For the right worshipfull his worthy maisters the commissioners for the customs of England at the custom house these London.

90. TO NEPHEW WILLIAM BYRD

[*Marginated*] Cardiff 24 December 1649

Cozen William

I wrote to you on the 8th instant; and in yours, to brother Pennant, and in that, i to Mr Sansom; and if my brother Pennant were out of towne I desier you to open his letter and to perfome what I requested him to doe. I hope these letters are come to your hands, pray a word therof in your next. I gave you therein an account of the receipt of your former letters etc. Nowe these are to desier you to deliver the inclosed to Mr Sansom or to the commissioners with all speede and please to write mee one word in answer to my former and receipt of this. Mr Hugh Lloyd hath received the ii letters signed by the lord generall: hee acknowledgeth himselfe very much oblieged to you and requested mee to give you thankes in his behalfe. Hee intended to have beene in London about this tyme but on Fridaie last [there] aryved at Swansey(1) a vessell of that port from the Caribbee Ilands with some tobaccoe, haveinge beene about a month at Milforde, which will cause him to staye a little longer before hee canne come up, soe that if eyther the commissioners for the excise or any other shall enquier after him, hee desireth you to endevour his excuse. Pray remember mee to all our freinds.

1. 'at Swansey' interlined.

91. TO THE COMMISSIONERS OF THE CUSTOMS

[*Marginated*] Cardiff 10 January 1650

Right worshipful

Pray please to take notice that a shipp of Lymbrick called the Eagle, in which Luke Roche was master, hir ladeinge beinge Irishe butter, rawe hydes, tand hydes, wooll and tallowe, besides severall chests and truncks belonginge to passengers which were abord bounde for Lymbrick to Rochell was by stormes dryven into the ryver of Seaverne and beinge leaky put into Ely woose nere Cardiffe on the 28th day of December last where Rees Griffith deputy searcher here with 3 men went abord that night, and by agreement betweene them and Major Gawler of this garrison, the said major with a partie of musketiers followed and boarded the shipp soe that the shipp and goods was seased by Rees Griffith and posessed by the major and the souldiers under his commaunde to the use of the states of England; and is founde to bee an absolute prize; and when I founde the major did intende to discharge some goods which laye beetweene the decks I conferred with him about the customes, whoe promised mee that the customs should bee paide when orders should bee graunted for disposall thereof.

On Tuesdaie last I heard that John Herbert esquier, high shereiffe for this county of Glamorgan had received order to lande the rest of the goods, whereuppon I conferred with him about the customes, whoe I finde conceaves noe custom is to bee paid for that it is seazed to the use of the state, wherein I humbly pray your speedy advice that if noe custom is to bee paid I may forbeare to prosecute it any further, or if custome is to bee paide that I may proceede therein as you shall order mee, wherein noe care shall bee wantinge which shall lye in the powers of your worshipps humble servant J B.

For the commissioners of the customes.

92. TO MICHAEL SANSOM

[*Marginated*] Cardiff [*No date*]

Mr Sansom

Yours of the 29th and 31st December last I received, whereby I finde the contynnuance of your true love for which I hartily thanke you; and according to your advice I will write to the commissioners; but to write more in substance and in truth then I have donne I cannott. My subject must be on your letter, wherein you write they utterly dislike allowance to paie my deputies. I pray advize me in that by your next. Here inclosed is a letter to my masters concerninge a prize that is here, to which I pray procure a speedy answer for I beeleeve those which have the mannagement of that busines here doe not intende any custom shall be paid; for things are carryed somme things privatly and somme things by power beinge not pleased that any custome officer take notice what is donne. I sende this by waye of Bristoll, but nowe a post is settled for our partes whoe will be at the oulde post house in London, by whome I pray please to sende hereafter and direct your letters to be left at the post house in Newport, with whome I will take order to sende them to mee, wheresoever I shall bee.

93. MEMORANDUM

12 January 1650

Wrote the 2 last letters againe on the 12 January 1649[-50] by the Welch post by Newport.

94. TO THE COMMISSIONERS OF THE CUSTOMS

16 January 1650

Wrote againe to the commissioners and inclosed Mr James Dennis (searcher of Cardiffe) his subscripcion to the Engagement; sent this by the post from Cardiffe.

Page 19

95. TO MICHAEL SANSOM

Caerleon 26 January 1650

Mr Sansom

Yours of the 21st instant I received by which I finde my 3 letters sent up this moneth came safe up. Pray please to present the remembrance of my humble duty and service to my worthy masters the commissioners, and acquainte them that theyrs of the 19th instant came very opportunely to my hands; for within an houre after I received it the governor of Cardiffe, Collonel Jones, Mr John Herbert the sheriffe, Mr Humphrey Blake one of the commissioners for prize goods and Mr Rees Davis one of the bayliffes of Cardiffe, mett togeither about the Irish prize, to whome I repayred to demaunde the customes; and after somme discourse with them I presented the commissioners letter to them, which put an ende to all theyr scruples and it was presently concluded that soe soone as order shall comme downe for sale or disposall of the goods the customes shall bee paide, to which purpose Mr Humphrey Blake gave mee a note of engagment under his hande for all goods which was discharged out of the holde of the shipp; and for the wooll which laye betweene decks Major Gawler hath promised payment of the customes due thereon when order is likewise graunted for disposall therof, soe that I hope this busines will bee cleared without any further trouble. Thus not haveinge else at present to enlarge I humbly take leave and rest yours faithfully to serve you J B.

96. TO THE COMMISSIONERS OF THE CUSTOMS

[*Marginated*] Caerleon 1 February 1650

Right worshipful

I pray bee pleased to take notice that I herewith sende my quarter booke to the 25th December last with my bill of charge and acquittances (for most parte of the moneyes which I have layde out) somme whereof should have beene sent up the other quarter but I had them not then; amongst which it will appear that my deputies in Cardiffe, Swansey and Neath have out of my sallary £26 per annum and I keepe a mare and a brace of geldings that I may bee ready at all tymes to ryde when and where this service requireth, which I humbly pray be pleased to take into consideracion and allowe mee wherewith to paie my deputies and what you thinke fitt to enable mee to performe the service. I formerlie lost my employment and all my personall estate and was most dangerously wounded, and all for my faithfullnes to the Parliament and I am still both willinge and ready to doe any service which may bee in my power for the commonwealth of England.

Our receipts are like to bee but little for that the excise is settled in our ports, but the trade from port to port is very much encreased and of that trade there is more in Neath than in any 3 places within my charge. Most worthy maisters I humbly pray you to afforde mee what encouragement you maye, with one word of receipt hereof to your worships humble servant J B.

97. TO MICHAEL SANSOM

[*Marginated*] Caerleon 1 February 1650

Mr Sansom

Sir I have herwith sent up my quarter booke (with acquittances for most of the moneyes which I have disbursed) to the commissioners and have written unto them accordinge to your advice. I pray opportunely to seconde what I have written and please to write mee one word of theyr pleasures therein for if they will not paie my deputyes, uppon my creditt I shall be a great looser in the service. Allsoe I pray procure the accomptant to cancell my first bill of charge which I sent up the other quarter, for nowe I have sent up the acquittances which were then wantinge and have charged them in my bill of charges this last quarter. Thus etc J B.

98. TO NEPHEW WILLIAM BYRD

[*No date*]

Cozen William

Yours with the last receipt (which is nowe right) with my brother Pennants letter and all things else according to your letters I have received; pray thanke my brother Pennant for his care of my letters and acquainte him that according to advice I have written to the commissioners. I pray desier him to take an opportunety to speake againe with Mr Sansom about the same busines. Alsoe pray deliver the letters to Mr Sansom at his house, or after the commissioners are risen, allsoe pray remember mee kindlie to Mr Thomas Bulkeley, whoe I hope is accountant to these commissioners as hee was for the last and acquainte him I should bee glad to heare of his wellfare and how my account standeth. I pray a word herein in your next and of the receipt and deliverie of the premisses. Allsoe pray deliver the other letter to Mr Morgan any daye before the terme endeth. I thanke you for your care of all my occasions above, the which I pray contynnewe and (God permittinge) the next quarter if not sooner, I will bee with you in London and then will all my accounts. If Mr Futter hath not paid in the money due on him I pray put him in mynde thereof, if hee doth not performe with mee herein it will breede a fraccion in the clearinge my accounts. I pray a word of this in your next; Mr Morgan will staye in London after the terme, pray faile not to deliver his letter soe soone as you canne.

99. TO THOMAS SHEWELL

[*Marginated*] Caerleon 2 March 1650

Mr Shuell

Yours of the 26th February last I received by Mr Mallory, by which I finde you have beene pleased to make stay of a parcell of Irish butter (which passed by certifficatt from Cardiffe) for that the neat weight thereof was not expressed in the certifficat. Sir uppon my creditt the butter was exactly weyghed but taken out whilest Mr Mallory our checquer and my selfe were busie in weyghinge out the rest of that butter soe that I cannott write you the exacte weit of that parcell in your custodie a part, yet it hath beene cleared with us according to the booke of rates. I observe that you permitt goods of severall sorts to passe from Bristol to our ports somme by port cockett and somme by certifficatt without expressinge the weight thereof eyther gros or neat; in particular by your certifficatt dated 12th January last, 180 rolls of Barbathoes tobaccoe amongest other goods without expressinge the weight eyther gros or neat, yet my confidence of your fidellity to the common wealth of Englande caused mee to forbeare stayinge thereof, assureinge myself that you would not confirme a certifficatt for passinge any goods before you had received the customs due thereon. I desier you please to harbour the like thoughts of mee and in soe doeinge you will deliver up the butter as in justice is requisite. Thus not haveinge else at present I rest yours assuredly J B.

Page 20

100. TO THE COMMISSIONERS OF THE CUSTOMS

[*Headed*] Cardiff 4 March 1650

Right worshipful

I pray please to take notice that I received a letter from Mr Sansom dated the 16th of February last by which I finde you take notice of the great charge and little receipt in our ports, the which in my judgement cannott bee helped, for most of the ports within my charge must have one officer or more in them, more for prevencion of fraude then for receipt, the greatest parte of our trade beeinge only from port to port. I make bould humbly to present unto you the state of our port and the members thereof, with howe many officers I conceave may bee necessary (with your worshipps approbacion) to acte in each of them: in Cardiffe and Swansey a collector, checquer and searcher, for that in these 2 ports will bee the most of our receipt; in Neath a collector and checquer to make bonds, confirme cocketts and certifficatts, there beinge in that port more trade by port cockett then in any 3 places within my charge; Newport and Chepstowe a collector and checquer in each[1]. I resideinge at Carlion for the most parte, where is farre more trade then in Newport, doe acte there by my selfe and servants, yet I spende much tyme here at Cardiffe and sommetymes in Swansey and elsewhere, when I heare of the arivall of any shippinge; Burry, Newton[2], Aberthawe, Barry, Sulley and Pennarth, a waiter to prevent fraude in each of them, for if any one port bee neglected, it will soone bee founde out by the merchants, to the prejudice of the common wealth, all which I humbly desier may bee taken into consideracion whereby that the officers and theyr deputyes may bee enabled to performe theyr severall dutyes herein.

Captain Hynde is comme hyther from Irelande to provide otes for supply of our army there and sayth that in Bristoll is an order from the counsell of state for passinge thereof to Irelande custome free. I am doubtfull whether I may permitt him to passe otes from hence free of custom without an order to the officers here for soe doeinge, wherein I humbly pray your speedy advice, with one word in answer to the premisses. Thus not haveinge else to trouble you with at present, I humbly take leave and rest J B.

For the right worshipful the commissioners of the customs.

1. 'in each' interlined.
2. 'Newton' interlined.

101. TO MICHAEL SANSOM

[*No date*]

Mr Sansom and faithfull freinde

My service and faithfull respects to you, with Mrs Sansom and all yours remembred, with harty thankes for all curtesies. Yours of the 16th of February last I received, by which you engage mee more and more, the Lord enable mee to expresse my thankefullnes to you. I here inclosed write[1] to my masters the commissioners, wherein I have stated the condicion of our port with the members and creekes thereto belonginge, which in my judgement cannott beee mannaged with fewer officers then I have expressed in the enclosed; whereas it is conceaved that the surveyor must[2] resyde in one place constantly and soe acte as collector there. I confesse he may doe soe if hee shall have order to doe soe, but then his office of surveyor must bee totally neglected. I pray please to write mee word by the first post of receipt hereof and wheither I may permitt otes (whereof here is a great quantety prepareinge) or any other provision to be exported to Irelande for the supply of our army there free of custome or not without speciall order to the officers here for soe doeinge, my last bill of charge and acquittances sent up therewith, setteth forth what fees are expected by the officers of each place, without which the service cannott bee performed, whereof I pray opportunely to speake your opinion to the commissioners; thus J B.

1. 'write' interlined.
2. Followed by 'bee totally' struck through.

102. TO MICHAEL SANSOM

[*Marginated*] Cardiff 22 March 1650

Mr Sansom

Pray please to take notice that I have received yours of the 16th and my masters the commissioners of the 11th instant, the contents whereof (by Gods assistance) shalbe carefully observed. Pray remember my humble duty to my masters and acquainte them that I have received theyrs. I wrote in my last to acquainte my masters that Captain Hynde was employed to provide otes in these partes to bee exported to Irelande for the service of our army there, and that he expected them custom free: since which tyme I received a letter from Mr Shuell wherein he writeth he hath received a warrant from the right honourable the counsell of state to permitt otes to passe from the port of Bristoll for the use of our army in Irelande custom free, but I conceave that extendeth not to our ports, wherefore I humbly desier one word from my masters or from you by the next post whether I may permitt otes to bee pased from hence as aforesaid without a warrant to the officers of our port for soe doeinge or not. I humbly pray you to write one word hereof with all speede to J B.

103. TO MICHAEL SANSOM

[*Marginated*] Chepstow 30 March 1650

Wrote to Mr Sansom that Captain Hynde providore for the horse in Irelande had shipped here about 2000 bushels of otes and I desired to knowe speedilye whether I might suffer him to passe therewith custom free or not in regard they were the states owne goods and sent only for supply of our army in Irelande.

Page 21

104. TO CAPTAIN HYNDE

[*Headed*] 31 March 1650

Wrote to Captain Hynde, nowe at the Crane in Chepstowe, acquaintinge him that I could not supply him with money without order from the commissioners of the customs of England, for that by a letter I received from them I expected bills of exchange from them on mee here, for what money I had in my hands.

105. TO THE COMMISSIONERS OF THE CUSTOMS

[*Marginated*] Caerleon 1 April 1650

Right worshipful

After my humble duty and service remembred unto you, I pray please to take notice that according to your commande I here inclosed sende you againe my account from the 21st of July to the 29th of September last. Allsoe I humbly acquainte you that there remayneth in my hands which I received for customs and subsedie in the port of Cardiffe and members before the 27th of July last £228 14s. 11¼d. which I have ready in cashe; and I formerlie wrote that my oulde masters (your worships predecessors) would bee pleased to order mee to paie the same in Bristoll, as formerlie by theyr order I did usually paie theyr moneys, for that I coulde not finde any secure waye to retorne it up from these partes, but as yet I have not received any order from them, but to retorne it up by good bills, which is not to bee had in these partes. Wherefore I humbly desier that they will bee pleased to charge bills of exchange uppon mee or else order mee to paie these moneyes eyther in Bristoll, Cardiffe or Chepstowe at vi daies sight of theyr bill or order, which (God permittinge) shall bee punctually performed by your worships humble servant J B. For the commissioners of the customs of England.

106. TO THOMAS PENNANT

[*No date*]

Brother Pennant

These are to request you to present the remembrance of my love and service to my loving freinds Mr Sansom and Mr Strelly, whose wonted love and assistance I desier in procureinge £10 which is now due in full of my £30 15s. 7d. ordered mee by the honourable committee for the navy and customs, in lieu of soe much paid by mee to the former commisioners for the customes for imp[ost] on coles, which I did not receave; a coppie of which order I left with you and uppon receipt of this £10 I pray gratifie the procurers thereof as you shall thinke fitt.

I thanke you for your love to my cozen William Byrd; pray remember mee kindly to Mr Thomas Bulkely and desier him to write mee one word howe my account standeth with him, and I pray enquier of him and of Mr Sansom to whome I am to paie the moneyes which I received before the 21st of July last, it beinge above £200 which I have readye in cashe, wherof I have written the nowe commissioners an account (by theyr commaunde). I have allsoe written them that I will paie these moneys at 6 daies sight of the former commissioners order eyther at Bristoll, Cardiffe or Chepstowe; uppon payment whereof I thinke fitt I should have up our bonde. I pray enquier of Mr Sansom herein, whoe I am confident will put us in the right waye. Pray a word by our Welch post whoe is constantly at the posthouse in London and please to direct your letters to bee left at the post masters in Newport, county of[1] Monmoth for J B. This daie I wrote to the commissioners as abovesaide.

1. 'com' [comitatus] in MS.

107. TO NEPHEW WILLIAM BYRD

[*No date*]

Cozen William

Since myne to you of 1st February I received 3 from you, by which as allsoe by letters from the commissioners and Mr Sansom I finde the contynnuance of your care for mee, for which I thanke you; but yours of the 12th February came not to my hande. Pray deliver the inclosed to my brother Pennant with your owne hande soe soone as may bee, with remembrance of my true love to him and all his. Allsoe if Mr Futter hath not paid Mr Sankey the £31 10s. 0d., I pray desier Mr Sankey to put his bonde in suite, for (if God permitt) I will bee in London next terme on purpose to cleare all my accounts. If an acte of parliament hath beene made since the 29th of September last for the manner of rateinge contrybucions togeither by the pounde rent or otherwise, I pray sende mee one by the first post. Pray desier my brother Pennant to call to Mr Futter to paie this money without suite, for hee is my brother Pennants acquaintance and I thinke his freinde.

108. TO THE COMMISSIONERS OF THE CUSTOMS

[*Marginated*] Caerleon 15 April 1650

Right worshipful

Pray be pleased to take notice that I sende here inclosed my quarter booke to the 25th of March last with acquittances for such moneyes as I have paide and disbursed this quarter and a list thereof to which I humbly desier Collonell Langhams hande, according to your direccions. There is nowe remayneinge in my hande from the 21st July to the 25th of March last £92 17s. 7½d. which with the money remayneinge in my hande before that tyme being £228 14s. 11¼d. makes the summe of £321 12s. 6¾d.

One Mr Dennis Gaurdon (a London merchant) hath undertaken to provide a good quantety of otemeale in these partes for the supply of our freinds in Irelande, and Mr Bunbury (whoe is his agent here) promised to write to Mr Gaurdon to paie somme moneyes unto you, to bee paide by me here. I humbly desier that you will be pleased to sende somme man to Mr Gaurdon to acquainte him that if he promise to paie you this summe I will at 6 dayes sight of your bill of exchange or your order paie it here. If this misse I humbly pray you to take somme course with our worthy freinde Collonell Harrison (whoe is nowe in

London), that hee will be pleased to retorne these moneyes. Thus humbly desireinge to know your plesure herin with a word of receipt herof I humbly take leave J B.

Page 22

109. TO MICHAEL SANSOM

[*Headed*] Caerleon 15 April 1650

Wrote to Mr Sansom desireinge him to further my busines in my letter to the commissioners that I may be rydd of the moneyes in my hande, and that hee would assiste my brother Pennant for my last £10, and that if he conceaved my goeinge up might give the commissioners better satisfacion concerneinge the state of our ports then my letters have don, then uppon notice from him to that purpose I would hasten up.

110. TO EDWARD HERBERT

[*Marginated*] For Edward Herbert esquire, Grange. Caerleon 27 April 1650

Worthy Sir

My service and faithfull respects to you and all yours remembred with humble and harty thankes for all curtesies. I formerlie made boulde to acquainte you howe unequally John Rosser, Thomas Raynolds and others had rated the contrybucion money towards the Brittish army, but before I had the acte, whereby I might observe the rule by which it ought to bee rated, most of that money was collected, soe that I could not seasonably make my farther addresses to you therein, but nowe the saide John Rosser, Thomas Raynolds and others have rated the contribucion for the army againe (in my judgement) very unequally, spareinge themselves and most of the able people in this towne and layinge the burthen on others; for redresse herein I humbly pray you to graunte your warrant to call before you the said raters; and I desier you please to commaunde the constables to bringe with them twoe severall warrants by which this money was to bee rated, and (God permittinge) I will waite uppon you when they are to comme before you, to acquainte you really theyr mistakeings herein. If it may stande with your conveniency, I desier it may bee on Mondaie next, for that urgent busines requireth mee elsewhere on Tuesdaie, and this money is speedily required. I would have waited on you nowe, but that I am on earnest busines and indeed I am doubtfull you are in Chepstowe this daie, wherefore I make bould to sende this bearer my servant, by whome I pray please to sende your warrant as aforesaid, wherein you will much obliege him that is sir yours faithfully to serve you J B.

111. TO MICHAEL SANSOM

[*Marginated*] Newport 6 May 1650

Mr Sansom and faithfull freinde

My service and faithfull respects to you with good Mrs Sansom and all yours remembred, with harty thankes for all favours. Sir I received a letter from my masters the commissioners dated 24 April last, concerninge petty customes, wherein noe mencion is made of coles, which is the only trade from our ports and allthough by the booke of rates aliens are to paie double subsedie to what the English paie, yet the aliens allwayes paid petty customs for coles accordinge to the subsedie paid by English merchants. Nowe my earnest request is thatt you will bee soe loveinge as to advertize mee whether aliens must paie a ¼ parte more for petty custome then they paie for subsedie on coles or whether only a ¼ parte more then English merchants paie (as formerlie) or not.

Yours of the 30th of April last I have likewise received by which I finde the commissioners have (by theyrs of the 10th of April which are not comme to my hands) beene pleased to order mee to paie such moneyes as are in my hands and what I shall hereafter receave for customes to Mr Shuell in Bristoll, to whome I have allready retorned a £100 and shall watch all opportunity to retorne or sende the rest to him from tyme to tyme as occasion shall require. I have written to my brother Pennant to trouble you againe in my former busines, wherein I desier your loveinge assistance. I allsoe farther desier that you will bee pleased to present my service to Collonell Langham accountant-generall, whoe I desier will bee pleased to signe my bills of charge and disbursements which I have sent up, which if my maisters may not allowe of I shall not bee able to contynew in the employment but (uppon my creditt) I shall bee a great looser in the service. I beseech you please to write one word in answer hereof by the first post to J B.

112. TO THOMAS PENNANT

[*Marginated*] Caerleon 6 May 1650

Wrote to brother Pennant desireinge him to proceede in seekeinge my £10, which Mr Sansom promised to assiste him in; allsoe to desier Collonell Langham accountant generall to signe my bills which I sent up and that one of them would send them downe to me, and if my bills of charge and disbursements would not bee allowed I should not bee able to contynnewe the employment, but should loose much in that service and allsoe that hee would doe what might bee donne concerninge the bond in Mr[(1)] Sankeys hande; sent this enclosed in a letter to William Byrd.

1. Followed by 'Futter', deleted.

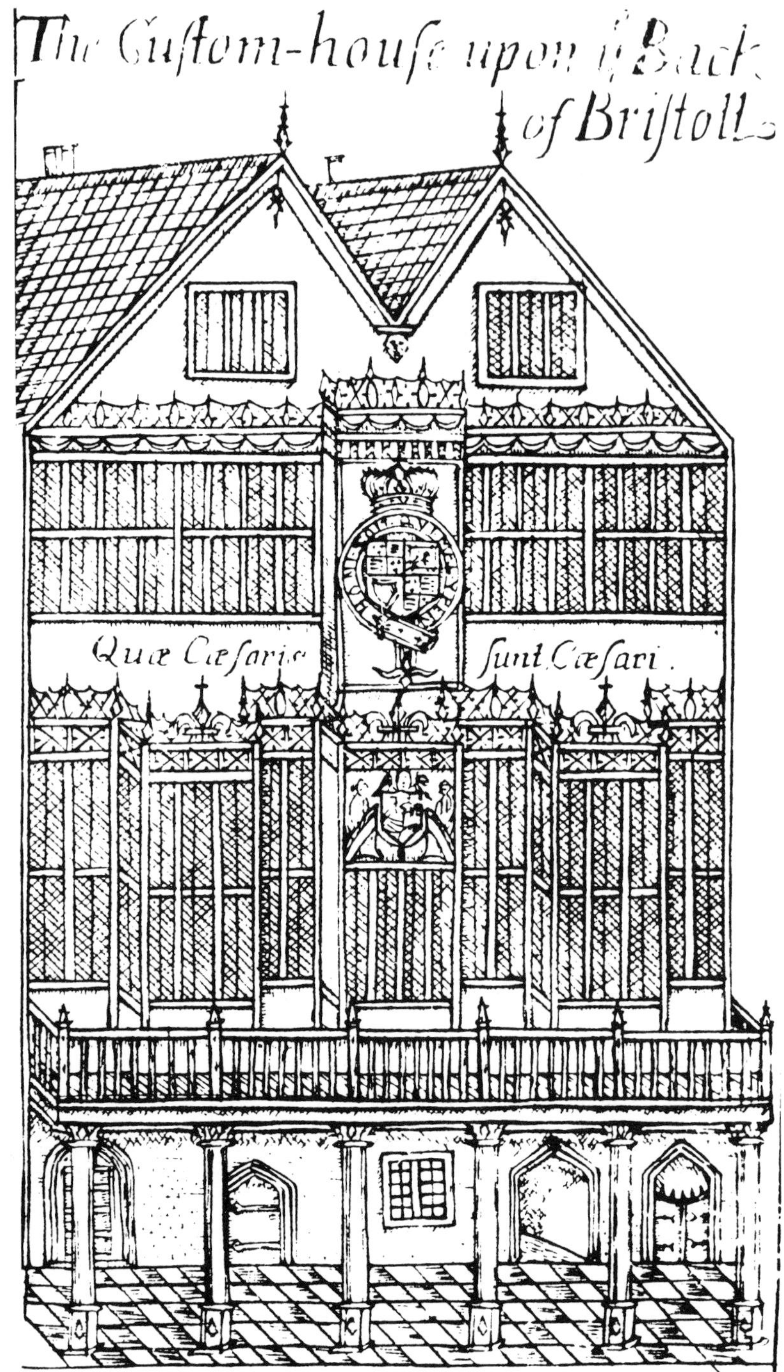

The Bristol custom house in the time of John Byrd.
From James Millerd, ***An Exact Delineation of the Famous Cittie of Bristol*** *(1671).*

113. TO EDWARD MORGAN

[*Marginated*] Caerleon 17 May 1650

Wrote to my unkle Mr Edward Morgan in Staple Inn, desireinge him not to proceede against Thomas Tate for that I had received parte of my money; I inclosed this to cozen William Byrd, desireinge to heare from him and brother Pennant before I shoulde comme up; and to sende me Mr Morgans answer.

114. TO THE COMMISSIONERS OF THE CUSTOMS

[*Marginated*] Caerleon 18 May 1650

Right worshipful

Pray please to take notice that yours of the 15th April last with books concerninge managment [of] the affairs of the customs I formerlie received, and have dispersed the bookes to the officers of the severall ports within my charge according to your commande. Allsoe I have received the copie of yours of the 10th of April last, for payment of my receipts to Mr Shuell in Bristoll, parte whereof I have allready retorned to him, and the rest shall eyther be retorned or sent over by the first opportunety. I further [desier] you please to take notice that my receipts of customs and subsidy from 25th March to 1st May instant is £38-8-9¼d. Thus etc.

Page 23

115. TO THOMAS SHEWELL

[*Headed*] Caerleon 25 May 1650

Mr Shuell

Pray please to take notice that on Thursdaie last I delivered Mr Thomas Wickam a carpenter of your citty £10 to bee paide you and nowe I sende you by this bearer Mr James Yong £210 more, for all which I pray sende mee your receipt as soe much paide on my account for and to the use of our worthy maisters the commissioners for the customes. Thus etc.

James Yong kept this £210 and Mr William Willett of Bristol merchant undertooke to paie it to Mr Shuell and to sende mee his receipt for the same before the 5th of June 1650.

116. TO THOMAS PENNANT

[*Marginated*] Caerleon 17 July 1650

Brother Pennant

I understande by my cozen William Byrd that you have ordered payment of your moneys in Bristol which had beene paide you ere this in London but that my cozen Williams wrote (by your order) to the contrary, for at that instant when I received his letter my cozen Williams his wife was sendinge the money to Bristoll to bee retorned up. I have received 40s. here to be paid in London, the which I have delivered to my cozen William to be paid to your use in in Bristol with your other money. Pray please to doe mee the favour as to deliver this 40s. to my cozen William Byrd whoe I have ordered to paie it to Mr William Francklyn eyther at Tower Hill or at the custome house, as I have beene desired. I pray opportunely to move Collonell Harvey and Mr Blackborne concerninge my peticion and please to write mee one word what hopes therein, that I may have a subject to write to them about it. Thus.

117. TO NEPHEW WILLIAM BYRD

[*No date*]

Cozen William

By this inclosed you may please to take notice that yours with the acte I received, for which I kindely thanke you. Your aunte thanketh you for the token you sent hir; soe doth my sonne. Your aunte is one of your mayne wittnesses to the bonde, as by hir faire handwriteinge you may perceave; God permittinge I will save you harmeles.

Pray deliver my brother Pennants letter to him to whome I have written to deliver you 40s., the which I pray paie unto Mr William Francklyn, whose wife keepeth the custom house and is commonly there all daie. Allsoe pray deliver him the letter directed to him and acquainte him that he was likely to have lost this 40s. for that hee did not write to his cozen according to his promise, yet by the money hee may perceave I prevayled without his letter. Let him thanke me for that and advize him to write his cozen word hee received this of mee on the 28th daie of June last. Paie yourselfe the portage of his letter for it is noe busines of myne.

118. TO COLONEL GEORGE LANGHAM

[*Marginated*] 20 July 1650

Honoured Collonell

I humbly and hartily thanke you for your several favours. I herewith sende you my quarter booke to the 24th June last, with an account currant to that tyme. At my beinge in London I left a peticion with Mr Blackborne the secretary to bee presented to the honourable committee for the navy and Collonell Harvey promised to endeavour to gett my desires therein graunted, which was for[(1)] moneyes which I paid my deputies. If this bee graunted there will be due to mee £30 9s. 7¼d. If this be not already graunted I pray be soe loving as to put Collonell Harvey and Mr Blackborne in mynde to gett my peticion heard that I may knowe what to trust unto, for unles provision shalbe made for payment of my deputies the service cannott be performed.

Sir I beeseech you be pleased to present the remembrance of my humble duty and service to my worthy masters the commissioners and acquainte them that butter is at 3d. per pound and under in all portes within my charge, and the merchants doe here affirme that entryes are taken in Bristol for butter, and both the merchants and gentry of those partes doe take it very ill that wee doe not take entryes for butter beinge natyve commodety of this country and by which the farmers paie most of theyr rents. I humbly desier the commissioners order herein which will give very much contente in those parts.

I allsoe send you herewith a coppie of soe much of the commissioners letter as concerned takeinge care of the service in these partes which in my judgement was not only an encouragement but a commaunde to doe what I have don in matter of deputyes, for I only did contynewe my former deputyes in each place, not addinge one man to the service, neyther cann the service be performed without soe many as I have formerlie employed. I humbly pray you to acquainte my masters herewith, that it may appeare unto them that I have not don things rashly nor all togeither of my owne head.

You shal receive herewith Collonell Tysons certificate concerning the hydes allso my receipt for £6 10s. for the tyme I executed the office of checquer: the blanke printed bondes which I formerly received are all most made use of. I humbly desier my masters will bee pleased to cause a rheame of printed bonds to be sent downe. Thus desireinge one word of receipt hereof and a word in answer hereto with my faithfull love and service to you with all our loving freinds at custom house remembred, I take leave and rest J B.

For his much honoured freinde Collonell George Langham accountant generall for the customes of England at the custome house these, London.

1. Followed by two words erased.

119. TO THOMAS SHEWELL

[*Marginated*] Newport 16 August 1650

Mr Shuell

Yours of the 15th instant wee have received by this bearer, for which wee acknowledge ourselves much oblieged unto you for your care of the generall good of our nacion. Wee shall observe what you have written and use all dilligence to performe what you advize. And for what the merchants saye they may doe with us what you deny them: they, on the contrary parte, affirme that they may doe with you what wee deny them, soe that wee may not put any confidence in what any of them saye, if theyr owne advantage bee concerned therein. Thus with our faithfull respects to you and yours remembred, with harty thankes for all curtesies, we remayne yours assuredly to serve you,

Francis Malory checquer John Byrd

Page 24

120. TO THE COMMISSIONERS OF THE CUSTOMS

[*Headed*] Cardiff 20 August 1650

[*Marginated*] For the commissioners of the customs

Right worshipful

I pray please to take notice that yours of the 10th instant I have received concerninge £4 which Mr James Dennis paid his deputy for executeinge the office of searcher in the port of Cardiffe in the ½ yeare ended the 25th of March last. I haveinge formerlie received the modell of officers in which James Dennis is appointed waiter and searcher in the port of Cardiffe and members[1] did acquainte him that I conceaved he ought to have a deputy at Cardiffe whereuppon he did appointe Rees Griffith senior to execute his office at Cardiff and paid him £4 for the ½ yeare; but at my last beinge in London, I humbly moveinge you herein, founde that it was not soe intended, allthough of necessity there must be a waiter at Cardiffe and if you please to order mee to paie Mr Dennis back his £4 I will sende up his deputies receipt for the same in my next account. Allsoe yours of the 13th instant, with the commaunde from the right honourable the counsell of state for stayinge all shipps which are bounde to Virginia, I have received and have communicated it to all the officers in each port within my charge. I hereby farther acquainte you that my receipt from the 24th of June last to the first instant amounteth not full to £20.

Worthy masters I humbly depende on your worshipps love and assistance for presentinge my peticion to the honourable committee for the Navy which I left with Mr Blackborne at my last beinge in London and if provision will not be made for payment of my deputyes according to my peticion the service cannott bee performed as it ought, neyther shall I bee able to undergoe the charge of the employment any longer. I cannott finde by what statute butter and calfeskins are exported, yet the merchants affirme that both are entred at Bristoll. I humbly desier one word from you whether I may not take entry for butter and calfeskins; if I may pray please to write mee one word what I must receive for customs on everye dozen of calfeskins. Thus desireinge to knowe your pleasures herein by the next post, I humbly take leave J B.

1. 'cum membris' in MS.

121. TO JOHN HOBBS

[*Marginated*] Caerleon 9 September 1650

Mr John Hobbs

On the 25th of August I rydeinge to the westerne ports within my charge on a speciall service concerninge the customes, by the way received yours of the 20th of August and on Saturdaie last I retourninge home from that service mett with yours of the 31th of August. Nowe according to desier you shall receive here inclosed my bill of charge or a breiffe of those receipts and vouchers which I sent last up with my account currant to the 24th of June last, which I would have sent you sooner if I had beene at home. I formerlie sent up my account currant with acquittances for all money paid and disbursed by mee, which I conceaved would have given satisfaccion. Pray remember my humble service to Collonell Langham, and desier that hee will bee pleased to sende mee a coppie of my account currant, subscribed by him according to the order of the commissioners that I may have somethinge to shewe for all the money which I have paide and disbursed. The money paid by Mr Tench was received by him for coles exported out of Llanelly alias North Burry, a member of the port of Millforde, as by his letter to Mr Blackborne here inclosed appeareth. Thus desireinge you to write one word of receipt hereof by the first post, wherein you will obliege J B.

For Mr Hobbs clerck to the accountant generall.

122. TO NEPHEW WILLIAM BYRD

[*Marginated*] 10 September 1650

Cozen William

Yours of the 10th, 17th, 24th and 31st of August with all things therein expressed I have received for all which I hartily thanke you. I formerlie sent inclosed to you a packett to be delivered to Mr Robert Franklyn at the custome house and then wrote to brother Pennant to deliver you 40s. to be delivered to Mr Franklyn. You wrote you had received the packett, but I have not heard at all of the 40s. If you had it of my brother Pennant I pray enquier of him whether he did not receive it back by my cozen Williams, with other money which he lent him, for before I wrote for the 40s. to brother Pennant, I delivered it to cozen Williams. Pray remember me hartily to brother Pennant and his wife, and if you finde his busines will not permitt him to call to Mr Blackborne, then I desier that you opportunely present the remembrance of my love and service to him and enquier what hopes of my peticion. Your aunte thanketh you for hir copies; remember us.

Page 25

123. TO WILLIAM JONES

[*Headed*] Newport 9 September 1650

Worthy Sir

After my service and faithfull respects to you remembered, with harty thanks for all your former favours, sir I make boulde humbly to present unto you the condicion and humble suite of a tennant of myne, one Thomas Williams, whoe was committed on Saturdaie last by John Plumley esquire, mayor of this towne, for the suspitious stealinge of a horse. This present daie the partie of whome Thomas Williams had this horse was brought before the mayor, and 3 wittnesses proved that Thomas Williams had this horse of him, soe that he is committed for the same. Nowe my humble suite in the behalfe of Thomas Williams is that you will accept of reasonable bayle for his present enlargement, and to afford him what favour you may lawfully doe. Your goodnes herein shall ever obliege mee to be sir, yours faithfully to serve you herein JB.

For the worshipful his worthy freinde William Jones esquire these, Usk.

124. TO THE COMMISSIONERS OF THE CUSTOMS

[*Marginated*] For the commissioners for the customs 9 September 1650

Right worshipful

After my humble duty and service remembred unto you, these are humbly to acquainte you that on the 22nd of the last moneth I received a letter from Mr Shewell your collector at Bristol by Captain Foxe, intymateinge that Richard Love of Neath had taken out a port cockett at Bristoll for severall goods laden abord the Eliza[beth] of Barnstaple for Neath (one of our member ports) but as hee understoode were intended to bee exported for Irelande. The 23rd of August Captain Foxe and I rode from hence to Neath hopeinge to meete the vessell there, but beinge not then arryved wee left order with Mr William Morgan, your waiter there, to take care therof, then wee rode to Swansey, thinkeinge the Elizabeth might arryve there, but noe newes of hir; but on the 25th of August shee arryved at Burton Ferry, where wee put a watch night and daie to attende hir. On the 29th shee came up to the Abbey neare Neath and on the 30th the goods were discharged there, Mr William Morgan then present, and tooke an exact account therof and findinge somme goods more then was expressed in the cockett made seazure therof, for that the merchants did intende to exporte the same to Irelande, and as wee conceave did not intende to paie any custom for the same.

A particular of the goods seazed I here inclosed sende you. Captain Foxe hath taken commissioners names and promiseth to take care that this seazure bee prosecuted, for the goods which came by cockett the merchants have entred and paid mee the customes, and have shipped the same in the Mary of Neath for Corcke. The captain and I have beene on this service from the 22nd of August till Saturdaie last, on which daie I came home.

I humbly desier you to thinke uppon my peticion which I left with Mr Blackborne that provision may bee made for soe many officers at least as I (by my severall letters and by my said peticion) have acquainted you are needfull for prevencion of fraude more then for receipt, otherwise assuredlie this kinde of fraude which wee have nowe mett with will encrease, and I am confident this is not the first that hath beene donne in this nature. I hereby humbly acquainte you that my receipt the last moneth commeth to about £35. A friggott for Silly commaunded by Captain Deamonde hath robbed many smale vessells betweene Silly and Swansey and hath taken one man or more out of each vessell and will not release them without money for each of them. I humbly hope the Lord will in good tyme cutt off all such theeves. I desier you please to write mee word wheither I shall paie Mr Dennis the £4 which he paid his deputy at Cardiffe or not and wheither I shall sende Mr Dennis his receipt or his deputies for the same.

125. TO OFFICERS OF THE CUSTOMS, PORT OF CARDIFF AND MEMBERS

[*Marginated*] Caerleon 11 September 1650

Gent[lemen]

I have received a stricte commaunde requieinge us not to permitt fullers earth nor tobaccoe pipe clay to be exported beyond seas on any termes, nor from port to port, but uppon extraordinary good securety in treble the vallewe of the earth soe shipped. Allsoe wee are required carefully to observe the com[mand] of the right honourable the counsell of state for stayinge all shipps bounde for Barbathoes, a coppie whereof is here under written. Allsoe we are required to take care that noe man enter goods in another mans name uppon payne of forfeiture therof, according to the inclosed printed paper, in all which your care is desired in[(1)] your port and adjacent places by him that is your faithful freinde and servant J B.

These are to will and require you forthwith to make stop in all the ports of Englande of any shipps goeinge to Barbadoes untill you shall receive further orders from this counsell, hereof you are not to faile and for which this shalbe your warrant. Given at this councell of state at Whitehall 3rd September 1650.

Signed in the name and by order of the councell of state appointed by authority of Parliament.

To the commissioners of the customs

A true copy made by John Byrd

Sent 3 coppies of the last letter and orders: 1 to Cardiffe, 1 to Swansey and 1 to Chepstowe.

1. In MS, parentheses opened, never closed.

126. TO JAMES YONG

[*Headed*] 14 September 1650

Wrote to Mr James Yong to call to Mr Moses Longman for £3 8s. 10d. for mee and on receipt therof, to deliver his note, which I inclosed to James Yong; allsoe desired James to paie Mr Deyos £11 for mee; allsoe to conferre with Mr Roberts about my sons and cozen Rees Jones.

127. TO MICHAEL DEYOS

[*No date*]

Mr Deyos

Pray these are to acquainte you that the 32 rolls which were seazed did weygh gros 1443 lbs. whereof i roll weight 23 lbs. gros was delivered to Mr Price, one of the parteners, and 5 cwt. gros was sent unto you soe that here remayned 920 lbs. gros, about a hundred weit whereof was rotten, and not worth any thinge. The money made of the rem[ainder] did amount unto £14 13s. 1d. out of which £3 13s. 1d. beinge deducted for the charge and clearinge thereof, the remainder in my hands is £11, which I will sende to you by the first opportunety.

The 2 casks are not in this account, in which the tobaccoe was sent to you, but are at your dispose.

128. TO ROBERT BLACKBORNE

[*Marginated*] 19 September 1650

Mr Robert Blackborne

Pray please to take notice that yours of the 14th instant I have received, by which I perceave my masters have beene enformed that a quantety of Fr[ench] tobaccoe was landed at Newport out of the North Starre of Dort from Pennarth, for satisfacion herein I humbly pray you to acquainte my worthy masters that here was a great quantety of pruens entred out of that ship[1] at Cardiffe, which was generally conceaved to bee tobaccoe, wherefore I caused all the vessells or caskes to bee searched and they proved all pruens according to the entry, the which were for the most parte carryed to Bristoll by carrier, the shipp only stayinge at Pennarth to discharge salt for the use of our country and for further clearinge this busines. Both the master and the merchant made oath that noe tobaccoe was laden at all on this shippe; neyther could our wayter nor any of us finde that any tobaccoe came in that shipp.

Whilst I was attendinge at Pennarth and Cardiffe about this shipp there arryved a parcell of tobaccoe at Newport in a smale barque of Byddyforde, the which Mr Plumley the waiter there tooke presentment of, and secured it till I came, then I examyned that likewise and those whoe bought this tobaccoe doe affirm it to bee ordinary and not French, which I beeleeve to bee true and have cleared it accordinglie. My masters former letters concerninge Mr Dennis £4 I have received and have written up an account thereof. A bill of charge cannott conveniently be drawen up with an account of everye vessell on which Mr Dennis his deputy did attende, nor howe many dayes hee attended, for that Mr Dennis agreed with his deputy for 40s. per quarter which if my maisters please to order mee to repaie I will sende up Mr Dennis his receipt for the same.

Pray doe mee the favour as to write mee one word what is becomme of my peticion which I left with you and whether any hopes of allowance of the money which I paide to my deputies or not. Thus pro[vok]inge you to present the remembrance of my humble duty and service to my worthy masters, I take leave and remayne, sir, yours assuredly to serve you J B.

Sir my last to the commissioners should beare date the 9th instant.

1. 'Out of that ship' interlined.

129. TO JOHN HOBBS

[*No date*]

Mr John Hobbs

Yours of the 14th instant with the inclosed direccions I have re[ceived] which I shall endeavour to observe with all care. Sir I have formerly sent up and delivered receipts and vouchers according to my severall quarter bills soe that I hope the accomptant generall will be pleased to sende mee a counterparte of my account currant, subscribed by himselfe. Pray please to present the remembrance of my humble service to him and desier him to graunte this my request which in my judgement is but just. Whereas it is expected that our surveyor should bee a wittnes to the payment of all the officers theyr sallaryes and other disbursements within our ports, it is impossible; for the extent of our port and members are above 60 miles and our surveyors and I are seldome in one place. Your love and furtherance in the premisses will obliege mee to bee sir yours J B.

130. TO NEPHEW WILLIAM BYRD

[*Marginated*] 26 September 1650

Cozen William

Yours of the 14th instant came this daie to my hands with the inclosed, for which I hartily thanke you; our botes not goinge to Bristol last weeke was the cause I received it noe sooner. Sir if Hugh Lloyd doth give over his employment in our portes soe that his place bee vacant, then if a commission may be had for Glamorganshere which is nowe in his charge and Mr Dittyes, and for Monmothshere which is nowe in Mr Davis his charge, I will embrace it and endevour to doe the common wealth the best service I canne therein; but if those gent[lemen] doe not freely and willinglie give over theyr employments in those 2 countyes then I desier you not to seeke any of theyr employments to pleasure mee.

My present employment extendeth through these 2 countyes soe that if (without prejudice to any other) I may have this employment I conceave it will enable mee to performe both the better if I may have any thinge considerable for my paynes herein, whereof I pray a word by first post, and if you canne agre[e] with the postmaster to carry a letter and a booke of newes on reasonable termes I pray please to sende constantly [*Page 27*] weekely or if you write of any busines of consequence pray sende it by the post, least it stay in Bristol till to late, as perhaps this hath don. I desier that opportunely, yet not to often, you remember my love and service to Mr Blackborne and put him in mynde of my peticion. I perceave my cozen Williams forgott the 40s., soe did you to write one word at all therof till your last, but I will call to my cozen Williams for it, in the meane tyme pray remember mee hartily to brother Pennant and all his and pray him not to harbour any ill thoughts of mee herein. I shall take the 1st opportunety to sende it up.

131. TO THE COMMISSIONERS OF THE CUSTOMS

[*Marginated*] Caerleon 18 October 1650

[*Subscribed*] For the Commissioners for the Customes of England

Right worshipful

Pray please to take notice that on the 7th instant Captain Foxe came with a writt of aprizement for valewinge the goods seazed at Neath, where wee have beene and have caused the goods to be aprized according to the said writt. The merchant Mr Moses Longman brought a letter of lycence to compounde for the said goods, which hath beene donne by Mr William Morgan your waiter there, whereof wee made certifficatt and delivered it to Captain Foxe to be sent up; and for the common wealths parte beinge £27 14s. 3d. I toke securety, and have ordered it to bee paid to Mr Shewell in Bristol and have desired him to retorne it up to Captain Langham which I am confident wil be performed accordinglie.

In our retorne from Neath wee rode to visitt the members and creekes and comminge to Aberthawe founde Captain Arthur Spencer newly arryved from Ireland in the newe Thomas of Aberthawe, with somme smale horses and coults, for which 10s. per piece is to be paide for customs by the booke of rates, but the merchant affirmeth he hath seene many horses landed at Mynhead and other ports without payment of custome or any other duty for the same. I have taken his engagement eyther to paie the custome or else to bringe me a sufficient discharge for the same before the 25th daie of December next. I humbly desier you to write me word by the first post whether 10s. per horse is to be paid according to the booke of rates or not, and what must bee paid for horses or cowes if any happen to arryve within my charge.

Since my comminge from London I discharged my deputies at Neath, Newton and Burry, but in visitinge of the ports I find of necessity men must bee employed to take care in those severall places, which I am not able to doe at my charge and unlesse provision bee made to enable men to looke to the severall places according to my peticion left with Mr Blackborne the service cannot be performed as it ought to bee; whereof I make boulde once more humbly to acquainte you. Worthy masters I humbly pray be pleased to give order to the accomptant generall to allowe on my account such moneyes as I have formerlie paide to deputies for performance of the service within the severall places expressed in my peticion, which if you may not doe then have I acted under you for lesse then nothinge which I pray consider of and please to afforde what encouragement you may to your worships humble servant J B.

132. TO JOHN HOBBS

[*Marginated*] Caerleon 19 October 1650

Mr John Hobbs

Yours of the 15th instant I received for which I hartily thanke you. Here inclosed I have written to my masters the commissioners: pray present it with remembrance of my humble duty and service to them. I formerlie left a peticion with Mr Blackborne to be presented to the honourable committee for the navy, which was for allowance of such moneyes as I had paid my deputies and the commissioners promised mee to present it opurtunely and did not doubt but that it should bee allowed mee. I pray remember my service to Mr Blackborne and enquier what hopes therein. Pray present the remembrance of my love and service to Collonell Langham, allsoe pray remember mee kindely to your brother honest Mr Thomas Swynmour and I desier you and him or one of you to write me one word howe this busines goeth and if any thinge hapneth concerninge mee, I pray a word thereof to J B.

133. TO ROBERT BLACKBORNE

[*Headed on page 28*] Caerleon 5 November 1650

Mr Blackborne

Pray please to take notice that yours of the 29th October last I received, concerninge the names of my deputyes and the quallety of theyr employments, whose employments in most of the ports within my charge hath beene and constantly is to take entryes and bonds, and to graunte cocketts and certificates whereof is great store in most of the ports within my charge, and where is but little employment, yet some man must take care constantly to prevent fraude. To draw bills per diem cannott conveniently be donne, for that my deputyes have beene employed quarterly and accordinglie I have sent up theyr particular receipts everie quarter under theyr owne hands which are with the accountant generall which I humbly pray may be accepted; for if I should agree with my deputies to acte by the daie, they will expect much more money[1] [*Page 28*] then I paie them by the quarter, for in some of our custome houses is contynuall employment, and I doubt those men which are nowe employed (nor any other men of credditt) will not acte by the daie, for the creditt of the service is more to them then the proffitt. I pray present the remembrance of[2] my humble duty and service to my worthy masters the commissioners, whose commaunds herein I humbly desier they please to laye on mee, which shall with all care and humillity bee observed. I herewith sende up my quarter booke to the 29th September last with my bill of fees and disbursments and account current. I pray one word of receipt thereof by the first post.

Alderman Arthur Roberts is pleased to act (in my absence for me in Cardiffe)

Alderman Patrick Jones in Swansey

Mr John Griffith in Neath Since my comminge from London I discharged these Mr Jenkin Arnold in Newton 3 hopeinge to spare the common wealth soe much Robert Basnett in South Bury as theyr sallaryes came to but I finde of necessity some men must be employed in those places wherein I humbly desier to knowe my masters pleasures J B.

1. 'money' repeated.

2. 'the rem of' interlined.

134. TO JOHN HOBBS

[*No date, probably 5 November 1650, from Caerleon*]

Mr John Hobbs

Yours of the 29th October last I have received, by which I finde my selfe more and more oblieged unto you. Sir I have herewith sent up my quarter booke, bill of charge and account current to the 29th September last which I hope will bee cleared accordinglie. I have allsoe sent acquittances for the moneyes paide and disbursed and I have written to my masters the commissioners humbly desireinge that my account may bee passed with allowance of the acquittances already sent up for the moneyes paid to my deputyes, whoe were employed quarterly and theyr severall quarter receipts are with Collonell Langham, to whome I pray present the remembrances of my faithfull service.

I doubt bills per diem cannott well bee made up, for that in somme of our customehouses wee have employment everye daie and my deputies were employed and paide by the quarter, as by theyr severall acquittances with Collonell Langham appeareth; howsoever if the commissioners will not give allowance of those moneyes by those acquittances then I pray please to doe mee the favour as to sende downe those acquittances which will not be allowed of, that I may deliver them back to whome I paid the moneyes, whereby to have bills drawne up as is expected; which in my simple judgement is the improprest waye, yet I shall humbly submitt to the judgement of my masters, and shall with all care endeavour to perform theyr commands.

Pray remember my true love to your honest brother, Mr Thomas Swynmowe, and I desier you not to bee weary in proceedinge to the perfectinge and cleareinge of my accounts; for which I will really appear to bee sir your thankefull freinde and servant J B.

135. TO OFFICERS OF THE CUSTOMS, PORT OF CARDIFF AND MEMBERS

[*Marginated*] 8 November 1650

Wrote to the officers at Cardiffe and Swansey and enclosed the acte for receipt of the 15 per cent, desireinge them to put the same in execucion and allsoe to receive 1s. in everye 20s. received for customs, by another acte of parliament, for redempcion of captives from Algier.

136. TO PHILIP WILLIAMS

[*Headed on page 29*] Caerleon 22 November 1650

Mr Phillip Williams

Sir, I was in Cardiffe on Wednesdaie in the audite weeke, where I hoped to have seene you according to your promise, that I might have communicated the orders enclosed unto you and have concluded the seazure made by you accordinglie, but since I sawe you I have not heard on word from you, wherefore I have sent you here inclosed orders which I received from the commissioners concerning seazures and if you will write mee one word when you have received lycence to compound for the wooll seazure and what daie you and the proprietors will bee in Cardiffe, I will give you the meetinge and there receive your oath as I am required. I have received letters from the commissioners, and alsoe from the accountant generall requiering us to receive 10s. per piece for horses, mare and coults[1] [*Page 29*] for subsedie, and 6d. per peece for redempcion of captyves. I pray remember my love and service to Mr Thomas Spencer and Captain Arthur, with theyr wives, and please to call to the captain for £5 5s. due from him for 10 horses.

Enclosed this in a letter to Mr Arthur Roberts, whoe I requested to procure Mr Williams's answer.

1. 'Coults' repeated.

137. MEMORANDUM

[*No date*]

On the 5th[1]1648 John Byrd of Carlion bought of William Brookes of Upton uppon Seaverne a ladeinge of soe good coles as the best coles were, which George Price lately soulde in Carlion. These coles are to bee delivered at the key in Carlion out of the Elizabeth of Upton within 6 weekes after the date hereof and hee is to weygh and deliver the coles within 3 dayes after the landinge thereof at 10s. 3d. per tonne, whereof John Byrd hath paid William Brookes in parte of payment 7s. 6d.

John Byrd[2]

Sworn by[3] William Meredith:

Thomas George sent the originall (whereof this is a copie) to Mr Deyos water bayleiffe in Bristoll 22nd November, desireinge him to procure the money from Brookes by course of lawe if it would not bee had otherwise. Received 40s. by Mr Deyos in satisfaccion for Brookes. J B.

1. Word missing.
2. 'John Byrd' preceded by large capital B.
3. 'Teste' in MS.

138. TO NEPHEW WILLIAM BYRD

[*No date*]

Cozen William

Yours without date I have received with ii bookes there inclosed. I most humbly and hartily rejoyce that the Lord hath made you an instrument of your fathers comfort and I humbly pray that the Lord will put in my brother's hart to accept what shall bee presented to him from the Lord.

As for the busines of excise (as I formerlie wrote to you) if Mr Lloyd and Mr Ditty doe laye downe theyr commission soe that[1] employment be totally voyde then if a commission may be graunted to mee for South Wales (but rather only for Glamorgan and Monmouthsheire) I will embrace it on the termes whereof you write. If South Wales shall bee farmed and noe other place (although it shoulde yeelde 3 tymes more then ever was made thereof) yet unles all England bee farmed, it will bee prejudiciall to the common wealth, for thes ports beinge farmed out and not Bristoll, Bridgewater, Barnstaple etc. what shall bee received in South Wales will be lost in those partes. This is a word of advice to you, which if you finde it convenyent you may communicate to the commissioners, and after that if Glamorgan and Monmothsheires will be rented out to farme, I will give as much as ever was clearely made thereof per annum, or else I had rather have those 2 countyes on sallary then any more, because of my relacion in them both only, and none in the rest, unles in Carmarthensheire be added.

Pray remember me kindely to Mr Lloyd and Mr Ditty, and I desier you to advize with them herein, for I founde them very honest and knowinge gentlemen, but if I had founde them other wise (the Lord hath taught mee to knowe) it is not lawfull to take another mans house over his head, wherein I desier you to take care. Pray remember my true love to your father, sister and ould couple; allsoe to my brother Pennant and all his family; allsoe I desier you opportunity to visitt Mr John[2] Hobbs, as I formerlie wrote you, and desier him to write mee and answer to my last letter. I desier to heare from you constantly by the Welch post with a diurnall, and a word in your letter of what busines or other newes current, for what cometh by way of Bristol (except heavy things) is as chargeable one way with the other as by the post, besides delayes. Pray enquire at Doctors Commons wheither probat of wills and letters of administration in Landaphe bee authenticall, or not; if not, what course is to be taken in those cases.

1. 'Yt' interlined.
2. 'Jo' interlined.

139. TO COLONEL GEORGE LANGHAM

[*Marginated*] Cardiff 5 December 1650

Honoured Collonell Langham,

Yours of the 23rd November last I have received and according to your freindly advice and your direccions formerly sent mee, I here inclosed send acquittances from the severall men which I employed in the severall ports within my charge, for transactinge and better securinge the customes, and allsoe my acquittance for the moneyes expressed in your letter, and another acquittance from James Dennis for the £4, for which I formerly sent a receipt from him; all which I humbly hope will bee allowed of. The receipts within my charge the last 2 moneths is about £23. I pray remember my humble duty to my worthy masters the commissioners whoe (God assistinge mee) I will not knowingely give any just cause of displeasure, but shall endeavour, as much as shall lye in my power, to performe theyr commaunds. Out of tobaccoes and allsoe corne and beare, which paid customs by statute, the 15 per cent was not allowed formerly; wheither it must be deducted, or raised over and above the former customs hereafter, I pray a word of advice, with a word [of] receipt hereof, by the first post to your faithfull servant, J B.

140. TO CAPTAIN EDWARD FOXE

[*Marginated*] Caerleon 23 December 1650

Captain Foxe

Sir you shall receive your 2 chayres by this bearer, which cost 15s. 6d. I have your 5s. from Mr William Morgan whoe remembers his love to you; if Mr Longman hath paid the moneys to Mr Shewell, I desier his receipt or a discharge for the same. If you canne spare any blanke bonds pray sende mee soe many as you may conveniently, for the ports within my charge doe vent great store. If you cannott spare any to us now, I pray sende for a rheame by the first for us. J B.

Page 30

141. TO NEPHEW WILLIAM BYRD

[*Headed*] Caerleon 24 December 1650

Cozen William

Your 3 last by our post and 1 by way of Bristol I received. I desier you to sende me by the first the acts for the assessment and militia; and if (in respect of my present employment) I may not bee employed in your affaires, yet I desier Newport and Carlion at rent, for which I will give as much as any, or at sallary, and if my name bee not [put forward] then to gett it in the name of Morgan Griffith yeoman, and I will engage for the busines and bee accomptable.

142. TO OFFICERS OF THE CUSTOMS, PORT OF CARDIFF AND MEMBERS

[*24 December 1650*]

Wrote the same daye to the officers of the customs in Cardiffe, Swansey, Neath, Newport and Chepstowe to looke to French tobaccoes, and to sende mee the entryes taken this quarter.

143. TO PHILIP WILLIAMS

[*No date*]

Wrote to Mr Philip Williams that I had received his 2 letters, and that he should againe call for customs of the horses landed at Aberthawe, or a discharge for the same; and appointe what daie I should meete him at Cardiff about the wooll seazure.

144. TO ARTHUR SPENCER

[*Marginated*] Caerleon 23 January 1651

Wrote to Arthur Spencer to paie the custom due on the horses to Captain Foxe, and wrote to Captain Foxe to demaunde it by that letter enclosed to him, and if hee did not paie it on demaunde to cause him to be arrested; allsoe desired Captain Foxe to sende some more blanke bonds.

145. TO HUGH ROBERTS

[*Marginated*] Caerleon 25 January 1651

Mr Hugh Roberts

You shall receive herewith £8 4s. 0d. to cleare my cozen Rees with you, Mr Powell and Mr Allen and my sons with you and Mr Allen, accordinge [to] the petition sent mee. In this money is 20s. for you towards scooleinge and when we meete (God permittinge) I will give you honest and reall satisfaccion. There will remain (all things discharged as abovesaid) 21d. which I pray deliver to the 3 youths from their mothers to buy the faier. Thus

£0 09s. 7d.	due to you by your note	our sons
£0 13s. 4d.	towards scooleinge	
£2 00s. 0d.	remains to Mr Allen for dyett last quarter	
£4 19s. 4d.	to cleare Rees his dyett, petty charge and 6s. 8d. towards scooleinge	
£0 01s. 9d.	amongest the youths	
£8 04s. 4d.		

146. TO WALTER SANKEY

[*Marginated*] Caerleon 27 January 1651

Mr Sankey and worthy freinde

You shall receive here inclosed a certificate of the apprizeinge and compoundinge for 8 sacks of wooll of Ed. Nicholls, seazed by Mr Philip Williams, waiter at Aberthawe. I have received the states parte beinge £6 10s. 0d. I desier order from the commissioners to paie money due on seazures to Mr Shewell, as I have all ready for payment of my other receipts. I desier you please to write mee word what will bee the charge of clearinge this 8 sacks of wooll, both for Philip Williams and my selfe.

Sir you shall receive here inclosed a letter of lycence to be renewed for compoundinge with Morgan Jenkins for his 8 sacks of wooll, the which was seazed heretofore by Philip Williams and after hee seazed the same he could not gett it on shore, soe that it was carryed to Mynhead whether it was boundinge and Morgan Jenkins gave bonde to Philip Williams to make good the vallewe thereof if recovered in the Exchequer, the which being thus gon and disposed of, it cannott bee weyghed and apprized as is directed, yet I beeleeve it may be apprized at guesse; which if you finde a writt to be proper to doe soe and that you please to sende one downe with the letter of lycence renewed and direct the writt to me and the 2 commissioners, in the inclosed certifficat expressed, with full direccions howe to proceede therein, I will take care and paynes to see it effected.

I pray please to remember my humble duty to my masters the commissioners, whose direccions I likewise desier herein, if you finde it convenyent. Sir by the direccions which I received Saturneday last I finde in the 4th article that the officer may not compounde for his owne parte under one third of what goods seazed shall bee vallewed at, without order from the commissioners, whose direccions I humbly desier herein likewise. It is desired that tyme bee given till midsommer terme in Morgan Jenkins lycence. I desier to knowe whether the officers of the customs here may take Philip Williams his oath for what composicion he shall make with Morgan Jenkins, or not.

Page 31

147. TO COLONEL GEORGE LANGHAM

[*Marginated*] Caerleon 27 January 1651

Honored Colonel George Langham

Pray please to take notice that I sende herewith my quarter booke to the 25th of December last, with acquittances, bill of charge, and account currant which I hope you will finde to bee right, which being soe I humbly desier your receipt accordinglie. Sir I pray please to present my remembrances of my humble duty and service to my worthy maisters the commissioners, and acquainte them that I received theyrs by the fast post with the acte concerning forraigne coyne and bullyon, and a coppie of orders concerning seazures, which shall be carefully observed.

I formerlie received commaunde from them for makeinge up my bookes yearely on the 24th of June, to that tyme; the port cockett bookes cannott bee made and delivered at the ende of the yeare, for that all men have 4 moneths tyme to bringe in theyr certifficatts; and wheither I am to have bookes out of the Exchequer as formerlie, or whether I must make bookes of paper or parchment for entryes and port cocketts yearely, I humbly desier to knowe the commissioners pleasure herein; and when I am to begin the midsommer account, for I have bookes here ready written both for entryes and port cocketts, in parchment out of the exchequer to the 25th of December 1649. At my last beinge in London Mr Kersley promised to sende mee word what course should be taken with these bookes but I heard not from him since.

148. TO NEPHEW WILLIAM BYRD

[*No date*]

Wrote to cozen William Byrd acquaintinge him I had received all things from him according to his weekely letters; and that I had sent up my quarterbooke etc to Colonel Langham and I [had] written to him and to Mr Sankey and I desired him to visitt Mr Hobs, Mr Swynmour and Mr Sankey, to desier them to answer my letters and allsoe that hee sende mee the next acts which shall comme out for contrybucion with remembrance to our freinds.

149. TO RICHARD, LORD HERBERT OF CHERBURY

[*Marginated*] Caerleon 28 January 1651

Right honourable

My humble service to you with your honourable lady remembered. I make boulde hereby to put your honour in mynde of a small debt (about £12) long since due from your honour to mee of which I formerlie gave you a particular; nowe my humble request is that you will bee pleased to give order to your steward here to paie mee this smale summe, which at present will much pleasure him that is your honour's humble servant J B.

For the right honourable Richard Lord Herbert, Baron of Cherbury and Castle Stands these.

150. TO NEPHEW WILLIAM BYRD

[*Marginated*] Caerleon 9 February 1651

Cozen William

I wrote to you the 28th January acquaintinge you that I had received all things from you according to your letters and that I had sent up my quarter booke to Colonel Langham and that I had written to him and to Mr Sankey about somme busines which required answer from them, and my request to you was to procure answer from them to mee; but I have not heard one word neyther from you nor them by this last weekes post, which makes mee doubt whether my letters came safe up or not. I pray enquire of Mr Hobbs or Mr Swynmoure and allsoe of Mr Sankey whether my letters came to hande or not, and if they are received I desier answers to them. I understande there is a new acte for the contynueinge the militia till May next; I pray sende mee one and if any acts shall passe for further contrybucion I pray sende mee one by the first opportunity. Pray lett mee heare from you by this bearer my neighbour Rowlande Williams, and if the acts are nowe to bee had I pray sende them by him.

151. TO PHILIP WILLIAMS

[*Headed, on page 32*] Caerleon 26 February 1651

Mr Philip Williams

You shall receive herewith the lycence renewed for compoundinge with Morgan Jenkins for the 8 sacks of wooll, for which you must receive of him 10s. for Mr Sankey. You shall allsoe receive herewith direccions in print (which I newly received) concerning seazures and allthough the direccions therein is that all goods ought to be apprized, yet the wooll beinge gon out of your possession, Mr Sankeys opinion is that the apprizeinge thereof may bee dispenced with, soe that there bee noe further prosecucion and you may compounde, which I pray doe soe soone as you may, for that I intende to bee with you about 3 weekes hence to performe herein what I am required. You shall receive herewith Ed. Nicholls indenture, [*Page 32*] allsoe an ordinance of parliament prohibitinge exportacion of wooll, fullers earth etc. wherein your care is desired in your port. In compoundinge with Morgan Jenkins, Mr Sankey writeth you may not compound for the states parte, but only for your owne. I pray doe mee the favour as to goe with this bearer to Mr Thomas Spencer, and desier him to bee soe loveinge as to sende mee by this bearer a coppie of a receipt and order which hee writeth he hath concerning armes delivered by Captain Moulton, and I will write him an answer.

152. TO THOMAS SPENCER

[*No date*]

Mr Spencer

After my true love and service to you, and all yours remembered, I pray please to take notice that yours of the 20th instant I have received, in which you write you have a receipt and order to receive money for armes delivered by Captain Moulton. I praye doe mee the curtesie as to sende mee a coppie of the receipt and order that I may write you an answer accordinglie, which (God permittinge) shall be performed by him that is and ever hath beene your faithfull freinde and servant J B.

153. TO COLONEL GEORGE LANGHAM

[*No date*]

Honored Colonel Langham

Pray please to take notice that yours of the 8th instant I have received by which I finde the commissioners pleasure is that I should make up my bookes on the 24th of June yearely in paper. My booke of entryes may be compleated and delivered then, but my booke for entryinge the port cocketts and bonds cannott[1] be then compleated and delivered, because 4 moneths tyme is given to all men for retorneinge certifficatts to theyr bonds as I wrote to you in my last; allsoe I desier to knowe whether the [ex]chequer bookes which I have here perfect to the 25th of December 1649 maye not be delivered by commission with my paper bookes from that tyme to the 24th of June next, or not.

My last bill of charge and disbursements did exceede my receipts, which sommetymes cannott be helpe[d], for as I formerlie wrote to my worthy masters that the officers in our ports are more for prosecucion of fraude then receipt, which if neglected, the state would suffer much in other ports. My receipt from the 25th of December last to the 1st instant will bee £98 0s. 10d. I pray present the remembrance of my humble duty and service to my masters the commissioners whose further direccions concerning my bookes abovesaid I humbly desier. Thus not haveinge else to trouble you with at present I take leave.

1. 'cannott' repeated in MS.

154. TO THOMAS PENNANT

[*No date*]

Brother Pennant

Sir I have forborne to trouble you soe long as I could and did impose my ordinary busines on my cozen William, dayly expectinge a good occasion to trouble you in which is not yet hapned but a busines of consequence, whereof I never thought is like to trouble mee, which is thus: above 5 yeares last past, I beinge sent as a messenger by somm gent (whoe then commaunded for the Parliament) in this county to Captain Robert Moulton, your worthy freinde and myne for some armes etc. which were delivered for the service of the Parliament, for which I conceaved satisfacion had beene made long since; but nowe by a letter from Mr Thomas Spencer, a coppie whereof is here under written it seemes satisfacion is not made.

Of late one of Mr Spencers sonns, owinge custome for which I tooke his word, refused to paie mee, soe that I was forced to take a course in lawe for it; by which meanes his father Mr Thomas Spencer (I doubt) will doe mee a discurtesie if hee canne; for prevencion whereof I earnestly pray you to take opportunety to speake with Captain Moulton herein, and present my love and service to him, and desier that hee will bee soe noble and soe just as to write his letter to the gentleman whoe wrote to him for the armes he delivered and who stands engaged for payment; and pray him to lay his command on mee to prosecute the busines which (God permittinge) shall be don with all care, and I will give him an account therof. Good brother if you cannott speake with Captain Moulton yourselfe I pray write to him herein and employ my cozen William Byrd to attende for his answer.

I understande my cozen William is out of employment for which I am hartily sorry. I pray afforde him your advice and best direcione and if the Lord shall enable me as I hope he will, I will bee a comfort to him. Thus dependinge on your love herein and desireinge one word in answer hereto soe soone as it may be had, I take leave and rest.

Page 33

155. THOMAS SPENCER TO JOHN BYRD

[*Subscribed*] Bristol 20 February 1651

Copie of Mr Thomas Spencers letter to mee John Byrd

Mr Byrd

Whereas I see by a receipt under your hande of certeyne armes you received of Captain Moulton when he was in Pennarth 1645, amounteinge to the summe of £404, the which you doe acknowledge by your receipt the 25th October 1645 and wheras I have order for receaveinge the saide moneyes from you, I desier you maye provide the said moneyes as soone as you may and that you give mee notice when you will paie them in unto mee, which money is to bee employed for the use of the state. I desier your answer, as soone as you maye and shall rest your freind Thomas Spencer.

If you bringe mee the money I shall deliver your bill under your hande, and spare further charges.

156. TO GEORGE TENCH AND ARTHUR ROBERTS

[*Marginated*] Caerleon 26 February 1651

Wrote to Mr Tench and sent him the entryes taken in Cardiffe and the easterne ports in ½ a yeare ended the 25th December last and desired him to sende mee this moneths account.

Wrote to Mr Roberts for the like.

157. TO NEPHEW WILLIAM BYRD

[Marginated] Caerleon 6 March 1651

Cozen William

Your 3 last letters with what you sent therein I received etc. About 5 yeares last past I was sent as a messenger by somme gent of this county whoe then commaunded here for the Parliament to Captain Robert Moulton a freinde of my brother Pennant and myne, for armes etc for the defence of this county which were delivered, which it seemes amounted to £404 as by a letter of the 20th of February last from Mr Thomas Spencer of Aberthawe to mee appeareth, wherein hee writeth hee hath order to receive this money from mee,by which I finde he intendeth to put a trick on me, for I am not engaged to paie for those armes, but was only a messenger sent to Captain Moulton for them, on the engagement of divers gentlemen of this county.

The last post I wrote to brother Pennant desireinge him (if he could conveniently) to speake with Captain Moulton herein and to request him to bee soe noble and soe just as to write to those gentlemen who wrote to him for those armes and who stand engaged for payment, and allsoe that hee would bee pleased to laye his commaunds on me to prosecute the busines which if he please to doe I would bee carefull therein and write him an account thereof. Allsoe I desired my brother Pennant (if he could not opportunely speake with Captain Moulton) that he would be pleased to write to him about this and desier you to to bee soe loveinge as to procure Captain Moultons answer to the premises, who knowes I was only a messenger herein and am not any way engaged to paie for those armes.

Nowe least my letter bee not comme to my brother Pennant's hands, or beinge received may bee neglected, I desier you to goe to my brother Pennant and put him in mynde hereof and if he cannott speake with Captain Moulton that then hee will write to him, which letter I desier you to carry to Captain Moulton, whoe I thinke lyveth in Reddriffe, and remember my service to him, and procure his answer as is above desired and sende it me soe soone as you canne. Your disbursements shall bee sent you up by the first freinde I shall finde comminge up; pray let noe paynes nor charge be spared to obtayne Captain Moulton's letter as abovesaid. Remember me kindly to father, sister and the ould couple with my true love to yourselfe.

158. TO CAPTAIN EDWARD FOXE

[*Marginated*] Caerleon 8 March 1651

Captain Foxe and worthy freinde

My true love and faithfull respects to you and Mr Shewell remembered, with harty thankes for all loving curtesies. Yours with the receipt for the £4 10s. I received, and am sorry that Mr Longman hath not performed. I pray put him in mynde thereof, for I long since wrote to the commissioners that I had ordered the payment of that money to Mr Shewell. Mr Philip Williams did by vertue of a lycence compounde for somme wooll seazed by him at Aberthawe and afterwards made oath before the officers of the customes at Cardiffe and wee wrote a certifficatt thereof and sent it up to Mr Walter Sankey, whoe writeth our certifficatt is alltogether invalyd and that the officers may not take an oath in such cases, without a commission from above for soe doinge; without which course, the officer which maketh seazure cannott be discharged on record; this beinge soe then the busines at Neath standeth in the like condicion, and Mr William Morgan cannott be discharged unles his oath bee taken by commission. I pray consider of it, and please to advize me herein by this bearer. If you have any store of blanke bonds I pray spare us somme. I pray write me word whether an English merchant bringinge in herrings unsalted in an Irish vessell ought to paie customs or not; and what a moy of herrings is, for a quantety is brought in within my charge, beinge fresh herrings.

Page 34

159. MARGERY BYRD AND OTHERS TO CATHERINE NICHOLLS

[*Marginated*] 12 March 1651

Sister Nicholls

It hath pleased God to take our deare mother out of this present world, whoe beinge displeased with you would not bee persuaded by us to give you any things by hir will. Howsoever (out of our sisterly love to you) in hope the Lord will soe blesse us as that we shall lyve togeither in true love, if you please to comme hyther yourselfe tomorrowe or the next daye and will accept of a ¼ parte of our mothers householde stuffe, wee are willinge and ready to present you therewith as a token of our true loves unto you; but if you comme not tomorrowe or the next daye wee take that for a refuseall and shall dispose of our mothers househoulde stuffe, according to hir will. Thus prayinge that wee may enjoye your company here, or else your answer by this bearer, with our true loves to you remembered wee rest your sisters.
sign[ed] Florence Morgan [*her mark*]
sign[ed] Florence Jones [*her mark*] for my mother Elynor Jones
Margery Byrd

160. TO COLONEL GEORGE LANGHAM

[*Marginated*] Caerleon 12 March 1651

Honoured Colonel Langham

I pray please to take notice that yours of the 1st instant I have received, by which I finde myne of the 26th February last came not to your hands, the coppie whereof is as followeth: after the coppie of that letter I wrote that my account and receipt thereon in the moneth of February last is £5 8s. 8d. and I desired to here from Colonel Langham soe soone as conveniently might bee.

161. TO CAPTAIN EDWARD FOXE

[*Marginated*] Caerleon 17 March 1651

Captain Foxe

Yours of the 14th instant with the letter and printed paper I received, the which I sende you back here inclosed, with many thankes. I long since wrote unto the commissioners acquainteinge them that I had ordered Mr Longmans money to be paid to Mr Shewell, whoe I had desired to returne it up to theyre casheere, but by a letter formerlie from Mr Sankey and another lately from the commissioners I finde it is not paid in, and the commissioners take it very ill at my hands that it is not performed according to my letter to them, wherein Mr Longman hath donne mee much wrong and I reape thereby somme disgrace. Wherefore I earnestly intreate you to call to him for this money, which if he doth not paie in a short tyme then I pray cause him to bee arrested uppon a staple accion, that I may bee cleared from this busines. I pray faile not herein.

162. TO HENRY VAUGHAN AND OTHERS

[*Marginated*] Caerleon 20 March 1651

Worthy Sir

I hereby make boulde to acquainte you that letters are lately sent downe; one from the committee for prize goods, the other for Captain Moulton for and concerning money due for armes and ammunicion delivered above five yeares since for and towards the reducement of this county to the obedience of the Parliament, which armes and ammunicion were to bee paide for according to an engagement confirmed by you and dyvers other gentlemen of this county. Many of them intende a meetinge at Chepstowe on Thursdaie next, where you are desired to bee then, that somme course may be advized on concerning the premisses. Thus dependinge on you herein I rest, J B.

Sent to Mr Henry Vaughan of Caldecott, Mr Henry Morgan of Riska and Mr Walter Jones of Magor; allsoe wrote to Mr Thomas Hughes of Moynes Court to meete.

163. TO THOMAS SPENCER

[*Subscribed*] Llancadle 21 March 1651

Mr Spencer

According to your advice and direccions I have conferred with most of the gentlemen named in the note you sent me, whoe desier that you will bee soe loveinge as to lett them see the letter of engagement to which theyre hands are, and the order by which the things were delivered, and the order by which you demaunde the money, the which I pray graunte them that they may give an answer thereto accordinglie. I am confident you will bee in Cardiffe at the assizes where (if God permitt) I intende to bee on Tusedaie next. I pray bringe the things abovesaid with you, that you and I maye advize therein.

Page 35

164. TO ROBERT BLACKBORNE

[*Headed*] Cardiff 25 March 1651

Mr Blackborne

These are to request you (in the behalfe of this bearer Mr Owen Jenkins, whoe hopeth to have somme employment from and under my worthy masters the commissioners) to bee so loveinge as to remember my humble duty and service to them, and to acquainte them that this man is a very honest man, and one that hath ever beene faithfull to the Parliament, and hath suffered exceedinglie by the cavileeres. Hee hath formerlie beene employed in the affaires of the customes in Llanelltly alias North Bury, which lyeth within the charge of the port of Millford. South Bury lyeinge very nere unto it (only a ryver runneth beetweene them) is within our port of Cardiffe, and I formerlie moved the commissioners that they woulde bee pleased to adde them both together and that they might bee both eyther under Cardiffe or under Millforde, the which I conceave would bee convenyent, for that one custome house would serve for both places, [as] they lye both within 8 miles of Swansey, the which I desier may bee considered, for the better secureinge the customes in both places. Thus earnestly desireinge your best assistance herein in the behalfe of this bearer I take leave and rest.

165. TO WALTER SANKEY

[*Marginated*] Caerleon 5 April 1651

Mr Sankey and loving friend

Yours of the 18th of February last with the lycence there inclosed I long since received, and nowe you shall receive here inclosed 3 lycences with endorsements what composicions were made by the officers. It is desired that you sende downe one commission (if it may be graunted) for takeinge the oaths on the 3 lycences, which when you sende downe againe I pray please to write one word of direcion what is to bee written after the oath is taken. I pray lett the commission bee directed to John Byrd, George Tench, David Price, Arthur Roberts, Richard Sheres and Francis Malory or any 2 of us and lett it bee retorneable in Michaelmas terme. The tobaccoe you wrote of is 48 rolls, in parte of the charges thereof I paid Mr Daniel Bubb 17s. at my last beinge in London; what else is due I will paie you. Mr Philip Williams sayth hee paide you 15s. towards the charge of his seazure and what else will becomme due, hee promiseth to paie it mee for you at the execucion of the commission for takeing his oath. I pray sende a particular note of your demaunds from him, with your commaunde on mee to call for it, wherein I will bee carefull. I pray cause or procure the severall defendants fynes to bee estreated accordinge to your last letter; pray one word of receipt hereof by the first post to yours assuredly to serve you, J B.

166. TO CAPTAIN EDWARD FOXE

[*Marginated*] Caerleon 5 April 1651

Captain Fox

Mr William Morgan of Neath remembreth his true love unto you and desireth you to file the enclosed certifficatt; his lycence with 2 more are enclosed in a letter herein to Mr Sankey. I have written for one commission to take the oathes on the 3, which if it may bee had will spare some charge. I pray reade myne to Mr Sankey and seale it and sende it by the first post, and if you thinke fitt I pray write one word to Mr Sankey, to sende downe one commission for takeinge oathes on the 3 lycences. I wrote to you on the 17th of March last, desireinge you to call to Mr Longman to paie in the money in his hande, which I hope is performed before this tyme. Good sir a word thereof and of receipt of the premisses to him that is J B.

167. TO HUGH ROBERTS

[*Marginated*] Caerleon 9 April 1651

Mr Hugh Roberts

My cozen Rees Jones and our sons entred into commons at Mr Allens on the 10th of October last, and came from thence on the 26th of March last, which is 5 moneths and ½ at 20s per peece everye moneth; 3 moneths was formerlie paid for, and nowe I sende money by my sonne William to cleare theyr quarter to this daie, beinge for the 3 youths 2 moneths and ½, £7 10s. and to you £1. Wheither it will give you contente or not I know not, if not at our next meetinge wee shall agree. I have allsoe sent money by my sonne William to cleare the taylors bill and all other petty charge, wherein I pray assiste him and cause him to sende mee a particular of everye disbursement, with a receipt for what money he payeth to each person. My sister Jones will not sende hir sonne Rees over nowe; shee desireth a receipt for what hath beene paide and what is nowe to bee paide, for the charge of hir sonne, the particulars of what was formerlie paid is here under written. I pray procure receipts for all to give hir contente. I pray instructe my sonns in the rules of arithmatick. Theyr quarters are very high; if you opportunely canne prevaile with Mr Allen to take £10 per peece I pray endeavour it. I canne have it soe, or cheaper, but that I am loth to remove them out of your presence. Thus

Due to Mr Charles Powell	00 - 14 - 10
To Mr Roberts for petty disbursements	00 - 05 - 04
To Mr Allen for disbursements in his sickness	01 - 02 - 06
To Mr Allen for 1⁄4 dyett	03 - 00 - 00
To Mr Roberts for scooleinge the last quarter	00 - 06 - 08
Sons Cozen Rees Jones	00 - 00 - 08
	05 - 00 - 00

Page 36

168. TO THOMAS PENNANT

[*Headed*] Caerleon 5 April 1651

Wrote to Brother Pennant that I had received his 2 letters with 2 from Captain Moulton and 1 from Mr Bulkeley, and I sent copies of Captain Moultons letters enclosed; for which to the gent[lemen] of our county they take it kindly and thankfully from the captain. I desired my brother to spare noe charge with Mr Bulkeley for our good, and desired him eyther by himselfe or cozen William Byrd to procure a coppie of the engagement signed in the same manner as the gent[tlemen] subscribed themselves, for that somme of them have forgotten the busines.

169. TO NEPHEW WILLIAM BYRD

[*Marginated*] Caerleon 10 April 1651

Wrote to cozen William Byrd concerninge the engagement that hee should procure it as above and sent enclosed a letter to Mr Samuel Neale in the excize office, or at the Angell in Lumber Streete, in which was Mr Maloryes quarter booke enclosed in a letter from mee to him, wherein I wrote that hee would remember mee to Mr Blackborne and procure him to move the honourable committee [for the] navy that 1 more officer might bee allowed in Neath, 1 in Newton and 1 in Bury, because of the new imposition of 2s. per chaldron on coles, and desired him to procure the acte and to advize thereon, as hee thought fitt or founde cause.

170. TO EDWARD HERBERT

[*Marginated*] Caerleon 14 April 1651

Mr Edward HerbertYou are desired to peruse the enclosed and if you finde any thinge improper therein to correcte it as you thinke fitt, and to advize with Collonell Jones herein, that letters may bee confirmed by the gent[lemen] of this county to Major-generall Harrison, Collonell Jones and Mr Henry Herbert, for theyr assistance herein.

171. TO OFFICERS OF THE CUSTOMS, PORT OF CARDIFF AND MEMBERS

[*Marginated*] 17 [April 1651]

Wrote to Mr Roberts at Cardiffe, and to the officers at Swansey and sent them the direccions concerning seazures and concerning the imposition on coles.

172. TO ROBERT BLACKBORNE

[*Marginated*] Caerleon 17 April 1651

Mr Robert Blackborne

Yours with the acte of parliament for receipt of the newe imposition on coles I formerly received,and yours of the 8th instant with the instruccions concerninge the same, and the direccions concerninge seazures, I have likewise received, and have communicated them to the severall officers in all the ports within my charge. Sir a question doth begin to arise here, which is whether any man ladeing coles within any of our ports and carryeth the same but 5 or 6 miles from the place where the same shall bee laden (not crossinge Seaverne) ought to paie the new imposicion or not, wherein I humbly desier my worthy masters the commissioners' direcions to whome I pray present the remembrance of my humble duty and service. I herewith sende my quarterbooke, bill of charge, account currant and receipt, which I pray please to deliver to Colonel Langham, with remembrance of my service to him. Thus desireinge one word of the receipt hereof, J B.

173. TO NEPHEW WILLIAM BYRD

[*Marginated*] Caerleon 18 April 1651

Cozen William

On the 5th instant I wrote to brother Pennant and inclosed coppies of the letters you wrote for me and on the 10th instant I gave you an account of your 2 letters with the actes etc which I receaved. I have nowe received yours of the 15th instant with the inclosed booke, for all which I kindely thanke you. Nowe you shall receive by this bearer Mr Thomas Jenkins (clerk to Mr Morgan of Pencreek, whoe you shall finde or heare of at Mr Walter Morgan's chamber, in Barnards Inne in Holborne) 40s. to cleare my scores, and 10s. to buy you and your sister each a paire of gloves. Pray remember mee kindely to brother Pennant and all his, and desier him to further my busines with Mr Bulkeley. 2 acts are nowe to comme forth, 1 for contribucions, the other for the militia of this nacion. I pray sende them mee soe soone as they may bee had. I heare there is an acte for doublinge money lent to bee repaid out of the chiefe rents of the king etc. I have £30 on the publique; if you canne finde a waie howe I may bee sure to bee paide on doublinge, I pray advize mee, in which I pray conferre with my brother Pennant, whose advice and assistance I desier herein. If I may bee paid out of the chiefe rents of Llyswery and Llebenyth, 2 lordships nere mee, I pray endeavour it. Remember me to father, sister and ould couple.

174. TO OFFICERS OF THE CUSTOMS, SWANSEA

[*Marginated*] Caerleon 20 April 1651

Wrote to the officers in Swansea, desireinge that noe lettpasses be graunted neyther there, nor in Neath, nor Bury, for that the commissioners have received somme lettpasses from the officers on the other side Seaverne, graunted in our ports with coles, which may not bee neyther for that, nor any other natyve commodityes, without cocket and bond.

Page 37

175. TO FRANCIS MALORY

[*Headed*] Caerleon 20 April 1651

Mr Francis Malory

I sent your account and quarterbooke on the 10th instant and would then have sent you this account of all seazures made in your tyme of beinge chequer if I had knowen your mynde, but nowe you shall receive that account herewith. If the newe imposicion must be paid for coles carryed but into the neighbourhood by water, not crossinge Seaverne, then to procure order it may be paid at ladeinge, for that noe officer resydeth[1] where such coles are landed.

1. 'recydeth' in MS, presumably for 'resideth'.

176. TO ROBERT BLACKBORNE

[*Marginated*] Caerleon 8 May 1651

Mr Blackborne and worthy friende

I pray present the remembrance of my humble duty and service to my masters the commissioners and please to acquainte them that my receipt from the 25th of March to the 1st instant is £35 15s. 3d. Good sir bee soe loveinge as to procure store of blanke bonds to bee sent downe soe soone as may bee for all those formerlie sent are used. Att my last beinge in London, I acquainted my masters that I was often sommoned to appeare at assizes and quarter sessions, from which and all other employments they then conceaved all officers of the customes were free. I am constantly sommoned to serve at the assizes and sessions and am threatned with other employments which I cannott performe without much neglectinge the affaires of the customes. Wherefore I earnestly desier you to procure the commissioners letter, directed to the high sheriffe and commissioners for the county of Monmoth, acquaintinge them that I am to be freed from all manner of service soe long as I am employed in the affaires of the customes, the which letter (I am confident) will be very authenticall in that busines. I pray please to write mee word whether the 2s. per chaldron on coles is to bee paid for such coles as shal bee exported to France and to Irelande, or not.

177. TO NEPHEW WILLIAM BYRD

[*No date*]

Cozen William

On the 18th of April last I sent you 50s. since which tyme I have received yours dated Tusedaie 10 a clock at night, with 3 acts of parliament, and since my wife received yours of the 25th April with your token, which is kindely accepted by yours. I finde you are drawen into trouble by him that shoulde have endeavoured your preservacion. I am hartily sorry for it and am very sensible howe he dealt with mee in the like nature. I pray God deliver and all your well wishers out of all troubles. I finde by yours to my wife that you hope for somme preferment, by a gent bounde for Irelande, which if you misse of then you are at leasure to visitt your freindes, if these parts would aforde any hopes of preferment. I would earnestly desier you to hasten hyther; howsoever if you misse of preferment, rather then to lye at expence without good hopes of doeinge yourselfe good, I advize you to comme downe to mee, and allthough noe gaine is to bee made in your comminge downe, yet I hereby promise you shall not loose any thinge.

If you comme by waie of Bristoll you shall finde your cozens William and Matthias with Mr Hugh Roberts at Mr Allens house in Wyne Streete, but if you comme not that waie you may please to sende any thinge you have to bring downe to bee delivered them. If you have not received the 50s. then enquier of Mr Walter Morgan at his chamber in Barnards Inne Holborne for Thomas Jenkins (clerck to Mr Morgan of Pencreeke) by whome I sent the money up.

178. TO NEPHEW WILLIAM BYRD

[*No date*]

Wrote to William Byrd and sent a coppie of an engagement for £20 lent by my mother in lawe Mrs Florence Seys, desireinge him to procure satisfaccion for that and £10 I lent, or to gett what might bee had for these 2 summes beinge in all £30; inclosed this to brother Pennant.

179. TO THOMAS BULKELEY

[*No date*]

Wrote to Mr Thomas Bulkeley desireinge him to gett my accounts cleared and to gett my ould masters discharge for the same, if it might be had without offence. Enclosed this to brother Pennant.

180. TO THOMAS PENNANT

[*Marginated*] Caerleon 14 May 1651

Brother Pennant

I make boulde to trouble you with the inclosed letters and coppie of a will. Pray reade Mr Bulkeleyes, and if you conceave it proper, pray deliver it sealed to him and (as formerlie I wrote) spare noe charge that maye doe us good. Pray employ my cozen William Byrd to gett a commission out of the court for probatt of wills above; for takeinge my oath belowe, on the same, directed to Mr Walter Cradock and Mr Henry Walter, ministers of the word of God, Roger Williams and Rees Williams esquires, John Warde and Philip Williams gent or any twoe of them. I have not sent up the originall will feareinge it may miscarrye. I conceave the coppie maye serve, for that my mother in lawe dyed without such debts or any other thinge, which may cause the will to bee questyoned. If a commission will not be graunted on this coppie, then I desier to knowe what tyme I may have for bringinge in the originall will. Perhaps somme occasion may invite me up; if not within the tyme proper for deliveringe in the will, then I will sende it up. Good brother if my cozen wanteth money to performe my busines, I pray creditt mee with soe much as will discharge what hee shall doe for mee. If you have opportunity to doe him good, I pray doe it as for mee, allsoe I pray afforde [*Page 38*] him your advice and assistance in the busines whereof I write to him here inclosed. Thus.

181. TO NEPHEW WILLIAM BYRD

[Marginated] Caerleon 23 May 1651

Wrote to cozen William Byrd an account of all letters etc received from him before this tyme and desired him to procure a coppie of a letter from the prize office, and I advized him to settle his sister in London and to come downe himselfe to mee[1] to save charge.

1. 'and to come downe himselfe to mee' interlined.

182. TO THE COMMISSIONERS OF THE CUSTOMS

[*Marginated*] Caerleon 21 May 1651

Right worshipful

These are humbly to acquainte you that in the sande which is in the bottome of the ryver of Uske, which runneth by Carlyon and Newport and from thence into Seaverne, is a smale cole taken up and cleansed in the water with sives by the poore of Newport, whoe lately sould somme of that cole for 1d. per bagg, to be carryed by water into the neighbourhood to bee used for burneinge of lyme in our county, and beinge waterborne I (according to your direccions that all cole waterborne must beare the new impost) did demaunde the imposition of 2s. per chaldron, which hath caused the poore to bee sommethinge clamourous and it hath beene argued by somme of the gentry of this county whoe doe beeleeve and humbly desier that noe imposition maye bee layd on this cole, which beinge cleansed soe well as maye bee is full of gravell, and it commeth by the providence of God from the colepitts in the mountaynes by great raynes washinge the croppe and other refuse cole from thence into this ryver.

The benefitt thereof redoundeth only to the poore; neverthelesse I might not omitt what I have donne herein, without your order, which I desier you will bee pleased to graunte, whereby our county may knowe there is noe intencion to laye a charge on this meane commodety which the Lord in mercy hath sent only for the reliefe of the poore as abovesaid. Thus prayinge your charitable order herein, I take leave and rest.

183. TO WALTER SANKEY

[No date]

Mr Sankey

On the 5th of April last I wrote to you by the conveyance of Captain Edward Foxe of Bristol and enclosed 3 lycences by which composicion was made on 3 seazures, but not haveinge heard one word from you since that tyme, maketh mee doubt myne came not to your hands, I pray a word thereof by the first post for my satisfaccion; for if these lycences are lost I doe not knowe what course is to bee taken therein. Pray present the reminder of my humble duty to my masters.

184. TO COLONEL GEORGE LANGHAM

[*Marginated*] Cardiff 29 May 1651

Honored Collonell Langham

Yours of the 22nd instant I received, by which I perceave somme mistake is committed which I hope will appear not to bee in mee, for on the 17th of April last, I enclosed my quarter booke to the 25th of March with an account current and receipts, desireinge Mr Blackborne to deliver them to you, which since that tyme hee writeth were received and delivered to you accordinglie, and on the 8th instant I wrote to Mr Blackborne againe and amongest other things which I desired him to present to the commissioners, I desired him to acquainte them of my receipts from the 25th of March to 1st instant, which was £35 15s. 3d. which it seemes he did not acquainte you of. I pray please to present the remembrance of my duty and service to my masters the commissioners, and if you finde any thinge amisse eyther in my accounts or any thinge else which concerneth mee, I pray please to write mee one word thereof which I shall with all care and dilligence amende, if it lyes in the power of your humble servant, J B.

185. TO THOMAS PENNANT

[*Headed, top of page 39*] Caerleon 6 June 1651

Brother Pennant

Yours of the 19th of May last I received by one of my neighbours but whoe brought it from you, I was not so happie as to knowe. Yours allsoe of the 27th May I received and allsoe my cozen William Byrds with the commission, which was executed according to the tenor thereof with a certificate on the back of the commission and nowe sent up by this bearer to bee delivered into the court. I pray please to employ my cozen William to see the commission delivered and to procure a coppie of the will under the authentique seale of the court, with an account of all charge both for the commission and what will bee the charge of puttinge in the inventorie that I may place it to the account of the proprietors.

I conceave Mr Bulkeley is mistaken in the great error spoken of, for he wrote mee it was in 46 which he hath passed and mist to finde any such thinge. Howsoever, I pray spare not the other quarto or any thinge else which you conceave may produce any good. I pray doe me the favour as to deliver the enclosed to Collonell Langham and enquire howe my accounts doe stande. If you have opportunety pray present him and the rest of the our loving freinds at the custome house with a cup of wyne or a breakefast. I wrote to cozen William to procure mee a coppie of a letter sent up (and subscribed by many gentlemen of our county) to the collectors of prize goods, with theyr names as exactly drawne as might bee; I pray desier him to gett it for mee, as hee did the other which was very exactly donne.

I pray good brother to supply my [*Page 39*] cozen William with what money shall bee requisite for performance of the premisses and charge mee therewith, which shall bee made good, with all other your disbursements for mee or on my behalfe whensoever you require the same, with faithfull love and harty thankes. Pray present my service to Mr Blackborne and desier that somme store of blanke bonds may speedily bee sent downe for here is great neede of them in all out ports. I formerlie wrote to him for somme but I received no answer as yet. I thinke honest Mr Parsons canne helpe mee to somme: I pray trye him.

As I was writeinge this I received a letter and 200 bonds from the commissioners which will serve only for Swansey, where is generally nothinge but coles to bee entred in the cockett, and condicion of each bonde. In Cardiffe and all the other ports within my charge are generally goods of severall sorts to bee entred in the condicion of each bond; to which ende, that blanke which is to entertayne severall sorts of goods must [*Marginated* 14 June] bee at least 3 whole lynes. I pray desier Mr Blackborne or Mr Parsons to procure mee somme store of such bonds with speede. The letter intended for Collonell Langham I sent by the post, for that the bearer could not go up tyme ynough; howsoever I pray opportnety to visitt him and the case is desired [*?words missing*]

186. TO PATRICK JONES AND GEORGE TENCH

[*Marginated*] Caerleon 6 June 1651

Mr Patrick Jones and Mr George Tench

Yours of the 30th May last with the account there inclosed I received, in which I finde these errors, vizt. out of the Truelove of Kinsale 2 Irishe horses 19s. which by the booke of rates is 20s. besides 1s. Algier duty; in the James of Swansey 10 chaldrons and in the Endeavour of South Bury 8 chaldrons of coles for which you charge the custome according to the booke of rates but the Algier duty is omitted. All customes are to bee paide according to the booke of rates, without any allowance and in every 20s. custom, 1s. must bee received for Algier [duty] according to severall acts of parliament formerlie sent you. This daye I received somme blanke bonds from London, whereof you shall receave herewith 50: you shall have more at our next meeteinge.

I should be very glad if I might spare my wonted journey which if Mr Jones and you will comme both hyther, may bee donne and not otherwaies, because of the oath which I must take of all our officers, both for theyr receipts and disbursements. I shal be very glad to see you both here, which if it may bee, pray write mee soe by the next post. If you cannott conveniently comme hyther, then (God permittinge) I intende to bee with you before midsommer. The certificatt you sent shal be filed. I have not heard from Mr Malory since his of the 12th of April. I feare hee is not well; I long to see the honest man whoe I am confident would have beene with us before this tyme if all were well.

If any coles shall bee laden with you or in any other port, eyther for Englande or for any other place allthough in the neighbourhood beinge once waterboarne, the imposition of 2s. per chaldron must bee paid before landeinge thereof according to the acte, to which purpose I have lately received a very stricte commaunde from the commissioners, wherein your care is desired in Swansey, Neath and Bury. I pray acquainte Mr William Morgan of Neath herewith. You shall receive here inclosed Mr Ed. Bowens entry of wyne, with any receipt for the Custome due thereon, according to your letter. Pray remember my service to Mr Walter Thomas and acquainte him[1] that his debiter Mr John Walter hath broken his word, soe that I intende to put his bond in suite, according to Mr Thomas his order. Thus etc.

1 February 1649[*?-50*]

Out of the Repulse of Swansey burthen 50 tons, John Snowe master; 5 full butts of sack, Ed. Bowen md[?] merchant.

Received of Mr Patrick Jones of Swansey alderman the summe of £6-7-6 of lawfull English money it being due to the Commonwealth of England for the Custome on the 5 butts of sack abovesaid. I saye received by mee John Byrd collector.

1. 'and acquainte him' interlined.

187. TO THE COMMISSIONERS OF THE CUSTOMS

[*Headed, top of page 40*] Caerleon 9 June 1651

Right worshipful

These are (in answer to Mr Blackbornes of the 31st of May last) humbly to acquainte you that the coles whereof I wrote to you on the 21st of May last is to bee distynguished from all other sorts of coles by the smoothenes thereof, which is soe made smoothe by the washinge thereof in rowleinge downe the ryver, and is of the bygnes generally of smale gravell. There is noe such coles in any place in all this county, neyther have I ever seene the like in any other place, and here it cometh by the mercifull providence of God, beinge a miraculous blessinge bestowed on the poore and they only reape the benefitt thereof, by takeinge great paynes to gather them out of the sande in the bottome of the ryver Uske, and wasshinge the sande from the cole through syves, which they sell sometymes for a 1d. sometymes 1½ and the dearest rate at 2d. per bushell and this place doth vent by botes into the neyghbourhood about 150 chaldrons per annum.

Dyvers commissioners of this county have taken notice of the meanenes of this sort of coles, who humbly desier that your goodnes may bee[1] [*Page 40*] (on the beehalfe of the poore) herein extended soe as that noe imposition may bee layde on this sort of coles, wherein I humbly desier your order. I further humbly desier that you will bee pleased to order a commission to bee sent downe for takeinge my oath for that I have noe other occasion in London at this present but to deliver in my bookes. I desier the commission may bee directed to Roger Williams and Rice Williams esquires, John Warde and PhilipWilliams gent or any twoe of them and to bee retorned the next terme, and presently after Midsummer I will prepare a booke of entryes and a booke for coast busines according to your former direccions. I received 200 blanke bonds by the last post, which will serve only in Swansey, where most commonly nothing but coles is to be entred in the condicion. I humbly desier you please to order somme score of bonds to bee sent downe, with large blankes in the condicion to enter severall sorts of goods in.

1. 'may bee' repeated, top of page 40.

188. TO ROBERT BLACKBORNE

[*Marginated*] Caerleon 14 June 1651

Mr Blackborne

Pray please to take notice that yours of the 7th instant I have received which intymateth that informacion hath beene given to my masters the commissioners that French tobaccoe was lately seazed in the river of Newport and afterwards cleared for 1d. per lb. which indeede is not soe, but a parcell of tobaccoe was lately brought into Newport, which was entred for French tobaccoe at 6d. per lb. whereof I pray acquainte my masters, with the remembrance of my humble duty to them.

189. TO COLONEL GEORGE LANGHAM

[*14 June 1651*]

Wrote the same daie to Colonel Langham that my receipt from the last of April to the 1st of June is £160-19-2¼.

Enclosed the 2 last to brother Pennant, desireinge him to deliver them and to proceede according to my last to him.

190. TO FRANCIS MALORY

[*Marginated*] 24 June [1651]

Mr Malory

I advized him to take care least his absence might cause his house to be taken over his head. Enclosed this in cozen Williams letter to bee delivered to Mr Samuel Neale.

191. TO NEPHEW WILLIAM BYRD

[*No date*]

Wrote to cozen William that I had received all his, and to deliver Mr Malloryes to be sent by Mr Neale to him with speede and to settle his sister in London; and if in a place of creditt not to trouble him selfe for great wages and to procure a coppie of a letter out of the prize office and to leave what money hee intended to bringe downe with brother Pennant on my account; which I will paie him at his arryvall here and desired him to speake with Mr Sankey about 3 lycences which I formerlie sent up to him by the conveyance of Captain Foxe of Bristoll.

192. TO GEORGE TENCH

[*Marginated*] Caerleon 26 June 1651

Mr Tench
You shall receave herewith the entryes taken in the esterne ports in the quarter from 25th December 1650 to 25th March 1651, which I conceave you had of mee before. Those with the tobaccoe entry I gave you at my last beinge with you is all that hath beene taken in all our ports (Swansey excepted) this last ½ yeare.

193. TO NEPHEW WILLIAM BYRD

[*Marginated*] Caerleon 7 July 1651

Wrote to cozen William Byrd to procure a coppie of the letter sent to the prize goods office and to procure a word from Mr Sankey concerning 3 lycences I formerly sent him by conveyance of Captain Foxe long since.

194. TO COLONEL GEORGE LANGHAM

[*Marginated*] 9 [July 1651]

Wrote to Collonell Langham and sent my quarter booke, bill of charge, acquittance and account currant to the 29th of June last.

195. TO THOMAS PENNANT

[*Marginated*] 9 [*July 1651*]

Wrote to brother Pennant and enclosed the 2 letters above to bee by him delivered, desireinge him to enquier how my accounts stand and allsoe to desier Mr Sankey to write mee one word concerning 3 lycences I long since sent him by the conveyance of Captain Foxe, surveyor of the customes in Bristol; allsoe sent brother Pennant a coppie of the inventory of Mrs Florence Seys personall estate, desireinge him to deliver it into the court. I desired him to direct his letters to my sonne William to be sent mee, for that the Welch post is layde aside. If my cozen William bee out of employment I have advized him to comme downe to spare charge, and to settle his sister in London, for that these partes affords neyther preferment nor profitt: I pray advize and direct them for the best. Thus.

196. TO ROBERT BLACKBORNE

[*No date*]

Mr Blackborne

Yours of the 21st of June last I have received concerning the cole gathered by the poore, and the commissioners pleasure therein, which shall bee carefully observed, and not only the poore doe take it very thankefully but allsoe the commissioners for this county are glad to see the godly inclynacion of my worthy masters herein. I pray present the remembrance of my humble duty and service to them, and please to acquainte them that the French tobaccoe was not under seazure at all. Allsoe I beeseech you to acquainte them that last... (1)

1. Foot of page.

Page 41

197. TO COLONEL GEORGE LANGHAM

[*Headed*] Caerleon 8 November 1652

Colonel Langham

I pray please to take notice that my receipts in the port of Cardiffe and members in the moneth of October doth amounte unto £17 11s. 5d. according to the particulars underwritten. I formerly sent up my quarter booke with what pertayned thereto. Only one acquittance was omitted the which I sent up to you about a fortnight since. I pray a word of receipt of them and this. I pray please to present the remainder of my duty and service to my worthy masters the commissioners; my true love to Mr Blackborne, Mr Parsons and all the rest of our loving friends at custome house.

11 - 08 - 00	subsidy outwards	Swansey
00 - 11 - 05	Algier duty outwards	Swansey
01 - 18 - 00	newe impost on coles for 12 October to 1 November	Swansey
03 - 14 - 00	newe impost on coles for 12 October to 1 November: Chepstowe	
17 - 11 - 05		

Nill in the port of Cardiffe, nor in any other of the members then what is abovewritten.

198. TO NEPHEW WILLIAM BYRD

[*No date*]

Cozen William

Given him an account of the receipt of all his letters and all things else sent by him and wrote to him howe our children have beene since his departure.

199. TO THOMAS PENNANT

[*Marginated*] Caerleon 15 November 1652

Brother Pennant

Yours of the 6th and 9th instant with my account from Mr Hobbs I received for which I hartily thanke you. I am hartily sorry that my sister is not well. I humbly pray God to restore hir to to hir perfect health to his glory and the comfort of you and yours. You shall receive by this bearer (my loving freinde and neighbour) Mr James Jones £5 towards clearinge disbursments made by you, for mee; pray remember mee to my brother William and cozen William, when you shall see them.

Sent 2s. to brother Pennant by Mr James Jones of Lanvihangell Llanter[nam], to drinke with him.

200. TO WALTER SANKEY

[*Marginated*] Caerleon 28 November 1652

Mr Sankey

Yours of the 18th instant I received which is all which came to my hands from you since I sent up the lycences, allthough I wrote severall letters to you. Sir for answer to yours I pray please to take notice that I have received the moiety due to the state on the 3 seazures and have long since paid to Mr Thomas Shewell, collector of the customes in Bristoll, to be retorned up to Captain Langham £27 14s. 3d., beinge the moiety due to the state for the seazure made by Mr William Morgan at Neath, which I hope is paid in accordinglie; I pray a word thereof in your next letter. I have not received any money from the officers which made

The London custom house in the time of John Byrd.
Engraved by Bartholomew Howlett from a print dated 1663.

those seazures towards the cleareinge thereof, but they have promised to paie what shall bee due after the fynes shall bee estreated soe that I desier you to sende downe a commission retorneable in Ester Terme for taking oath to the 3 lycences. Pray please to name John Byrd, George Tench, Robert Barker and Benjamin Streater authorizinge us or any 2 of us commissioners for takeinge the oathes and please to write me somme direcions what is to bee written on the lycences after oath is taken to them.

You doe not charge any thinge concerning the seazure made by Mr William Morgan, soe that I suppose Captain Foxe hath paid the charge thereof. Howsoever I pray sende downe one commission for the 3 lycences. Good sir please further this busines according to desier, which if you cannot conveniently doe then I pray please to give direccions to the bearer hereof, my kinsman, who I desier to proceede according to your direccions. Thus.

Page 42

201. TO NEPHEW WILLIAM BYRD

[*Headed*] Caerleon 28 November 1652

Wrote cozen William an answer to his of the 16th instant and enclosed a letter to Mr Walter Sankey. I gave my cozen an account of what letters I sent him since our departure and that I sent them to brother Pennant for him, allsoe gave him an account of receipt of his letters and all things sent by him to my wife and children; allsoe wrote him the rates of butter and corne according to his desier.

202. TO COLONEL GEORGE LANGHAM

[*Marginated*] Caerleon 6 December 1652

Colonel Langham

Pray please to take notice that my receipt the last moneth amounteth to £42 8s. 3d. according to the particulars underwritten. Allsoe (if God permitt) I will paie the moneyes remayneinge in my hands to Mr Thomas Shewell collector at Bristoll forthwith according to yours of the 27th of November last. But my charge is not soe much as you write it is. I shall make good the whole receipt, although parte thereof remayneth in somme of the officers hands according to my last account current sent up to you, for whome I conceave I am not lyable to make good more then I receave of them, yet I will paie in all at this tyme, that my accounts may be cleared to the 29th of September last. I pray please to present the remembrance of my humble duty and service to my worthy masters the commissioners, with my love and service to Mr Blackborne, Mr Parsons etc.

00 - 02 - 06	subsidy inwards	Cardiffe
00 - 00 - 01½	Algier duty inwards	
39 - 12 - 00	subsidy outwards	Swansey
01 - 19 - 07½	Algier duty outwards	
00 - 14 - 00	newe impost of 2s. per chaldron on coles	Chepstowe
42 - 08 - 03		

203. TO COLONEL GEORGE LANGHAM

[*Marginated*] Caerleon 13 December 1652

Colonel Langham

Sir, on the 10th instant I paide into the hands of Mr Thomas Shewell collector in Bristoll to those of my masters the commissioners of the customes £114 5s. 10½d. which is the ballance of my account, for all my receipts to the 29th daie of September last, in which summe nowe paide by mee is £12 13s. 4½d. which remaynes in the hands of Mr Streater and Mr Lloyd, which summe (I conceave) I am not lyable to make good, yet I have paide it in at this tyme for the cleareinge of my account, soe that I earnestly desier that you will bee pleased to sende mee my discharge to the 29th daye of September last soe soone as conveniently you maye. I pray present the remembrance of my humble duty and service to my worthy masters the commissioners and please to acquainte them herewith. Thus not haveinge else to trouble you with at present I take leave and am J B.

204. TO THOMAS PENNANT AND NEPHEW WILLIAM BYRD

[*Marginated*] Caerleon 6 December 1652

Wrote to brother Pennant by Mr Thomas Yong and to cozen William Byrd to assiste Mr John Morgan to compounde for his estate, and my wife sent 22s. in gould in my letter to cozen William which Thomas Yong brought backe againe.

205. TO THOMAS PENNANT

[*Marginated*] 27 December 1652

Wrote to brother Pennant desireinge him to sende me word what is like to becomme of Mr John Morgans busines and requested him to deliver 20s. to cozen William Byrd as a token from my wife on my account and desired him to gett mee a chapman for my publique faith bills etc.

206. TO NEPHEW WILLIAM BYRD

[*No date*]

Wrote to cozen William an account of receipt of all things sent by him and acquainted him that I wrote to brother Pennant to deliver him 20s. as abovesaid and gave him order to procure £5 13s. 4d. due from Joseph Evans eyther in love or by lawe etc.

Page 43

207. TO WILLIAM JONES AND OTHER CUSTOMS OFFICERS

[*Headed*] Caerleon 1 January 1653

Wrote to Mr William Jones in Chepstowe that the Algier duty is contynnewed till 26th December 1653 by acte of parliament.

Sent 1 acte to Cardiffe and 1 to Swansey with letters to all the ports within my charge for receipt of the Algier duty as abovesaid.

208. TO COLONEL GEORGE LANGHAM

[*Marginated*] Caerleon 3 January 1653

Colonel Langham

Sir you shall receive herewith my quarter booke to the 25th of December last, with my bill of charge, account current and acquittance for that quarter only in which Mr John Lloyds receipt for his sallary is wantinge, which I pray please to call to him for when he commeth to the custome house, for I understand by your letter that the commissioners have beene pleased to graunte him somme tyme to followe his owne occasions in London; his employment with us is carefully looked unto in his absence. I have beene lately in those partes and received the account from those employed by him. His brother Mr Walter Lloyd allsoe taketh care thereof in his absence. Pray present my service to Mr Blackborne and please to acquainte him that I received the the acte for the receipt of the Algier duty till 26th December 1653, whereof I have sent an account to all the ports within my charge, according to direccions therein. Allsoe I desier you will bee pleased to put the remembrance of my humble duty and service to my worthy masters the commissioners. I formerly sent up all my abstracts and if any have miscarryed uppon notice from you which one wantinge I will sent you an account thereof againe.

209. TO THOMAS PENNANT

[*Marginated*] Caerleon 26 January 1653

Brother Pennant

I wrote to you formerly to request you to deliver 20s. to my cozen William on my account, the which you shall receive here inclosed and 2s. to drinke a glasse of wyne with our brother and sister Wooddall, to whome I pray remember mee kindely, and I pray give them thanks for the fish dynner they bestowed on mee at my last beinge in London. On Monday last my wife shipped abord our bote 2 cheeses out of hir dairy, and a dolphyn which was taken where our kyne graze. They are nayled and mayled up in a faire boxe and directed to you and are to bee sent by Bristol carryer to the 3 Cupps, and I hope will bee received by you, before this commes to you; if not, I pray sende to enquier after them, and beinge received, my wife desiers you to present them to my sister as a poore token from Wales.

The last quarter I paid in all moneyes due on my receipt to the 29th September last, and Collonell Langham wrote mee word hee would shortly after sende mee my duplicatt and discharge, the which as yet I have not received. Good brother take an opportunety to give him a visitt and enquire howe my accounts stande, and doe your best endevour to gett my discharge from him to the 29th of September last. If my cozen William bee not yet gon out of London, pray remember us to him and tell [him] I desier to receive one word from him. Allso I pray remember mee to my brother William when you shall see him.

Page 44

210. TO THE COMMISSIONERS OF THE CUSTOMS

[*Marginated*] Caerleon 26 January 1653

Right worshipful

After my humble duty and service rendered unto you I pray please to take notice that yours of the 5th instant I have received, by which I finde the right honourable committee for the navy have beene pleased to order that you appointe a collector to reside in Swansey and that £10 bee deducted out of my sallary to bee added to £20 allowed by them, which is to make up £30 per annum for your collector at Swansey.

You have beene allsoe pleased to direct that I take the charge of Cardiffe, Newport and Chepstowe, by which I conceave your pleasure is that I shall not have any thinge to doe neyther in Penarth, Aberthawe, Neath, Swansey not Llanelltly (as formerly I had) but that these places bee added to Swansey as members thereof, which if soe then I humbly pray that I may bee ordered to deliver my quarter booke, with acquittances for our sallaryes and incident charges, which shall bee due in the ports nowe committed to my charge, to Mr Shewell your collector in Bristoll, with your order to him to paie what shall bee due each quarter, for that the receipts in those ports are generally soe smale that it will not cleare sallaryes, yet are places of much trade from port to port; and Caerlion (the port wherein I lyve) is of greater concernement then any other port within my charge for exportacion and importacion of vallewable goods by port cocketts.

Mr Bowen did request mee to write unto you desireinge to knowe what ports you are pleased to adde to Swansey as members thereof and allsoe to knowe to whome he is to make his accounts. I humbly pray you will bee pleased to write him your direccions therein. Thus desireinge you will bee pleased to graunte mee your order as abovesaid, I humbly take leave and am your worshipps humble servant J B.

211. TO COLONEL GEORGE LANGHAM

[*No date*]

Colonel Langham

You shall receive herewith an abstract of what hath beene received within my charge from the 25th of December last to the 23rd instant, in which tyme nothinge hath beene received in any of our ports, but only in Swansey, an account whereof is underwritten.

From the 25th of December exclusive to the 1st of January inclusive:	34 - 06 - 00
From the 1st of January exclusive to the 8th inclusive:	nill
From the 8th exclusive to the 15th inclusive:	00 - 15 - 09
From the 15th exclusive to the 22th inclusive:	02 - 10 - 05
From the 22th exclusive to the 29th inclusive:	nill
	37 - 12 - 02

JB.

212. TO COLONEL GEORGE LANGHAM

[*No date*]

Colonel Langham

Pray please to take notice that accordinge to yours of the 18th instant I hereunder written sende you the abstract of my receipts from the 25th December to the 30th January last, in which tyme nothinge hath beene received in any place or port within my charge, but only in Swansey. Sallaryes and incident charges in the port of Cardiff and members[(1)] will amounte unto £5 10s. 0d. per weeke or thereabouts.

1. 'in the port of Cardiff and members' interlined.

Page 45

213. ABSTRACT OF CUSTOMS RECEIPTS AMD PAYMENTS

[*Headed*] Caerleon 1 February 1653

An abstract of the receipts and payments in the port of Cardiffe and members thereof
from the 25th
Portus Swansey outwards
From the 25th of December exclusive to the 1st of January inclusive 1653

For subsidy outwards	27 - 15 - 04
For 15 per cent outwards	04 - 18 - 00
For Algier duty outwards	01 - 12 - 08
From the 1st of January exclusive to the 8th inclusive	nill
	34 - 06 - 00
From the 8th of January exclusive to the 15th inclusive	
For subsidy outward	00 - 12 - 09
For 15 per cent outwards	00 - 02 - 03
For Algier outwards	00 - 00 - 09
	00 - 15 - 09
From the 15th of January exclusive to the 22th inclusive	
For subsidy outwards	02 - 00 - 09½
For 15 per cent outwards	00 - 07 - 02½
For Algier outwards	00 - 02 - 05
	02 - 10 - 05
From the 22nd of January exclusive to the 29th inclusive	nill

Noe other moneyes have beene received in the tyme abovesaid then what is charged in this account, neyther in the port of Cardiffe nor in any other member thereof.

Disbursements for sallaryes and incident charges in the said port of Cardiffe and members doth amounte unto five pounds tenne shillings per weeke, or nere that summe. JB.

214. TO COLONEL GEORGE LANGHAM

[*No date*]

Colonel Langham

Pray please to take notice that nothinge hath beene received for subsidy etc in the ports of Cardiffe, Newport, Caerlion nor Chepstowe (which are the ports nowe in my charge) from the 29th of January exclusive to the 5th of February inclusive. The sallaryes due to the officers which acte in these ports with other incident charges will amounte unto 30s. per weeke or thereabouts. I received a letter from Mr Griffith Bowen nowe collector in Swansey, acquaintinge mee that my worthy masters the commissioners have commaunded him to sende up a weekely account for that port and its members, which I conceave is from all the ports formerlye in my charge except those above named, which are expressed in the commissioners letter to mee to be in my charge, but if anythinge else bee expected from mee herein, I humbly desier to knowe what it is, and I shall carefully observe commaunde and bee yours assuredly to serve you. JB.

Page 46

215. TO THOMAS SHEWELL

[*Subscribed*] Caerleon 3 March 1653

Mr Shewell

Our worthy maisters (the commissioners for the customes of England) have beene pleased to order mee to sende monthly abstracts both of my receipts and disbursements and allsoe my quarter bookes unto you, in pursuance of which theyr commaundes I pray please to take notice that nothinge was received for subsidy etc (in the ports nowe in my charge) from the 25th daie of December exclusive to the 29th daie of January inclusive, in which moneth custome house rent and other incident charges did amounte unto about 24s. besides sallaryes. And from the 29th daye of January exclusive to the 26th daye of February inclusive, I received 21s. as underwritten. Custome house rent and other incident charges this last moneth amounteth unto about 20s. Thus not haveinge else in commaunde from them I take leave and am, yours really to serve you, JB.

00 - 17 - 00	subsidy	Caerlion outwards
00 - 03 - 00	15 per cent	
00 - 01 - 00	Algier duty	

216. TO THE COMMISSIONERS OF THE CUSTOMS

[*Marginated*] Caerleon 1 March 1653

Right worshipful

After my humble duty and service presented unto you, pray please to take notice that according to yours of the 15th of February last I have enquired after such vessells which you have beene enformed went out of some ports in South Wales for Lysbone, Portugall and Spayne and doe finde that noe such things hath beene donne in any port (now within my charge). Att Swansey the shipp Reformacion of that place did enter for Lysbone the last quarter, which only is in my quarter book above, the same vessell was entred againe at Swansey for Lysbone since the 25th of December, the dutyes due thereon I retorned up in Januaries abstract, hir ladeinge beinge coles, calfeskynns and herrings. I did not knowe of any other vessell which went for any of those ports, yet for your further satisfacion herein I sent your letter to Swansey and to the rest of the westerne ports, which is retorned with answer that dyvers vessells have laden great quantetyes of coles by bond for England, whereof Mr Griffith Bowen, your collector at Swansey (in answer of yours to him to this purpose) hath given you an account. Thus not haveinge else to trouble you with at present, I take leave and am your worships humble servant JB.

Page 47

217. TO THE COMMISSIONERS OF THE CUSTOMS

[*Marginated*] Caerleon 2 May 1653

Right worshipful

I hereby make boulde humbly to acquainte you that accordinge to your order I delivered my quarter booke, with acquittances for sallaryes, custome house rent, my bill of charge and account current, for the quarter ended the 25th of March last, to Mr Thomas Shewell, your collector at Bristoll; in which my account current there is due to mee in ballance of that quarters account £19 1s. 10d. which Mr Shewell would have cleared, but sayth hee hath not any direccion from you, to pay any moneyes to mee, but only to receive my accounts and moneyes from mee. Nowe my humble request is that you will bee pleased to sende mee your order for Mr Shewell to paie what is and shall bee due to mee, as well as to receive what shall bee due from mee, that I maye cleare my accounts quarterly, which (by Gods permission) I shall bee very carefull to doe.

218. TO COLONEL GEORGE LANGHAM

[*No date*]

Wrote Colonel Langham for my discharge to 29th September last, for that I paid the cleare of my accounts to that tyme to Mr Thomas Shewell, collector in Bristoll about 5 moneths since, and sent him Mr John Lloyd collector at Llanelthy his receipt for £5 due to him in the quarter to the 25th December last.

219. TO THOMAS PENNANT

[*No date*]

Wrote to brother Pennant and sent the 2 letters above to him desireinge him to procure answers thereto and desired to heare from my brother and his sonne.

220. TO THOMAS SHEWELL

[*Marginated*] Caerleon 9 May 1653

Mr Shewell

Please to take notice that the ports within my charge hath not afforded any receipt from the 25th of March to the last of April, both inclusive; petty charge the same tyme amounteth to about 22s. I desier a word from you what answer you received from the commissioners concerning clearinge my accounts.

221. TO THOMAS SHEWELL

[*Marginated*] Caerleon 18 May 1653

Mr Shewell

I received Aprils account for Swansey and members thereof from Mr Bowens deputy, by which it seemes hee is from home at present. His receipt from the 25th March to the last of April both inclusive by this account, is as underwritten. Pray please to write mee one word whether you wrote to the commissioners concerning cleareinge my account or not; if you did I desier to knowe what is theyr pleasure therein.

01 - 13 - 08½	subsidy inwards	Swansey
00 - 05 - 11½	15 per cent inwards	
00 - 02 - 00	Algier duty inwards	
00 - 09 - 11¼	petty custom inwards	
19 - 03 - 11	subsidy outwards	
03 - 07 - 09	15 per cent outwards	
01 - 02 - 07	Algier duty outwards	
02 - 13 - 10	petty custom outwards	
00 - 08 - 00	newe impost of 2s. per chaldron	
29 - 07 - 08¼		

Nill in all the members of Swansey this moneth of April 1653.

Page 48

222. TO COLONEL GEORGE LANGHAM

[*Headed*] Caerleon 27 May 1653

Colonel Langham

Pray please to take notice that according to yours of the 21st instant I here inclosed sende you the account of my receipt of the newe impost on coles, from the 29th of September 1652 to the 1st of April 1653.

223. TO GEORGE TENCH AND SYMON JONES

[*Marginated*] Caerleon 9 June 1653

Mr George Tench and Mr Symon Jones

Gentlemen, your letters I have received by which it seemes Mr Griffith Bowen hath received the moneyes due on the entryes which I charge Symon Jones with. If it be soe, then I must have an acknowledgement thereof under his hande to the particular entryes, by which I shall charge him and free both Symon and myselfe, otherwaies the entryes will charge him and the bonds will charge mee, soe that the dutyes will be paid twice. John Bynons certificate sheweth hee is willinge to paie the dutyes, by which it seemes the custome is not paid, yet I have received 1 entry formerly for for 5 chaldrons on the 27th of July 1652, the which I supposed was for this voyadge. But you write if custom be paid what neede your certificate, and that you use to write on your bonds custom paid, which you have not donne on Bynons bonde, which makes mee doubt the entry on the 27th of July is not for this voyadge, which if it bee, then of necessity you must sende your certificate under your hands and seales of office to cleare the bonde, otherwaies you will doe the merchant wronge.

You shall receive here inclosed 3 certificates to which I have not the bonds. You shall likewise receive back Thomas Groats certificate for I cannott cleare him without custome for all his goods, or an order for the same. The officers of your port (as I conceave) maye releeve him, but I cannott, unlesse I will paie the dutyes for him, which I must doe if I file his certificate, wherein I desier to be excused; 10 chaldrons were entred for Garnesey at Llanelthy, and Mr Lloyd saith hee did not receive the custom for the same. Pray please to remember mee to him, and acquainte him it must bee paid, for the bond will charge mee and then I shall leave it to fall in its right place. Hee promiseth by his letter to mee to paie the former money due on my account to Symon Jones, next quarter daye or sooner; I pray desier him not to faile mee herein.

Robert Basnett writes that hee paid Mr Lloyd for one entry of[(1)] the first of February 1653 for 18 chaldrons of coles laden at Burry the 6th of October by bond for England, but went for Ireland, in the Endeavour of Burry and that it is accompted to Mr Bowen. I desier his acknowledgement of receipt of this entry with the rest, or else if you please to sende mee an acknowledgement under your hands that this and all the entryes which I charge Symon Jones with, are accounted to Mr Bowen, it will bee suffitient. I pray remember my true love to all the rest of the officers and I earnestly desier both you and them to perfect our accounts soe as the states may have theyr dues, and that neyther of us be wronged. Pray present my service to Mr Walter Thomas and his wife, and please to acquainte him, his letter was sent to Pencreeke according to desier.

1. 'for one entry of' interlined.

224. TO THOMAS SHEWELL

[*Marginated*] Caerleon 9 June 1653

Mr Shewell

These are to acquainte you that the port of Cardiffe and members thereof have not afforded any receipt from the last of April exclusive to the 28th of April inclusive. Incident charges the same tyme amounteth to about 20s., which is all at present from yours to serve you JB.

225. TO THOMAS PENNANT

[*Marginated*] Caerleon 22 June [1653]

Wrote to brother Pennant by Rowland Williams, desireinge him if hee had my discharge from Colonell Langham, to sende it by Rowlande, or by the post, and desired to heare of my brother and his children.

226. TO SUSANNA BYRD

[*22 June 1653*]

Allso wrote to cozen Susanna Byrd, desireinge to knowe howe hir father etc doeth, and directed to sende to mee by the post of Newport.

Page 49

227. TO THOMAS SHEWELL

[*Marginated*] Caerleon 6 August 1653

Mr Shewell

These are to acquainte you that my receipt from the 24th of June to the 30th of July both inclusive is 18s. 4d. subsedy, and 11d. Algier duty, beinge for one entry inwards in Chepstowe; noe other entry in any other port within my charge in this tyme. Incident charge the same tyme amounteth to about 29s. Good sir, if you have received my discharge from Colonel Langham, I pray please to sende it mee by this bearer; thus desireinge your love herein.

228. TO EDMUND HARVEY

[*Marginated*] Caerleon 12 August 1653

Right worshipful etc

Pray please to take notice that yours of the 5th instant concerning prizes brought into the ports within my charge by the shipps of the commonwealth I have received. These are humbly to acquainte you that noe prize at all hath bene brought into any port within my charge since the Eagle of Lymbrick which was taken in the ryver of Cardiffe in December 1649, and the goods thereof was entred at Cardiffe on the 23rd of January 1650 in the name of John Herbert esquire and I received for the subsidy and other dutyes of that entry £31 6s. 4d. and by another entry made in the name of the said John Herbert, on the 5th of April 1650, I received £1 10s. 8¾d. which I have formerly charged my selfe with and cleared the same, as by my severall bookes and accounts above with Colonel Langham will appeare. Thus etc JB.

To the right worshipful Colonel Edmund Harvy.

229. TO THOMAS PENNANT

[*Marginated*] Caerleon 22 August 1653

Brother Pennant

Yours of the 5th of July last I received, but heard nothinge of yours sent by way of Bristoll. You write that Colonel Langham desired I would sende up my quarter booke to the 24th of June last, and then hee would give mee a discharge to that tyme. By order from my masters (the commissioners), I (on the 28th of June last) delivered my quarter booke and my yeares account, with my bill of charge and account current, to Mr Thomas Shewell, collector of the customes in Bristoll, and cleared all my accounts to the 24th of June last, all which I am confident Mr

Shewell hath delivered above, soe that I earnestly entreate you to procure my discharge from Colonel Langham accordinge to his promise. Good brother pardon my bouldenesse herein, for I have not any freinde in London that I may depende uppon but your selfe. Thus etc.

230. TO THOMAS SHEWELL

[*Marginated*] Caerleon 5 September 1653

Mr Shewell

These are to acquainte you that noe receipt hath beene in the ports within my charge from the 30th of July exclusive to the 27th of August inclusive. Incident charges in the same tyme amounteth to about 22s. Thus etc.

231. TO SIMON JONES

[*Marginated*] Caerleon 14 September 1653

Symon Jones

I have conferred with the father and mother of the partie whoe take kindely your loving request and promise you shall bee wellcomme and if the Lord soe order that you and the partie doe agree, they will bee contente therewith on reasonable termes; but for a particular encouragement (whereof I conceave you meane), I did not put the busines to that. I shall bee glad to see you and more glad if things fall out herein to Gods glory, and both your comforts. Remember mee kindely to your father in lawe and your mother.

232. TO NEPHEW WILLIAM BYRD

[*Marginated*] Caerleon 14 September 1653

Cozen William

Yours of the last of May I received on the 28th of July and yours of the 30th of August came this daye to my hands, both which cause your aunte and my selfe to give thanks to the Lord on your behalfe, for before your first letter came to my hands wee did much doubt that you weare dead, calling to mynde your weake constitucion of body, and change from this ayre to that which is reported not to bee soe agreeable to the English as ours is. Joseph Evans hath beene with mee, and hath given mee satisfacion; as for what you wrote in your last letter, I will sende speedily to Bristoll that you may bee supplyed with the first vessell that shall saile from thence to Dublyn.

I wrote a letter of enquiry for you and the rest of our family in London, which my messenger sayes was delivered to my cozen Susan, and that shee was writeinge mee an answer, but hir aunte(1) sendinge for hir suddenly to Boe, it was layde aside and since your last to mee before you left Englande I have not heard one word from any one of them, which makes me doubt they are all dead. If I shall finde a mayde fitt for the service whereof you write and shall finde a passage for hir from Bristoll to you within the tyme prescribed in your letter I will endeavour to provide hir over. [*Page 50*] Wee and our children are in health, and many in the country very sick.

1. 'aunte' interlined.

233. TO THE COMMISSIONERS OF THE CUSTOMS

[*Marginated*] Caerleon 14 September 1653

Right worshipful

After my humble duty and service remembered unto you, I pray please to take notice that by a letter which I received from Mr Samuel Whittell dated the 2nd instant, I understand that the account I gave you of the goods in the shipp Eagle, by my letter dated the 12th of August last was not according to your expectacion but that you require a larger account thereof. First you desier to knowe the name of the shipp and what shee together with hir tackle, furniture and gunns were appraised at; howe sould and what custome was paid for the same; secondly the quantety and quallety of the goods, wares and merchandize on bord the said shipp, at what sould, howe disposed, what customes was paid for the same and under the order of what commissioners.

In pursuance of which, your commaunde, I humbly acquainte you that the shipp Eagle of Lymbrick sprunge a leake at sea, by which meanes shee was brought up Seaverne, and so put in to the mouth of the river of Cardiffe in December 1649, where shee was seazed uppon by souldiers of that garrison. Afterwardes John Herbert esquire then high shereiffe of the county of Glamorgan saide hee had a commission from the right honourable the counsell of state to sell the shipp and goods, and to deliver the proceade thereof to the use of the garrisons of Cardiffe, Chepstowe, Caermarthen and Tenby. The shipp with its furniture, tackle and gunns hee soulde to John Gawler, major of the garrison of Cardiffe for £100 or within 40s. thereof, which hee hath ript up for that shee was not serviceable, but noe custome was paide for the same, for that before I received your commaunde by your letter dated 31st of May 1651 to receive custom for prize shipps and shipps bought beyonde sea, I conceaved noe custome was to bee paid for the same. Howsoever, if it must bee paide, then I humbly pray that you will bee pleased to laye your commaunds on mee to demaunde the same, eyther of Mr John Herbert who soulde or major John Gawler who bought the same, which you conceave is most fitt to paie it, and I shall use all dilligence to procure it.

Hereunder written is a particular of the goods and the customes I received for the same, as nere as I canne remember the rates at which the goods were sould. I must confesse I did not take any expresse account at what rates the goods were soulde, for that I received the customes according to the booke of rates.

04 - 10 - 00 360 rawe hydes
12 - 00 - 00 480 tanned hydes
00 - 15 - 00 60 Barbary hydes
12 - 12 - 00 678 casks of Irish butter, weight neat 50400 lbs.
04 - 04 - 00 21 baggs great and smale of Irish wooll uncombd weight 3000 lbs.
02 - 15 - 10 33 barrels of Irish tallowe weight neat 6700 lbs.
36 - 16 - 10 full subsidy
05 - 10 - 06 15 per cent
31 - 06 - 04 subsidy paid by and in the name of John Herbert esquire on the 23rd of January 1650 for the goods abovesaid landed out of the Eagle of Lymbrick, burden 80 tons, Mark Roche master.

On the 5th of April 1650 John Herbert aforesaid entred out of the same vessell these goods following and paid custom and Algier duty thereon due:

01 - 02 - 4¾ 3 baggs of Irish wooll uncombed weight neat 800 lbs.
00 - 08 - 04 2 hogsheads and 1 firkin of Irish tallowe weight neat 1000 lbs.
01 - 10 - 08¾ full subsidy
00 - 04 - 07¼ 15 per cent
01 - 06 - 01½ subsidy paid this last entry

butter per lb. 3d; tallowe per lb. 5½d; wooll per lb. 7d; rawe hydes per peece 7s.; Barbary hydes per peece 17s.; tanned hydes per score £7 7s. 6d.

Thus not haveinge else to trouble you with at present I take leave and am your worshipps humble servant JB.

Page 51

234. TO THOMAS PENNANT

[*Headed*] Caerleon 18 October 1661

Brother Pennant

Yours of the 3rd instant I long since received by which I finde you sawe my sonne in health from whome we have not heard one word since the 20th August last, which very much troubleth us for which I pray good brother chyde him. I received another letter from you last night without date, by which I finde the contynuance of your true love to mee and myne, for which and all other curtesies my wife and I render you all harty thanks. I finde by your last that the accomptant is troubled at the variablenes of our custome house rent at Cardiffe, which I did rent at £3 per annum, it beinge the most convenient roome in Cardiffe for that service. The present commissioners beganne on the 23th July 1660, from which tyme to 29

September beinge ⅔ of the quarter the rent is 10s. and the next quarter is 15s., but about the middle of the third quarter the customer and searchers deputy tooke the kings armes out of the custom house which I had rented and carryed them to his owne house, which (I conceave) was only to affront mee; soe that I paid but 8s. which was for that parte of the quarter for which I was engaged to paie, since which tyme I have not charged any thinge for custom house rent. I pray acquainte the accountant generall or the commissioners herewith, and I hope they will not blame mee herein.

I pray present my service to the accountant and Mr Whittle, and give them 10s. per peece, as a smale token from mee, and if you have an opportunety I desier you to bestowe a collacion on them, with Mr Kerseley, Mr Parsons, Mr Sankey and Mr Thornbury wherein I pray bee not spareinge; they are my loving freinds. My sonne wrote that Mr Kerseley had obteyned my lord treasurers warrant for my sallary, beinge £10 per annum, which is to bee paid from 24th June 1660; I pray gett Mr Kerseley to assist you or my sonne to procure the said sallary for the 5 quarters to 29th September out of which I pray paie my parte for procureinge that warrant and gratifie Mr Kersely as you see fitt. I should likewise have 10s. per quarter from Mr John Dawes for quarter bookes, which is unpaid likewise for the same 5 quarters. My last booke is not yet sent, but shall bee shortly.

The ports nowe in my collecion, some of them afforde great quantetyes of butter, frize cloth, calfe skynns and other commodetyes, which are carryed to Bristoll by coast cocketts and from thence shipped for beyond seas; not any merchant at all nowe lyveinge in any of these ports, which is the cause of noe receipt with mee; soe that I desier that my accounts bee cleared in London or in Bristoll. As you have desired, here inclosed is a receipt for the ballance of my accounts with the commissioners, with a blanke for the summe, and if my sallaryes as comptroller may bee obteyned I pray give receipts for the same and subscribe them, as in the margent[(1)], which I shall justifie accordinglie. If Swansey were added to Cardiffe and the rest of the members to my collecion as formerly, it would spare mee a trouble and[(2)] I shoulde bee very thankefull if it may bee had and would remove my habitacion to Swansey, wherein I earnestly desier you to use your endeavour. Thus dependinge on your love herein, with etc.

I sent 4 letters to my sonne since I heard from him which troubleth mee.

1. 'John Byrd comptroller' in margin.
2. 'mee a trouble and' interlined.

235. TO WILLIAM THORNBURY

[*Marginated*] Caerleon 26 October 1661

Mr Thornebury

I here enclosed sende my quarter booke to 29th September last, which I pray present to Mr John Dawes with my service, and I desier your assistance that the bearer hereof my sonn William may receive my fee of 10s. per quarter for the 5 last quarters.

236. TO SON WILLIAM BYRD

[*No date*]

Wrote to my sonne William by my neighbour William Morgan, and sent my sonne 2s. 6d. by him. My wife sent him by cozen Charles Williams 5s. on the 21st October.

237. TO THE COMMISSIONERS OF THE CUSTOMS

[*Marginated*] Caerleon 28 October 1661

Right worshipful

Please to take notice that here enclosed is the account of coles which were taken in the port of Cardiffe and members thereof in the quarter ended 29th September last; and in the quarter to 24th June last not any coales, eyther laden or landed in the said port of Cardiffe nor any of the members thereof which are nowe in my collecion, Swansey and other members of Cardiffe from whence coales are constantly exported beinge nowe taken out of my collecion. The money due by this account I have ordered the bearer hereof, my sonne William Byrd, to paie to whome you please to appoint it, which etc.

To Sir Job Harbie knight and baronet; Sir Nicholas Crispe and Sir John Shawe knights.

238. TO THE COMMISSIONERS OF THE CUSTOMS

[*Headed*] 2 July 1661

[*Marginated*] 00 - 02 - 06

Michael of Croisick 15 tons Francis Nowell about 5 chaldrons coales London measure for France	01 - 10 - 00
Sent this entry to Sir Job Harbie and order my sonne W B to paie him	00 - 18 - 00
Sent the same to Mr Edmond Turner for Sir John Shawe and ordered W B to paie	03 - 15 - 00

Page 52

239. TO THE COMMISSIONERS OF THE CUSTOMS

[*Marginated*] Caerleon 28 October 1661

Right worshipful

Please to take notice that here enclosed is my quarter booke to the 29th of September last, with my bill of sallaryes and incident charges with my account current, the ballance whereof is 49s., which I desier you to order that it may bee paid to this bearer, my sonne William Byrd, whoe will deliver receipts according to the said account. Thus etc.

For the Commissioners for the Customs of England.

240. TO SON WILLIAM BYRD

[*No date*]

Sent all the last quarters accounts and letters to William to be delivered and I desired him to paie the 3 severall summes before expressed beinge £6 5s. 6d. out of my receipts at the custom house.

241. TO SON WILLIAM BYRD

[*Marginated*] Caerleon 5 November 1661

Sonne William

Above a yeare since I retorned up money to you to paie Mr Wharton and to cleare the charge of the fine etc. concerning that busines, which (in regard that I heard not from you that any thinge remayned unpaid) I did conclude that all was cleared; but last weeke I received a letter from my brother Pennant which (beside the expression of his true love to us) intymateth that £4 10s. 0d. is unpaid to him in the busines between mee and Mr Wharton with Mr Butler and his lady, in which you are very much to bee blamed in that you makeinge use of that money which was to cleare this busines, ought to have given mee an account thereof, that I might have satisfied my brother Pennant, butt you never wrote mee one word thereof. I received a letter from you dated 13th October last, which is all since yours of the 20th August last and in this not one word concerning the fine which was imposed on mee for not appearinge to the grand jury last great sessions at Monmoth, which I by severall letters desired you to take of[f] above.

Alllsoe I desired you to procure somme blanke bonds from Mr Parsons or somme other freinde at custome house, or else from Mr Godfrey Richard statyoner whoe dwelleth at the signe of the Pecocke in Cornehill, whoe the commissioners ordered mee to make use of for such things as hee selleth fitt for the affaires of the customes, but on whose charge I knowe not. I desired you to sende mee word on what account they were to bee had. Wee stande in great neede of bonds, and I am confident somme may bee had amongst our acquaintance at the custom house. A word of this in your next.

On the 28th October I wrote to you and enclosed my last quarters accounts, which I hope you have received and delivered the severall letters and accounts according to theyr direcions. By some of them there is a little money to bee paid which I ordered you to paie out of the ballance of my account, which you wrote you were to receive before this tyme, but my brother Pennant had notice from the custom house that order was given to the collector at Bristoll to paie mee, which if I finde to bee soe, then will I retorne up money by the first conveniency to cleare all the accounts above, and allsoe for your supply. As for the busines concerning the woman, I have (according to your advice) referred it totally to the searjeant, whoe promised faithfully to speake with Sir Philip therein. Present your mothers faithfull respects and myne to him and all his; and as occasion requireth put him in mynd thereof, wherein alsoe I desier your care. Present your mothers true love and myne to my brother Pennant and all his, and desier him to excuse your error above, which (God permittinge) shall bee made good to him (if not by you) by JB.

242. TO THOMAS PENNANT

[*No date*]

Brother Pennant

Yours of the 29th October with the enclosed order to Mr Mansell I received for which I and all other your loving favours to mee and myne I do most hartily thanke you. Good brother, pardon the error committed concerning the money about Esquier Butler. Upon my creditt, I did beeleeve it was paid, for that I heard not one word thereof but in your last letter. Howsoever, (God permittinge) that and all other your disbursements for mee shall bee made good unto you, with all faithfull love and harty thankes. I pray reade the enclosed and please to seale it and send your porter eyther with it or [call] for my sonne to comme to you, that you may advize him to bee more punctuall in writeinge to us. Hee formerly wrote to mee that Mr Kerseley procured the warrant for payment of our sallaryes. I here enclosed sende my receipt according to your direccions which I pray cause to bee delivered to Mr Thornbury on receipt of the money, out of which must bee deducted my parte for procureinge the warrant.

I sent my last quarter quarter booke with other accounts to my sonne William to bee delivered, which I hope is perfected accordinglie; and I then wrote to Mr Thornbury to paie my fee to my said sonne. I shall write to Mr Isaack Morgan to morrowe to knowe what order hee hath received concerning mee, and what answer I shall receive, I will give you an account thereof in my next.

Page 53

243. TO THE COMMISSIONERS OF THE CUSTOMS

[*Marginated*] Caerleon 8 November 1661

Right worshipful

Pray please to take notice that not any coales have beene laden nor landed, neyther in the port of Cardiffe, nor any member thereof (which are nowe in my collecion) from the 29th September to the 31st October 1661 (both dayes inclusive) in which tyme not any shippinge hath arryved in any of the places aforesaid, by which any became due, according to the Act for increase of shippinge and navigacion etc.

To Sir Job Harbie knight and barronett, Sir Nicholas Crispe and Sir John Shawe knight.

244. TO THE COMMISSIONERS OF THE CUSTOMS

[*8 November 1661*]

Wrote the same daye to acquainte the commissioners for his majesty's customes that not any thinge was received for customs etc. in the port of Cardiff and members aforesaid in the tyme aforesaid.

245. TO SON WILLIAM BYRD

[*Marginated*] 13 November [1661]

Wrote to my sonne William and sent £5 by Mr James Jones to him; my wife sent him 5s. and I [sent] 2s. 6d. by Mr James Jones his wife.

[*Marginated*] £5 7s. 6d.

246. TO THE COMMISSIONERS OF THE CUSTOMS

[*Marginated*] Caerleon 20 November 1661

Right worshipful

Pray please to take notice that yours of the 13th instant I received, which intymateth that you have not received any account of coales from mee. My worthy masters, since 25th day of March I have written 4 severall tymes to acquainte you with that busines, from which said 25th day of March to this present daye, but only one entry of coales was taken, neyther in the port of Cardiffe nor any member thereof (which is nowe in my collecion) which is under written, the coppie whereof I formerly sent up at least 4 severall tymes; neyther in all this tyme hath any other vessell arryved at any of the places aforesaid, by which any money became due according to the act for the encrease of shippinge and navigacion, but only the vessell underwritten.

Swansey, Neath and Burry, 3 of the members of Cardiffe (from whence great quantetyes of coales are exported somme for beyond sea, and somme for Englande[)], are not in my collecion, but are in the collecion of Mr Philip Mansell, his majesty's searcher; yet if it shall bee your pleasure that I shall give you an account of what coales have beene and shall bee exported from thence; uppon receipt of your order to that purpose I shall doe it with all care and faithfulnes. The money due on this one entry I formerly ordered my sonne William Byrd of Lincolnes Inn to paie out of moneyes which hee was to receave at the custom house, London. For the ballance of my accounts which if not donne before this commeth to your hands I shall take care that it shall be paid. I humbly desier one word of your pleasure in the premisses to JB.

247. TO SON WILLIAM BYRD

[*Marginated*] Caerleon 2 December 1661

Son William

Yours of the 26th November (being your second letter since the 20th of August) I received. I was Thursedaie last with Mr Isaack Morgan in Bristoll, whoe shewed mee the commissioners order to paie me £21 8s. 9d., the ballance of my accounts to the 24th June last, which I made up to him £22, which summe hee promised to retorne up to my brother Pennant this weeke. I did beeleeve that my ballance would have beene paid you in London, otherwayes I had sent your allowance by our neighbours, and whereas you write you paid Mr Wharton £25 my bond beinge only for £24, and that you paid the remainder to such uses whereof you never wrote mee one word, Sir Job received but £23 8s. 1d. and by myne of the 9th October 1660 I dyrected you to paie the remainder towards the charge for the fine from the Lady Morgan (but noe more of this).

Wee are exceedinglie oblieged to my brother Pennant and I have requested him, uppon, the receipt of the £22 to deduct what hee hath disbursed for mee, and to paie you the remainder out of which you are to paie the 3 smale summes which I ordered you by myne with the packett, which I desier may be donne with all speede, for allthough the summes are but smale, yet my creditt lyes at stake. Write mee word in your next what you paid po[st] for the packett; endeavour still to gett barronett Morgans order to Mr Thomas Morgan to paie mee, for I stande in great neede of money. Present my service to his brother and acquainte him that if I were in a capacity to furnish him I would not write to his brother the barronett for the smale summes which hee oweth mee.

I desier to knowe howe Mr Richards selleth the blanke cockett bonds. Bee carefull of our busines. Present your mothers faithfull respects and myne to the searjeant and as you shall finde cause desier him to speake with Sir Philip and if you canne, employ somme man to procure from the woman the certificate and affidavit. Use your endeavour. Present your mothers faithfull love and myne to my brother Pennant and all his, and I desier you and him to endeavour to gett the commissioners order to Mr Isaack Morgan to cleare my accounts quarterly, from the 24th of June last, for our ports yealde noe receipt at all. Thus.

[*Marginated*] £33 13s. 07d. due to mee from Barronett Morgan by bond.

248. TO ISAAC MORGAN

[*No date*]

Sent Mr Isaack Morgan my receipt dated 29th November 1661 for £21 8s. 9d. beinge the ballance of my accounts, as collector at Cardiffe and members (nowe in my collecion) from 23rd July 1660 to 24th June 1661.

Page 54

249. TO THOMAS PENNANT

[*Marginated*] 2 December 1661

Brother Pennant

Yours of 26th November I received, the contents whereof hath (if it were possible) doubled my obligacion: whoe was more oblieged to you before then I knowe how to deserne. Sir I wrote twice to Bristoll, but not receaveinge a satisfactory answer I rode thyther on Wednesdaie last, where Mr Isaack Morgan shewed mee the commissioners order to paie mee the £21 8s. 9d. whereof you write, which I made up to him £22, which summe hee promised to retorne up to you this weeke by bill of exchange, which I am confident hee will performe accordinglie; for I founde him very cyvill and very ready to serve mee on your account, of which (if you have any occasion to write to him) I pray take notice; and when you shall have received this £22, I pray deduct what you have paid and spent on my occasions, and I pray accept of 20s. out of it for you and my sister to drinke a cup of sack together with your Christmas pye, and please to deliver what remayneth to my son William, whoe should have beene supplyed sooner, but that I did hope this money woulde have beene paid above.

Mr Morgan hath noe order to paie mee any thinge since 24th June last. I earnestly desier that the commissioners will bee pleased to give him theyr order to cleare my accounts quarterly from that tyme, for our ports (which are nowe in my collecion) yealde very little or noe receipt at all. I pray good brother assiste my sonne to obteyne this order, if it may bee had. I make boalde to trouble with the inclosed, for that I finde my letters have beene intercepted. I pray send your porter therewith.

250. TO THE COMMISSIONERS OF THE CUSTOMS

[*Marginated*] Caerleon 6 December 1661

Right worshipful

Please to take notice that not any custom hath beene received neyther in the port of Cardiff, nor any member thereof (which is nowe in my collecion) from 29th September to the 30th November 1661 (both dayes inclusive), neyther hath any vessell arryved within the tyme aforesaid in any of the said places, whereby any money became due according to the act for encrease of shippinge and navigacion; neyther hath any coales beene laden or landed in any of the said places within the tyme aforesaid, neyther did I take any bonds at any tyme for the addicional duty etc.

For the right worshipful the commissioners for his majesty's customs.

251. TO THOMAS PENNANT

[*Marginated*] Caerleon 3 January 1662

Brother Pennant

On the 2nd December last I wrote to acquainte you that I had beene in Bristoll with Mr Isaack Morgan, to whome I delivered soe much money as made my ballance £22, since which tyme hee wrote to you and enclosed a bill of exchange for payment of this £22 to you, which my sonne Edward sawe delivered to the post, and I hope this money is received by you accordinglie. In myne to you, I sent one to my sonne. I have not heard from him, nor you since, neyther have I received but 2 letters from him since 20th August last, and if hee hath written oftner, his letters are myscarryed. I desired you to deduct out of this money what you disbursed and spent on my busines and that you would accept of 20s. to drinke a cupp of sack with my sister at eateinge of your Christmas pye, and that you woulde deliver the remainder to my sonne. I doe allowe him £15 per quarter, whereof I sent him but £5 by Mr James Jones last quarter, dependinge that this money would have beene paid above; but I hope you have before this tyme received and disposed of this £22, as is above desired. Good brother write mee one word hereof by the first post, for my wife is much troubled that hee doth not write oftner to us; and I must confesse I am not well pleased with his neglect herein. Thus etc.

252. TO THE CUSTOMS OFFICERS AT GLOUCESTER

[*Subscribed*] Caerleon 'sub Cardiffe' 6 January 1662

Honoured freinds

I understande that a parcell of iron is stayed in your port for want of a cockett therewith, which belongeth to Mr Caple Handbury, whoe had ordered Francis Vickers of Tewxbury to receave the same abord his trowe here for Gloucester; but our neigbour Reece Gwynn (contrary to Mr Handburyes intencion) caused the said iron (beinge 12 tonns) to bee laden aborde his vessell called the Giuft of Caerleon, in the name of Robert William, on the 11th daye of December last, whoe went master in the said vessell, and tooke a cockett from hence, therewith for Bristoll, and toulde mee it was to bee put abord a vessell there for Gloucester, which cockett I beeleeve is in the custom house at Bristoll; and I knowe there hath not beene [*Page 55*] any intencion to deceave his majesty herein in the least, which (at the request of the said Mr Handbury) I make boulde to certifie you of, which I desier may bee considered and that all lawfull favour may bee afforded him. I knowe this quantety of iron was intended for Gloucester only, and shall make oath thereon, if neede requier. Thus leaveinge the premises to your consideracions, I take leave for present and am,gentlemen, yours really to serve you, John Byrd comptroller and collector.

253. TO WILLIAM THORNBURY

[*Marginated*] Caerleon 7 January 1662

Mr Thornebury

I here enclosed sende my booke for the last quarter, which I pray present to our worthy freinde Mr Dawes with my humble service. I thanke you for paieinge my fee for my former quarter bookes to my brother Pennant, to whome I pray please to paie my fee for this quarter booke and hee will deliver my receipt for the same.

254. TO THE COMMISSIONERS OF THE CUSTOMS

[*No date*]

Right worshipful

Pray please to take notice that not any custome, nor any other money for custom causes hath bene received, neyther in the port of Cardiffe, nor any member thereof (which is nowe in my collecion) in the quarter from the 29th September to the 24th December 1661 (both dayes inclusive) neyther hath any vessell arryved in any of the places aforesaid in that quarter, by which any money became due according to the act for encrease of shippinge and navigacion;

neyther were any coales laden or or landed in any of the places aforesaid in that quarter, but only 15 chaldrons laden at Neath by coast cockett, dated 25th October, and 12 chaldrons laden at Swansey by coast cockett dated 21st November last, which were landed at Chepstowe, one of the members of Cardiff, for the supply of his majesty's garrison there. My bill of sallaryes and incident charges the last quarter is here enclosed, which commes to £7 8s. 0d., which with 49s., the ballance of my account in Michaelmas quarter, makes £9 17s. 0d., which summe I humbly desier your order to Mr Philip Mansell, your deputy in Swansey, to paie mee.

My worthy masters: Mr William Williams, waiter at Newport, acquainted mee that in regard the sallary was smale, and his occasions such at present that hee coulde not attende that service, soe that I did not paie him his sallary this last quarter, parte whereof hee coulde not attende on that service; and if it bee your pleasures to contynewe a waiter there, I humbly present unto you one Moses Nicholas, a man whoe suffred for his late majesty's sake, of blessed memory; in whose service hee lost the benefitt of one of his hands; and if you will bee pleased to sende him your commission to bee waiter in Newport in stead of Mr Williams, I am confident hee will prove very carefull in that service. Thus humbly desireinge one word of your pleasures herein by the first post, I take leave.

255. TO THOMAS PENNANT

[*Marginated*] Caerleon 11 January 1662

Brother Pennant

Yours of the 24th December and yours of the 7th instant I received, and am glad the £22 is paid to you, on the bill of exchange; and I doe hartily thanke you for furnishinge my sonne before you received the bill. Your love embouldeneth mee to trouble you with myne to the commissioners, and to Mr Thornebury, in which are my last quarters accounts. There is due to mee from the commissioners to ballance my 2 last quarters accounts, £9 17s. 0d., and I have written to them, desireinge theyr order to Mr Philip Mansell, theyr deputy at Swansey to paie mee, for I finde him nowe very ready to pleasure mee. I desier your endeavour with our freinds at custom house to procure theyr order accordinglie, which being obteyned, pray deliver Mr Tanners receipt for 25s. and myne for £5 (which are here enclosed) to the accountant generall, and my receipt to Mr Thornebury for 10s. on receipt thereof, and whatsoever you thinke fitt to give to or spende on our freinds herein, I pray doe it freely, and charge all to my account, which shall bee made good to you on receipt of your bill of charge.

I have formerly written many letters to the commissioners and (as they write) scarce any commes to theyr hands, which makes me desier your love herein; for

I finde that yours to mee and myne to you are received, but I doubt that myne to my sonne and his to mee are stayed in some place, for I have received but 2 letters from him since 20th August, in which tyme I have written many to him. Wherefore good brother pardon my boaldnes herein, and when you may with conveniency please to write one word of receipt of the premises, that I may knowe they are received and delivered according to theyr dyrecions. In your next, I pray write mee word what you paie for postage of this packett, for I am to be allowed it on my next account.

256. TO SON WILLIAM BYRD

[*Marginated*] 16 January 1662

Sent my sonne William £10 by my cozen William Lucas
Sent £5 more to my sonne William by Mr Isaack Tomkins, and 5s. to drinke with him.
[*Marginated, added later*] 3rd February £15 5s. 0d.

Page 56

257. TO A SCHOOLMASTER

[*Marginated*] Caerleon 27 January 1662

Honoured Sir

A worthy freinde of ours advized mee to trouble you with a sonne of myne which is a poore scoller, and desiers to bee more learned; and if you will bee soe loveinge as to entertayne him, both for dyett, lodgeinge and learneinge, uppon reasonable termes, I shall make boulde to sende him to you. I pray please to write mee one word of your mynde herein by the first post, with the lowest rate of the premises, wherein you will very much obliege him that desiers to bee sir, yours to serve you JB.

258. TO THE COMMISSIONERS OF THE CUSTOMS

[*Marginated*] Caerleon 10 February 1662

Right worshipful

Pray please to take notice that not any money hath beene received in the port of Cardiffe nor any member thereof (nowe in my collecion) for custom, or any custom cause, from the 25th day of December to the last daye of January last (both dayes inclusive) in which tyme not any shippinge hath arryved by which any money became due, according to the act for navigacion and encrease of shippinge, neyther hath any coales beene laden or landed in any of the places aforesaid within the tyme aforesaid.

Richard Charleton a carryer dwelleth about a mile from Chepstowe.
Phineas Rogers is an attorney in the county court for Monmothsheire.

259. TO THOMAS PENNANT

[*No date*]

Brother Pennant

Yours of the 28th January with the courts order there enclosed I longe since received, for which I must hartily thanke you, in token whereof I sende you by Thomas Burleigh (one of the Monmoth carryers, whose lodgeinge in London is at the signe of the St Paules head in Carter Lane) a newe salmon (beinge the first I coulde procure this season) in a pie nayled and mayled up in a boxe and dyrected unto you. I pray you and my sister to accept thereof as a smale token of thankefullnes, for you to conclude Lent withall, which hath beene very sharpe in these partes, fish beinge at a most unreasonable rate.

My sonne Ned is at Monmoth, from whome you shall receave a letter with the pie; howesoever pray sende your porter on Thursdaie night or Fridaie morneinge to the carryer (whoe beginns his journey this day) for it. I understoode that the last pie I sent you was kept soe longe by the carryer before it came to you that it stunke exceedinglie, which did discourage mee from sendinge any more, but this was sent to the carryer soe soone as it was ready, and I hope you will receive it in a gallant condicion. It weigheth 80lbs. for carriage whereof the carryer is paide. I did hope to heare from you by my neighbour Mr James Jones according to your last, but it seemes he did not see you.

Pray please to present Mr Samuel Whittle with 10s. as a token from mee, untill I shall sende it up to you which (God permittinge) shall bee by the first opportunety. Pray present my due respects to Mr Keresley and Mr Thornebury, and as for my quarter bookes my smale fee was constantly paid mee every quarter by Mr Thornebury, whoe I desier to deduct out of my fee what is due on mee towards procureinge my Lords warrant, and I desier him to accept of 5s. as a token of thankes for his love and care therein, and I desier to knowe when hee is pleased that I sende up my acquittance for my fee for quarter bookes, which I shall observe accordinglie.

Good brother in your next pray please to write mee word howe much money you paid my sonne William, for hee lately wrote to his mother that hee received but £5 from mee in the quarter to Christmas, which I confesse is truth; but I retorned up to you wherewith to supply him and to cleare some smale accounts with the commissioners wherewith I chargedhim, whereof hee hath not written one word at all, which sommethinge troubleth my mynde. Thus etc

The salmon cost	00 - 07 - 00
flower	00 - 04 - 06
spice and eggs	00 - 00 - 06
the cooke	00 - 02 - 00
the baker	00 - 01 - 00
16 lbs. of butter	00 - 05 - 04
carriadge to Monmoth	00 - 03 - 00
carriadge from thence to London	00 - 10 - 00
	01 - 13 - 04

Page 57 is blank

Page 58 is torn out except for the following fragment

260. FRAGMENT

[*No date*]

of the ... oryginall copie ... in armes against the ... have beene refer ... bee soe loveinge as to ... acquainte them that ... [W]orcester I was at home ... [o]ffice of comptroller ... restored by order from ... [of]fice, and I hope I shall ... [my]selfe; I was allsoe collector ... are nowe commissioners for his majesty's ... to one Mr Griffith Bowen.

Page 59

261. TO EDWARD HERBERT

[*No date*]

Mr Edward Herbert

I have conferred with Mr Morgan, as by the enclosed noate you will perceave, by which it seemeth that those of whome you bought the lands intende to leave that parte of the charge of the suite on you, which if you are contented to paie and please to write mee your order therein, I shall observe and performe it accordinglie; howsoever I pray please to write your mynde, eyther to Mr Morgan or to mee what answer to give him herein. I cannot give you any account of your other busines, but soe soone as I shall speake with the parties I shall write unto you thereof.

262. COPY OF A CERTIFICATE

[*Subscribed*] 30 May 1662

To the right honourable the Lord High Treasurer of England

Wee whose names are under written, beinge justices of peace and commissioners for the monthly assessments in the countie of Monmoth, doe understande that an

informacion is given in against John Byrd (comptroller of his majesty's customes in the port of Cardiff and members thereof) that hee was in armes at Worcester against his majesty, and that hee was a sequestrator in the late troubles, of which crymes the said John Byrd is wholly innocent; for when his majesty was at Worcester wee are certayne that the said John Byrd was not there, neyther was hee a sequestrator at all, neyther doe wee knowe nor ever heard that hee wronged any person. Allsoe hee beinge comptroller of his late majesty's customes in the ports aforesaid was sequestred from his saide office and the execucion thereof for many yeares, untill by order of his majesty that nowe is, hee was restored to his said office. This was thought fitt (at the request of the said John Byrd) to certifie your honours, and that wee are your lordshipps humble servants
of Uske: Trevor Williams. Thomas Morgan: of Tredegar
of Newport: Edmond Morgan. Thomas Morgan of Penrose
of Tynterne: William Herbert. Charles Vann of Coldrey
of Peacefeilde: John Walter. Thomas Williams of Caerlion
William Williams of Abergavenny. William Morgan of Pencreege
Charles Hughes of Trostre. Roger Williams of Kevan Hylith and Sir George Probert of Pennalt

The names of the places of aboade of the gentlemen whoe subscribed the above written certificate is not in the originall. This certificate was not full in answer to what was layde to the charge of J B, which is further certificate in January 1665, the coppie thereof is in this booke.

263. COPY OF A CERTIFICATE

[*Marginated*] 'Cardiffe villa' 30 May 1662

To the right honourable the Lord High Treasurer of England

Wee the bayliefs and aldermen of the towne and port of Cardiffe doe understande that an informacion is given in against John Byrd (comptroller of his majesty's customes in this port and members thereof) that hee was in armes at Worcester against his majesty, and that hee was a sequestrator in the late troubles, of which crymes the said John Byrd is wholly innocent; for wee are certaynely informed that hee was in his owne house when his majesty was at Worcester, and that hee never was a sequestrator at all; neyther did hee wronge any person that wee knowe (or ever heard) of. Allsoe we knowe that hee was comptroller of his late majesty's customes in this port and members, and that hee was sequestred and kept from the execucion of that office above 11 yeare, all which tyme one Mr Francis Malory enjoyed the same, untill by order of his majesty that nowe is, hee was restored to his said office. This wee thought fitt (at the request of the said John Byrd) to certifie your honours. And that wee are your lordshipps humble

servants
Herbert Evans constable of the castle[(1)]
Lewis Jones }
John Woolluyn } bayleifes
John Gibbs }
Arthur Lloyd } justices
Miles Morgan
Henry Morgan
Arthur Roberts
Rice Davis
Roger Sheere
John Sheere
William Jones
Nathan[iel] Wells aldermen
[*Marginated*] 2 June 1662
[*Marginated*] These certifficatts were sent to my sonne William 2 June. Allsoe I wrote them to the searjeant for his assistance with a request (if neede soe required) to furnishe William with money to proceede in my busines. Sent these letters by Giles Phi[llips] and £5 in money to W B and coppies of this certificate to bee kept by him to bee produced if neede requier hereafter.

1. 'const[abularius] castr[i]' in MS.

264. TO THOMAS PENNANT

[*Marginated*] 3 June 1662

Wrote to brother Pennant concerning the certifficatts abovesaid, and desired him to assist W B therein and I acquainted my brother Pennant that I had received his of the 24th and 29th May last.

My wife sent 5s. to W B by yonge Mr Sissell.

3 June [1662]. I sent W B £1 by Mr Philip Mansell.

Page 60

265. TO EDWARD HERBERT

[*Marginated*] Caerleon 3 June 1662

Mr Edward Herbert

I spake with widdow Gent, whoe at first said I shoulde doe what I pleased in that busines, but woulde not conclude any thinge with mee without the advice of a freinde which shee said shee had besides mee. After shee had spoken with him, shee concluded that if you please to paie 40s. which shee sayth shee paid for reparacion of sea walls, or somme such charge which was imposed on that land,

and paide the charge allready expended in that suite and paie her £4 5s. 0d. per annum dureinge hir life, you shall have the lande, otherwayes shee will wage lawe with you; for shee sayth you helde hir lande but from yeare to yeare, and if you cannot prove your bargaine to bee otherwaies, I wish you to lett hir enjoy it quiettly, for some reasons which I coulde shewe you.

Yeasterday I went to Newport where [lives] Mr William Jenkins, and I spake with David Williams whoe after somme debate concluded to accept of 40s. to cleare accounts betweene you and him, which if you please to give one notice thereof from you, eyther to Mr Jenkins or my selfe, that busines shall bee ended. As for your busines with Mr Morgan, I wish you woulde bee pleased to write your mynde to him, and set forth the charge which you were at with him; and if it were my case as it is yours, I would reserve it to himselfe, and I beeleeve (as hee is a gentleman) hee will deale cyvilly with you; if not (unles you canne avoyde it by lawe) I would paie what is demaunded. Mr Morgan sayes that you bought somme of those lands for 9 or 10 yeares purchase, and that those whoe soulde those lands left the charge of the suite to goe with the lands, which since the decree will yealde (as hee saith) 16 yeares purchase I pray consider of the premises and please to dyrect what you please to have donne therein; wherein Mr Jenkins and my selfe shall serve you with all faithfullnes according to understandinge.

266. TO THE COMMISSIONERS OF THE CUSTOMS

[*Marginated*] Caerleon 6 June 1662

Right worshipful

28s. was received in the month of May last, which is all since 25th March last in which tyme noe shipping hath arryved neyther in the said port of Cardiff nor any member thereof (which is nowe in my collecion) by which any thinge became due according to the act for encrease of shippinge and navigacion, neyther hath any coales beene laden or landed in the tyme aforesaid in any of the places aforesaid.

267. MEMORANDUM

[*No date*]

Paide Thomas Browne whoe dwelleth at the signe of the Dyall nere the Tolesey in Bristoll, watchmaker, for puttinge my clock in order 3s. 6d. agreed with him for 2s. per annum to keepe my clock cleane and in order.

268. TO SON WILLIAM BYRD

[*Marginated*] 10 June 1662

Sent W B £9 by Mr Isaack Tomkins and sent the coppie of a will enclosed in a letter to W B to bee delivered to Elizabeth Drewe widdowe, whoe dwelleth at the back side of the rounde court, right against the 3 Kings in Lees Yard in St Martyns in the Feilds and ordered W B to call to hir for 3s. 6d. which I paid for that coppie. I allsoe desired William to cleare accounts with brother Pennant, and if it were not prejudiciall to comme downe soe soone as conveniently hee might.

269. TO THE COMMISSIONERS OF CUSTOMS

[*Marginated*] 27 June [1662]

Right worshipful

Please to take notice that yours of the 21st instant I received this daye and the oath herein written shall bee tendred to all persons relateinge to his majesty's customes with all speede, according to your dyreccions. Your former letter with the act for regulateinge abuses in his majesty's customes (which you write was formerly sent mee) is not comme to my hands, wherefore I humbly pray that one of these acts may bee sent mee, soe soone as may bee; that I may performe my duty accordinglie; which etc.

270. MEMORANDUM

[*Marginated*] 27 June 1662

Mr William Jenkins of Newport paid Mr David Williams of Caerleon 35s. in full payment and satisfaccion for all his demaunds from Mr Edward Herbert and he gave David Williams 11s. to retayne him in all his causes where hee practized. This was donne at Mrs Joane Pryddies house in Newport in the presence of JB.

271. TO THE COMMISSIONERS OF THE CUSTOMS

[*Marginated*] Caerleon 14 July 1662

Right worshipful

Pray please to take notice that here enclosed is my last quarter booke with my bills of sallaryes and incident charges, and account current. My worthy masters, I was last weeke at Swansey with the customer whoe dwelleth there, before whome, with the comptroller, you have beene pleased to order that all officers relateinge to the customes within my collecion shoulde take the oath by you prescribed; but the customer is soe aged and feeble that he cannot travell at all, and for all the officers relateinge to the customes within my collecion to ryde to

Swansey (somme of our ports beinge above 50 miles from thence) it must needes bee prejudiciall to his majesty's service. Wherefore I humbly conceave (with your worshipps approbacion) that if the said oath be really taken before the mayor or somme justices of peace in somme place in my collecion, it may bee satisfactory. Wherein I pray please to sende mee dyrecions by the first post, which shall bee faithfully observed by [JB].

Page 61

272. TO EDMUND TURNER

[*Marginated*] Cardiff 16 July 1662

Mr Edmond Turner

According to dyreccions I here enclosed sende you my quarter booke to 24th June last, for which 10s. fee is due to mee, which I pray please to paie to my worthy freinde, Mr Samuel Whittell, who will deliver you my receipt for the same.

273. TO SAMUEL WHITTELL

[*No date*]

Mr Whittell

By the post that bringeth this I sende my quarter booke to Mr Edmond Turner for which 10s. fee is due to mee, for which I here enclosed sende my receipt, prayinge you to accept therof as a smale token of remembrance from mee. By the last post I sent my quarter book with my bill of sallarye and incident charges and account current to the commissioners; and I then wrote to acquainte them that I had beene at Swansey with the customer who dwelleth there, and is so ould and feeble that hee cannot travell at all, and somme of the officers which are in my collecion live above 50 miles from Swansey and for all the officers to goe to Swansey to take the oath which the commissioners prescribed must needs be prejudiciall to his majesty's service; and that if they woulde bee pleased to write mee theyr order that the oath might bee taken before the cheife magistrate or somme of our justices, in the places where the officers relateinge to the customes doe live, [all] might with their approbacion bee satisfactory.

All the officers at Swansey and adjacent ports tooke the oath the last weeke before the customer and myselfe at Swansey, and all the officers at Cardiffe and Pennarth tooke it before the customer's deputy and my selfe at Cardiffe. I allsoe offred it to the officers at Newport before a justice of peace and my selfe, where the customers deputy refused it, because the customer himselfe was not in place as by the commissioners letter to mee was dyrected. Wherefore I pray procure the commissioners dyrecions herein with all speede to JB.

Impression of the controller's cocket seal , creek of Swansea, port of Cardiff, c.1649.

Impression of the customer's cocket seal for tonnage and poundage, creek of Chepstow, port of Cardiff, c.1605.

274. TO SON WILLIAM BYRD

[*Marginated*] 30 July 1662

Sent 5s. to W B by Mr Lyson Evans and desired my sonne W B woulde comme downe with him, if it might not be prejudiciall to him nor mee.

275. TO THE COMMISSIONERS OF THE CUSTOMS

[*No date*]

Right worshipful

My receipts of customs in the port of Cardiff and members (nowe in my collecion) is 23s. 9d. from 24th June to 31st July (both dayes inclusive) in which tyme one French vessell arryved at Newport within my collecion, but not any coales eyther laden or landed, in any port within my collecion in the tyme aforesaid, which etc.

276. TO THE COMMISSIONERS OF THE CUSTOMS

[*Marginated*] Caerleon 25 August 1662

Right worshipful

Please to take notice that according to your letter of the 18th instant I sende you here enclosed duplicates of my former accounts, both outwards and inwards from 24th July 1660 to Michaelmas 1661. I desier to knowe whether you please to have duplicates from that tyme, and soe hence forward quarterly or not. Wherein I humbly desier your dyrecions, which shall bee carefully observed by JB.

277. TO THE COMMISSIONERS OF THE CUSTOMS

[*Marginated*] Cardiff 18 September 1662

Right worshipful

Please to take notice that yours of the 18th August last I formerly received, and on the 25th of the same I sent duplicatts of my accounts both inwards and outwards from the 24th July 1660 to the 29th of September 1661, as was dyrected, but by yours of the 12th instant (which I likewise have received) I finde that myne came not to your hands, soe that I here enclosed sende the like duplicatts of my accounts both inwards and outwards for the tyme abovesaid. And after Michaelmas day I shall sende duplicatts of my accounts for this present yeare according to your dyreccions; and shall in all your affaires committed to my care performe my duty therein with all faithfullnes, soe long as you shall bee pleased to contynnewe mee as nowe I am, and was formerly for many yeares, your worships most humble servant JB.

278. TO THE COMMISSIONERS OF THE CUSTOMS

[*Marginated*] Caerleon 26 September 1662

Right worshipful

I pray please to take notice that yours with my lord treasurers enclosed I have received and communicated them unto all the officers within my collecion as was thereby dyrected. My worthy masters, my humble suite unto you is that you will bee pleased to contynnewe mee in your service in the port of Cardiff and all the members thereof, whereof Swansey is one; which was taken from Cardiffe in the tyme of the late troubles; but I beinge your worshipps servant formerly when most of you were farmers to his late majesty, Swansey was then in my collecion, beinge then (and still is by our accounts delivered into the exchequer) but a member of Cardiff; and if it shall please you to confirme mee your servant as I was formerly when most of you were farmers to his late majesty, I shall give you securety for performance of my duty therein, to your own content and shall contynewe as I am etc.

[*Marginated*] £4 Edw[ard] B[yrd] had when he went hence.

Page 62

279. TO EDMUND TURNER

[*Marginated*] Caerleon 13 October 1662

Mr Edmond Turner

Yours of the first instant I received of Friday last, in answer whereunto pray please to take notice that only one French vessell arryved within my collecion this last quarter, which is under written. Not any foreigne liquors have beene imported into any port within my collecion this quarter. I knowe not anythinge concerning 3d. per tonn for Dover harbour. I pray please to sende mee one of the acts with dyrecions what is to bee donne therein, and I shall with all care put it in execucion. I have ordered money to bee paide to the bearer hereof, Mr Thomas Pennant dwellinge in skynners hall, and soe soone as hee shall receive it I have requested him to paie you the £3 15s. due on the former French vessell and the £5 due on this. I understande that the £10 is allowed for collecting these moneyes, which if it bee soe I pray afforde the benefitt thereof to him that is your JB.

I shall very shortly sende up my quarter booke to you.

Newport 25 June 1662

The Trynity of Croisick, burden 20 tons, Peter Abuo master and merchant, bound from France: £5 tonnage.

John Byrd collector.

280. TO THOMAS PENNANT

[*No date*]

Brother Pennant

Yours of the 7th instant I received, and on Thursdaie last I had notice from Swansey that Richard Dutton had the day before produced a pattent for my office of comptroller there. I came from Swansey the same daye that hee came thyther and then noe newes of him in any of our ports, soe that till I see his pattent I cannot tell what to saye to it. You knowe by my certificates that I am unjustly put out and I hope my oulde masters the farmers will not deale soe unkindely with mee; to which ende I pray (according to your woonted love) to advize with Mr Whittle. Mr Philip Mansell intends to bee in London this weeke.

Here enclosed is a letter to Mr Michael Pynder haberdasher of smale wares, whoe dwells at the signe of the Blackamores Head in Bread Streete, whoe had a tickett for my sonne Matthias's wages in his majesty's service abord the shipp Princesse, for which tickett Mr Pyndar gave a receipt, the coppie whereof is under written. I pray add your helpe to procure my sonns money which Mr Pynder is by the enclosed from his freinde my ould servant William Merredith desired to paie you, which when you shall have received I pray please to paie my sonn William £12. I have allready sent £4 both beinge for this quarters allowance. I pray call to him for your £10 and let him not knowe that you have given mee notice thereof. He constantly receives his allowance of £15 per quarter and somme smale tokens from his mother and mee besides. I did hope hee was soe good a husbande that hee had money lyinge by him and not to bee in want. Good brother, please to write mee word whether hee is to bee called to the barre the next terme or not, that if hee bee, I may order him somme more money for I conceave hee will bee at more charge then ordinary at that tyme.

In obteyneinge my sonne's money somme charge will bee which must bee allowed; allsoe I desier you after receipt of the money to paie £8 15s. 0d. to Mr Edmund Turner at the custom house according to the letter enclosed and please to deliver the letter open to him, and if 2s. per pound may bee had I pray put him in mynde thereof. Mr Dawes owes mee 20s. for my 2 quarter bookes to 25th March last, which if it may bee had, it will make us drinke. I sent Mr Whittle my receipt for my last quarter booke fee, to 24th June, which was to bee paid him by Mr Turner, but I heard nothinge thereof; it was for him to drinke. I pray write mee word by the first of receipt hereof and of what hopes to receive my sonnes money. Brother, it is your goodnes which makes mee thus troublesomme to you, wherein I beeseech you to pardon mee. My wife presents hir faithfull love to you and all yours, soe doth JB.

Received 29th July 1662 of Mr William Merredith a bill to receive of the navy office comminge to £39 10s. 0d. due to Mr Matthias Byrd, which money when received I promise to retorne to Mr William Merredith or to paie to his order. I saye received the abovesaid bill, eyther to retorne the bill or money for it. Pray deliver my brother W[illiam] 20s. and remember my love to him. For Michael Pynder.

Page 63

281. TO EDWARD BYRD

[*Marginated*] Caerleon 9 March 1663

Sonn Edward

Yours of 21st February (by my cozen William Lucas) I received, which puts mee in doubte that you have quite layde aside those dyreccions which I gave you in writeinge. I paid £3 10s. 0d. to my cozen Lucas which you borrowed of him, whereof you coulde not have needed if you had not spent my money vaynely. I expect that your habitt may bee fitt for a servant; if you exceede therein I shall not maynteyne it, and if you borrowe money againe (without my order) I shall not paie it; wherefore p[eruse] my dyreccions sure againe and endeavour to observe them.

I wrote to you by Mr Tomkins concerning severall things which concerne mee, but you have not written one word concerning any one of them, wherein you appear to be very careles. I expect in your next (and that soe soone as may bee) an answer to everye particular in my former letter. I desier to knowe when the searjeant and your master intende to begin theyr journeyes to the country. Present your mothers true love and myne to the searjeant and to your master. I sent you 10s. by Mr Tomkins to buy you a deske, which you write was bought with parte of what you had of my cozen Lucas at 9s., soe that you charge mee double. I allsoe sent you £6 to buy you a suite and 30s. to buy you a clerks gowne.

Bee carefull to studdy humillity and beware of drinkinge, to which you will bee induced by your countrymen; bee carefull to serve God and then hee will blesse and dyrect you in all his wayes, for which shall bee the prayers of your father JB.

Your mother and brothers remember you.

282. TO THOMAS PENNANT

[*Marginated*] Caerleon 24 March 1663

Brother Pennant

Yours of 17th instant with the enclosed I received, and have here enclosed sent the 2 accounts current, which your noate expresseth to bee wantinge, but the vouchers which are wantinge were delivered with my quarterly accounts to Mr Philip Mansell, according to the commissioners order, to Michaelmas last, without which hee coulde not cleare my accounts and if there bee a necessity for haveinge them above, good brother procure Mr Whittell or the accomptant to write one word to Mr Mansell for them. The farmers did (since Michaelmas) commande mee to sende up my accounts and vouchers to themselves, in pursuance whereof I made boulde to trouble you to receive and deliver them for Christmas quarter accordinglie, and I hope that the £8 7s. 5d. ballance of that quarters account due to mee will bee paid to you according to my former request.

As for the 13s. 4d. customs money received in Chepstowe for my account, Mr Mansell gott it from my deputy I knowe not howe, and I have charged him therewith in my account current to Christmas last. Here enclosed is the quarter booke which Mr Thornebury wanteth. I serve him the same formerly. Pray present my due respects to him, to Mr Whittell, Mr Parsons and Mr Sankey and I pray gratifie the accountant freely on receipt of my ballance. Good brother sende your porter with the enclosed, and for my sonne to comme to you, and I pray advize him to bee very carefull of his masters busines, whoe is gon the circuite and my sonne left to himselfe, which I doubt may prove prejudicall unto him and unto mee, for youth are apt to bee led aside if noe man lookes to them. I pray deliver him 20s. on my account and advize him to use it carefully, and I pray write mee word howe hee beehaveth himselfe etc. Since the writeinge hereof I understande that Mr Mansell is nowe in London, and I hope will give satisfaccion concerning the vouchers. JB.

283. TO EDWARD BYRD

[*No date*]

Sonne Edward

On the 9th instant I wrote to you that I had paid my cozen William Lucas the money which you toke up of him. I advized you not to take up money of any person without my order, which if you doe I will not paie it. I allsoe advized that your habitt may bee fitt for a servant and if otherwaies I will not mayneteyne it. Yours of the 3rd and 12th instant are received by which I finde you have spent all the money which you had. You must learne to bee more frugall and humble, otherwayes I shall not bee able to mayneteyne you. I have desired my brother Mr Thomas Pennant to deliver you 20s.; use that well and it will produce more to doe you good. I shall endevor to supply you with what is fitt and what may doe you good and not otherwayes.

I formerly wrote to you to enquier in the exchequer for a suite commenced there against mee by Richard Dutton, my successor, in Michaelmas terme, and another suite commenced against mee in common pleas the last terme, by George or Roger Whittley and I desired that you would go to the Fleete and enquier for Mr Edward Rumsey and desier him to remember howe that Whittley forcd him and mee with Mr Edmond Waters to give him £20 per peece and enter in bonde dated 30th October 1644[(1)] to paie him more, on which bonds Whittley nowe sueth mee and Mrs Susanna Waters, but you never wrote mee one word concerning any busines of myne, neyther canne I receive any handsome account from Mr James Jones whoe I employed herein for mee. Pray desier my brother Pennant to advize you herein. Whittley with a party of horsemen carryed us to Worcester prisoners and there forced us as abovesaid. Faile not to give mee an account hereof with all speede.

If the searjeant bee yet in London present your [*Page 64*] mothers service and myne to him and write mee word when hee intends to bee at Gloucester; if I had knowne what daye Mr Smythies had beene in Hereford I would have waited on him there.

1. 'dated 30th October 1644' interlined.

284. TO EVAN SEYS

[*Marginated*] Caerleon 17 April 1663

Honoured Sir

In October 1644 Roger Whittley of Aston in the county of Flint (beinge then a major under generall Gerrard) sent 3 troupes whoe arrested mee, pretendinge that I must appear before the generall (beinge then at Abergavenny) but the said Whittley carryed mee and one Mr Edmond Waters to Worcester, and before hee would let us goe he had from us there £20 a peece and our bonds to paie him £20 a peece more, whereof hee had from mee in May next after, £10 in parte thereof, and nowe he sueth mee for the remaynder. Nowe I humbly pray one word of advice what answer I may make, my money beinge forced from mee for nothinge.

Allsoe Richard Dutton my successor commenced an accion in the exchequer in Michaelmas terme last, for what I received after the date of his pattent, and before hee produced it in any of our ports, I and my deputyes haveinge donne the service and neyther Dutton nor any person for him did appeare in any of our ports, yet hee expecteth the benefit of the place as aforesaid. Mr James Jones my attorney sayth hee appeared for mee in both these accions, but as yet I cannott have coppies of the bills which are put in by them against mee. Good sir, please to write one word of advice herein soe soone as conveniently you may to JB.

My wife and sonne William presents theyr true loves and services to you and allyours; soe doth JB.

For the right worshipful Evan Seys searjeant at lawe these Gloucester.

285. TO SIR WILLIAM, FIFTH BARON PAGET

[*Marginated*] Caerleon 'sub Cardiffe' 21 April 1663

Right honourable

Please to take notice that yours of the 18th instant I received, in answer whereto Sir Job Harbie gave mee his order on the 28th day of August 1660 (I beinge then in London), to receive the duty of 4s. per chaldron on coales in the porte of Cardiffe and Swansey with the members thereof, together with Llanelthy (alias North Burry) and on the 17th daye of September then next followinge Sir Job gave his order to major Robert Manwareinge to collect the said duty on coales in Llanelthy (alias North Burry aforesaid); and before Christmas then next after, Sir Job gave his order to Mr Philip Mansell of Swansey to collect the said duty in the ports aforesaid, since which tyme I have not had any thinge to doe therein and what money I received for that duty in that little tyme I was employed I retorned it up to Sir Job[(1)] about the tyme that I was dismissed as abovesaid, and I have Sir Job Harbies receipt for the same. I humbly thanke your honour in that (if I were nowe in that employment) you are pleased to contynnewe mee therein; and if I may doe you any service in this, or any other thinge in my power, none shall bee more ready to serve you then is your honours humble servant JB.

For the right honourable William Lord Pagett at the signe of the Golden Lyon at the Savoy in the Strande these London.

1. 'to Sir Job' interlined.

286. TO THOMAS PENNANT

[*Marginated*] Caerleon 28 April 1663

Brother Pennant

Yours of the 14th instant I received by which I finde the contynnuance of your care and trouble in my busines, for which I hartily thanke you. According to your advice I here enclosed sende Philip Mansells receipt for the 13s. 4d. I was served with process out of the exchequer in Michaelmas terme last, at the suite of Richard Dutton, and before the last terme, the deputy sheriffe served mee and Susanna Waters with 2 processes, at the suite of George Whittley, in common pleas, to all which accions my attorney, Mr James Jones, sayth hee appeared for mee, but I cannott gett any coppies of theyr bills or declaracions, Mr Jones telling mee still that I shall have them tyme enough. I am advized to search the affidavit office to finde whether oath were made that I was served at the suite of Dutton or not. I understande that there [is] a charge on mee in the exchequer of £1500, but for what yeares I cannot learne as yet. I do not owe any thinge for customes: you knowe (to your great trouble) that I was unjustly charged there before nowe, for which I have my quietus. I beeseech you good brother to employ somme person of your acquaintance to search after these suites and for what tyme this money is charged on mee, and I pray pay whome you employ, that I may knowe certaynely howe all things stande in the premisses, for I doubt things are not right. My sonne Edward hath endevoured to finde out the truth of these things, but beinge a stranger cannot finde it. Wherefore I pray employ somme knoweinge person and put the charge thereof to my account, which (God permittinge) shall bee honestly and thankefully repaid you. Pray lett mee heare from you concerning the premisses, soe soone as conveniently you may.

287. TO EDWARD BYRD

[*Marginated*] 6 May [1663]

Sent Edward Byrd £5, whereof £3 5s. 0d. for a quarters dyet to 20 April last; 23s. for 3 bookes, and 12s. for what else hee wanted.

Page 65

288. TO EDWARD BYRD

[*Headed*] 24 May 1663

Sent Edward Byrd by Mr Isaack Tomkins

[*Marginated*] 2s. 6d.

289. TO EVAN SEYS

[*Marginated*] Caerleon 9 June 1663

Cozen Seys

This morneinge your mare cast a stone horse coult, of a chesnutt couller, a black mane and a black tayle and a little white on his forehead. Mr Jones acquainted mee that Whittley hath declared against mee and conceaves it will comme to tryall the next assises, and if it cannot bee avoyded(1) I conceave the sooner, the better, whilest our witnesses are alyve.

1. 'if it cannot be avoyded' interlined.

290. TO LADY MARY MORGAN

[*Marginated*] Caerleon 19 June 1663

Right worshipful

Mr William Morgan of Pencreeke lately acquainted mee that you are to paie him 6s.8d. per annum for tythe on sores mills which hath not been paid about 7 yeares last past, for which hee intendeth to proceede against mee at the bishopps next court, which is to bee on Thursday comme 7 nights, unles hee shall receive satisfacion in the meane tyme, and if this bee due to him, I humbly pray that you will bee pleased to sende your order speedily eyther to Mr Barton or to my selfe to paie it; and if it bee not due, then I pray write mee direcions what you please to have mee to doe therein, or else I pray please to write to Mr Morgan himselfe to prevent the charge of a sute. Thus prayinge your answer hereto by the next post, I take leave for [the] present, and am

your ladyshipps most humble servant and tenant JB.

For the right worshipful the Lady Mary Morgan of Llanternam, at hir lodgeinge in Drury Lane these, London.

291. TO THOMAS PENNANT

[*Marginated*] Caerleon 22 June 1663

Brother Pennant

On the 28th April I sent Mr Philip Mansells receipt for 13s. 4d. received by him of my deputy at Chepstowe. I lately received yours of the 4th instant, in which is noe mencion of that receipt which makes mee doubt it is lost. I formerly delivered my accounts and vouchers to Mr Mansell by order of the commissioners to 29th September last, but my last quarters account with vouchers for my owne sallary and what I paid out of my purse, the farmers commaunded mee to sende up to themselves, which I did accordinglie, by troublinge you therewith, the which you delivered to Sir John Harryson, soe that if all things shall be justly weyghed (I haveinge performed my masters commaunds) I hope my accounts will bee cleared without further trouble. I am ashamed of the great trouble that you have beene pleased to undergoe in my busines, and I had rather give one halfe of what is due to mee then to make use of Mr Mansell at all, for hee hath dealt soe unworthely with mee, and with all persons formerly employed by mee, that I may not expect any kindenes from him at all. I leave it wholly to your discretion to make what ende you canne in the premises.

292. TO EDWARD BYRD

[*No date*]

Sonne Edward

Yours of the 3rd instant I received from Mr Tomkins by Arthur Jones, but broken open before I received it. Yours of the 16th instant I received by the post, in which you write for money to paie for washinge, which by yours and the searjeants letters you both write that your master is to finde you washinge for your whole tyme. You shall receive £4 by this bearer to paie for your quarters dyett, the overplus to helpe to furnish you with what shall bee most needefull; if you shall ryde your circuite with your master, bee sure to gett my cozen Richard Lucas, or somme one of the searjeants people to hyer a horse for you at Gloucester for that journey, for I cannott conveniently spare a horse from hence. Desier your master that wee may see him here in his circuite, and write mee one word of his mynde herein. If you cannot conveniently deliver the inclosed to my brother Pennant, then sende a knowne porter therewith that I may bee sure it is delivered. When you shall see my brother Pennant enquier whether hee received myne of the 28th April, with Mr Mansells receipt or not.

Sent this by John Waters, clerck to Mr James Jones.
[*Marginated*] £4.

Page 66

293. COMMISSIONERS FOR THE RELIEF OF INDIGENT OFFICERS TO JOHN BYRD

[17 June 1663]

Mr John Byrd

By the commissioners appointed by act of parliament for releife of the truely loyall and indigent commissioned officers, you are assessed for your office of comptroller of the customes at Monmoth, the summe of seaven pounds fower shillings, which you are to paie to John Cooper esquire, collector for Englande and Wales and towne of Berwick upon Tweed, or his deputy, whereof this is to give you notice this 17th daye of June 1663.
[*Marginated*] For Mr John Byrd at his house in Carleon bee these.
The collectors house in Pell Mell.
Francis Lovelace registrar.

The above written is the coppie of a noate which I received by the post from William Morgans postmaster in Caerleon the 23rd day of June 1663. I delivered the originall to Mr James Jones to endeavour to discharge mee from payment of the money, for that Richard Dutton hath the office of comptroller.

294. TO EDWARD BYRD AND THOMAS PENNANT

[*Marginated*] Caerleon 29 June 1663

Sent coppies of the noate above to Mr Thomas Pennant and Edward Byrd, desireinge theyr endeavours that I may bee cleared and the charge layde on him whoe hath the office. Sent this to Edward Byrd by Richard Davis and 5s.

295. NOTE OF A BOND

[*Marginated*] Monmoth

Hillary[(1)] [Term] 14 and 15 Charles II

John Byrd lately of Carlion in the said county of Monmouth gentleman and Susan Waters lately of Cophill in the said county widow, executrix of the will lately made by Edmund Waters of Cophill in the parish of Howick in the said county gentleman, by George Whittley esquire £40.

By an obligation made at Monmoth 30th October, 20 Charles I, 1644, under the following condition:

The condicion of this obligacion is such that if the above bounden John Byrd his heires or assignes shall and doe well and truely paie or cause to bee paide to the above named Roger Whittley his heires or assignes they or eyther of them demaundinge the same, by the tender of this bonde, the summe of £20 of lawfull

English money on the seconde day of February next ensuinge the date hereof without any delaye, that then this present obligacion to bee voyde or else to remayne in force.
Sworn by[2] Ratcliff Gerard, Ellis Edwards.
The like verbatim on Susanna Water and John Byrd the same daye the same summe and the same witnesses.
J B received them 25th June 1663 and sent them up to Mr James Jones and requested him to communicat this and all other my businesses to Mr Searjeant Seys.
Sent these to Mr James Jones by Mr Isaack Tomkins and sent Edward Byrd 2s. 6d.

1. 'Hillary......condition', Latin in MS.
2. 'Testes' in MS.

296. TO THOMAS PENNANT

[*Marginated*] Caerleon 7 July 1663

Brother Pennant

Yours of 30th June I received and according to the dyreccions therein I sende here enclosed copie of the severall orders by which I acted and with which you have beene formerly troubled. Here is allsoe a copie of my account current with Mr Mansell, all which I hope will bee satisfactory. I did not deliver any account to Mr Mansell for the last quarter to Christmas, but sent it up to the farmers with vouchers according to theyr enclosed dyreccions, which you delivered them accordinglie. Pray please to present my humble duty to my ould masters, whoe I am confident woulde not have displaced mee on any informacion of Mr Mansells, if they had knowne him soe well as they knewe mee.

297. MEMORANDUM

[*Marginated*] 19 July 1663

Sarah Edwards, the daughter of Mrs Mary Dryver, came to us from Bristoll and retourned thyther againe on the 23rd daye of September 1663.

Page 67

298. MEMORANDUM

[*Headed*] 6 July 1663

Mr James Jones, vicker of St Brides, came to Caerlion church portch where hee caused the institucion of Morgan Thomas clerck to bee read, and afterwards caused the bishopps order to bee reade by which the said Mr Jones was authorized to induct the saide Mr Morgan Thomas to the vicaredge of Caerlion, which hee did this day accordingly in the presence of Hugh Powell clerck, John Byrd, Jeffrey Price (then churchwarden), William Merredith, William Byrd, Richard James and others. [(1)]

1. 'et alii' in MS.

299. TO THOMAS PENNANT

[*Marginated*] Caerleon 10 August 1663

Brother Pennant

Yours of 23rd July I received, and according to dyreccions I wrote to Mr Mansell desireinge that hee would sende up the vouchers which are wantinge, or else that hee woulde be pleased to sende them to mee, that I might sende them up to the accomptant, but I heard not one word from him, and whether hee hath sent them up or not I cannott tell; and for the £2 5s. 3d. to ballance my accounts to Michaelmas 1662 I delivered my receipt to Mr Philip Mansell for 50s. due to mee as comptroller in the quarter to Michaelmas 1662, the which hee hath not charged himselfe with, as it appears by the account which you sent mee, by which you may perceave what justice I may expect from him; soe that I desier the £2 5s. 3d. may bee deducted out of the £7 14s. 1d. due to mee for the ballance of my account in the quarter ended at Christmas 1662; and if I cannott procure my 50s. hereafter then I must loose it.

As for the £7 4s. 0d. which I am to paie Mr Cooper I shall according to your freindly advice sende it up by the first opportunety unto you, to bee paid to Mr Cooper. I doubt I shall not have an opportunety to sende up this money till towards Michaelmas terme, and if you conceave I may bee prejudiced by not sendinge it up sooner I pray a word of advice therein, and I will sende it up by an expresse, wherein I shall request your love to paie it, that I may bee sure of my discharge for it. Thus.

300. TO THOMAS PENNANT

[*Marginated*] Caerleon 27 August 1663

Brother Pennant

Underwritten is the coppie of a bill of exchange for £7 4s. 0d. which I hope will bee paid to you before this commes to your hands; if not I pray bee soe loveinge as to sende your clerck for it, and soe soone as may bee to paie it to Mr Cooper the collector in Pell Mell, and I pray sende mee his receipt for this £7 4s. 0d. soe soone as may bee for I understande that a messenger is to comme for it, and if hee commeth before I have a receipt for it beinge imposed on the office of comptroller I shall bee dampnified. Wherefore good brother (according to your woonted love) assiste mee herein. If my accounts at the custome house cannot be cleared without the vouchers which are wantinge, then I must procure newe ones from the severall parties to whome I paide the moneyes; or else I shall take my oath that I paid the severall summes expressed in my accounts.

301. [COPY OF A BILL OF EXCHANGE] WALTER HARRIS TO JOHN BETTLEY

[*Marginated*] Gloucester 23 August 1663

Brother

I pray paie to the bearer Mr Thomas Pennant or his assigne the summe of £7 4s. 0d. on sight of this my bill, for soe much I have received here and the retorne of it, of Matthias Byrd, I pray faile not, and place it to the account of your brother Walter Harris.

This for Mr John Bettley haberdasher at the Blewe Bore and Mayden Head, nere Fleete bridge, London.

302. TO JOHN TANNER

[*Marginated*] Caerleon 31 August 1663

Mr Tanner

I formerly received vouchers for salaryes which I paid to you and others which at present are not to bee founde, for want whereof my accounts above cannott bee cleared. I want 2 from you, which are for the 2 quarters to Christmas 1661. Good sir bee soe loveinge as to sende mee 2 more, for Michaelmas and Christmas quarters 1661, soe soone as may bee according to the forme under written. Good sir, faile not herein. Your JB.

Sent this by the post.

303. TO JOHN TANNER

8 September [1663]

Wrote againe to Mr Tanner and sent it by Alexander, Searjeant Seys his servant.

Page 68

304. TO THOMAS PENNANT

[*Marginated*] Caerleon 15 September 1663

Brother Pennant

Yours of the 3rd instant with a receipt for £7 4s. 0d. there enclosed I received, for which etc. And according to your freindly advice I procured newe vouchers from the parties to whome I paid the sallaryes therein expressed, which I sende you herein enclosed, and doe hope that my account will bee nowe cleared without any farther trouble. I regayned these vouchers by accident; for William Williams was beyond sea, and arryved at Newport about a weeke before I received your last, and Mr John Tanner was very sick in bed, and I doubt is dead nowe. I formerly gave my receipt to Mr Philip Mansell for 50s. due to mee as comptroller in the quarter to 29 September 1662; for my successor Dutton, nor any person for him, did appear neyther in the port of Cardiff, nor any member thereof till 8th October 1662 to which daye the service was performed by mee and my deputies in Cardiff, and all the members thereof.

Good brother, £7 14s. 1d. is due to mee from the farmers beinge the ballance of my account in the quarter to Christmas 1662, as by the account and vouchers which I long since troubled you with appeareth. I desier your loving endeavour to procure it, and if you canne receave that money I pray gratifie those whoe shall assiste you therein, as you see fitt, and out of it I pray deliver 40s. to fr[iends] to dispose thereof according to former order.

305. TO THOMAS PENNANT

[*Marginated*] Caerleon 13 October 1663

Brother Pennant

Yours with the receipt for £7 4s. 0d. I longe since received and wrote you an account thereof on the 15th September last, in which I enclosed newe vouchers in lieu of those which were wantinge which letter I kept, expecting that Mr Smythies and my sonne Edward would comme this waye toward London, but they come not, soe that I sent it by Mr Roger Rogers, clarke to my cozen Mr Searjeant Seys, whoe promised to deliver it to your owne hands. I durst not send it by the post least it shoulde bee lost, and noe hope to procure vouchers againe.

Mr Thomas de la Vale (surveigher generall for the customes) was lately here, and promised to assiste you in the cleareinge of my account. Hee intended to bee in London about the next weeke. I pray enquier for him at the custome house, whoe I am confident will doe what shall lye in his power herein. Pray present my humble duty to my maisters, the farmers; my service and due respects to Mr de la Vale, Mr Whittell, Mr Parsons, Mr Sankey and the accountant generall and all our other loving freinds at custom house, in particular to Mr William Thornebury, and my account beinge cleared I pray bestowe a collacion on them, which with our faithfull love to you and all yours presented is all at present from JB.

306. TO THOMAS PENNANT

[*Marginated*] 19 [October 1663]

Wrote to brother Pennant and enclosed a letter from Mr Henry Bassett register to Mr William Cooke, deputy collector for the indigent officers at Pell Mell, by whome I sent 5s. to brother Pennant to drinke a cupp of wyne together with theyr wyves.

307. TO EVAN SEYS

[*Marginated*] Caerleon 6 November 1663

Cozen Seys

Here is a report that I am in the list for sheriffe of Monmothsheire, which with the unhappie death of our Nedd very much troubleth us. I beeseech you to use your best endeavour to gett mee of from that office and what charge you shall bee at therein (with your former disbursements) shall be repaid with harty thankes. I hope that (in regard Nedd served Mr Smythies at my charge, and the charge which I have beene at in my seekeinge to save his life) Mr Smythies will repaie the £20 which you paide him. I pray opportunely to speake with him, and conclude howe you thinke fitt concerning the agreement you made with him concerninge our sonne Nedd; if the party which did committ the fact on Nedd bee not in hande wee desier to knowe his name, his quallety and place of aboade, which I pray if you knowe it, to sende by the first post with one word of advice herein, to JB.

308. TO THOMAS PENNANT

[*Marginated*] Caerleon 20 November 1663

Brother Pennant

Yours of the last of October I received, by which I perceave Mr Whittells brother conceaves that my accounts are involved in Mr Manselles, and that withoutt him my accounts coulde not be cleared, which I conceave is a mistake, for the ports within my collecion were distinct from his, and by the farmers commande I sent up my last quarters account and vouchers to themselves, which were delivered by you accordingly. I received a letter from Mr Samuel Whittell this weeke, by which I finde Mr Mansell hath lost the collecion. I pray present my love and service to Mr Samuel Whittell who I desier to assist you to cleare my accounts. Mr Thomas de la Vale (surveigher generall) promised to assiste you herein, soe that I hope beetwene all you my loving freinds my account will bee cleared without Mr Mansell.

I pray present my humble duty and service to my oulde masters the farmers and please to acquainte them of that truth concerning my account, and I am confident they will order my account to bee cleared according to the vouchers which I have sent up. My successor Dutton is nowe in London, who I suppose received from Mansell 50s. which was due to mee as comptroller in the quarter to 29th September 1662, for that neyther hee nor any person for him did appear in that service till October 1662. Wherefore I pray get that 50s. allowed in my account in the quarter to 29th September 62. I sent 5s. by Mr Cooke and the like by Mr James Jones to drinke a glasse of wyne with them. Pray deliver brother William 40s. on my account.

Page 69

309. TO RICHARD LUCAS

[*Marginated*] 4 December 1663

Cozen Richard Lucas

My sonne Matth[ias] borrowed £5 of Mr John Turner inkeeper in Farringdon (where my poore Ned had his death), for which hee gave his bill. Mr Turner hath ordered it to bee paid to Mr John Cornewell, carryer for Gloucester. Nowe my request is that you will doe mee the favour as to receive £5 which I sende by this bearer, Mr Henry Dobbins, and paie it to Mr Cornewell, or to sende it to Mr John Turner and take up Matthias his bill. Pray present my wife['s] faithfull love and myne to the searjent and all his, and wee pray you to write us word by the first post when the searjeant intendeth to comme this way. Good sir, doe this curtesy for JB.

310. TO THOMAS PENNANT

[*Marginated*] Caerleon 29 December 1663

Yours by my neighbour Mr James Jones I received, by which I finde that I am like to loose my money due to mee at the custom house, which is contrary to the wonted justice of the farmers, and I hope that when they shall bee made acquainted therewith I shall not loose it. You write that you finde Mr Whittell to bee my reall freinde, which if hee bee, I pray present my love and service to him and endeavour to gett from him coppies of the informacion which was preferred against mee and the reference to the commissioners and of theyr report therein concerning the office of comptroller, for I am advized to endeavour to recover the office back, to which purpose (if God permitt) I intende to give you a visitt before I dye.

On Saturne day last I sent a dish of fowle (which were scarcer here at this tyme then in any winter since I came to Wales) in a pye, and in a boxe nayled and mayled up, and dyrected unto you, which one Robert(1) Longe the carryer of Monmoth promised my messenger to deliver unto you in London this weeke, whose lodgeinge I conceave is at the signe of St Pauls head in Carter Lane. I sent money by my messenger to pay for carriadge of the pye up, and wrote in my letter to you that the carryer was paid, but my messenger was soe simple that because hee could not have it carryed for 1d. per lb. brought back my money with a note from the carryer that he would have 8s. for carryadge thereof. Good brother, please to sende your servant to the carryer of Monmoth for this pye, and laye out this 8s. for mee for carryadge thereof, for uppon my creditt I doe not intende that you shall paye for the pye, beinge a smale token of love which I sende to you and my sister to bee merry with. The pye weigheth 65 lbs. I pray write one word in answer to the premises to JB.

1. 'Robert' interlined.

311. TO THOMAS PENNANT

[*Marginated*] 8 January 1664

Brother Pennant

The same as above, with this added (namely) and please to acquainte Mr Whittell that I beinge in Glamorgansheire yesterday did understande that Mr Philip Mansell had soulde his office of searcher. I conceave Mr Whittell will doe well to acquainte the farmers therewith.

312. MEMORANDUM

[*Marginated*] 16 November 1663

Mary and Richard Barnes came to Caerlion. Richard went away about 7th December 1663, and Mary went away the 5th of January 1664. I sent Giles Philipp of Caerlion to Oxonforde with hir.

The charge of the pye abovesaid

Imprimis flower	00 - 02 - 00
cloaves and mace	00 - 01 - 00
a turkey	00 - 02 - 06
2 ducks and 2 snipes	00 - 01 - 06
17 wood cocks	00 - 06 - 02
15 lbs. of butter	00 - 05 - 00
paid the cooke	00 - 03 - 06
for carryadge to Monmoth	00 - 03 - 00
for carryadge from thence to London	00 - 08 - 00
for a boxe to put the pye in	00 - 02 - 00
for a cord to mayle it	00 - 00 - 04
	01 - 15 - 00

Page 70

313. ACCOUNT

[*1 February 1664*]

Account current betweene Thomas Morgan of Penrose esquire and Mr Thomas Shewell of Bristoll wollendraper 1 February 1664

Mr Thomas Shewell debitor

1 February 1664

Imprimis by bonde beinge for merchandize which hee soulde in Bristoll for Thomas Morgan juniour	76 - 10 - 00
Item by charge of a suite at lawe for this money	04 - 07 - 00
Item by charge in goeinge severall tymes to Bristoll for this money	06 - 00 - 00
	86 - 17 - 00

Mr Thomas Shewell creditor

1 February 1664

Imprimis by money sent to cleare the bonde etc	77 - 10 - 00
Item by money delivered Mr Thomas Morgan juniour since sealeinge the bond abovesaid	01 - 00 - 00
Item by money to ballance this account	08 - 07 - 00
	86 - 17 - 00

314. TO THOMAS SHEWELL

[*Subscribed*] Caerleon 2 February 1664

Brother Shewell

On Sunday last Mr Mayor of Newport came hyther according to promise to meete Mr Thomas Morgan, and wee agreed with him concerning your busines, and yesterday I delivered him your money due by bonde, and I paid £4 7s. 0d. charge of the suite, and Mr Mayor and I gave our bills to paie him £3 per piece, beinge in all £6 towards the charge which hee and his sonne were put unto, in goeinge[1] to Bristoll for this money. Wee got tyme till 25th March for payment of this £6, hopeinge that in the meane tyme you may gett it remitted, which if you coulde speake with him yourselfe, I hope it will bee donne. Here enclosed is your bonde, the 2 letters, the bill of ladeinge and the account of the charge. Please to write one word of receipt hereof to JB.

1. 'inge' interlined.

315. MEMORANDUM

[*Headed*] 1 October 1663 'beinge Thurseday'

[*Marginated*] Edward Byrd slayne

Edward Byrd was wounded at Farringdon in the county of Berks. (beinge at the house of Mr John Turner inkeeper at the signe of the Crowne) by one Humphry Davis, of which wounds hee dyed the 14th of October 1663 for which the said Davis was indited for manslaughter at the assizes helde at Reddinge for the county of Berks. on the 25th of February 1664 by the name of Humphry Davis late of Farringdon aforesaid.

The witnesses of this unhappy fact were Mr Thomas Lloyd whoe was in the chamber when it was donne, John Turner chamberlayne and Robert West tapster in the Crowne aforesaid.

Richard Worthen constable whoe had this Davis in custody and then beinge conceaved that the wounde was not dangerous, was let goe and hath not beene founde since. Mr John Hobbs was the coronner whoe examined this fact, Sir Robert Pye justice in whose buryinge place in the church of Farringdon Edward Byrd was buryed.

316. TO THOMAS SHEWELL

[*Marginated*] Caerleon 31 May 1664

Brother Shewell

Yours of the 17th instant with Mr Thrustons I received and presented the same to Mr Morgan according to your desier, whose answer is that you should not loose any thinge by his sonne, whose comminge home hee expecteth dayly. I conceave you will doe well to lett Mr Thrustons letter remayne with mee till Mr Charles Morgans comminge home, that thereby hee may give his father a perfect account, that soe your money may bee paid you without any further trouble, which is the desier of JB.

Page 71

317. TO JOHN WHITTLE

[*Marginated*] Caerleon 30 June 1664

Mr John Whittle

By the enclosed you will perceave that I spake with Mr Eyvis according to my promise. Hee acquainted mee that Mr William Willett of Bristoll promised to bee here this weeke and had order to discharge him from his first bonde concerning his shipp, which beinge donne, hee is to have your bonde up, which will spare further trouble as to counter securety. Pray present my humble duty and service to my oulde masters the farmers, my due respects to your good brother, with Mr Lancelott, Mr Cooke, and Mr Mountney, not omittinge my faithfull respects to your selfe, and I thanke you hartily for the love which I received from you all, and if I may doe any service for you or eyther of them, pray freely commaunde him that is sir, your JB.

318. TO THOMAS SHEWELL

[*Marginated*] Caerleon 4 July 1664

Brother Shewell

I shewed Mr James Thrustons letter (which is here enclosed) to Mr Charles Morgan whoe sayth that for what moneyes hee received of Mr Thruston on account, hee gave him a bill of exchange which his father hath made good to Mr David Arthur, and if you conceave other wayes. Mr Charles Morgan promiseth to comme to Bristoll to give you further satisfacion herein by the particulars of his account with Mr Thruston, and indeede I finde him very ready to doe you all the right which lyeth in his power.

319. TO COLONEL THOMAS STRADLING

[*Marginated*] Caerleon 10 July 1664

Honoured Colonel

The just answer which you were pleased to write to a paper which Captain Price sent unto you (whereof the enclosed is a coppie) embouldeneth mee to pray that you will bee soe loveinge as to write soe much under the enclosed, and please to subscribe it with your name and I pray sende it to mee by the first post, wherewith you will doe an act of justice to JB.

To the honourable colonel Thomas Stradlinge these St Donetts.

In the paper above written was a coppie of a false certificate which Major Richard Dutton presented to the Kinge against JB.

320. TO HERBERT SPRINGNETT

[*Marginated*] Caerleon 10 July 1664

Cozen Herbert Springnett

Yours of the 16th and 19th July, with those to your wife I received, and delivered them, and went with hir to Mr James Jones, whoe sayth that an order was graunted for an allowance towards mayntenance of your brother, which is referred to one of the masters in Chancery to consider what is fitt to bee allowed and to make his report therein the next terme, but this not tendinge to your present liberty, I conferred with the mayor, whoe sayth that by the decree hee is to have the custody of your brother which if delivered to him, hee will accept of the bond of £10 in parte of the £14 odd money, which is likewise ordered him by the said decree; and for the rest hee promiseth to referre it to mee or to any other reasonable person. I acquainted your wife and Mr James Jones therewith, whoe saye that your brother will not goe to the mayor, and your wife sayth that shee knoweth not where your brother is; and if the mayor's expectation abovesaid will bee performed, hee promiseth to take order for your present liberty, which is earnestly desired by JB.

321. TO JOHN MANSELL

[*Marginated*] Caerleon 1 September 1664

Mr John Man[sell] collector at Swansey

Yours of the 23rd August I received last night, and according to your desier, the above written are the formes which I used in makeinge up my accounts, and if you want anythinge else which you conceave I cann assiste you in for the furtherance of his majesty's service or the farmers, then bee pleased when you ryde this way to visitt the ports to call on mee, and you shall have any assistance that is in the power of J B. When you write up, I pray present my love and service to both Mr Whittles and allsoe to Mr Launcelott the accountant generall. JB.

322. TO MATTHIAS BYRD

[*Marginated*] Caerleon 5 September 1664

Sonne Matthias

On Fridaye last your chest trunke and hatt in the leather case were delivered to George James a carryer in Bristoll whoe was paid there for carryadge up. All those things were dyrected to bee left with William Jones porter, at the signe of the 3 Cupps in Bread Streete, to bee kept till you call for them. Present my due respects to your captain and lett us heare from you often.

Page 72

323. TO MATTHIAS BYRD

[*Headed*] Caerleon 12 September 1664

Wrote by John Lawrence, Captain Wood's servant, to Matthias Byrd that I received the captain's letter dated 31st August, and Matthias's letter dated 7th instant, both desireinge to sende the captain a peece of flannen which wee intende to sende to Abergavenny faire for on Wednesday next, beinge the 14th instant, which shall (if it may bee had) bee sent to William Jones porter at the signe of the 3 Cupps in Bread Streete London soe soone as may bee.

324. TO MATTHIAS BYRD

[*Marginated*] Caerleon 15 September 1664

Sonne Matthias

This daye I sent by way of Bristoll a peece of flannen, the best that coulde be had yesterdaye in Abergavenny faier. It cost here 15½d. per ell, beinge 36 ells and 13d. I sent with it to pay for carryadge from Bristoll up; it is dyrected (as your former things were) to be left with Mr William Jones the porter at the signe of the 3 Cupps in Bread Streete London till you call for it. You will doe well to bestowe it on your captain, whoe I finde is your very good freinde, for thankefullnes and humillity are the only meanes to gaine love and preferment, and the contrary to them doe produce contrary effects. I desier to heare that you receive all things sent you. Present your mothers true love and myne to your captain. Wee trust that the Lord will blesse the whole fleete and make the voyadge prosperous for which shall be the prayers of your father JB.

325. TO GEORGE GWYN

[*Marginated*] Caerleon 9 November 1664

Honoured sir

I understande by our loving freinde Mr George Morgan that you expect that I shoulde paie the arreares due from William James for the house and garden which hee holds by lease graunted by Mr Christopher Morgan and Elizabeth his wife. I humbly conceave that you never intended that I shoulde paie the rent for what William James helde unles I coulde gett it from him, but hee was soe poore that hee coulde not paie it, neyther woulde hee parte from his interest untill the 19th daye of October last, on which daye hee did surrender his interest to Mr George Morgan for your use, and if you will bee pleased that I may enjoy it according to your graunte and warrant, I shall hereafter paie the rent accordinglie, or if you bee pleased to take William James his house and appurtenances into your owne hands, I shall willingly submitt to your pleasure therein, and shall paie you 6s. 8d. yearely for the garden plott which I houlde from you according to our reall intencion when hee first agreed. I humbly desier one word of your pleasure herein, and that you will bee pleased to give your bayleife order to receive your rent from mee for what I houlde, which shall bee paid on demaunde by JB.

For his worthy freinde and landelord George Gwynn esquire these, Llanelwith.

326. TO THOMAS PENNANT

[*Marginated*] Caerleon 30 December 1664

Brother Pennant

Yours of the 26th November last(1) with my brother Williams enclosed I received. Sir I have spoken with Colonel Thomas Stradlinge, Mr Robert Thomas and Major-generall Laugharne, whose 3 names are to the certificate which Major Dutton presented to the kinge against mee, all which persons doe affirme that they never subscribed nor knewe of any certifficatt against mee; and Colonel Stradlinge (a person of much honour) hath given it mee(2) under his hande accordingly. Mr Thomas and Mr Laugharne have likewise promised to vindicat themselves and mee herein, soe that every particular in Duttons peticion and certificate are false, by which my great wronge is apparent, and som freinds do advize mee to endeavour to bee restored to my employment.

Pray remember my love to my brother William and desier him to gett Mr Plummer to acquainte Sir Philip Warwick herewith, and humbly pray his advice herein; and if you finde any hope of justice to bee donne mee herein, then (on notice thereof) God willinge I will comme up and waite on it myselfe; and if Sir Philip will bee pleased to dyrect mee herein, I shall not bee ungratefull. I pray furnish my brother William with what my bee convenient to waite on this busines, and what money you shall furnish him herein, on notice from you howe much it shall bee, I will sende it up by the first opportunety. I heare that Dutton intends to sell the comptrollershipp, by which men may judge howe unjustly hee got it. Pray write by the first post of receipt hereof.

1. 'of the 26th November last' interlined.

2. 'it mee' interlined.

327. TO EVAN SEYS

[*No date*]

Wrote to my cozen Mr Evan Seys searjeant at lawe the contents of the letter to my brother Pennant and prayd him to speake with Sir Philip Warwick and desier his advice in the premises.

328. TO EVAN SEYS

[*Marginated*] 13 January 1665

Wrote againe to searjent Seys the contents of the letter abovesaid.

Page 73

329. COPY OF CERTIFICATE

[*No date*]

[*Marginated*] Monmothshire

Right honourable

Upon the viewe of a peticion presented to his majesty against John Byrd within named, that hee contrary to his alleageance did promote in this country a peticion for the execrable murder of his late sacred majesty kinge Charles the first, of ever blessed memory, wee further certify that to the utmost and best of our informacion there was noe such peticion attempted(1) publiquely here, and if there were any, wee are confident hee was a person of another temper then to subscribe any such hydeous paper.

Sir George Probert of Penalt, Sir Trevor Williams of Llanguby, Edmond Morgan of Newport esquire, John Clegg doctor of devinity, Roger Williams of Kevan Hylith esquire, Charles Hughes of Trostre esquire, Charles Van of Coldre esquire, William Morgan of Tredegar esquire, Thomas Morgan of Penrose esquire

The tytles nor places of aboade of the persons abovesaid are not in the oryniginall certificate.

1. 'attempted' interlined.

330. TO THOMAS PENNANT

[*Marginated*] Caerleon 7 March 1665

Brother Pennant

Pray acquainte my brother William that I received his by Mr James Jones etc and what hee hath promised Mr Turner shall bee perfomed if I shall bee restored , and I shall gratify whomesoever shall asiste my brother in my busines as Mr Turner shall advize. Good brother bee soe loveinge as to afforde my brother William your advice and assistance herein, and whether I shall bee restored or not (God permittinge) you shall not lose by mee. I beeleeve my peticion must bee presented to his majesty and if £5 or £10 bee requiset more then I left with my brother for proceedinge herein; good brother doe mee the creditt to supply it if you finde hope of restauracion, and what you shall disburse for mee shall bee honestly repaid with harty thanks.

It is beeleved here(1) that Dutton was in London when I was there, and is not retorned as yet, and if my brother William shall not have sent the act for the assessment before this shall comme to your hands, pray desier him to sende it by the carryer to Bristoll, dyrected to be left with Mr Michael Deyos at his house on the back in Bristoll whoe will conveigh it to mee.

1. 'here' interlined.

331. TO THOMAS PENNANT

[*Marginated*] Caerleon 17 March 1665

Brother Pennant

On the 7th instant I wrote to desier your love to advise and assiste my brother in my busines, since which tyme I understande that Dutton is retorned from London to Swansey. Nowe my request is that you will advize and assiste my brother to have the coppie of Duttons proceedings against mee fairely written and attested by Sir Philip Warwick (if his hande may bee procured) and his clarcks, and allsoe Mr Samuel Whittells hande, that the coppie of his proceedings against mee, which was had at the lord treasurers, is a true coppie; for I doubt that Dutton will deny the unjust wayes hee used to out mee; and if it bee possible to procure the originall certifficatt and Duttons peticion against mee, (which I conceave is at the lord treasurers) I desier you and my brother William to endeavour it, but if neyther the coppie attested nor the originalls may bee had for love nor money, then I desier that my peticion may not bee presented to his majesty till I bee further advized. If my brother William canne procure any good to bee donne mee by the lord treasurer or Sir Philip I desier his endeavour with them, all which I leave to your loving advice and discretion. I pray a word from you or my brother William of receipt of this, and my last, by the first post which etc.

332. TO MATTHIAS BYRD

[*Marginated*] Caerleon 24 March 1665

Sonne Matthias

Yours of the 24th February and 13th instant I received but not yours of the 10th instant. You shall receive here enclosed Mr Creedes letter which you desired. I did reade it before sealed, it beinge very authenticall for your purpose. Present my love and service to your captain, and procure his letter to bee presented with the enclosed for that he knoweth your abillityes and I hope both will doe you good. Mr Creede desiers to heare from his brother, and desiers if hee please to write that you woulde enclose it in yours to mee for him.

333. TO BROTHER WILLIAM BYRD

[*Marginated*] 24 March [1665]

Brother William

Yours of the 2nd and 26th instant I received. On the 17th instant I wrote to brother Pennant as in my last to him etc, only I added that my brother William woulde gett Mr Rowes proceedings, and that when I shoulde bee thus armed (before wee proceede any farther) I woulde take advice thereuppon etc.

Sent the 2 last letters enclosed to my brother Pennant, prayinge his advice and assistance with my brother William therein.

Page 74

334. TO THOMAS PENNANT

[*Marginated*] Caerleon 2 May 1665

Brother Pennant

You shall receive by this bearer Mr Isaack Tomkins 10s. parte to cleare your disbursements for mee, and the remainder to drynke a glasse of wyne with my sister and brother William whoe I desier to procure coppies of Mr Rowes bill and his adversaryes answer thereto.

My brother Pennant received the 10s. and the coppies were sent as desired to mee JB.

335. TO EDMUND THURLOWE

[*No date*]

Dyrect letters to bee left with Mr John Scurluck in Caermarthen mercer to bee sent to Mr Edmond Thurlowe dwellinge in Laugharne.

336. TO MATTHIAS BYRD

[*Marginated*] 27 June 1665

Wrote to Matthias that I received his of the 22nd May and 12th June but not his of the 10th June.

337. TO THOMAS PENNANT

[*Marginated*] 23 November 1665

Brother Pennant

Yours of the 16th instant I received etc. My sonne Matthias sayth that Mr Ellis was (with severall other persons) lost at Shettlande or the north of Scotlande about July last.

338. TO THOMAS PENNANT

[*Marginated*] 2 January 1666

Brother Pennant

I formerly gave you an account that I received yours of the 16th November last since which tyme I heard not one word from you, neyther did I receave one word from my brother William since his of the 5th August, yet wee trust in the Lord that you are all in good health. Wee shoulde bee very glad to receive a word from you and another from my brother William in writeinge. I pray remember mee to my brother William and cause him to write (if hee may with safety from infeccion) by the first post after this shall comme to your hands, and to enclose a bill of mortallety. The post commes through our towne constantly, by whome wee have the dyurnalls twice every weeke, but not a bill of mortallety. My brother William hath disbursed some money for mee, and in my last I requested you to supply him with 30 or 40s. on my creditt, which if it bee not donne I pray doe mee the kindnes to furnish him and God permittinge I will repaye you by the first opportunety.

339. TO MATTHIAS BYRD

[*Subscribed*] Caerleon 2 August 1666

Sonne Matthias

Yours of the 16th April and 27th of May I longe sence received, and wrote you an account thereof by my letter which was delivered in Wappinge according to your order, since which tyme I received yours of the 8th of June, and this daye I received yours of the 8th of June, and this daye I received yours of the 17th of June. Our freinds and neighbours doe generally rejoyce at your wellfare, and doe pray for the good successe of our navy. I desired you in my last to make use of my antient freinde Mr Thomas Pennant, from whome I shall bee sure to heare from you by the first post. My cozen William Seys is marryed to Elizabeth Jenkins, and are settled in his house at the Gare. Your mother and brothers are in health and desier to heare from you as often as conveniently you may; soe doth JB.

For his loving sonne Matthias Byrd aboard his majesty's shipp Henrietta. Leave this with Mr Richard Grassingam dwellinge neare Sir William Warrens house in Wappinge, whoe is desired to conveigh it according to its dyrecions.

Sent this to Mr Thomas Pennant, and desired him to gett my brother William Byrd to deliver it at Wappinge and to enquier howe Matthias doeth, and what employment hee hath, and to write us an account thereof by the first post.

340. TO BROTHER WILLIAM BYRD

[*Marginated*] 14 September 1666

Wrote to my brother William to comme downe etc., and that I received his letter of the 11th instant.

341. TO BROTHER WILLIAM BYRD

[*Marginated*] 17 September [1666]

Wrote againe to W B to comme downe, and in both these letters to acquainte my brother Pennant that if it might bee convenient I hartily wish that hee with his family were heare, whear I woulde furnish him with a house and what necessaryes I coulde, for which hee shoulde not paye any thinge, and I desired my brother William to write (as at my request) to Mr John Williams chaplyn and to Matthias Byrd aboard the shipp Henrietta, desireing that they would write to us by all opportunetyes that wee might knowe howe they doe etc.

342. TO BROTHER WILLIAM BYRD

[*Marginated*] 23 September 1666

Wrote againe to W B to the same purpose as is above written.

Page 75

343. TO LEYSHON SEYS

[*Marginated*] Caerleon 4 October 1666

Cozen Seys

My worthy freinde, Mr William Jones of Lanarth, acquainted mee that his unkle (Mr John Morgans[)] stock at Kil lan was distrayned on, for none payment of rent due to your brother, my cozen William Seys. Esquire Jones oblieged mee to write to your brother William (if hee were in your(1) partes) or unto you in his absence, desireinge that what hath beene distrayned on may bee kept and not disposed of for one month or thereabouts, in which tyme Mr John Morgan promiseth to make your brother William full satisfaccion. In pursuance of esquire Jones his request, I earnestly request your brother (if hee bee in your partes) to graunte what is herein desired, and if your brother bee not in your parts, then I request you to procure your brothers agent to preserve Mr Morgan's stock (which was distreyned on) for one moneth and not to sell, or dispose thereof in that tyme. Good sir, please to write mee one word by the first post, that you have received this my letter, and what hopes of grauntinge what is above desired(2), that I may give esquire Jones an account thereof accordingly. I depende on you to doe your best herein for Mr Morgan.

My cozen William Seys answered this on the 9th October, which letter I sent to Mr William Jones.

To Mr Lyson Seys these Swansey.

1. 'your' interlined above 'these', deleted.
2. 'what is above desired' interlined.

344. TO EVAN SEYS

[*Marginated*] Caerleon 9 October 1666

Wrote to Searjeant Seys to put him in minde of our sheriffe.

345. TO MATTHIAS BYRD

[*Marginated*] 29 October [1666]

Wrote to Matthias that I received his by way of Bristol, dated 8th instant, which was all synce 17 June last. I desired him to write where I may sende letters to bee conveighed to him.

Sent this with Charles, servant to Thomas Morgan of Penrose esquire.

346. TO MATTHIAS BYRD

[*Marginated*] 5 November 1666

Wrote againe to Matthias by my cozen Mr William Williams.

347. WILLIAM JONES TO JOHN BYRD

[*No date*]

Mr Bird

I thanke you for your kindnes in writeinge to your kinsman in the behalfe of my unkle whoe doth informe mee that hee hath satisfied Mr Seys of the 1st yeare rent to a farthinge, and what hee is in Mr Seys debt hee sayth that suddenly hee will satisfy him to a farthinge, provided he doth not put him to unnecessary charge in the lawe, which if hee doth hee must bee forced to doe the like. It is his further desier that Mr Seys woulde bee soe kinde to him as to keepe the boxes which hee speakes of in his letter in his custody, for there are somme things in them of a great concernement to him, untill further order. Sir to my knowledge hee will bee suddenly in a condicion to pay all persons where hee is indebted unto, therefore lett mee intreate you to write unto your kinseman to desier him to stopp any further proceedinge against him for somme tyme and assure him that I will bee uppon his back to satisfy him the 1st that shall bee satisfied, and in soe doeinge you will further oblieg him whoe is your loving freinde, William Jones.

348. TO LEYSHON SEYS

[*Marginated*] Caerleon 1 November 1666

Cozen Lyson Seys

If your brother my cozen William bee in your partes, I pray shewe him this letter. The above written is a coppie of esquire Jones of Lanarths letter to mee; my earnest request is that your brother will bee soe lovinge as to graunte what is above desired, and if your brother bee not in your partes, then I desier you to use your endeavour that the boxes may bee kept safe, and that noe proceedinge may bee against Mr Morgan. I pray a word of receipt hereof by the 1st post that I may give an account hereof to my goode freinde Mr Jones accordingly. Thus etc.

349. TO MATTHIAS BYRD

[*Marginated*] 9 November 1666

Sonne Matthias

Somme person wrote a letter in your name to Mr James Jones dated 30th October which I received from him this daye. It intymateth that you had not received any pay, that you were above a moneth sick in Rochester, and that you want money. In June you wrote that you had received pay and 3rd October that you were in good health and I hope you are soe still. If not, his majestys care was that provision shoulde bee in all his ports for all persons sicke or wounded in his service, by which meanes I conceave you cannot want. Dyrect your letter to Mr Roger Rogers the searjeants clercke nowe in London, whoe will sende them unto mee. Lett us heare from you in what condicion you are and where I may dyrect letters in London, that you may bee sure to have them.

Page 76

350. TO MATTHIAS BYRD

[*Marginated*] Caerleon 13 November 1666

Sonne Matthias

You formerly wrote that you were to receive somme pay and on the 8th October last you wrote that you were in good health and I hope you are soe still, but noe other letter have I received since 17th June last, but on the 9th instant I received a letter which was written in your name to Mr James Jones dated 30th October last, which intymateth that you had not received any pay, that you were above a month sick in Colchester, and that you want money. The letter written to Mr James Jones and not one word of your writeinge makes mee doubt the truth thereof, wherefore I desier you to write mee the truth of your condicion, and dyrect your letters to your unkle Mr Searjeant Seys at his chamber in Searjeants Inn in Chancery Lane, from whome I shall bee sure to have them. This day (before concludeinge this letter) I received yours of the 8th instant, by which I finde that the letter to Mr Jones abovesaid was not right, yet it was sealed with your seale.

Your mother, with all our freinds and neighbours here doe rejoyce to heare of your recovery and wee all desier the contynnuance of your health and wellfare. This is the 4th letter which I have sent to you within this 16 dayes. My coresponds in London have beene unhappily fired from thence, soe that when the searjeant shall leave the citty (which I conceave will not bee dueringe the sittinge of the Parliament) I knowe not to whom I may dyrect letters that you may be sure to have them, wherefore I desier (if you have any freinde in London) that you will write to whome I may sende letters that you may bee sure of them. Thus.

351. TO EVAN SEYS

[*No date*]

Cozen Seys

Yours of the 13th November and 3rd instant I received for which and all other favours I humbly and hartily thanke you. My coresponds whoe dwelt in London beinge unhappily fired from thence forceth mee to begg the favour of you to reade and seale the enclosed and cause it to bee delivered at the post house. Pray pardon this my bouldenes.

352. TO THOMAS PENNANT

[*Marginated*] Caerleon 17 November 1666

Brother Pennant

According to your dyeccions in your last letter to mee I herewith sende by my neighbour Mr Isaack Tomkins to bee left at the Rolls the 30s by you disbursed and 2s. 6d. to drinke a glasse of sack with my sister. Sir I understande that my sonne Matthias lyeth sick at the signe of of the Mermayde nere the bridge in Rochester, and it is reported that he hath not received any pay haveinge beene in his majestys service aboarde the Henrietta since August last was 2 yeares, and is lately comme from that shippe into the Cambridge friggatt, which vessell is neare Quimbourrough. Good brother (if you meete with any of your freinds whoe ought to pay the seamen) bee soe loveinge and [true] to your former kindenes to endeavour to procure him somme parte of his pay for I doubt hee may wante money if hee hath not beene paid any in all this tyme. I did supply him with severall summes of money since hee went into the service for want of his pay. Good brother herken after him and please to write mee word howe you finde things to bee with him.

Leave this with Mr Selinger the Master of the Rolls chapplyn; or in his absence with Mr William Adams, the porter at the gate, for his good freinde and brother Mr Thomas Pennant.

353. TO [ROBERT] AMBERSON

[*Subscribed*] Caerleon 21 January 1667

Mr Amberson

You and I knowe that my neighbour Rees Gwyn was a careles man, by which meanes hee left his widdowe in a very sadd condicion and amongst other of hir troubles shee wanteth a certificate for goods laden here and landed at Bristoll by cockett. I am not acquainted with any officers in your custome house but only Mr Isaack Morgan to whome I pray present my humble service and I earnestly pray him (at the request of my neighbour the widdowe Gwyn) to graunte hir a certificate which I conceave will bee an act both of justice and charety to helpe the widdowe out of trouble. I pray present my humble service to all the rest of the officers in your custome house, whose assistance (allthough unacquainted) I humbly begg on the beehalfe of my poore neighbour herein, which beeinge graunted will not only obliege hir but mee allsoe to bee theyr and your servant to commande, JB.

Page 77

354. TO MATTHIAS BYRD

[*Marginated*] 22 January 1667

Sonne Matthias

Yours of the 22nd December I received. Wee desier to heare from you by all opportunetyes.

Leave this with Mr Philip Williams at the signe of the White Dragon in Holborne for Matthias Byrd aborde the Cambridge friggott.

355. TO THOMAS PENNANT

[*No date*]

Brother Pennant

On the 17th November last I wrote to you by my neighbour Mr Isaack Tomkins, by whome I sent the 30s. which you disbursed on my account and 2s. 6d. to drinke a glasse of sack with my sister, the which hee left with Mr William Adams the porter at the Rolls gate, according to your order in your last letter which I received from you, since which tyme I have not heard one word from from you, which makes us doubtfull of your health. Wherefore good brother write mee word by the first post howe you all doe, at whose health and wellfare none shall rejoyce more then shall JB.

Deliver this to Mr Henry Burgen haberdasher at his shopp under Bishopsgate church or at his house in Wallnutt tree Yard, beinge neere the Countesse of Devon without Bishopps gate London for Mr Thomas Pennant, London.

356. TO LEYSHON SEYS

[*Marginated*] Caerleon 27 January 1667

Cozen Lyson Seys

I received a letter from your brother William[1] dated 26th December which I sent to esquire Jones whoe retorned it back to mee with his further request that my cozen William will bee pleased to sende hyther a particular of what Mr John Morgan oweth him, and both hee and my worthy freinde and neighbour Mr Thomas Morgan of Penrose have promised to use theyr best endeavours to cause theyr unkle Mr John Morgan to pay my cozen without suites at lawe. I pray present the due respects of my wife, sonne and selfe to your brother and to all his family, and pray him to graunte what my freinds above named have requested, and I am confident that they will cause Mr Morgan to give satisfaccion without suites at lawe. I pray desier your brother to sende your particulars above desired soe soone as may bee. Thus.

1. 'Wm' interlined.

357. TO THOMAS PENNANT

[*Marginated*] Caerleon 4 February 1667

Brother Pennant

Yours of the 24th January I received and wee are all hartily glad to heare that you and all yours are in good health. My wife and I doe hartily thanke you for loving intencions to supply our sonne Matthias at Rochester, whoe is longe since gon from thence and I conceave is nowe neare the Weight, to which coast they were longe boundinge, as by his last letters to mee appeares. Howsoever I acknowledge my obligacions to you on his behalfe in the most freindely measure and shall bee ready to shewe my thankefulnes in any thinge which shall lye in my power. I pray lett us heare from you by this bearer my neighbour Mr Isaack Tomkins whoe hath a great desier to see you.

358. TO WILLIAM SEYS

[*Marginated*] 13 May 1667

Cozen William Seys

Mr Robert Morgan wrote to my cozen William Seys that hee had beene with his father at Abergaveny concerneinge the difference betweene them, and that his father conceives somme errors to bee in the accounts, as that the wheate and other goods which were Mr John Morgans were worth more then is charged in the account, for reconcilinge whereof Mr John Morgan desires my cozen William Seys to meete him at Cowbridge on the 4th June next, where eyther himselfe or somme freinde for him would bee then to examyne the accounts betweene them in order to my cozens satisfaccion.

This letter I sent enclosed in a cover to my cozen Lyson Seys in Swansey, desireinge him to sende it to my cozen William.

Page 78

359. TO EVAN SEYS

[*Marginated*] Caerleon 13 May 1667

Cozen Evan Seys

Yours of the 4th instant I received etc., the bill which I received of my cozen William Lucas is £123s. 10d. which my sonne sayth ought not to bee soe much, howsoever I pray bee soe loving as to agree with the party soe well as you may, and if you canne conveniently spare soe much money as hee must have, I humbly beseech you to pay him, and I will repay it to you or to your order on demaunde. If you cannot conveniently doe this, then I desier the parties order to pay it to whome hee please in Bristoll, which (God permittinge) shall bee performed with all convenient speede. I pray please to write mee word by the first post of the receipt hereof, and what must be donne in the premisses, for I woulde not have the party to suffer by my noneperformance herein. Your contynuall love to mee and myne hath created this trouble to you, wherein I humbly begg your pardon. My cozen William Morgan was on his fathers wharth on Friday last where hee sawe your geldinge very well as hee toulde mee. Thus etc.

360. TO WILLIAM SEYS

[*Marginated*] Caerleon 23 May 1667

Cozen William Seys

On the 13th instant Mr Robert Morgan (the sonne of your late tenant Mr John Morgan) wrote to acquainte you that his father desired that you woulde give him the meeteinge at Cowbridge on the 4th of June next, but my worthy freinde Mr Thomas Morgan of Penrose toulde mee yesterday that his kinsman Mr Jones of Lanarth earnestly desires that you will bee soe loveinge as to comme to Caerlion about the 20th of June next, where Mr Jones, Mr Morgan and your late tenant will meete you, and will settle your busines soe as that you shall bee sure of your money. Mr Jones is for London the beeginninge of June and intends to bee at home before midsommer. Wee shall bee hartily glad to see you here, and I desier you to bee soe loveinge as to comme hyther as our loving freinds have desired, and I am confident you will not repent your journey. Good sir write mee one word of receipt hereof by the first post that I may acquainte these gentlemen of your pleasure herein, which etc.

361. TO MATTHIAS BYRD

[*Marginated*] Caerleon 10 June 1667

Sonn Matthias

Yours of the 23rd May last, and yours without date and from noe place came both to my hands on Monday last, by both which I finde that your oulde infirmityes have not yet left you, but I hope the Lord will in his good tyme cure you. Our country is soe much impoverished that our tenants cannot pay rents, howsoever I will endeavour to pay your £5 to Mr Deyos soe soone as I can gett money in. I advize you to bee carefull if you expect any thinge here: you knowe my meaneinge. My brother Pennant lyveth nowe in Acorne Alley right against the Spittle, to whome I have written to assiste you for your pay, if neede bee. Lett us here from you by all opportunetyes.

362. TO MICHAEL DEYOS

[10 June 1667]

Wrote to Mr Michael Deyos that I woulde pay the £5 to him or to his order here soe soone as I coulde gett in money.

363. TO EVAN SEYS

[*Marginated*] 15 June 1667

Cozen Evan Seys

According to dyreccions in yours of the 25th May I sende by this bearer (my neighbour Mr Isaack Tomkins an attorney in common pleas) £12, which I pray cause to bee paid to the party whoe you wrote to mee about, and receive his generall discharge for the same. Your geldinge was lett blood according to your order, and is nowe well with our horses in the marches. The £12 is sealed up in a purse.

This was to pay Thomas Jones my sonne Williams tayler.

364. TO THOMAS HANDS

[*No date]*

Cozen Thomas Hands

Yours of the 6th July last I longe since received, by which I finde your great care of and love to my cozen Mary, for which I hartily thanke you. Ollyver Gadbury whoe was marryed to Sir Thomas Curson of Waterperryes sister (and as I understande lyveth with Sir Thomas Curson[)] oweth a summe of money to a freinde of ours. Nowe my request is that you will enquier howe Olliver lyveth and whether hee bee in a condicion to pay his debt or not. I beeleeve my cozen Thomas Symms canne acquainte you howe it is with Olliver Gadbury. This bearer Francis Launder is to comme often from Oxonforde hyther this summer, by whome I desier to heare from you.

Page 79

365. TO EVAN SEYS

[*Marginated*] Caerleon 24 June 1667

Honoured cozen Evan Seys

I make boulde to acquainte you that Mr Perkins our high sheriffe is dead, and I am doubtfull whoe shall succeede him. My earnest request is that you will bee soe loveinge as to herken after it, and (according to your woonted love[)] to prevent the evell that is threatned.

I wrote to you on the 15th instant by my neighbour Mr Isaack Tomkins whoe is nowe in Staple Inn, by whome I sent £12 according to your dyreccion to cleare with the party whoe you wrote to mee about, which I hope came safe to your hands. Your geldinge is very well with our horses in the marches. I pray write one word of receipt hereof, with a word of the treaty and what else is current by the first post.

366. TO THOMAS PENNANT

[*Marginated*] Caerleon 13 August 1667

Brother Pennant

Yours of the 6th instant wee received for which I render you harty thanks and I earnestly pray you to write mee word by the first post what is to bee had towards my brothers maytenance. My reason herein you may imagine; hee intends (if God enable him) to bee in London the next moneth. I received a letter from my sonne Matthias (whose quarters is at the White Lyon in Ratclif) that the shipp which hee commanded was burnt in the late service against the Dutch in the Hoape, and nowe hee attends on the commissioners with whome (if you have any interest) I pray afforde him your assistance, according to your wonted love.

367. TO MATTHIAS BYRD

[*Marginated*] Caerleon 13 August 1667

Sonne Matthias

Yours of the 10th instant I received which is all I received from you since yours of the 6th June last from Gosp[ort]. This hath given your mother great satisfaccion, who desireth to heare from you by all convenient opportunetyes. In June last I paid Mr Pearson himselfe £5 according to your order. My brother Pennant dwelleth in Acorne Alley right against the Spittle, to whome I have written to assiste you with the commissioners, and whether you have occasion to trouble him or not you will doe civilly to give him(1) a visitt and to render him thanks for his former love to you with the commissioners in procureinge your pay; when if hee had not beene our true freinde and one that had an interest in somme of the commissioners you had lost above one halfe of your pay. Ingratitude is hatefull both to God and man.

1. 'him' interlined.

368. TO MATTHIAS BYRD

[*Marginated*] Caerleon 3 September 1667

Wrote to Matthias againe to the purpose aforesaid, and that I had not heard from him, nor from my brother Pennant since my last to him.

Leave this with Mr Philip Williams at the signe of the White Dragon in Holborne, for Matthias Byrd lately aboarde the Cambridge friggatt, London.

369. TO EVAN SEYS

[*No date*]

Cozen Evan Seys

Yours of the last [of the month] I received on the first instant.

370. TO EVAN SEYS

[*Marginated*] Caerleon 7 October 1667

Honoured cozen Evan Seys

Yours of the [last of] September last I received on the 1st instant, and did communicatt the same to my cozens William Morgan and Rice Jones according to dyreccion, whoe will use theyr endeavours to procure scrawlings to the purpose. The aquitaine apple is conceaved to be best for syder, of which sorte my cozen William Morgan is promised a dozen and ½ and will endeavour to gett more against your messenger commeth for them. I conceave my hussie apple to bee very good for syder, of which sorte[1] or any other which wee have your messenger shall take his choise when hee shall bee here. My nursery will afforde somme store of smale grafted trees, which if you please to make use of, they shall bee at your service; and soe is yours etc. JB.

1. Followed by 'your messenger' deleted.

371. TO EVAN SEYS

[*Marginated*] Caerleon 21 October 1667

Honoured Sir

Yours with Mr Rogers and all things therein I received bearinge date 15th instant, for which and all other favours I humbly thanke you. I have spoken againe with my cozen William Morgan, whoe doubteth not but to procure your number of aquitaynes scrawelings and for jennet moyles beetwene my cozens and my selfe wee shall furnish you and for stocks my nursery will afforde the number which you writt for; and when you please to sende for the premisses pray please to order the man whoe shall comme for them to stay here a day or 2 for the cuttinge of the scrawelings and takeinge up the stocks, that they may bee had fresh to sett, wherein noe helpe shall bee wantinge which shall ly in the power of your etc. JB.

Page 80

372. TO RICHARD LUCAS

[*Marginated*] Caerleon 11 November 1667

Cozen Richard Lucas

Our good freinde the searjeant is to have about 3 horse loades of scrawelings and crab stocks in these partes, which when you conceave the season to bee best for settinge them, you will doe well to sende a man or two with horses for them. The scrawelings are to bee gathered out of severall orchards, and if you please to write me word when you will sende for them, I will procure our freinds to gett them ready. The searjeant writt mee word that hee hath given you order that your messenger shall stay a day or 2 here, for gatheringe the premisses togeather. Pray write a word by the post when you intende to sende. Thus etc.

373. TO BROTHER WILLIAM BYRD

[*Marginated*] Caerleon 19 December 1667

Brother William

Yours by way of Bristoll with all things sent therewith I received and allsoe yours of the 5th instant, in which you write that you delivered a paper to my good freinde the searjeant concerning custom officers. I knowe not what you meane by that unles you intende to turne informer, which I hope you will not bee in your olde age. I pray doe not trouble my freinde with frivolous busines, for you finde by what you wrote mee that I am troublesome enough to him in what concernes mee.

Here enclosed is a letter to my sonne Matthias landlord and landlady, with whome hee left a tickett for his pay, beinge about £26, which hee hopeth they have received for him. If soe that it bee received, then his desier (in the inclosed) is that all charges in procureinge it and wherewith for his landlorde and landlady to drinke a glasse of wyne beinge deducted, that they doe pay the remainder unto you, which if you receive, please to keepe 40s. and desier the searjeant to bee soe loveinge as to receive the rest from you and to pay it to Matthias here. I pray write mee word what you intende by the paper which you delivered the searjeant, and allsoe what is donne concerning Matthias's pay.

374. TO THOMAS PENNANT

[*No date*]

Brother Pennant

I pray reade and seale the enclosed and cause it to be delivered, and I pray write mee word what hee meaneth by the paper which hee delivered the searjeant and advize him not to meddle with unhandsome busines. Allsoe (if neede requireth) I pray assist concerning Matthias's pay.

Brother Pennant his house is in Acorne Alley right against the Spittle.

375. TO RICHARD LUCAS

[*Marginated*] Caerleon 9 December 1667

Cozen Richard Lucas

Our worthy freinde the searjeant wrote that hee had ordered you to sende a man on purpose for crab stocks and scrawelings, which hee was to have from hence, and on the 11th November I wrote to you accordingly and did expect a man from you before this tyme, but I not heareinge from you and the season beinge nowe very good for setting trees, I sende this bearer on purpose with the crab stocks, being 50 in number. I have noe skill concerning scrawelyngs, but our planters heer are of opinyon that the season for settinge them is after Christmas. Pray write mee word by this bearer when you intende to sende for them, that wee may bee ready to fitt your messenger. Thus.

376. TO JAMES HARRIS

[*Marginated*] Caerleon 13 January 1668

Mr James Harris

Your neighbour, captain(1) John Morgan of Pentre bach, oweth £30 to Mr William Seys (my wifes cozen jerman), on ½ whereof Mrs Morgan promised shoulde bee paid about All Saints tyde last, and the other ½ 15 dayes after May day next, and shee promised that your sonne Mr John Harris shoulde undertake payment accordingly, but not any thinge as yet performed. I am not acquainted with your sonne; howsoever I received a letter from him, wherein hee promised to use his endeavour that this money shoulde bee paid my freinde, whoe I have perswaded not to put Mr Morgans bonds in further suite, hopeinge that hee shoulde bee paid without farther trouble. Nowe my request to you is that you will doe me the kindenes to present my due respects to your sonne Mr John Harris and acquainte him that my freinde relyeth wholly on his promise, and I desier one word from you what hopes there is of satisfaccion; and if noe hopes then I must deliver Mr

Morgans bonds to my cozen which I am very unwillinge to doe for the respect I beare to him and his relacions. Thus.

1. 'Capt' interlined.

Page 81

377. TO THOMAS PENNANT

[*Headed*] 24 January 1668

Brother Pennant

Yours by Mr Tomkins I received. Pray remember my true love to my brother and please to acquainte him that his by the post and his by Bristoll with the packett I received, in both which hee acquainted mee that hee delivered £19 19s. 0d. to you for my sonne Matthias, the which I pray please to keepe till Mr Tomkins commeth up, by whome I shall trouble you with a word for disposall thereof which etc.

378. TO THOMAS PENNANT

[*Marginated*] 2 February 1668

Brother Pennant

Yours by Mr Tomkins I received[1]. Pray acquainte my brother William that I received his of the 31th December by the post and his of the 1st January with the packett, in both which hee wrote that hee had delivered you £19 19s. for my sonne Matthias, and on the 24th January I wrote to you by the post that you should receive order by Mr Tomkins for disposall of the money abovesaid, which order from my sonne Matthias is here enclosed, wherein hee desires that you please to pay Mr Tomkins £19 to my brother William 15s. to cleare his disbursements for mee, and the other 4s. to drinke a glasse of wyne with my sister, my brother William and Mr Tomkins, which I pray you to performe accordingly.

1. 'I received' interlined.

379. TO MATTHIAS BYRD

[*Marginated*] Caerleon 20 April 1668

Sonne Matthias

Yours of the 4th and 18th instant (but not yours of the 11th) I received, by both which I understande that you were in good health, the which I pray God contynewe, and blesse all your faithfull undertakeings in his majesty's service. This day my cozen William Williams junier brought his wife from Colbroke hyther in a very noble manner, beinge accompanied with many persons of good quallity. I praise God wee are all here in good health. Your mother and brothers remember you and wish you all happines; soe doth JB.

Leave this with Mr Philip Williams at the signe of the White Dragon nere Grayes Inn in Holborne, to bee delivered as above is dyrected. London.

380. TO MATTHIAS BYRD

[*Marginated*] Caerleon 18 May 1668

Sonne Matthias

On the 20th of April last I wrote to you that yours of the 4th and 18th of that month I had received and since that tyme I received yours of the 8th instant, by which wee understande that you were then in good health, the which we hope you still enjoy. I wish (and I beeleeve you doe) that you had beene advized by mee here, howsoever the Lords will bee donne. When you write next, lett mee knowe what letters and of what date you received from mee. Our freinds and neighbours remember you often, and wish you all happines, soe doth JB.

Leave this with Mr Richard Stiles at the White Lyon neare Rattcliffe Crosse to bee delivered to Captain Matthias Byrd abord the St David, Captain John Walterworth commander, London.

381. TO MATTHIAS BYRD

[*Marginated*] Caerleon 25 May 1668

Sonne Matthias

In my last I gave you an account of 3 letters (with theyr dates) which I had received from you, and this day I received yours of the 21st instant, but not one word in any of yours that you received any one from mee, this beinge my 4th to you. I understande by your last that your former resolucion is altered, which wee hope will bee for the best. You writt for for your chest and other things, but not one word which way you will have them sent: neyther where, nor to whome to bee delivered. Wherefore if you intende to have your things sent, give speedy notice which way, whether and to whome that you may receive them accordingly.

Page 82

382. TO EVAN SEYS

[*Marginated*] Caerleon 31 May 1668

Mr Searjeant

Since I sawe you I received 2 letters from you, with what was therein enclosed, and of late I received a letter from my sonne Matthias intymateinge that you have beene soe loving as to appeare for him, endeavouringe his good, for which and all other curtesies my wife and I render you our humble and harty thanks, and doe pray that you will bee pleased to write us one word, that wee may knowe howe you and yours doe, and when (God permittinge) you intende to comme this way, where none shall rejoyce more to see you then shall my wife and J B.

383. TO MATTHIAS BYRD

[31 May 1668]

Wrote the same day to Matthias to the same purpose as my last was, which I enclosed in myne to my brother William desireinge him to deliver it and to write mee word concerninge him, and enclosed both to my brother Pennant.

384. TO MATTHIAS BYRD

[*Marginated*] Caerleon 11 June 1668

Sonne Matthias

This day Rees Lewis had your chest abord the boat for Bristoll, and from thence to bee sent to London according to you dyreccions. I desired Rees to sende by wagon rather then by horse, least any thinge in the chest shoulde bee spoyled. Your busines beinge urgent and your hast very great when you departed hence, made you forgett to leave the key of your chest here, which caused a newe key to bee made, which you shall receave here enclosed. In your chest you will finde £5 to pay for the carryage of your chest etc.

385. TO MATTHIAS BYRD

[*Marginated*] Caerleon 16 June 1668

Sonne Matthias

On the 11th instant I sent your chest to Bristoll and all things in it which you wrote for. It was delivered to Thomas Beesurd a wagoner whoe put it in his wagon on Friday last. I thinke his quarters is at the Swan at Holborne bridge, where you may expect your chest in which is £5 to pay for carryage thereof. It weighed 1 hundredweight, 1 quarter, 14 pounds, for which Rees Lewis agreed for 5s.6d. per hundredweight. In myne to you of the 11th instant I sent you a newe key to your chest which etc.

386. TO JOHN POINTS

[*Marginated*] Caerleon 6 July [1668]

Captain Points

Yours of the 27th of May last with 4 other letters I received on Friday last from Bristoll, which I sent to the severall persons to whome they were dyrected. I communicated what you wrote to mee, to your sonne Mr Steeven Points, whoe promised to write to you by this bearer John Greene. Your wife is long since departed this life, and I hope is with the Lord. I heard that my cozen William Byrd is an attorney in the Exchequer in Dublyn. I have not heard from him in 8 yeares; hee did lodge somme tyme at Mr Thomas Dancers house, in Bride Streete, over against St Patricks church, and somme tymes at the Bell, in Fish Shamble Streete. I pray endeavour to finde whether hee bee lyveinge or dead, and please to write mee one word thereof by the post for London; and please to dyrect your letters for mee, to Mr Thomas Pennant at his house in Acorne Alley right against the Spittle in London, from whome it will be carefully sent to yours as above J B.

To his much honoured freinde Captain John Points, servant to his Grace the Duke of Ormonde, at the castle, present these, Dublyn.

387. TO ELIZABETH CAYSUM

[*Marginated*] Caerleon 11 July 1668

Elizabeth Caysum

Yours of 28th May and 2nd of July instant I received, both intymateinge your desire to lyve in this county by the trade of a silke weaver, which is soe meane in this place that here beinge but one of that trade, whoe had 2 prentices whoe after they had served theyr tyme wear forced to fall to labour for theyr lyveinge, and theyr master tooke uppon him another callinge by which hee nowe lyveth in this towne. These partes are served both from Bristoll and London with silke weavers at such reasonable rates which causeth that trade to bee little worth here, and as for semsters, most women in these partes make theyr owne lynnen clothes, soe that if a person cannot lyve in Englande reasonably by any trade, here is little hopes to lyve at all by it in these partes, where all works are scarce and money scarcer and workemen plentifull. My brother William lyveth in London in the skynners rents, but in what place of the citty I cannot tell. Thus for present I rest. Your unacquainted J B.

To Elizabeth Caysum, present these, Arlingham.

Page 83

388. TO MATTHIAS BYRD

[*Marginated*] Caerleon 1 September 1668

Sonne Matthias

Yours of the 13th and 24th August I received, by both which I understande that you are bounde to sea. Wee wish you a prosperous voyadge. Your mother desires you to write word in your next what employment or office you have in the ship you are to goe in. I communicated your [love](1) to our freinds and neighbours according to your desier, whoe doe wish you all happines and soe doth J B.

Leave this with Mr Richard Styles at the signe of the White Lyon nere Rattcliffe Crosse, to bee delivered to Captain Matthias Byrd aboard the ship Transport.

1. Word missing between 'Your' and 'to'.

389. TO CHARLES VAN

[*Marginated*] Caerleon 5 October 1668

Honoured Sir

I am advized (by learned counsell) not to pay any money without order from the person to whome I stande oblieged, which I pray please to procure for what summe you expect from mee, which order shall bee carefully performed by J B.

For Mr Charles Van.

390. TO HENRY DRAPER

[*Subscribed*] Caerleon 'Friday morneinge' 29 October 1668

Mr Henry Draper

My wife and I remember our true loves to you and yours with thanks for all former curtesies, to which my wife prayeth you to adde one more, which is that you will be soe loveinge as to present our due respects to my lords commissioners, whoe I hope have considered the great charge which I have beene at, in improveinge what I houlde from my lord and the dayly charge I am at in mayneteyneinge the same. I did offer £70 to add Matthias his lyfe into my lease, but they insisted uppon £100. My wife is very desirous to have Matthias's life added, and rather then faile shee will give £10 to make it up [to] £80, which accepted, I shall waite on the commissioners on Monday, or if required I will (God willinge) comme to Cardiffe tomorrowe, and pay in one halfe according to our treaty therein. I pray write mee word by this bearer what they please to doe herein etc.

Postscript

Good sir, if what is offred bee refused, then I pray treate with them (as of your owne love and not by my desires) what will bee the least which must bee given, and desier 2 or 3 dayes tyme to answer theyr expectacions, which is the request of my wife and yours J B. My wife depends very much on Mr Henry Rumseyes love herein, to whoe I pray remember hir and allsoe J B.

391. TO EVAN SEYS

[*Marginated*] Caerleon 2 November 1668

Cozen Seys

On Tuseday last I came from Cardiffe, where I did treate with my lords commissioners (namely Mr John Herbert, Mr John Jesse and Mr Henry Rumsey) for puttinge my sonne Matthias's life in the lease on the mills and marches. They demaunded £100, I offred £70. I did then agree with them for a smale thinge which I hould from my lord, lyeinge in the lordshipp of Uske, for which I sent the fine and money for the lease to them on Friday last and I wrote to Mr Draper desireinge him to offer £10 more(1) at my wifes request, the one _ in hand and the other in May next, on receipt of a newe lease, provided if Matthias did happen to dye before receipt of the newe lease, then another life was to bee added for halfe soe much money more; which (if I had agreed to give what they demaunded) they were pleased to doe.

In answer to myne to Mr Draper I received a letter from Mr John Jesse, intymateinge that my fine for addinge one life would bee £120, yet loveingly promised to improve his interest with the other commissioners for mee. I have bestowed above £100 in repairinge the mills, and in cribbs and sea walls to preserve the marches from the ryvers, and I hope shall not bee turned of for doeinge good. Uppon my creditt, there is noe such profitt to bee made of the premisses as the commissioners doe conceave it is. My wife beeleeveth that you will see my lords commissioners above, and desiers your endeavour with them that £80 may bee accepted, or to procure it as reasonable as may bee under £100, and please to write one word what must be donne herein.

The commissioners requier our leases up without which (Mr Jesse writes that) my lord will not confirme any lease, which I conceave to bee sommethinge unreasonable. I beeseech you to bee myndefull of the yearely trouble which I am forced to put you unto. My wife, sonne William and selfe present our faithfull respects to you and all yours, and pray you to pardon herein the bouldnes(2) of your troublesomme alliesman and servant JB.

1. 'more' interlined.

2. followed by 'herein', deleted.

Page 84

392. TO THOMAS HANDS

[*Marginated*] Caerleon 2 November 1668

Cozen Hands

Yours of the 11th of October I received, by which I understand that you have beene ill, yet uppon recovery. I pray God to graunte you perfect health. I am glad to heare that your wife and our relacions at Whateley are in health. I doubt (by what you write) that all is out of order at Whateley. I wish my silly cozen had beene advized by mee, which was not to breake the entaile, which would have prevented what hath hapned. I prayse God wee enjoy our healths in a comfortable manner. My wife, sonne William and selfe with our neighbour James Wattkins and his wife remember our true love to you and to your wife; pray remember my love to my cozen Symms, to my sister, and theyr familyes, whose welfare and happines none desireth more then doth JB.

393. TO BROTHER WILLIAM BYRD

[*Marginated*] Caerleon 14 November 1668

Brother William

I pray enquier of Mr Richard Stiles at the signe of the White Lyon neare the crosse in Rattcliffe for Matthias, whoe in the last I received from him wrote that hee was shipped aboard a shipp called the Transeport for the Canaryes. I pray write us word what you heare of him, eyther by my neighbour Mr Tomkins the bearer hereof, or by the post. Pray sende the enclosed to my cozen Thomas Hands at Oxenforde by the first post. Enclosed this in my letter to my brother Pennant.

394. TO MATTHIAS BYRD

[*Marginated*] Caerleon 10 March 1669

Sonne Matthias

Yours of the 1st instant I received, from Dall roade at Millforde and have communicated it according to your dyreccion. I praise God we are all in health here and noe newes here at present but that your aunte Florence Morgan departed out of this woolde on the first instant and was buryed on the 4th instant at Tredonock. Your mother, brothers and freinds desier the Lord to sende your ship and all in it safe to its desired port; soe doth JB.

395. TO EVAN SEYS

[*Marginated*] 30 March 1669

I sent a coppie of the articles of agreement to Searjeant Seys, by which I holde sores mills and the lands thereunto belonginge (which are Mr Pierce Buttlers in the right of the Lady Morgan his wife[)] for 12 yeares which are expired; yet Mr Gunter (agent for Mr Buttler here) refuseth to take them up, alleadgeinge that I ought to have given Mr Buttler a quarters warneinge. My time beganne in the premises 1st May 1656; I desired the searjeant to sende his opinnyon under his hande, whether Mr Buttler coulde force mee to houlde the said mills etc, or not. Sent this by the post.

396. TO EVAN SEYS

[*Marginated*] 12 April 1669

I not haveinge received any answer from the searjeant, wrote againe to him, and sent the like coppie, by his servant Edward Vorst.

397. TO MATTHIAS BYRD

[*Marginated*] 20 April 1669

Wrote Matthias word that I had received 2 letters dat[ed], and Milforde, and nowe his dat[ed] at Ratcliffe 15th instant. His mother desires to knowe what voyadge hee intendeth and in what shippe.

This day I sent moarneinge for my sister Morgan to my sister Katheryn Nicholls at Lantwitt from my brother Mr Giles Morgan, by Edward Vosse, servant to Searjeant Seys.

398. TO THOMAS GUNTER

[*Marginated*] Caerleon 21 April 1669

Mr Thomas Gunter

I pray present my humble service to Mr Pierce Buttler, and his good lady, and please to acquainte them that the tyme which was granted mee on soores mills determyneinge, I cannot holde them longer then May day next. Wherefore I pray cause the lands to bee looked unto. Indeede Mr Gunter I have paide £40 more then I receaved from those mills, which I hope Mr Buttler will confirm when I cleare my accompt, wherein I hope you will bee my freinde, which with my due respects to you presented is all at present from your freinde and servant John Byrd.

The letter whereof this is a coppie was carryed to Lanternam this day and left with Elizabeth Jones there for Mr Gunter by mee Mirick John.

Page 85

399. TO BROTHER WILLIAM BYRD

[*Headed*] 17 May 1669

Wrote to my brother William and sent him a token by Mr Isaack Tomkins.

400. TO MATTHIAS BYRD

[*Marginated*] 18 May 1669

Wrote to Matthias that I received his of the 10th instant, beinge his 4th from Ratcliffe. I desired him to write when hee intends to retorn to Englande.

401. TO MATTHIAS BYRD

[*Marginated*] Caerleon 28 May 1669

Sonn Matthias

Yours of the 25th instant I received, the contents whereof shall bee communicated according to your dyreccions. I was yesterday at Cardiffe where I had an opportunety to put your life in the lease on the mills and marches, which will cost about £100, and must bee paid in October next. I was very unwillinge to loose this opportunety, hopeinge that you will bee soe carefull a husbande as to provide somme money towards payment for the newe lease, that you may bee the more assured of my estate in the 2 lordshipps of Llyswery and Lebenyth. I desier you to write mee word howe much money you can furnish mee with against October next, which etc.

JB and M[argery] B[yrd].

402. TO RICHARD STILES

[*Marginated*] Caerleon 1 June 1669

Mr Richard Stiles

Although unacquainted, yet I finde myselfe much oblieged unto you for your love to my sonne Matthias, for which I render you my harty thanks. I received a letter from my brother, intymateing that on my sonne Matthias's behalfe, you desier that I would furnish him with £200, which is according to the last advice I gave him, at his last goeinge from hence, and I hope this mocion proceedeth from himselfe, and if hee shall not bee gon to sea before this shall comme to your hands, and that my sonne resolveth to followe my last advice, then I pray cause him to write soe much to mee, and I will endeavour to furnish him with £200, for I knowe that soe much money present may bee farre better for him then £40 per annum hereafter.

Yet the last weeke I purchased his life to bee added in the lease on the mills and marches (a thinge which hee well knoweth) and if hee lyve, will bee a comfort to him in his ould age; and if hee resolveth as abovesaid (God permittinge) I will provide for him against his retorne from his voyadge nowe in hande. I wrote to him on Friday last and hope he received it. I pray please to write mee one word of receipt hereof, wherein you will obliege him that is already sir yours oblieged to serve you, JB.

403. TO BROTHER WILLIAM BYRD

[*Marginated*] Caerleon 15 June 1669

Brother William

On the 1st instant I wrote to Mr Stiles concerning £200 which you wrote to mee of in your last for Matthias; and on the 28th May last I wrote to Matthias acquainting him that I had purchased his life in the mills and marches, but I have not heard from eyther of them, which makes mee doubt they did not receave my letters. My request is that (on receipt hereof) you please to goe to Ratcliffe, and present my due respects to Mr Richard Stiles, to whome I acknowledge myselfe much oblieged on Matthias's behalfe, and acquainte him that if Matthias had taken my advice when hee went last from hence, I had then furnished him with £200 to buy him parte of a vessell, and soe I shall doe yet, if hee will observe my last advice to him. I pray write mee word by the 1st post whether my 2 letters aforesaid were receaved or not, and if they were, then I desier to knowe my sonne Matthias's answer thereto. I suppose hee is gon to sea; if soe, pray write mee word what day hee went from Ratcliffe. Present my wifes true love and myne to my brother Pennant and all his, and write mee word howe he doeth; I should bee hartily glad of his recovery.

Page 86

404. TO ROBERT VICKRIS

[*Headed*] 23 July 1669

Honoured Sir

After my faithfull respects presented to you with my harty thanks for all curtesies, it is soe that (if I goe through a busines which I have in hande) I shall want a £100 money more then I have at present. Nowe my humble request is that you will bee soe loveinge (if you may conveniently) to furnish mee with that summe which, if you please to doe, I will secure your repayment with reall satisfaccion for use thereof, eyther by bonde or by lande to your owne content. I shall neede it about a moneth hence; I pray pardon this my bouldnes, and please to write mee your favourable answer by this bearer, wherein you will double the obligacion which lyeth already on JB.

For his much honoured freinde, Mr Robert Vickris merchant, these, Bristoll.

405. TO NEPHEW WILLIAM BYRD

[*Marginated*] Caerleon 12 September 1669

Cozen William

Yours of the 13th July last, from Mr William Powell of Langattog juxta Neath by Morgan Edward of the same, to whome I gave 2s. I received[1]. Please to take notice that your father lyveth in the Skynners rent, without Algate; and your sister (as I beeleeve) lyveth in somme place in Kent, but where I knowe not. My sonne Edward was kilde at Faringdon long since; Matthias is beyond sea; I praise God wee are in good health. I never received any letter nor any newes from you since May 1660, at which tyme I sawe you in London. Please to dyrect your letters for us to bee left with Mr Thomas Pennant at his house in Acorne Alley nere Bishoppsgate, by which conveyance wee shall receive them. Thus etc.

To his loving kinseman, Mr William Byrd, at his chamber at Mr George Savells, over against the Coach and Horses in Goldinge Lane, these, Dublyn.

1. 'I received' interlined.

406. TO BROTHER WILLIAM BYRD

[*Marginated*] Caerleon 11 October 1669

Brother William

I lately received a letter from your sonne William dated 13th July last, at his chamber in Mr George Savells house, as above, which is all I ever heard or received from him since May 1660. Hee desired to heare from you and us, and I gave him an account accordingly. I advized him to dyrect his letters for us to bee left with brother Pennant. I allsoe received a letter from my sonne Matthias dated 30th July last[1] at Newe founde lande, intymateinge that hee hoped to bee at Bilboa in September last, soe that I conceave about this tyme the shipp wherein hee is may arryve at London. I pray enquier after him and present my true love and faithfull respects to Mr Richard Styles at the White Lyon in Rattcliffe, and acquainte him that the advice which I gave Matthias before hee went last from hence was to take £200 (which I then offered to furnish him with) to buy parte of a vessell, conceavinge that soe much money then might with Gods blessinge beene better for him then £40 per annum hereafter. Howsoever, I acknowledge myselfe very much oblieged to Mr Stiles for his love to Matthias, for which I pray render him my harty thanks. Pray write mee word by the first post what you shall heare from Matthias. I am hartily glad that my brother Pennant is well recovered. Pray sende mee a bill of mortallety, with such newes as is current.

1. '30th July last' interlined.

407. TO BROTHER WILLIAM BYRD

[*Marginated*] Caerleon 12 November 1669

Brother William

You shall receive a token by this bearer Mr Isaack Tomkins for your selfe and 5s. to drinke with Mr Styles at Ratcliffe, to whome I pray remember mee kindely, and enquier for my sonne Matthias, and write us word what you heare of him.

408. TO THOMAS HANDS

[*No date*]

Cozen Hands

Yours of the 7th November last I received, and am hartily glad to heare of your healthes and wellfare. I pray God sanctify all his mercyes both to you and us. I am glad to heare that my cozen John is a better husbande then formerly; I pray houlde fast what you have from Margaret and hir daughter, or else I doubt all will bee gon. My sonne Matthias is beyond sea; William and Andrew are here and wee all desier to bee remembered to you and all our relacions in [*ends here in mid-sentence; there are no longer any traces of any missing pages in the MS* .]

Page 87

409. TO THOMAS DENNETT

[*Marginated*] Caerleon 23 August 1671

Honoured Sir

After my due respects presented to you, I pray bee pleased to present my humble duty to my honourable lord and acquainte him that according to his lordshipps commaunde (by his letters to Sir Trevor Williams) I have with great trouble and charge brought the busines concerning the weare (for turneinge the water out of the ryver called Avon Lloyd to the towne of Caerlion and to his lordshipps mills there) to a tryall, for which I was ready with my wittnesses and counsell at the assizes helde at Monmouth in March last, but was then put of, for the jury then sworne for our tryall to viewe the weare, which was donne accordingly; and at the assizes helde in Monmouth on Friday last a verdict passed for us concerning my lords weare, and but £5 dammadge given by the jury. Thomas Morgan of Penrose esquire caused the constables of the towne to present against the last quarter sesssions, and hee himselfe indited and fined mee at the same sessions for cuttinge the watercourse streight cross my lords wast and the high way there, alledgeinge that I did it by my owne authorety, whereupon I produced the order which I had from my lords commissioners at Cardiffe for draininge thereof, which order hee slighted.[1]

I had[2] made a very strong bridge over this water course for all people, and all manner of carryadges and drawing of tymber doe passe securely. I depende on my lords favour to protect mee in what I have donne, and shall doe, in defence of my lords right and hope that his lordshipp will bee pleased to give order to his commissioners the next audit at Cardiffe to repay mee what I have disbursed about the premisses, wherein I earnestly pray your opportune assistance. Mr Henry Rumsey did attende on our tryall at both assizes with great care and faithfulnes, and I hope will [provide] my lord a full account thereof[3]. I desier a word of dyreccion (by this bearer) what is best to bee donne with the inditement about the newe water course abovesaid. Sir Trevor Williams hath written an account of our tryall to my lord by this bearer; I pray assiste him to procure my lords pleasure in the premisses, and sende him back soe soone as may bee, wherein you will obliege etc.

To Mr Thomas Dennett auditor to the right honourable William, Earl of Pembroke and Montgomery.

Complayned at a court of sewers that I had cutt a newe water course crosse the highway alleadgeinge that I had donne it by myne owne authorety, where uppon I produced the order which I had from my lords commissioners at Cardiffe for doinge thereof. The commissioners of sewers then agreed to viewe the said water course themselves, which is not yet donne. Mr John Rumsey (my lords agent here) was present at this court of sewers, since which court of sewers the said Mr Morgan caused the constables of Caerlion to present mee against the last quarter sessions and he himselfe indited and caused mee to bee fined at the same sessions, not withstandinge that I had ... [ends here]

1. 'caused the constables .... slighted' deleted.

2. 'had' interlined.

3. 'and I hope will [provide] my lord a full account thereof' interlined over about seven words, expunged.

410. TO EVAN SEYS

[*Marginated*] Caerleon 20 October 1671

Cozen Seys

Your letter founde very kinde acceptance at Chepstoll where 2 months tyme was graunted to finish the water course. A newe tryall is still threatned. The eleccion of sheriffs is at hande. I humbly pray your woonted love in both. I humbly pray one word from you of the receipt hereof, that wee may knowe howe you and yours doe.

411. TO HENRY DRAPER

[*Marginated*] Caerleon 30 October 1671.

Kind sir

Mr Edmond Lewis promised to write to my lord about a busines wherein I am concerned, and advized mee to procure somme freinde to put him in mynde thereof. Nowe my earnest request to you is to present my humble service to Mr Lewis, and to put him in mynde of his loving promise, and I pray acquainte him that whereas Mr John Rumsey did acquainte him and the rest of my lords commissioners that hee coulde have saved £30 of the charge of our suite, if hee had beene employed, which summe hee conceaved was fines imposed on persons indited, and soe would have fallen to my lord; wherein Mr John Rumsey mistooke, for the persons indited were cleared and noe fine at all imposed on any one of them, and the money charged in my attorneys bill was paid to the clercke of assize and other officers for fees, and not for fines, as Mr Henry Rumsey (whoe acted on my lords behalfe with mee at the severall assizes) knoweth right well. Here enclosed is 5s. to drinke a glasse of wyne with Mr Lewis, Mr Henry Rumsey and the rest of my lords commissioners with my humble service to them all. Thus etc.

To Mr Henry Draper at the Angell present these, Cardiffe.

412. TO NEPHEW WILLIAM BYRD

[*Marginated*] Caerleon 15 November 1671

Cozen William

Yours of the 25th September last I received by this bearer your neighbour, Mr Rowlande Jones, and am hartily glad to heare of your good health. Your father was in health the last terme, since which tyme I have not heard from him. My wife and 3 sonns being here at present (and in health I praise the Lord) remember theyr true love to you, so doth your unkle JB.

To his loving nephew Mr William Byrd at his chamber over against the Coach and Horses in Goldinge Lane present these, Dublyn in Irelande.[1]

1. 'in Goldinge Lane ....Irelande' interlined.

Page 88

413. TO EVAN SEYS

[*Marginated*] Caerleon 16 November 1671

Cozen Seys

Yours of the 24th October I received, since which tyme Mr Tomkins received an execucion for £22 for which I hartily thanke you. Mr Thomas Gunter promised to pay this money to Mr Tomkins, but yesterday hee toulde mee that hee had received a letter from Mr Buttler forbiddinge him to pay it, for that hee did intende to move the court for an abatement of the cost, wherein I humbly pray your wonted love. I am still threatned with a new tryall.

414. TO EVAN SEYS

[*No date*]

Cozen Seys

About a weeke since, I (at the request of my loving freinde and neighbour Mr Henry Walter) wrote to you, desireinge you to bee of counsell for him in a cause wherein the Marques of Worcester is concerned, a copie whereof was then enclosed in myne to you. Mr Isaack Tomkins toulde mee since I wrote to you that Mr Walter hath beene served with an injunction, and that (God permitting) hee intends to waite on you herein the next weeke. Mr Tomkins tells me likewise that Mr Herbert Jones (nowe deputy sheriffe) did execute my execucion on Walter Edwards, at our last quarter sessions, and that Mr Thomas Gunter promised to deliver plate to the sheriffe, for his securety, which makes mee doubtfull that somme mocion will bee made against my execucion, wherein I humbly pray your wonted love for my defence. Thus etc.

415. TO MATTHIAS BYRD

[*Marginated*] Caerleon 15 December 1672

Sonne Matthias

I beinge in Newport yesterday mett accidentally with Mr Cradock, a gentleman whoe dwelleth nere Margam, whoe toulde mee that you lay with him Monday night last, and that you were in good health, which wee here are glad of. Wee all here enjoy the like mercy, for which wee praise God. Mr Cradock toulde mee that you have not heard from us, at which wee admire, haveinge sent severall letters to you, the last of which was by Elizabeth Thomas (alias Couch), wife to Thomas Davies, tayler, whose mother departed last night out of this worlde, not leaveinge behinde hir wherewith to bury hir. I received severall letters from you, the last whereof was dated the 22nd of November last. Edmond Harvey remembers his love to Meirick, and marvells that hee forgetteth his freinds here. You will doe well to cause him to write to Edmond, and his other freinds in these partes: many enquier for him. In your next pray write what letters you have received from us since you went last from hence.

JB and M[argery] B[yrd].

416. TO MATTHIAS BYRD

[*Marginated*] Caerleon 7 January 1673

Sonn Matthias

Yours of the 20th December last and 16 letters before that I received, but doe not finde that you received any from mee since your last goeinge from hence, although I wrote severall letters to you. My last was dated 15th December last, and my last before that I sent by Elizabeth Thomas etc. Edmond Harvey remembers his love to you and Meirick, and marvells that Meirick forgetteth his freinds in these partes etc as above.

417. TO EVAN SEYS

[*Marginated*] Caerleon 10 January 1673 'this to Gloucester per post'

Cozen Seys

Yours of the 7th instant I received, and wee are glad to heare that you and all yours are in good health; I praise God that I and all my family here doe enjoy the like mercy at present, and trust in the Lord that his mercyes will contynnewe to us all. Wee shoulde have beene hartily glad to have seene you here. Sir I lately spake with a gentleman whoe spake with my son in London, whoe complayned that hee had not heard from us since hee went last from hence, yet I have sent up severall letters which it seemeth are eyther stopt or miscarryed. The enclosed will give him some satisfacion. I pray please to lett it remayne with your clerck in your lodgeinge till he commeth thither, for I am confident hee will bee troublesomme to you etc.

418. TO MATTHIAS BYRD

[3 February 1673]

Sonne Matthias

Yours of the 2nd and 23rd of January last I received. By your last you desier a peece of flannen, the which was sent to Monmoth on Saturneday last, and there delivered to Thomas Burley the carryer, whoe lodgeth at the Crosse Keyes in White Crosse Streete. It is dyrected to bee left at the searjeants lodgeinge for you; the peece is 31 yards, the carryage was paid for at Monmoth etc.
[Marginated] Sent this per post 3rd February 1673 and another of the 4th February 1673(1) to Searjeant Seys per Isaack Tomkins.

Flannen	34s.
Carryage to Monmouth	02
Carryadge to London	02

4th February sent this to the searjeant and acquainted him that I received his of the 25th January.
1. '4 February 1673' substituted for 'month and date' deleted.

419. SON WILLIAM BYRD TO EVAN SEYS

[*Marginated*] 11 February 1673 'to the searjeand'

Sir

Yours of the 8th instant my father received, for which and all other favours hee and my mother give you harty thanks. I understand by yours that my unkle William desiers my consent that his sonne may have my chamber in Lyncolnes Inn. I doe freely give my consent that my cozen may have it. I knowe not where the key of my studdy is; my cozen may breake open the dore. I have a bed and appurtenances in the chamber, which my cozen may please to make use of etc. WB.

Page 89

420. TO MATTHIAS BYRD

[*Marginated*] Caerleon 14 February 1673

Wrote to Matthias to enquier for the flannen etc, and to write word whether hee received it or not.

421. TO THOMAS HANDS

[*Marginated*] Caerleon 14 February 1673

Cozen Hands

Yours of the 21st December last with your kinde token and allsoe one from our worthy freind Mr Alderman Griffin of the 23rd December last I longe since received, whereof I formerly gave you an account by the post by way of Abingdon, but by yours of the 21st January last, which I lately received, I finde that my last came not to your hands. My wife and I doe give you and Mr Griffin and both your wives our harty thanks for all your loving rem[embrances] of us, and wee wish you much happines with your newe honour, and wee are sorry that you are troubled about your purchase. Pray please to write us word in your next howe our relacions in Whateley doe etc.

422. TO EDMUND LEWIS

[*Marginated*] Caerleon 20 May 1673

Worthy Sir

After my humble service to you and the rest of my lord's commissioners presented, I humbly pray that you please to doe mee what right you may in the charge I was at in defendinge my lords right and title to the weare and water course to his lordshipps mills in Caerlion, which was by mee donne by my lords order and dyreccions, as by letter herewith sent will appeare. I intended to waite on you herein, but findeinge my selfe not well able to travell, am forced to sende this bearer, my sonne William Byrd, to waite on you herein, whose assistance I pray afforde him on the account of Sir your humble servant JB.

To the worshipful Edmond Lewis esquire, one of the commissioners for the revenewe of the right honourable William Earl of Pembroke and Montgomery present these Cardiffe.

423. TO THOMAS HANDS

[*Marginated*] 1 June 1673

Wrote my cozen Hands word (by Mr William Williams) that I gave him the account abovesaid by way of Bristoll, which was sent thence by Mr Wharton the Oxforde carrier. I sent by Mr Williams 5s. to drinke a glass of wyne with Mr Alderman Griffin, and both theyr wyves etc.

424. TO BROTHER WILLIAM BYRD

[*Marginated*] '9th' [June 1673]

Wrote to my brother William by Mr Tomkins, requestinge him to enquier after Matthias.

425. TO EVAN SEYS

[*Marginated*] '9th' [June 1673]

Cozen Seys

My longe silence may give you just cause to thinke that I have forgott myselfe, wherefore I make boulde to write nowe to give you an account of our present condicion, which is my sonne Andrew departed this life on the 6th day of April last; my sonne Matthias is at sea. I pray God sende us good newes from him and our whole fleete. My wife, sonne and selfe are all in good health, I prayse God, and I hope this shall finde you and all yours in good health allsoe, to which purpose my wife desiers to receive one word in writeinge from you, and shee desiers allsoe to knowe when (God permittinge) you intende to comme this way for shee longs to see you; soe doth JB.

426. TO MATTHIAS BYRD

[*Marginated*] Caerleon 23 June 1673

Wrote to Matthias that I longe since received his of the 12th of May last and this eveninge I received his of the 17th instant, by which it appears that what letters hee sent beetweene these 2 dates miscarryed; a word is desired from Meirick etc JB.

Since the writeinge of this letter I received yours of the 9th instant, which hath given our freinds and neighbours here great satisfaccion JB.

427. TO MATTHIAS BYRD

[*Marginated*] 22 July [1673]

Wrote to Matthias an account of my last and of receipt of his of the 4th instant etc.

428. TO NEPHEW WILLIAM BYRD

[*Marginated*] Caerleon 6 October 1673

Cozen William

Yours of the 13th of July 1669 I received from Mr William Powell of Langattog juxta Neath, and I paid Morgan Edward of Langattog for bringinge that letter to mee 2s., and on the 10th of September 1669 I wrote you an answer of that letter at large by Mr Powell, and yours of the 4th of March 1671 I received, and on the 29th of April 1671 I wrote you an account at large of both those letters; and yours of the 25th September 1671 I received by Mr Rowland Jones, by whome I wrote you an answere thereunto, and nowe yours of 5th of September 1673 I received from Mr James Gough, by which I finde my 3 letters abovesaid nor any one of them was received by you, at which I marvell beinge all sent by your owne messengers.

Your father was lately in good health, my sonne Matthias is nowe in London, the shipp which hee commaunded beinge sunke under him. Admirall de Ruyter sent boates and saved him and his company which were left alyve, and sent them prisoners to Holland. My wife, sonne William and selfe are here in good health I praise God, which is all lyveinge of my family. Please to dyrect your letters to your father whoe dwelleth in the Skynners Alley in Great St Hellens nere Bishopsgate, from whence I shall be sure to receive them.

To my loving nephew Mr William Byrd at his chamber in the house of George Savell a shooemaker, over against the Coach and Horses in Goldings Lane, these, Dublyn, in Ireland.

429. TO ELIZABETH HERBERT

[*Marginated*] 2 February 1674

Mrs Elizabeth Herbert

Your letter and bill of exchange for £3 to bee paid to the order of William Morgan I longe since received by this bearer Mrs Tomkins and have performed accordingly. Here enclosed is William Morgans bill, which I pray please to deliver to him with remembrance of my love to him. My wife and I present our faithfull respects to you and your sister Mrs Anne, whose health and happinesses none woulde bee gladder to heare of then shoulde yours really to serve you, John Byrd.

[Page 90]

Since the writeinge above I received yours of the 24th January last, and have paid Mr Rowland Morgan £3 to the use of Mr John Morgan of London merchant according to your order; this is all that I received from you since yours of the 14th of November 1673. This is all at present from yours as above JB.

430. TO THOMAS HANDS

[*Marginated*] 5 April 1674

Cozen Thomas Hands

I coulde not omitt the opportunety of writeinge to you by this bearer (my cozen Mr William Williams) to whome you shewed much kindenes at his beinge at Oxforde for which I render you my harty thanks. I pray present my due respects to Mr Alderman Griffin, and to both your wives. You shall receive here enclosed a peece of 5s., to drinke a glasse of wyne togeather with my cozen Williams. My sonne Matthias is lately marryed here, whoe with my wife and sonne William remember you all very kindely. I pray write mee word by this bearer howe you at Oxforde and all our relacions at Whately doe.

431. TO ELIZABETH HERBERT

[*Marginated*] 23 May 1674

Mrs Herbert

Yours of the 26th of April last I received and according to your order have delivered to my neighbour Mr Isaack Tomkins £11 in money. I shoulde bee glad to see you here; I pray please to write mee word when (God permittinge) you intende to comme to this country etc.

To his much honoured freinde Mrs Elizabeth Herbert, at the house of Mr Botsforde a lawyer at the upper ende of Grayes Inn Lane, nere the almsehouse, present these, London.

432. TO THOMAS FLETCHER

[*Marginated*] Caerleon 18 July 1674

Kinde sir

Yours of the 25th of June last I longe since received, with the paper therein enclosed, the party which was therein concerned beinge then in London. Since his returne home I did communicate yours to him, whose answer is that when your sonne in lawe Mr Layton commes to these partes hee will speake with him about the busines, which I hope will bee to the satisfaccion of Blanche Edwards which with my servis to you and yours presented and my kinde remembrance to Blanch, is all at present from yours really to serve you J B

I pray present my wifes hartie love and service (with myne) to Mr Searjeant Seys and all his family.

To his honoured freinde Captain Thomas Fletcher present these, Gloucester.

433. TO THOMAS HANDS

[*Marginated*] Caerleon 10 September 1674

Cozen Hands

Yours of the 19th and one from our worthy freinde Mr Alderman Griffin of the 18th of August I received last night from Cardiffe, in answer to both which, it is soe with me that a smale purchase which I formerly made and a great and tedious[1] suite in lawe which I was lately forced to undergoe hath soe disabled mee at present that I cannot doe what you desier, for which I am hartily sorry. I pray present my service and due respects to Mr Alderman Griffin and his wife, and please to acquainte him that I received his letter. My wife and sonnes present theyr true loves to you and your wife and to all our relacions at Whateley; soe doth JB.

I pray write mee word of receipt hereof by your bearer and howe our relacions doe at Whateley JB.

1. 'and tedious' interlined.

434. TO THOMAS HANDS

[*Marginated*] Caerleon 13 September 1674

Cozen Hands

Yours dated in the yeare 1674 I received on Tuseday last beinge the 10th instant,[1] and according to your dyreccion doe sende here enclosed a certifficatt subscribed by Mr John Morgan, one of the sonnes of Edward Morgan of Lanternam esquire. Thomas Morgan esquire one of the justices of peace in this county, and Mr Robert Morgan, are 2 grand children of the said Edward Morgan of Lanternam. Mr James Jones, one of the attorneys in this county,[2] and Mr William Jones were borne nere Lanternam aforesaid. Pray present my true love and service to Mr Alderman Griffin and his wife, and I give him and[3] you harty thanks for your loves in dyrectinge my neighbours Lewis Younge and Roger Younge in this theyr busines etc.

1. 'beinge the 10th instant' interlined.
2. 'one of the attorneys in this county' footnoted.
3. 'him &' interlined.

435. TO THOMAS HANDS

[*Marginated*] Caerleon 9 December 1674

Cozen Hands

Yours of the 19th of August dyrected to bee left at Christ Church I received from Cardiffe the 9th of September last, whereof I wrote you an account on the 10th of the same September, but by yours of the 12th of November last which I received by my neighbour Roger Younge, it seemes that myne came not to your hands. The contents of myne were that a smale purchase and a tedious suite in lawe which I was forced to undergoe disabled mee from performeinge what you desier. Wherefore I hope you will excuse mee beinge unprovided at this tyme to doe what you desire. I hartily thanke you for the great paynes which you have taken for my neighbours Lewis and Roger Younge and if it shall ly in my power I will endeavour to requite you. My neighbour Roger Younge commeth provided with that which I hope will give full satisfaccion to all whome it concernes. My wife and sonnes remember theyr true loves to you and your wife; soe doth your unkle JB.

I pray remember my true love to all our relacions at Whateley and in your next I pray write mee word howe all doe there.

436. ?TO ROGER GRIFFIN

[*No date*]

Honoured sir

Yours by this bearer (my neighbour Roger Younge) I received, by which and Rogers thankefull acknowledgements I finde my former obligacion to you trebled, which if God enable mee and you please to commaunde any thinge which shall ly in my power I shall expresse my thankefullnes for all your kindnesses. Sir here are severall auntient persons which say they will prove Lewis Younge and Roger Younge to bee the sonnes of Christopher Younge and Anne Barefoote of Northly (his wife)[1] and[2] Walter Harris an honest neighbour of ours sayth that hee is descended from the Barefootes of Northly and nowe commeth with Roger Younge to testifie the truth herein. Here is allsoe Mr Richard Harris, a person of creditt whoe sayth hee is descended in the same Barefootes of Northly and will prove if cause bee that Lewis Young [*Page 91*] and Roger Younge are the sonnes of Christopher Yonge and Anne Barefoote of Northly his wife. I hope that these with a certifficatt which Roger Yonge bringeth with him will give full satisfaccion in my neighbours just cause.

1. '(his wife)' interlined.
2. Followed by 'nowe commeth with Roger Younge' deleted.

437. TO THOMAS HANDS

[*Marginated*] Caerleon 28 February 1675

Cozen Hands

Yours of the 7th instant I received by this bearer Roger Younge whoe acknowledgeth the great kindenes which hee and his brother Lewis received from you and from Mr Alderman Griffin and from both your wives, for which I render my harty thanks to you all on the behalfe of my neighbours. Younge William Seys is a student in Lyncolnes Inn in London and I suppose is nowe there. His father dwelleth above 40 miles from us, whome I have not seene nor heard from since you wrote to mee concerning his sonnes debt, but if I shall happen to see eyther of them I shall bee myndefull of your busines. My wife and sonnes present theyr true loves to you and yours, and to all our relacions at Whateley. My cozen Mr William Williams presents his due respects to you and your wife and to our worthy freinde Mr Alderman Griffin with his wife and daughter and desires the Lord to contynewe all in health and happines; soe doth JB.

438. TO NEPHEW WILLIAM BYRD

[*Marginated*] Caerleon 17 April 1675

Cozen William

Yours of the 5th of September 1673 I longe since received from Mr James Gough, by whome I wrote to you at large, since which tyme I have not heard from you at all, but nowe this bearer Mr William Pritchard comminge from Irelande acquaintes mee that hee sawe you in good health in June last, which wee here are hartily glad of, and desier that wee may receave the like account from your selfe. This bearer promiseth to conveigh your letters to us here, his mother haveinge an estate in these partes. My sonne Matthias was marryed on St Matthias his day was 12 months to the daughter of Mr Edward Morgan of Pencreeke, by whome hee hath a daughter, whoe with my wife and sonne William desier to bee remembered to you; soe doth your unkle JB.

To Mr William Byrd at his chamber in the house of George Savell a shooemaker over against the Coach and Horses in Geldinge Lane, these, Dublin.

439. TO NEPHEW WLLIAM BYRD

[*Marginated*] Caerleon 13 November 1675

Cozen William

On the 17th of April last I wrote to you by William Pritchard whose father Roger Pritchard was a captain in Irelande (but longe since deceased). His widowe hath an estate in these partes and William Pritchard promised to conveigh your letters to mee and toulde mee allsoe that hee sawe you in good health in Dublyn, but by yours of the 21st of July last (which I received from Mr Jeffries) it seemes that William Pritchard miscaryed or else was a false messenger. Since the last terme I received a letter from your father whoe was then in good health and I hope is soe still; hee lyveth in Skynners Alley in Great St Hellyns nere Bishops Gate, by which way it is best to sende your letters. I praise God that I with my wife and sonnes are in good health, soe is my sonne Matthias's wife and daughter, whoe all remember theyr true loves to you, with desier to heare of your health and welfare; doe doth your unkle John Byrd.

To his loving nephewe Mr William Byrd at his lodgeinge at George Savills, at the Golden Ball in Goldinge Lane these, Dublyn, in Irelande.

440. TO ROGER GRIFFIN

[*Marginated*] Caerleon 29 August 1676

Honoured Sir

Yours of the 18th instant I received, in answer whereunto my neighbour Mr James Jones (an attorney in common pleas) hath written a discharge which was confirmed here by Roger Youngs widdowe and attested by Mr Jones, Mr Williams and myselfe, and doe hope it will give full satisfaccion to William Richards and all other persons therein concerned. Wee all doe render you our harty thanks for the love which you shewed to our poore neighbour Roger Younge and allsoe to his widdow. JB.

Written likewise to my cozen Thomas Hands that I had received his of the 17th instant, with my thanks and remembrances.

[*Marginated*] To Mr Roger Griffin alderman present these, Oxonforde

441. TO THOMAS HANDS

[*No date*]

Cozen Hands

Yours of the 30th of June and of the 20th of July I received and am very glad to heare of your good healths and wellfare. I am hartily sorry for the death of our worthy freind Mr Alderman Griffin, to whose widdowe my cozen[1] (Mrs Jane Pennant and hir daughter) I pray present the remembrance of my faithfull love and service. I pray God comfort them after soe great a losse. Pray remember us kindely to our relacions at Whately, and in your next I pray a word howe they doe etc.

1. 'my cozen' interlined.

442. TO NEPHEW WILLIAM BYRD

[*Marginated*] Caerleon 10 November 1677

Cozen William

Since yours of the 21st of July 1675 I have not heard one word of nor from you since whereof I formerly gave you an account. I desier to heare from you by this bearer Llewellyn ap Thomas ap John. JB.

443. TO THOMAS HANDS

[*Marginated*] Caerleon 13 February 1678

Cozen Hands

Yours of the 27th January I received and am glad to heare that our freinds in Gatehampton[1] are in health; I pray present the remembrance of my due respects to them all, and in your next pray write mee word howe our relacions doe in Whately. This I sende to Mr John Rousworth in Bristoll to bee sent to you according to your direccion.

1. 'Gapton' in MS.

Page 92

444. TO THE COMMISSIONERS FOR THE REVENUE OF THE EARL OF PEMBROKE

[*Marginated*] Caerleon 5 June 1677

[*headed]* 1 Ju[ne or July] 1670

Pierce Butler esquire, then lord of Edlogan (in the right of the Lady Morgan his wife) did cause the weare which turned the water (out of the ryver called Avon Lloyd) to the Earl of Pembrokes mills in Caerleon to bee broken 3 tymes soe that noe water was suffred to run to the said mills, alleadgeinge that in regards one(1) ende of this weare was fixed to the lordship of Edlogan hee ought to bee compounded with for the same, whereof the then lord was made acquainted, whoe wrote to Sir Trevor Williams desireinge him to advize John Byrd, tennant to the said mills to indite the persons whoe had donne this wronge and to proceede against them accordinge to lawe and not to compounde with Mr Buttler or any other person herein, which was donne accordinglie, the charge and dammadge whereof to the said John Byrd beinge above £100, which the then commissioners for his lordships(2) revenews promised shoulde bee considered to the content of the said tennant; but the lord dyed and not any thinge donne therein, which the said John Byrd then and nowe tennant to the said mills humbly prayeth his lordship that nowe is, and his commissioners, will bee pleased to take into consideracion the premisses whereby the said tennant may be releaved herein.

Right worshipful

I humbly pray you to present my humble duty to my honourable lord and to present the premisses to his lordship, wherein you will very much obliege him whoe is your worshipps humble servant John Byrd.

To the right worshipful the commissioners for the revenewe of the right honourable the Earl of Pembroke etc present these, Cardiffe.

1. 'one' interlined.
2. 'for his lordships' interlined.

445. TO RICHARD SEYS

[*Marginated*] Caerleon 21 January 1678

Honoured cozen

Accordinge to your request by your letter dated 12th November last I spake with my cozen Mr William Williams and his wife, whoe seemed to bee very willinge to graunte theyr consents to your desier, referringe it to theyr daughter to whome

I spake likewise, whoe very modestly was silent; yet I doe suppose that after you have conferred with my cozen Williams and considered of things for theyr future comfort that the match will goe on. This bearer canne acquainte you of his further proceedings[1] herein, to which I must referr this matter, wishinge them (beinge both[2] allyed to mee) all happines. I thanke you kindely for the pickled oysters which I received from you; my wife presents hir true love to you and all yours; soe doth your alliesman and servant John Byrd.

To the worshipful (his loving freinde and alliesman) Richard Seys esquire present these, Rheedinge nere Neath.

1. 'proceedings' repeated in MS.
2. 'both' interlined.

446. MEMORANDUM

[*Subscribed*] Caerleon 14 October 1680

Mr Kanerley a minister left five pounds in money with my father in lawe Alexander Seys esquire, the interest to bee paid to such poore as hee and his heires etc. shoulde thinke fitt for ever. The said Alexander Seys gave five pounds by his will, the use thereof to bee to the poore of Caerlion for ever, which tenne pounds I woulde have paide to the overseers of the poore, but our neighbours desired mee to keepe it and to pay the interest therof to the overseers of the poore of the saide towne, which I have donne accordinglie; and for the future secureinge the interest of the said tenne pounds I will eyther paye it to the overseers or secure the interest to bee paide out of any house or any parte of my estate for ever, John Byrd.

[*Marginated*] My sonne Matthias Byrd delyvered a noate to the commissioners for pious uses at the court kept this day at Uske, whereof this is a coppie. JB.

447. TO RICHARD JENKINS

[*No date*]

Kinde sir

I did beeleeve that I shoulde have seene you here before this tyme, that I might have confirmed the newe lease by us agreed uppon. The tyme is neere when it is to begin, wherefore I send this bearer unto you by whome I pray write mee word what day you intende to bee heere, that I may cause the lease to bee ready against your cominge, which with my due respects to you and yours presented is all at present from yours really to serve you John Byrd.

[*Marginated*] To his loving freinde Mr Richard Jenkins present these, Glacecoed.

NOTES

1. Luke Hodges (d. 1656) was MP for Bristol, 1646-53. He was the third son of John Hodges of Shipton Moyne, near Tetbury, Glos., and was trading in Bristol by 1639 at the latest. He was nominated to the first local tax and sequestration committees of parliament in February and March 1643, and sat on many Bristol committees for taxation subsequently. In 1643 he was removed from his place on Bristol city council when the city fell into royalist hands. In December 1645, when Bristol was again under parliament's control, Hodges was re-instated, and by September 1646 he had been made an alderman. From that year he was also customer for Bristol, and its MP. In 1646 and 1648 he was made a commissioner for excluding 'improper persons from the sacrament' (on the authority of presbyterian-inspired parliamentary ordinances). His posting as cheque or check in the Bristol customs establishment in June 1649 instead of Thomas Shewell seems not have been carried through. He accepted Pride's Purge and became a member of important parliamentary committees of the Rump for the army and the sale of bishops' lands. Under the protectorate he became a commissioner for removing 'scandalous ministers'. Crucially for JB, Hodges was a member of the committee for the navy, which had oversight of customs' appointments. He became an excise commissioner in 1652.

F&R i, 91, 113, 853, 1209, ii, 64, 153, 562, 689, 974; Bodl. MS Rawl A 224, fos. 33v-109v [I am grateful to Dr A P Barclay of the History of Parliament Trust for this reference]; *Merchants and Merchandise*, 91; *Merchant Venturers,* 190-2; *Deposition Books 1643-1647,* 264, 266, 267; D. Underdown, *Pride's Purge* (Oxford, 1971), 376, 393.

2. 'Mr Kellam' was George Kellam, clerk to the committee for the navy and customs until December 1648, and acting in a temporary capacity in that post until February 1649. He may have been related to Richard Kellam, a petitioner for the place of messenger to the accounts committee in 1649, and a former soldier in the cavalry regiment of Sir Arthur Haselrige.

Bodl. MS Rawl. A 224 fo. 48; Aylmer, *SS*, 66.

3. Sheriff Avery was Samuel Avery, a customs commissioner between 1645 and 1649, and sheriff of the City of London in 1647. Dudley Avery, his son, was receiver to the customs commissioners in London. In February 1656 Dudley Avery was arrested for fraud; Samuel denounced the 'foul miscarriage' of his son, which brought down both the Averys.

CSPD 1655-6, 172, 248-9, 578; *CSPD 1656-7, 84-5.*

5. Sir Thomas Dawes was collector inwards for the customs of the port of London, and John Dawes was surveyor of the outports. By February 1648, both had been sequestered for royalism, and their estates and salaries were managed by Thomas Abberley. After 1660 John Dawes recovered the post of collector of subsidy inwards in the port of London, and was appointed briefly surveyor of the outports, before being succeeded by Edmund Turner: see **234** below.

PRO E 351/648; *CSPD 1660-1661,* 149, 559, 576, 580, 602; BL Add. 33590 f. 181.

7. The nearest assize meetings were held at Monmouth; at Cardiff met their Welsh equivalent, the courts of great sessions.

8. John Morgan of Trostrey, gentleman, and John Morgan of Pentrebach were two Monmouthshire recusants listed in 1650s compilations of sequestered individuals: the estate of the latter was farmed by John Plumley of Newport, JB's deputy there.

PRO SP 28/213. See also **204, 205** below.

9, 11. JB is here describing Thomas Lewis of St Pierre, near Chepstow , who shortly after this joined the royalist rising led by Sir Nicholas Kemys of Cefn Mabli. Kemys seized Chepstow Castle, and Lewis was one of the defenders against the forces of Oliver Cromwell. In the autumn of 1644, St Pierre had provided quarters for royalist officers, seemingly with Lewis's consent, but his visitors were uneasy about the loyalty of the area. Lewis's estates were afterwards sequestered for his part in the 1648 episode, and he was still under suspicion in 1655. He was rewarded at the restoration by a place on the Monmouthshire bench of magistrates. He was high sheriff in 1666.

BL Add. 18981 ff. 259, 308; Add. 34013 p.120; Bradney iv, 76-7, 81; *CCC*, 311, 2350; Phillips, *Justices; List of Sheriffs.*

10. A Robert Hampton was on the committee for the Middlesex militia in 1644: (F&R i, 383, 556). Francis Parsons was assistant secretary to the customs commissioners at the London custom house, in 1657 on a salary of £50. He was a close associate of Michael Sansom, solicitor to the customs commissioners in 1649-50; Sansom left mourning clothes to Parsons in his will.

PRO E351/658; PROB 11/ 212 fo. 369v.

12. William Knight was a Bristol merchant: a linen-draper.

Bristol Deposition Books 1650-1654, 97; *Merchants and Merchandise,* 115-6.

13. 'Andrew' was Andrew Seys of Cwrtybela; JB's mother-in-law was Florence Seys: see 159 below. *Limbus Patrum,* 228-21; Bradney ii pt. i, 94-5.

15. William Toomes was surveyor general of customs in 1649, on a salary of £125. He was still surveyor-general at the restoration, but was succeeded by Christopher Metcalf and by William Rumbold.

PRO E 122/236/19; *CTB* i, 548.

27. n.2: a Thomas Young gent. of Newport was in 1655 suspected of disloyalty to the protectorate.

BL Add. 34013 p. 243.

28, 136: William Meredith held some lands in Caerleon of the earl of Pembroke in 1668, was collector of the subsidy in the town in 1661, and as a 'gentleman' paid 5s. towards the 'free and voluntary present' for Charles II, of 1661.

Gwent RO MAN/B/16/0001; PRO E179/148/91, E179/253/32.

30. Col. Henry Herbert (1617-56), was the eldest son of William Herbert of Coldbrook, Abergavenny, and a leading parliamentary soldier in South Wales, rewarded for his services with a grant of lands from the estate of the Marquis of Worcester, including Coldre lordship. He was MP for Monmouthshire in the Long Parliament, serving through until the dissolution of the Rump, and served on the council of state in 1651-2. He was MP for his county in the first protectorate parliament, a member of several county committees and of the commission

for the propagation of the gospel. When he died in 1656, Evan Seys was one of the trustees of his estate. JB is here asking Herbert's agent for clarification about a possible heriot due on the death of his relative, Hulls.

DWB; PRO PROB 11/1656/267.

31. Mathew Franklin was a leading Swansea merchant and alderman, and portreeve (mayor) there in 1642-3. He seems to have been a parliamentarian at least as early as 1645 and had shipping interests.

M. Price (ed.), *The Account Book of the Borough of Swansea, Wales, 1640-1660* (Lampeter, 1990), *passim; Deposition Books* i, 29, 114.

32. William Yeomans or Yeamans had been admitted into the Society of Merchant Venturers of the City of Bristol in 1646, and from that year he was also a city councillor. His name recurs through the 1640s and 50s as a prominent merchant in the city. In 1656 he was accounting for sums at the exchequer on behalf of Thomas Shewell, customs collector at Bristol, presumably because of his easy access to bills of exchange.

Merchant Venturers, 44; *Merchants and Merchandise,* many refs, *passim; Deposition Books* i, 268; PRO SP 18/131A.

40. Francis Buckeridge was in 1648 the collector of customs at Milford Haven. In 1657 he was paid a salary of £25.

PRO E 351/648, 658.

46. Francis Yeomans or Yeamans was a notary public in Bristol, helping many of its leading citizens to draft legal documents.

Deposition Books i, 52, 68.

47. Mr. Barker: Robert Barker was in 1657 searcher for the customs at Swansea (salary: £25), but his service as a customs officer went back at least to 1638, when he was a searcher at Aberthaw.

E 134/ 22, 23 Charles I/ Hil. 2.

49. The list of small harbours or 'pills' shows the extent of Byrd's territory. 'Horse Pill' must have been above Chepstow on the Severn, possibly near Pillhouse Rocks.

55. 'Father, mother, sister and the ould people': William Byrd, JB's brother, his wife and daughter Susanna. Perhaps the 'ould people' were the parents-in-law of William Byrd senior. A Thomas Palmer was a tidesman in the London custom house in 1659, complaining with others that the position was unestablished.

BL Add. 15888 fo. 232.

56. The *Charles* was presumably the vessel still loyal to the king in December 1648, whose complement was 120 naval officers and men and 20 soldiers.

BL Add. 18982 ff. 133, 145.

57. Colonel Richard Deane (1610-53) had commanded artillery at the battle of Naseby, and was enthusiastic for the trial of Charles I. He was appointed general-at-sea in 1649, and in May of that year he and his two fellow generals-at-sea blockaded Ireland. Deane returned to England in June; at the time of JB's letter, he was in Bristol preparing for the invasion of

Ireland. He was to be killed in action during the first Dutch war, in 1653. He is not to be confused with his cousin, Captain Richard Deane, who was treasurer-at-war and receiver-general of assessments.

DNB; M. Ashley, *Cromwell's Generals* (1954), 122-24; Aylmer, *SS,* 99.

60. Mr Lloyd: Hugh Lloyd, sub-commissioner for excise in South Wales: see **130** below.

63, 64. Thornbury was an official in the London custom house, and Sankey was the customs commissioners' solicitor. Foxe, Swynmoure and Palmer were also junior customs officials in London. Richard Bateman and Samuel Avery, both London aldermen, were customs commissioners from 1645 to 1649. Unlike the three other commissioners, who were accountable for port of London customs, Bateman and Avery were treasurers for money from the outports. Bateman was, like Thomas Pennant, also a member of the Skinners' Company and its master in 1643. The protracted references to Futter evidently concerned a sum long overdue to the Cardiff customs collector, thus payable to the commissioners.

Beaven, *Aldermen* i, 185, ii, 67, 69; Wadmore, *Skinners*, 192.

67. 'The Importing of any Wines, Wooll or Silk from the Kingdom of France, prohibited', 28 August 1649.

F&R ii, 239-40.

68 (see also **118**). This seems to be a sidelight on the long-standing dissatisfaction with the Bristol merchants' two-thirds monopoly on sales of Welsh butter (assessed at 6000 kitterkins per annum) from c. 1618. In 1639, Charles I supported the merchants by prohibiting exports, but the following year the Long Parliament suspended the merchants' privilege. By the early 1650s there was developing a three-cornered dispute over the terms of the monopoly between the government, the merchant venturers and the corporation of Bristol: the Bristol merchants would look for reasons for any decline in the supply of Welsh butter to the city.

Latimer, 76, 136, 149-50, 242-3, 246.

In 1629 the owners of the *Abraham* of Bristol had been Humphry Hooke, Andrew Charlton, John Goninge, Edmund Petre, Thomas Heathcott and Mrs Butcher.

The Bristol Channel has one of the largest tidal ranges in the world: a spring tide, rather than rough seas, would have been the most likely cause of Williams's difficulty in landing the cargo at Aberthaw.

69. George Strelley (b. 1609) was of Nottinghamshire parentage, but was born in the city of London. He married Elizabeth Reading, of Clewer, Berks., in 1634, and four children were born to them in the parish of St Olave Hart Street in the city. He seems to have advanced in the customs service: from 1652-7 it seems likely that he was customs collector at Plymouth. George Strelley was related to John Strelley, who died in Ireland in 1650 while commanding a troop of horse in the regiment of Col. John Reynolds.

Boyd's Inhabitants of London, 39173; Aylmer, List; PRO PROB 11/ 212 fo. 369v.

70. This refers to a principal stipulation of an ordinance on establishing tonnage and poundage collection between 1648 and 1651, dated 16 December 1647.

F&R i, 1032-1042.

74. The committee of sequestrations sat at Goldsmiths' Hall, in the City of London, and was responsible for dealings with royalists whose estates were sequestered. Early in 1650 the committee was replaced by the commissioners for compounding, who appointed subsidiary local committees (F&R i, *passim; CCC* preface to vols. i and v). JB was worried that although he had obtained a judgment against Morgan, he could not recover the value of his goods.

76. Colonel Tyson was probably Edward Tyson, a leading Bristol merchant and partisan of Parliament from at the latest 1644, when he was named a member of the Bristol committee. He served on every committee for the city subsequently, through the 1650s, and was mayor in 1659. His military title would have been derived from the command he shared with others of the Bristol militia. Following a dispute between the Bristol merchant community and the military presence, the militia at Bristol was reduced to one regiment of eight companies, and Col. Tyson accepted the lower rank of lieutenant-colonel. In 1656 he became one of the commissioners to Major-general Boteler. There was another Edward Tyson in the New Model Army, but he was a lieutenant in the dragoon regiment of Colonel Okey, and a link between him and the Severnside area cannot be traced.

F&R i, 460, 545, 974, 1234, ii, 42, 308, 477, 1378; *Thurloe State Papers,* iii, 259-60, 299, iv, 379; Firth and Davies, *Reg. Hist.* ii, 724-5.

79. JB required writs of appraisement to be able to value cargoes; the commissioners he nominated for insertion in the writ for Monmouthshire were his neighbours in Caerleon. Of those for Glamorgan, he had brushed with the Spencers of Aberthaw in the 1630s and they later became his enemies; Robert Corrock took exchequer depositions in the Spencers' complaints against JB in 1646 and acted after 1660 in the Vale of Glamorgan on behalf of the king against those who had handled tithes and other public revenues during the Interregnum. Corrock lived in St Athan. Although James Gibbon remains obscure, his surname was common in the Vale.

PRO E 113/2; *Glamorgan Hearth Tax.*

81. Thomas Harrison (1606-60), colonel of horse, regicide and leading light among the radicals of the Rump Parliament was at this time the foremost military figure in South Wales, and three months after this letter was the first named among the lay commissioners for the propagation of the gospel in Wales. Harrison's troops were by virtue of their armed strength a useful means of transporting to London specie, in the form of customs dues or the rents collected from the South Wales tenants of Philip, earl of Pembroke (1584-1650), another Rump MP and member of the council of state.

DNB.

89. On 14 December 1649 an act was passed which confirmed the form of words for an oath or 'engagement' to be taken by officials and others in public office, as resolved in parliament on 11 October: 'I do declare and promise that I will be true and faithful to the commonwealth of England, as the same is now established, without a king or house of lords'. This was shortly afterwards extended systematically to all officeholders.

F&R ii, 319-20, 325-9; S.R. Gardiner, *History of the Commonwealth and Protectorate. Volume One: 1649-50* (1903), 176.

On 20 September 1649 Parliament passed an act against the printing and publication of 'scandalous' (i.e. blasphemous, seditious or libellous) material. It affected JB insofar as it stipulated that no books were to be imported anywhere except at the port of London. The act represented a step towards the reimposition of censorship after its breakdown during the civil war.

F&R ii, 245-54.

91. Major John Gawler commanded a company of soldiers at the Cardiff garrison, lived at St Fagans, and rented church lands at Whitchurch in 1648 and 1652. From 1656 to 1660 he was a magistrate and commissioner for assessments. He was the brother of Francis Gawler, feltmaker, an eminent early South Wales quaker, and by the early 1660s seems to have joined his brother in the Friends' cause.

N. Penney (ed.), *The First Publishers of Truth* (1907), 324, n.8; S.K. Roberts, 'Godliness and Government in Glamorgan' in C. Jones *et al., Politics and People in Revolutionary England* (Oxford, 1986), 249 and sources cited there.

John Herbert was in 1650 sheriff of Glamorgan, mayor of Cardiff, and nominated as a lay commissioner for the propagation of the gospel. He was the seventh son of Philip, fourth earl of Pembroke, and was a magistrate for the county from 1649 throughout the 1650s. Richards, *Puritan Movement,* 94; Phillips, *Justices.*

95. Colonel Philip Jones (1618-74) was the Cardiff garrison commander. Originally of Llangyfelach, near Swansea, he was rapidly rising to a position of pre-eminence in South Wales committees, and was second only to Thomas Harrison on the list of lay commissioners for the propagation of the gospel . Like John Herbert, he became a magistrate in 1649.

DNB; DWB; A. G. Veysey, 'Colonel Philip Jones', *Trans. Hon. Soc. Cymmrodorion* (1966), 316-40.

Humphrey Blake was the brother of Robert Blake, the most eminent sea-commander of the commonwealth. Blake was named to Somerset county committees from 1648. From April 1649 Humphrey Blake was a treasurer, accountable to the commissioners, for prize goods. The commission for prize goods investigated cases of wreck or capture when the vessel was considered an enemy.

F&R i, 1092, ii, 76-8; GRO D/DF F/37.

107. 'rateinge contrybucions': JB is asking whether any change has taken place in the basis of monthly taxation to support the army.

108. Denis Gauden was a victualler for the navy from this period through the 1660s. He was a London merchant, who became an alderman of the city of London from 1667, and was sheriff, 1667-8. In the same year he was knighted and became master of the clothworkers' company. As surveyor for victualling in the navy from 1660, he became an associate of Samuel Pepys, whose diary contains much on him. Denis was the brother of John Gauden, bishop of Worcester and possible author of Eikon Basilike, the hagiographical work which appeared shortly after the execution of Charles I.

Beaven, *Aldermen;* Pepys, *Companion.*

110. Under the system of taxation by monthly assessments, a sum was levied by Parliament on each county, which was divided by commissioners into sums to be apportioned to the individual hundreds and parishes. In each parish the 'raters' would set the sum on individual taxpayers: JB is objecting to the method adopted by the Caerleon raters.

115. William Willott or Willett (d. 1679) was admitted to the freedom of the city of Bristol in 1642, as a consequence of his marriage to the daughter of a late alderman, William Pitt. He became a merchant venturer in 1647, sheriff 1668, master of the merchant venturers 1670-71.

Merchants and Merchandise, 237.

116, 117, 122. William or Robert Franklin: JB seems confused about the forename.

118. see **68.** Colonel Harvey: Edmund Harvey was a customs commissioner from 1649 to 1655 and brother-in-law of Henry Langham, cashier-general of customs whose own brother, George, was as accountant-general, one of JB's correspondents. Another brother-in-law, Robert Tichborne, was a leading London citizen and master of the skinners' company in 1650. Harvey and Henry Langham were central figures in a corruption scandal in the customs establishment from 1655, which also touched Tichborne.
Aylmer, *SS,* 161-2; *Second Narrative of the Late Parliament* (1658), quoted in Wadmore, *Skinners,* 124-5.

122. 'Cozen Williams': probably William Williams of Caerleon, gentleman, eldest son of Thomas Williams esquire, and brother of John Williams of Caerleon, related to JB through his wife. William Williams was clerk of the peace for Monmouthshire in 1640-41; either he or a namesake was a commissioner for sewers with JB in 1662 and was on the assize grand jury with JB in 1665.
GRO D/DF 2919; PRO ASSI 5/2, C 181/7 p.132; L.E. Stephens, *The Clerks of the Counties.*

123. This was the same John Plumley who served as JB's deputy collector in Newport (see **49**). Plumley was of sufficient local importance to be nominated to a commission of sewers, dealing with sea- and river-banks and other watercourses, for Monmouthshire in 1655. One of his name was among the first nominated aldermen of Newport when it acquired its charter in 1623.

PRO C181/6 p. 105; [W.N. Johns], *Historical Traditions and Facts relating to Newport and Caerleon* (Newport, 1880), pt. v, 35.

124. In 1670 Margaret Love occupied the largest house (with ten hearths) in the High Street, Neath.

Glamorgan Hearth Tax, 12.

125. Parliament passed an ordinance prohibiting the export of wool, or any kind of clay that could be used for fulling, in January 1648 (F&R i, 1059-61). Trade with Barbados and with other colonies was stopped as a response to royalist-inspired rebellions against the commonwealth there, and JB and other customs officer received this order a few weeks before an act was passed to confirm the prohibition.

F&R ii, 425-9, S.R. Gardiner, *History of the Commonwealth and Protectorate,* i, 316-7.

126. For James Young see biographies of JB's correspondents; Moses Longman was a Bristol mercer; Rees Jones was JB's nephew, the son of JB's sister-in-law, Eleanor, and her

husband, William Jones of Cwrt Bleddyn; Hugh Roberts was a schoolmaster in Bristol.

Merchants and Merchandise, 20; Bradney ii pt. i, 94-5.

130,138. Hugh Lloyd was excise sub-commissioner, 1650-53, for the counties of Glamorgan, Carmarthen, Cardigan and Pembroke, with Edward Ditty. Mark Davis filled the same office for Monmouthshire and Herefordshire, and in August 1649 had summoned Herefordshire excise payers to account at Bromyard . JB is here contemplating a request to be made farmer of the excise for the two counties, having heard of or seen the act of 20 September to permit this.

PRO AO 1 /891/7 [I owe this reference to Dr G E Aylmer]; Birmingham City Archives, Hanley Court MSS, Box 4, 398337; F&R ii, 422-3; M. Braddick, *Parliamentary Taxation,* 170.

131. At the discretion of customs officers, merchants were allowed to 'compound' for duties payable: in other words they could reach a settlement which gave the officers revenue, but often involved a reduction in what they might have gained by strict adherence to the Book of Rates. By Books of Rates current from as early as 1610 to as late as 1782, an imported horse was valued at £10. The rate charged the merchant by the customs officer varied. Under the terms currently prevailing, JB was charging Spencer 5 per cent of the supposed value of the animals.

University of London Library, Goldsmiths' Library, has Books of Rates of 1610, 1620, 1635, 1782.

133, 135. The customs commissioners were trying to change the conditions of their officers' employment, so that they made accounts for each day they worked, rather than quarterly. They were responding to the fitful volume of business transacted in the South Wales ports. The effect of the change would have been to add to the paperwork of the local officers.

135. In order to build up the navy to protect English merchant shipping, an act of 31 October 1650 removed the rebate of fifteen per cent on customs receipts which had been allowed merchants, and by another act of March 1650, a levy of one shilling in the pound of customs duties paid was to be made to fund attempts to release the hostages of foreign pirates.

F&R ii, 368, 444.

137. See **28** for William Meredith.

138. See **130.**

141. In 1650, acts for the militia and assessment had been passed on 11 July and 26 November, respectively. The militia act continued in office those commissioners nominated earlier. Morgan Griffith was a Caerleon man who paid 1s. towards the 'free and voluntary present of 1661'.

F&R ii, 397-402, 456-90.

146. In this composition case involving the waiter at Aberthaw, JB and his colleague were attempting to compound for wool that had been carried across to Minehead and then distributed before duty had been paid.

147. 'An Act touching the Importation of Bullion' (9 January 1651) guaranteed free passage into the country of all foreign coin and bullion. Merchants were to pay one per cent customs

duty, but had to send one third of their consignments to the mint at the Tower of London.

F&R ii, 495.

Henry Kersley or Kersey (d. 1670) was clerk of bonds and certificates for coast business, based at the London custom house and in 1657 paid an annual salary of £120. He was it seems of Lancashire parentage, but married in 1632 at Stepney, Middlesex. He was a member of the bowyers' company, and lived in St Olave Hart Street, near the London custom house, where seven children were born to him and his wife. He was probably the man who in 1650 bought Kersley's Farm, West Ham, formerly crown property, for £54 12s; when his widow died in 1680 she was brought back to St Olave's from Leyton for burial.

Boyd's Inhabitants of London, 12945; *Visitations of Middlesex 1663,* 51; Cambridge University Library, MS Dd. viii.30.5 f. 25v.

148. JB wants first hand information on any new acts for the monthly assessment.

149. An act of 28 January 1651 continued until 1 May of that year the terms of the militia act of July 1650.

CJ vi, 528.

151, 154, 155. Robert Moulton (c.1592 -1652), a Cornishman, had emigrated to New England in 1629 and in the 1630s was involved in attempts to break up the monopoly of the East India company in the far east. He served in the navy of Parliament from 1643, and was a leader in suppressing the naval mutiny of 1648. Moulton was helping to break the power of the royalists in South Wales from the spring of 1644, organising a strong naval presence in the Bristol Channel. At the end of 1645, as Glamorgan fell into the hands of the parliamentarians, Moulton kept a watchful eye on developments from off-shore. He supported Pride's Purge and from 1651 to 1652 was navy commissioner at Portsmouth; at the time of JB's difficulty he was living in Rotherhithe.

Phillips, *Civil War*, i, 216, 235-6, 273, ii, 159, 191; Capp, 19, 30, 39, 44, 49, 54-5, 176, 197; *Glam. Co. Hist.* iv, 272.

152, 154, 155, 157, 163. The hostility shown JB by Thomas Spencer, which seems to have taken the former by surprise, had antecedents back in the late 1630s when Spencer's trade in tobacco was significantly damaged by the customs officers at Aberthaw, including JB, who detained his cargoes. In January 1647, depositions were taken at Penmark in Spencer's exchequer case against JB and his colleagues.

E 134/ 22, 23 Charles I/ Hil. 2.

159. The deceased was Florence Seys, JB's mother-in-law. She was the daughter of Andrew Vaen, archdeacon of St David's in 1577, and vicar of Christchurch, Monmouthshire. She was the wife of Alexander Seys (d. 1632) of The Gaer, St Woollos. Florence Morgan (JB's sister-in-law) was the wife of Giles Morgan of Tymawr, Tredunnock. Eleanor Jones, another sister-in-law, was the wife of William Jones and the mother of Rees; Margery Byrd was JB's wife. In her will Florence Seys expressly denied a bequest to her daughter Catherine. JB was sole executor, and the will was proved on his oath on 21 June 1651.

Bradney ii, pt i, 94-5, iii, 262, 264; *Limbus Patrum,* 218-21; PRO PROB 11/217/131.

163. JB uses the word 'assizes' to mean the court of great sessions for Glamorgan.

167. A Charles Powell was the son of Walter Powell (1581-1655) the diarist of Llantilio Crossenny. Charles was an apothecary in Bristol. Walter Powell's nephew, James, was the founder of a school.

J.A. Bradney, *A History of the Free Grammar School in the Parish of Llantilio-Crossenny* (1924), 38.

169. The excise office was located at Broad St., London. Samuel Neale was cashier in the office there for mercery and silk, 1647-50, 1653-4 at a salary of £60 pa.

PRO E 351/1295-6. I owe this reference to the kindness of Dr G.E. Aylmer.

In March 1651 an act stipulated that cargoes of coal entering home ports were to pay an extra duty of 2s. per chaldron or 1s. per ton at customs houses, in order to finance an expansion of the navy to protect shipping against piracy. Seized cargoes were to be split equally between the seizing officer and the state.

F&R ii, 505-9.

170. Col. Jones is Philip Jones (see **95** above); Harrison is Thomas Harrison (see **81** above); For Henry Herbert (1617-56), see **30** above.

DWB.

173. 'Mr Morgan of Pencreek': William Morgan of Pencrug, parish of Llanhennock, Monmouthshire (d. 1665), son of Giles Morgan (d. 1641), who was sheriff of the county in 1614. The Dutch visitor Lodewicjk Huygens met him in 1652 and considered him 'a very decent man' (Bradney iii, 252; Huygens, 124). On 15 and 18 April respectively, acts for continuing the monthly assessments and empowering militia commissioners to press soldiers for service in Ireland appeared (F&R ii, 511-4). By an act of 6 February 1651 those who had already lent the government money would by advancing an identical sum be guaranteed interest at eight per cent on the security of confiscated crown rents.

F&R ii, 498-500.

179. 'Ould masters': JB is referring here to the commissioners for the customs who left office in 1649.

180. During the 1650s the probate of wills was centralised, at what was until 1653 called the Prerogative Court of Canterbury. To avoid the need for travelling long distances to obtain grants of probate, the court appointed commissioners, often clergy, to administer oaths to executors. JB, pursuing the will of his mother-in-law, suggests for this role Cradock and Walter, two well-known Puritan ministers. They were settled as ministers at, respectively, Usk and Newport in the spring of 1653, although their appearance here confirms their prior activism in the area. Rees or Rice Williams of Newport was a commissioner for the propagation of the gospel, a sequestration official and lay preacher. Philip Williams of Monmouth was another preacher. Roger Williams was alleged to have been involved with the sequestration of the marquis of Worcester's property in the late 1640s, and John Ward was treasurer of sequestered rents in Monmouthshire in 1655. JB was here naming the most radical supporters of the government in his area. Cradock wrote to Oliver Cromwell to recommend Rice Williams for a post as registrar of deeds in Monmouthshire, commenting sympathetically on the limited clerical skills of that 'renowned ancient saint'.

Richards, *Puritan Movement,* 82, 95, 98, 99, 146, 159 [Walter Cradock, Rice Williams]; *Diary of Walter Powell,* 40, 41, 43; PRO E112/569/1077 [Ward]; E112/569/1076 [Roger Williams]; B. Worden, *The Rump Parliament 1648-1653* (Cambridge, 1974), 114-5.

182. The same phenomenon was noted by Lodewijck Huygens on his visit to Newport in 1652:

> 'Near the bridge and still further down the river every twelve hours at certain places coal is washed up by the sea; people come to collect it in small boats without knowing why and from whence the coal comes' (Huygens, 124).

In 1708 the poor were still collecting coal in this way: Nathan Rogers, *Memoirs of Monmouthshire* (1708), 32.

185. For JB's mother-in-law's will, see **159** and **180** above.

186. Algiers duty was a 5 per cent *ad valorem* surcharge on the tonnage and poundage payable on all imports and exports, established in 1640 to fund the rescue of hostages of north African pirates. The books of rates laid down fixed values of commodities, ignoring market prices. Customs duties were percentages based on valuations in the book of rates. Walter Thomas had filed a bond with JB on the credit of John Walter, who had defaulted; JB would then enter legal process to recover the money due to the state.

187. JB's 'oath' is presumably the Engagement (see **89** above). Those he suggests as commissioners were, with the exception of his colleague Philip Williams, magistrates

(Phillips, *Justices*). See also **180** above.

197. 'Subsidy' in this context means the main customs duty, consisting of tonnage and poundage.

199. James Jones gentleman stood fourth in the subsidy or direct tax list for Caerleon in 1661, and held tenements in Jany Crane St. there. He was an attorney in the court of Common Pleas. In 1655 he was the guardian of William Morgan, whose late father, also William, had been sequestered as a catholic. PRO E179/148/91; Gwent RO MAN/B/15/0007; *CCC*, 3238; **285**, **300**, **441** below.

200. Robert Barker was in 1657 searcher for the customs at Swansea (salary: £25). Benjamin Streater was collector at Aberafan, on a salary of £20.

PRO E351/658.

203, 204. By an act of 18 November 1652, the estate of John Morgan of Pentrebach, Monmouthshire, was forfeited to the commonwealth for treason. Morgan was the brother of Sir Edward Morgan of Llantarnam, and was a catholic. Those named in the act were allowed to 'compound' or pay a fine instead, and catholic recusants were to sell their estates within one year or be subject to the full penalties of anti-catholic legislation. The estates of those named in the act were to be security against new loans encouraged by the government from those who had already loaned on the 'public faith'. JB's interest, as such a lender, in Morgan's affairs probably derived more from material interest than from friendship, since in 1651 he acquired over eleven acres of his in the lordship of Liswerry, but **205** suggests that he was hoping to sell his public faith bills, not buy more. In the event, Morgan did pay a fine, of £287.

F&R ii, 623-52; *CCC* iv, 3003, 3088; PRO SP 28/213; Bradney iii, 231; NLW Tredegar Park

107/24.

207. The act 'for the redemption of captives' was renewed on 21 December 1652.

CJ vii, 231; F&R iii, xc.

208. John Lloyd had by this time been appointed collector of customs at Llanelli. He was presumably John Lloyd of Faerdref, since 1649 a JP and member of Carmarthenshire county committees.

Phillips, *Justices*; Dodd, *Studies*, 148.

209. Thomas Woodall was upper beadle of the London skinners' company. In 1644 the company granted him and his wife Anne a house near skinners' hall, for life. In 1646 he was paid a salary of £10, and he seems to have acted as Thomas Pennant's assistant. By 1655 he had died, and his wife, 'being poore' was granted a pension of £6. Widow Woodall was still alive on the eve of the Great Fire, living in a one-hearthed property in St Botolph Bishopsgate parish. One can only assume that JB's description of the Woodalls as 'brother and sister' (unless meant jocularly) refers to a marital link between one of them and Pennant's wife.

Guildhall Library, Skinners' Company records, court book 3, f. 212, receipts and payments book 6, pp. 1-24; court book 4, f. 46v; PRO E 179/147/617.

210. By this time the collectorship of Burry Port and Llanelli had been given to John Lloyd, and the collectorship of Swansea had been taken by Griffith Bowen. Bowen (c. 1600 - c.1676) and his family left Gower in 1638 for Boston, Massachusetts, where he was admitted into the first church. He returned to Wales in 1650, and by December of that year was involved in a business transaction with Col. Philip Jones, who may have been the instrument of Bowen's advancement in government service. In 1651-2 he acquired the post of farmer of the inland excise for south west Wales, and kept the collectorship of the Swansea customs until 1657. He joined the Ilston baptist community in 1653, and suffered religious persecution after 1660.

Publications of the Colonial Soc. of Massachusetts, vol. 39; *Collections: Records of the First Church in Boston* (ed. R.D. Pierce, 1961), 23, 283, 286, 306; A. H. Dodd, *BBCS*, xvi, part 1 (1954), 31, 34; E. S. John, 'Croesi'r Iwerydd: Piwritaniaid Cymreig, 1630-40' in J.G. Jones (ed.), *Agweddau ar Dwf Piwritaniaeth yng Nghymru yn yr Ail Ganrif ar Bymtheg* (Lampeter, 1992), 47; B.G. Owens, *The Ilston Book* (Aberystwyth, 1996), 7; Aylmer, List.

213. See **135** for '15 per cent'.

221. Petty customs: despite the name, the petty customs were quite substantial. They were duties originally agreed between the king and foreign merchants in 1303, and by Byrd's time the petty customs meant the combined duties on cloth.

M. J. Braddick, *The Nerves of State:Taxation and the Financing of the English State, 1558-1714* (Manchester, 1996), 51.

234. JB's son William, admitted to Lincoln's Inn in 1655, and by this time practising as an attorney, is presumably the son meant here. *(Records of ...Lincoln's Inn vol. i. Admissions* (1896), 271.) The 'accomptant' is the accountant-general of customs. The office of customer at Cardiff was revived at the restoration; in 1660 it reverted to its pre-civil war holder, Edmund Wogan, and by 1672 it was held by Rice Guy.

CTB i,10; BL Add MS 6133, f. 45r.

236. Charles Williams was a relation of JB's wife's, probably the son of Thomas Williams of Caerleon, who headed tax lists for the town in the 1660s. In 1672 Charles Williams killed Edmund Morgan of Penrhos Fwrdios in a duel, and fled to Smyrna, Turkey, where he built up a powerful trading interest. He died in 1720, and was buried in Westminster Abbey.

PRO E179/148/91; Bradney iii, 198-9, 255.

238. 'London measure': the London chaldron was a fixed volumetric measure for coal, of 48 Winchester bushels, in practice weighing roughly 28 cwts.

J. Hatcher, *History of the British Coal Industry Volume One: Before 1700* (Oxford, 1993), 567-9.

241. Mr Butler would be Piers Butler, third husband of Lady Mary Morgan of Llantarnam. JB frequently confuses great sessions with assizes; both involved the impanelling of grand juries, to consider bills of indictment against alleged offenders, and to make 'presentment' of any political, administrative, religious, economic or social issues of public concern. Great sessions meetings were held for Glamorgan; assizes for Monmouthshire. There were occasions when he certainly did sit on the assize grand jury for Monmouthshire: in the summer of 1665, for example, when the jury presented a number of roads in the county (PRO ASSI 5/2). The 'searjeant' is Evan Seys, JB's wife's cousin; 'Sir Philip' is probably Sir Philip Warwick (see **247** below).

242. Philip Mansell had been appointed searcher or deputy collector of customs in Swansea, under JB's supervision, in September 1660, at a salary of £10 per annum. Isaac Morgan was an officer at the Bristol custom house.

CTB i, 56; E 351/660.

243. The act of 13 September 1660, 12 Car. II c. 18, known as the Navigation Act, confirmed provisions of the act of 1651 of the same name, but went further in stipulating that certain specified colonial products should be shipped to home ports and should pass through the customs system.

Chandaman, 13.

247. Sir Edward Morgan of Llantarnam was the second baronet, and a former royalist delinquent. He married Frances, daughter of Thomas Morgan of Machen. It is probable that JB is referring here to Sir Edward's brother-in-law, Thomas Morgan; Bradney does not record a Thomas Morgan of Llantarnam.

Bradney iii, 231, v, 70.

'Sir Philip' is Sir Philip Warwick (1609-83), at this time managing the treasury for the earl of Southampton and also a clerk of the signet. These offices made him a very significant figure for anyone seeking a treasury warrant or a grant of government office, or trying to influence the course of administrative business in chancery: see **327** below. DNB; G. E. Aylmer, *The King's Servants: The Civil Service of Charles I* (1961), 14, 16-18.

250. The additional duties were imposed in the tonnage and poundage act of 1660 (12 Car. II c. 4) on wines, linen, silk and tobacco.

Chandaman, 12-13.

252. Capel Hanbury (1625-1704) was the third son of John Hanbury of Kidderminster, Worcs. He established an iron and tinplate making dynasty at Pontypool (*DWB*).

Rees Gwyn lived in Caerleon, and was significantly less well-off than JB, if tax records can be relied upon (PRO E 179/253/32, E 179/148/95, E 179/148/91). In this case a cargo from Caerleon was detained at Gloucester because its accompanying cockett had only authorised the journey to Bristol. It arrived at the next port, Gloucester, without documentation. For a cockett issued against a cargo carried by Francis Vickers of Tewkesbury to Gloucester, see BL Add. Ch. 63664, 63665.

254. William Williams may have been a relative of Philip Williams, JB's former colleague.

256. Isaac Tomkins of Caerleon (d. 1684) was an attorney in the court of common pleas with property interests in the town. He was counted among the gentry and was undersheriff of the county in 1671. He was steward of the court leet of Coldra manor, for Henry Milborne, the lord, in 1675.

Bradney iii, 195, 205; Eton College MSS 42/80.

257. The 'poor scoller' was probably Edward Byrd, and the school at Monmouth, as 259 suggests. Of JB's other sons, William was in London, Mathias in the navy, and the eldest son, Andrew, was by the autumn of 1662 living in his own house in Caerleon.

PRO E 179/148/95.

259. 'My lord's warrant': JB wanted a warrant from the lord treasurer, and this may link with **247**.

The Usk was a noted salmon river. The poet Thomas Churchyard (d. 1604) wrote:

'A thing to note when salmon fails in Wye

(And season there goes out as order is)

Then still, of course, in Usk doth salmon lie

And of good fish, in Usk, you shall not miss.'

Quoted in [W.N. Johns], *Historical Traditions and Facts Relating to Newport and Caerleon* (Newport 1880), pt. v, 25.

260. This is a damaged fragment of JB's first attempt in 1662 to defend himself against allegations that he was active in arms against Charles I, and that he was at the battle of Worcester against the future Charles II in September 1651.

261. In November 1661 Edward Herbert of Grange, Magor, was reported to have been arrested. He had bought lands confiscated by the state from the marquis of Worcester, and perhaps from other royalists. The marquis and his creditors presented a private bill to parliament in order to recover the lands, and they were permitted in March 1662 to create a trust to administer the estates, from which the latter were to be repaid. Most royalists did not succeed in recovering their property this way.

Dircks, 230-1, 238, 245-6, 249; Joan Thirsk, *The Restoration* (1976), 92-99; P. Seaward, *The Restoration 1660 -1688* (Basingstoke, 1991), 36-7.

262, 263. JB's claim that he had been sequestered from the office of comptroller for eleven years and that Francis Malory had enjoyed it in his place, although true, was something of a technicality. JB is described as comptroller throughout the 1630s. Malory had 'entred on the employment' in August 1649 (**77**) and was in 1650 still describing himself as check (**119**), not comptroller. By 1651 he was still in post, but not as check (**175**). In 1657 he was check under Griffith Bowen at Swansea, on a salary of £40. JB and Bowen were undoubtedly the customs officials making returns to London. By 1648 JB held the title collector, rather than comptroller. There was a reduction in staffing in the Cardiff customs establishment - the post of customer was laid aside - probably because of the low volume of business, on which JB himself often commented. JB recovered the title of comptroller in 1660. No fewer than nine of the thirteen gentry mentioned in this list were new to the bench of magistrates in 1660.

PRO E 190/1274/18, E 190/1275/11, 1275/15, 1276/ 1, 4, 5 for sample signatures on port books by JB; E 351/648, E 351/653, E 351/658, AO1/605/56; *CTB* i 1660-1667, 16; Phillips, *Justices.*

263. Herbert Evans of Gnoll was married to Anne Morgan of Pencrug, who inherited that house on the death of her father, William Morgan. The Morgans were related to JB's wife. The constable of the castle was chief magistrate of Cardiff, and the nominee of the lord, the earl of Pembroke. Arthur Roberts had served as JB's deputy.

Bradney iii, 252; S and B Webb, *The Manor and the Borough* (2 vols., 1908) i, 255.

265. See **261** for related material on Herbert's attempts to legitimise purchases of land made in the interregnum. David Williams was an attorney (**271**).

271. The oath of allegiance to the king was being taken by regiments of the army as early as June 1660. The customer at Swansea was Edmund Wogan, it seems, as the establishment reverted to the pre-civil war pattern.

W. L. Sachse (ed.), *The Diurnal of Thomas Rugg, 1659-1661* (Camden 3rd series, xci (1961), 93; E 351/660; *CTB* i,10.

279. 3d. per ton for Dover harbour: by a statute of 1662, Dover harbour was declared to be of particular value to the kingdom, as it provided protection to shipping from tempest, pirates and wartime enemies. The king's grant of funding for repairs proving inadequate, the statute authorised a tax on shipping of 3d. per ton of the burthen of the ship, on ships between 20 and 250 tons. Customs officers were to collect the duties, and provide a cockett to the master, owner or shipper as a receipt.

Statutes of the Realm v, 422-3.

280. Richard Dutton (d. 1703) was the fourth son of Edward Dutton of Hatton, Cheshire, and Mary, his wife, daughter of Hugh Calveley of Lea. Dutton was a kinsman of Lord Gerard (**284** below), and with Roger Whitley (**284** below) he was active in royalist plots during the 1650s, including the Ship Tavern conspiracy of February 1654 and the New Action Party, 1657. After the latter plot he was released from prison in straitened financial circumstances. After arresting the regicide Daniel Axtell in duplicitous circumstances, and acquiring Byrd's post, Dutton rose through connections with the marquis of Worcester and through military office to become governor of Barbados. It seems that William Byrd was never called to the bar.

Visitations of Cheshire, 1613 (Harleian Society, 1909); D. Underdown, *Royalist Conspiracy* (1960), 98-9, 203; [Morgan], *Memorials of the Duttons of Dutton in Cheshire* (Chester 1901), xxv; S. S. Webb, *The Governors General* (Chapel Hill, North Carolina), 470-1.

281. Isaac Tompkins or Tomkins was an attorney, a Caerleon resident, and undersheriff of Monmouthshire in 1671. He was named in a list of Monmouthshire gentry in 1673, and his will was proved in 1684.

Bradney iii, 195, 205.

283. Roger Whitley (1618-97) was the eldest son of Thomas Whitley and his second wife, Elizabeth Brereton. He was a royalist captain, in the foot regiment of Colonel Charles Gerard, his brother-in-law, and in 1644 was promoted to major. After commanding regiments of horse and foot, he became governor of Aberystwyth. In 1648 he was involved in the royalist rising, and was taken at Beaumaris. He was released and left the country to become during the interregnum a principal plotter on behalf of Charles Stuart. Whitley was back in the country in time to be involved in the Booth rising of 1659. After the restoration he was an MP, a farmer of the post office and four times mayor of Chester. George Whitley was Roger's brother.

N. Tucker, *Royalist Officers of North Wales, 1642-1660* (Denbigh, 1961), 64-5; P. R. Newman, *Royalist Officers*, 409; *House of Commons 1660-1690*, 709-11.

Edward Rumsey was probably the son of Walter Rumsey of Llanover, Mon., judge and MP in the Short Parliament of 1640. He was a lawyer, of Gray's Inn, and he died in 1677. He was first cousin once removed to Henry Rumsey of Sudbrook, in Portskewett parish, south-east of Chepstow (see **391** below). JB's instructions to his son to enquire for Edward Rumsey at 'the Fleet' suggests that the latter was at work on cases of debt, as Fleet prison was London's debtors' gaol.

Bradney i pt. ii, 384.

Edmund Waters: this is probably Edmund Walter, of Cophill, brother to the minister, Henry Walter, ejected from the living of St Woollos in 1661. JB's civil war sufferings with Edmund Walter may have helped cement his friendship with the family after 1660: see **414** below.

Bradney iii, 77, iv, 36-8.

Mr Smythier: Edward Byrd's employer. John Smyther or Smither was a leading member of the Scriveners' company of the city of London, and the son of a former master of the company. The Smithers were originally a Surrey yeoman family. John Smither junior was apprenticed to his father, became free of the company in 1637, was a steward of it in 1653, assistant in 1658 and warden in 1664. Given the clerical, quasi-legal backgrounds of JB and Thomas Pennant (the latter being described sometimes as a scrivener), it would be natural for a son of JB's to be articled to a scrivener. Smither in turn was probably in the employ of Evan Seys, to explain the choice of master for Edward Byrd.

PRO E 179/251/22/104; F.W. Steer (ed.), *Scriveners' Company Common Paper 1357-1628* (London Record Society Publications, iv, 1968), 48, 61, 114, 115, 120, 121, 123.

284. Charles Gerard (1618-94), of Halsall, Lancashire, was wounded in the royalist cause at Edgehill, and fought subsequently at the siege of Bristol and the battle of Newbury. In 1644 he was appointed commander-in-chief in South Wales, replacing the earl of Carbery, and by August 1645 had acquired notoriety for his plundering of the Pembrokeshire countryside. To his enemies he was the 'grand papist', and his catholic allegiances stood him in good stead after the restoration. With the title Baron Gerard of Brandon, later Viscount Brandon, he was

gentleman of the bedchamber to Charles II until 1679. He abandoned the Stuarts in 1685, and became captain of William III's bodyguard in 1688. As Lord President of the Council of Wales in 1689, he remade Welsh connections forged fifty years previously.

Newman, *Royalist Officers,* 151.

290. 'Sore mills' were the mills called Lansôr mills on the 1839 tithe map of Caerleon. They were in an isolated position on Afon Llwyd in the north east of the parish. These mills were owned by Piers Butler, by right of his wife, Lady Mary Morgan of Llantarnam. JB also held a lease from the earls of Pembroke on the mills much nearer the town, off Mill St.

291. Sir John Harrison (c.1590-1669) was a farmer of the customs, 1633-8, 1640-1 and 1660-2, and between 1662 and 1667 was a commissioner of customs. He worked his way up from a minor post in the customs service in his youth to become, in 1640, a linchpin in Charles I's reliance on customs revenue to fund the war against the Scots. He was described as 'a great accountant, of vast memory, and an incomparable penman', and the placing of the customs administration out of farm and under direct government supervision was on his advice.

House of Commons 1660-1690, ii, 501.

292. JB is here giving his son advice if he were to ride the summer 1663 assize circuit with his employer, John Smither. Assizes were organised into groups or circuits of counties, which judges visited in turn. Berkshire, Oxfordshire, Gloucestershire, Worcestershire, Herefordshire, Monmouthshire Shropshire and Staffordshire comprised the huge circuit called the Oxford circuit, and the judges visited twice a year, from late February to late March, and again in July and August. Smither would have worked for one of the judges or perhaps for Evan Seys, who as a serjeant-at-law was named automatically on the commission of oyer and terminer issued to leading JPs of the circuit, entitling them to try cases brought before them while the circuit was being covered.

J.S. Cockburn (ed.), *History of English Assizes* (Cambridge, 1972), 23-5, 60; idem (ed.), *Calendar of Assize Records....Introduction* (1985), 18-19; PRO C 181/7 p. 205.

293. Commission for the relief of indigent officers: by a statute of 1662 (14 Car. II c.8), £60,000 was to be raised by a tax on officeholders whose posts were worth £5 per annum or more. County commissioners (among them for Monmouthshire, Sir George Probert, William Jones of Llanarth, Thomas Morgan of Lansôr, Roger Williams of Cefn Ila, and Charles Hughes) were to identify worthy recipients of the revenue, who had to prove that they had commanded soldiers and had no other means of support. Certificates of worthiness were to be despatched to London before 29 September 1662: none were to be valid after that. Officeholders were to be taxed at 12 per cent of the annual value of their posts. For Monmouthshire, JB was one of only seven named officeholders (among them the registrar and chancellor of Llandaff diocese), and his post was assessed as being worth £60.

Statutes of the Realm v, 380-88; BL Add. 33590 f. 184v.

295. For the background of this document, see **283** above.

298. James Jones vicar of St Brides: a James Jones was rector of St. Brides Netherwent, 1662-69, and must be distinguished from JB's colleague of the same name (note to **199**). Bradney iv, pt. 2, 226. I owe this reference to the kindness of Mr B. Ll. James.

305. Thomas de la Vale (Delavale, Delavall), surveyor-general of the customs, was

presumably the same individual who in the early 1660s was the customer at Dunkirk, held by the English from 1658 until November 1662; he was in July 1663 surveyor to the farmers of the customs duties on tobacco, and he was seeking help in finding a place or reward of some sort in 1675.

CTB i, 264, 374; *CSPD 1663-4*, 189-90; *CSPD 1675-6,* 469. I am grateful to Dr G.E. Aylmer for help with Delavale.

313, 314. Thomas Morgan of Penrhos [Fwrdios]: sheriff of Monmouthshire in 1679 (*List of Sheriffs*, List and Index ix, 84). JB was a neighbour of Morgan's and seemingly by this time a relative of Shewell's. Although this seems to be a private business matter between Morgan and Shewell, the former customs collector at Bristol, there is a customs dimension to it, indicated by the reference to the bill of lading.

315. Great Faringdon, then in Berkshire and now in Oxfordshire, was on the main route between London and Gloucester, and the Crown was the principal inn there in the seventeenth century. The Pye family held the manor and the advowson of Faringdon, and their 'burying place' was the north chapel of Faringdon church. The lord of the manor at this time was Robert Pye, son of Sir Robert (d. 1662), an MP and staunch parliamentarian in the civil war. No memorial inscription to Byrd has survived, nor, oddly, is there any record of his burial in the parish register. A search of the minute book, the process book and indictment files covering the February 1664 Berkshire assizes at Reading has failed to trace any details of the case.

Victoria County History of Berkshire, iv, 489-90, 493, 497, 498; personal communications, Berkshire Record Office, chairman, Faringdon Local History Society; PRO ASSI 2/1, ASSI 4/14, ASSI 5/2.

318. Charles Morgan of Penrhos Fwrdios and Lansôr, son of Thomas Morgan and his first wife, the daughter of Walter Griffith of Llanfrechfa. He was a neighbour of JB's. Bradney iii, 255.

319. JB had discovered that Stradling, Rowland Laugharne and Robert Thomas had signed the petition orchestrated against him by Richard Dutton.

PRO SP 29/53/68.

321. Launcelott the accountant general: it is possible that Byrd was confusing the office with some other, as there does not appear to have been an office of this title in the 1660s.

323. Captain Wood: Walter Wood, lieutenant 1660; captain of *Princess,* 1660, *Convertine,* 1664, *Henrietta*, 1664: died of wounds in battle with the Dutch, June 1666. J.R. Tanner (ed.), *A Descriptive Catalogue of the Naval Manuscripts of the Pepysian Library at Magdalene College, Cambridge Vol. I* (Navy Records Society XXVI, 1903) i, 46; *Sea Officers*, 478. Pepys vii, 154.

324. 15 September 1664: this was written at a point when the English fleet was returning from its campaign against the Dutch in the Second Dutch War R. Hutton, *The Restoration* (Oxford, 1985), 224.

325. George Morgan: probably of the Penrhos Fwrdios family, and thus a neighbour of JB (Bradney iii, 255), or perhaps George Morgan of Newport, gentleman. (Bradney v, 55.) One GM was steward of the Monmouthshire manors of the Marquis of Worcester in 1663.

NLW Badminton Manorial, 1716, 1717.

326. Robert Thomas (c.1622 - after 1684) of Llanmihangel (Llanfihangel Y Bontfaen), Glamorgan, was the eldest son of Sir Edward Thomas of Betws, who in 1646 led the rising against the Glamorgan county committee, put down by Rowland Laugharne before his change of sides. Thomas was an active royalist conspirator by the late 1650s, acquired office at court at the restoration of Charles II, and served as MP for Glamorgan boroughs, from 1661 to 1681.

House of Commons 1660-1690, iii, 547-49.

Rowland Laugharne (c.1607-1675), of St Brides, Pembrokeshire, was a parliamentarian commander and general until 1648, when he became the principal agent of rebellion against Parliament in the second civil war. He was defeated at St Fagans in May 1648, and was fined for his offences against Parliament. After the restoration he petitioned successfully for financial help from the king; he remained in financial difficulty until his death. He was MP for the Pembrokeshire boroughs from 1661 until he died.

Newman, *Royalist Officers,* 224; *House of Commons 1660-1690*, ii, 712-3.

On the face of it the trio of signatories against JB were activists in South Wales in 1648 against rule by Parliament, at a time when JB had stayed loyal.

For Sir Philip Warwick see also **241**, **247** above.

329. Sir George Probert of Penallt (c.1617-77), royalist in civil war, knighted at Oxford in 1643. Paid a fine of £134 as a royalist 'delinquent', and was MP for Monmouthshire, 1661-67: it is thought, through the patronage of Lord Herbert of Raglan.

Bradney ii, 141, 156; *House of Commons 1660-1690*, iii, 292.

Sir Trevor Williams (1623-92) of Llangybi was the son of Sir Charles Williams and Anne, daughter of Sir John Trevor of Plas Teg, Flints. In the civil war Williams seems to have been a turncoat, at different times *persona non grata* to either party in the conflict. Sir Trevor was MP for Monmouthshire, 1667-79.

DWB; Bradney iii, 100; Williams, *MPs*, 126; *House of Commons 1660-1690*, iii, 727-31.

Edmund Morgan of Newport was a magistrate there, and unsympathetic to quakers when they disturbed the minister Walter Cradock.

G. F. Nuttall, *The Welsh Saints 1640-1660* (Cardiff, 1957), 61.

John Clegg DD: prebendary of Llangwm, diocese of Llandaff, to 1667.

Le Neve, ed. Hardy, *Fasti Ecclesiae Anglicanae* (Oxford, 1854), 268.

Roger Williams (d.1682) of Cefn Ila, Llanhennock, was a royalist in the civil war, who paid a fine of £206 for his part in the conflict. His son, Roger (1634-c.1715) married the daughter of Trevor Williams of Llangybi. JB may have been corresponding with either father or son.

Bradney iii, 77-8.

Charles Hughes of Trostrey: see Thomas Hughes in biographies of JB's correspondents.

Charles Van of Coldra: see biographies of JB's correspondents.

William Morgan of Tredegar (d.1680) was the son of Thomas Morgan of Tredegar Park and Machen. Like Sir Trevor Williams, his orientation in the civil war was ambivalent: he was named on the Monmouthshire county committee from 1647, but was also regarded by royalist conspirators as sympathetic to their cause. He was certainly among the leaders of the county gentry, and to be counted among the interest of the earls of Pembroke. He was MP for Monmouthshire in parliaments from 1659 to 1679.

Bradney v, 70; *House of Commons 1660-1690*, iii, 99-100.

Thomas Morgan of Penrhos Fwrdios, Caerleon and Lansôr Fawr, Llanhennock, was the son of George Morgan, second son of Edward Morgan of Llantarnam. Thomas married first Cicil, daughter of Walter Griffith of Llanfrechfa (issue: three children) and secondly, Florence, daughter of Henry Morgan of Penllwynsarff (issue: three children).

Bradney iii, 221, 231, 255, v, 135.

332. Richard Creed (1620-90) was a naval civil servant during the 1650s, serving as deputy treasurer of the admiralty and secretary to the generals-on-sea. He worked under Robert Blake and Richard Montagu, Earl of Sandwich. He was the son-in-law of Walter Cradock, the celebrated Independent minister, and after 1660 Creed retired to Llangwm, Monmouthshire, to the estate of his late father-in-law. It was probably he who was appointed a schoolmaster at Llangwm in 1664, although in order to serve thus he would have had to tone down the fifth-monarchist views he held in the 1650s. Creed's background would be useful to Mathias Byrd in advancing his career. Richard's brother, John, also worked in naval administration. He was deputy treasurer of the fleet, 1660-3, but failed to advance further in his career, mainly because of his puritanism. He was a rival and close associate of Samuel Pepys.

Pepys, i, 86, 91; x, 79-80; index for many refs. to John Creed; Glyn Parry, 'Richard Creed: Mab yng Nghyfraith Walter Cradoc', *National Library of Wales Journal* xxiv (1985-6), 392-4.

339. This William Seys was the son of Roger Seys, the brother of Margery Byrd, JB's wife. William inherited the Gaer, St Woollos, on the death of his brother Alexander, who had been a legatee of his uncle, another Alexander. The Gaer had been the home of Alexander and Florence Seys, parents of Roger, Margery and Alexander.

PROB 11/189/56, Bradney ii, pt. i, 94-5; *Limbus Patrum,* 218-221. Both Bradney and *Limbus Patrum* are deficient in their pedigrees of the Seys family of Caerleon. The will of Alexander Seys (d. 1642) provides additional information.

Sir William Warren (1624-?): a timber magnate of Wapping and Rotherhithe. Master of the London company of drapers in 1648-9. 'The greatest of contemporary timber merchants', dealing in the New England and Baltic timber trades. He was virtually a monopolist supplier to the navy after 1664, and there are many references to him in Pepys's Diary. He was reputedly a baptist.

Pepys, *Companion*, 468.

343. John Morgan, uncle of William Jones: Jones's mother was Elizabeth, daughter of William Morgan of Llantarnam. John Morgan was of Trostrey.

Bradney ii, 303, ii pt 2, 231.

350. 'Coresponds unhappily fired': JB is referring to the losses suffered by Thomas Pennant in the Great Fire of London.

353. Rees Gwyn witnessed the will of Florence Seys, JB's mother-in-law, in 1651.He was a merchant of Caerleon, with interests in shipping there. In the 1661 subsidy list for Caerleon

he was listed eighth, and paid ten shillings towards the Free and Voluntary Present of 1662 (JB paid £10).

PRO PROB 11/217/131, E 179/148/91, E 179/253/32; J. W. Dawson, *Commerce and Customs. A History of the Ports of Newport and Caerleon* (Newport, 1932), 19.

358. William Seys the recipient of this letter was the brother of Leyshon and Serjeant Evan Seys. The William mentioned in the letter was the son of Roger Seys and the nephew of Margery Byrd, JB's wife. The first William was the first cousin once removed of the second. At Cowbridge, mutually convenient for a meeting for men coming from Newport and Swansea, lived Margaret Seys, widow of Matthew, Evan Seys's brother.

359. Cousin William Morgan: this was the son of Giles Morgan of Tredunnock, the second husband of Florence, Margery Byrd's sister.

361. Acorn Alley was off Bishopsgate Street, in the parish of St Botolph's Bishopsgate, and was largely owned by the Company of Skinners. The parish lay outside the city walls, and was by Byrd's day teeming with people. It was noted before the civil war for its large population of immigrant weavers. Where the medieval hospital of St Mary had been (the Spittle) were many substantial houses, and sermons were delivered in the open area of Spitalfields.

Guildhall Library, Skinners' mss, volume of plans 'East Walk' fo.15; R. Hyde, J. Fisher, R. Cline (eds.), *The A to Z of Restoration London (the City of London, 1676)* (London Topographical Society Publication no. 145, 1992), 36; J. Stow, *Survey of London* (2 vols., ed. C.L. Kingsford, Oxford, 1908) i, 164-68; 174; 230-1; V. Pearl, *London at the Outbreak of the English Civil War* (Oxford, 1961), 10-15.

364. Sir Thomas Curson (1611-83) baronet, of Waterperry, Oxfordshire, son of Sir John Curson of Waterperry, was high sheriff of Oxfordshire in 1675. His sister, Frances (d. 1678) married Oliver Gadbury, one of a family numerous in the Wheatley area of the county.

Visitations of Oxfordshire (Harleian Society v, 1871), 131, 246, (Harleian Society n.s. xii, 1993), 29.

Thomas Symms (1603-?) was the son of John Symms (d. 1638) and the grandson of Thomas Symms (d. 1628), all of Wheatley, Oxfordshire. John Symms's sister, Ann, married John Lankford in 1602.The relationship between the Symmses and JB was therefore through his mother's family. The Thomas Symms mentioned by JB was a substantial householder in Wheatley, occupying a five-hearthed house: he was overseer of the poor there, 1647-50 and 1657.

Cuddesdon PR; W.O. Hassall (ed.), *Wheatley Records* (Oxfordshire Record Society, xxxvii (1956), 49, 66, 70; Oxfordshire RO, MS Wills Oxon 60/2/6.

365. Christopher Perkins of Pilston esquire had married Cicil (Sisyl), daughter of William Morgan of Pencrug (Bradney iii, 352). Perkins died at a time when Monmouthshire politics were highly charged. At the by-election for the county in November 1667, when Sir Trevor Williams was returned against the wishes of the powerful marquess of Worcester, of Raglan castle, there was bitter animosity between the parties. JB is here probably fearing that the sheriff's death could aid the Raglan interest.

House of Commons 1660-1690, i, 317-8.

370. John Beale, *Herefordshire Orchards, A Pattern for All England* (London, 1659), 5, 24 notes that jennet moyles (Gennet Moyle) were the best apples for cider, and remarks on the Welsh practice of grafting the variety on to rootstock of the same variety, to improve cropping. The variety is mentioned also in John Parkinson, *Theatrum Botanicum* (1640), 1502, and John Ray, *Historia Plantarum* (1693), ii, 1448, and is still extant. Hussey's Pearmain is recorded in 1880 but is no longer extant, and no record seems to have survived of Aquitaine.

Ex info. Brogdale Horticultural Trust.

376. For John Morgan of Pentrebach, see **8**, **204**, **205** above.

379. William Williams, son of William Williams, presumably married a daughter of the Herbert Family of Coldbrook: see **122** above for a note on the Williams family.

380. Captain John Walterworth or Waterworth: commissioned in 1662 as a lieutenant in the *Fairfax*, promoted to captain 1665, killed in action, 1672.

Catalogue of Naval Manuscripts, i, 419; *Sea Officers*, 459.

390, 391. JB is here renegotiating the terms of the lease, in the right of his wife, from the earl of Pembroke of the water grist mills at Caerleon. The lease on the mills had been left by Alexander Seys (d. 1639) to his son Alexander (d. 1642) who in turn bequeathed them to Margery Byrd. The property consisted of two mills under one roof, a mill pond, a forty-acre pasture called the Marches, two other pastures and a fulling mill in disrepair. JB had to pay an annual rent of £16 3s. 4d., and had the lives of Mathias and his son William inserted in the lease, but did in the end pay the £100 the earl's commissioners were demanding for the privilege.

PROB 11/162/107, PROB 11/189/56; Bradney iii, 193; Gwent RO, Williams and Tweedy Ms 1111, MAN/B/16/0002, MAN/B/15/0007.

Henry Rumsey was of Sudbrook, in Portskewett parish, south-east of Chepstow. He and his relative John Rumsey were agents for the earl of Pembroke's Monmouthshire estates, and in the mid-1650s Henry Rumsey held the lordship of Liswerry and Lebenyth, of which JB was a free tenant. Henry Rumsey had been a surveyor of confiscated lands on behalf of Parliament; yet another Rumsey, James, was the receiver of the sequestered rents and revenues of Llandaff and St David's bishoprics in the late 1640s.

NLW Badminton Manorial 1739; PRO AO 1/367/1; Bradney iv, pt.ii, 290.

392. Wheatley was a village then in the parish of Cuddesdon, Oxfordshire. The 'silly cousin' is almost certainly Thomas Symms.

See **364** above.

394, 397. Florence Morgan, sister of Margery Byrd and wife of Giles Morgan of Tredunnock. Catherine Nicholls, widowed since at least 1651, seems not to have remained outside the family circle after her mother's death.

See **159**, **180**, **185** above; PROB 11/217/131.

395. Soares or Sôr mills were separate from those JB's wife held directly by lease from the earl of Pembroke: see **290** above.

396, 397. Edward Vosse or Vorst: Evan Seys's grandmother was Elizabeth Voss. Edward, his servant, was thus likely to be a member of his extended kinship network.

Limbus Patrum, 218-21.

404. JB here seems to have had to go to the Bristol merchant community to borrow the £100 he needed to renew the lease on the mills at Caerleon.

409. John Rumsey: one of that name was under suspicion of disloyalty to the government in 1655 (BL Add 34013 p. 182), but this one was agent for the earl of Pembroke, so was more likely to be of the Sudbrook than the royalist Llanover branch of his family. See **390** above.

414. Henry Walter (1611-78) was chosen by Parliament to preach in South Wales in 1646, was the leading minister in the list of itinerants appointed by the Act for Propagating the Gospel in Wales, and after 1653 settled as minister in Newport. At the restoration he moved; he is described as living at Parc y Pil, Llantarnam, in 1669, which was wrongly described by contemporaries as being in Caerleon. The evidence of this letter suggests, however, that as a 'loving friend and neighbour' of JB's, he did, after all, have an address in the town, and in any case, the two parishes were contiguous.

DWB.

415. The Edmund Harvey mentioned here would not be the same as the London customs official with whom JB dealt in the 1650s.

419. 'Uncle William' would be William Seys, brother of Evan. His son was another William, as **437** makes clear.

428. Admiral de Ruyter: Michiel Adriaanszoon de Ruyter (d. 1676), the Dutch naval commander in the war with England.

429. It is possible that 'Mrs Anne' is Ann Llwyd, widow of Morgan Llwyd, minister at Wrexham in the interregnum, friend and brother-in-law of Edward Herbert of the Grange, and a man who by his own account spent some time among the religious radicals of south east Wales.

434. Edward Morgan of Llantarnam became the third baronet. The existence of his son John and grandsons Thomas and Robert cannot be squared with the pedigree in Bradney iii pt. ii, 231, where the third baronet had only a daughter, who married Edmund Bray and had one son, Reginald.

441. Jane Pennant (1628-?) was the sixth child of Thomas Pennant and his first wife, Barbara. She and Roger Griffin seem to have had one daughter, Ursula, who by June 1679 had married one Walker.

Boyd's Inhabitants of London, 40097; Oxfordshire RO, MS Wills Oxon 166/2/11.

445. JB is here match-making, between the son of Richard Seys and the daughter of William Williams.

446 . Alexander Seys in fact gave £5 each to the towns and parishes of Cardiff, Llantwit Major and St Woollos, as well as to Caerleon.

PROB 11/162/107.

JOHN BYRD'S CORRESPONDENTS: BIOGRAPHICAL NOTES

ABBERLEY, THOMAS

Sequestrator of the estate of royalists Sir Thomas Dawes and John Dawes esquire, former collector and surveyor respectively of the customs in the port of London. Stephen Abberley, a London grocer, was a creditor of Sir Thomas Dawes in August 1641.

PRO E351/648; *CJ* ii, 241.

AMBERSON, ROBERT

An officer in the Bristol custom house, described in 1672 as clerk to 'the cheque upon the coast and to keepe an accompt of all the proceedings of the porte', on a yearly salary of £30.

BL MS Add. 6133 f.67r.

AVERY, SAMUEL (c. 1596-1659)

Of a family from Somerset, Avery was apprenticed to a London merchant in 1610. By 1630 he had become very prominent as a merchant, and became known for his opposition to Archbishop Laud's policy of enforcing uniformity on English congregations overseas. From 1643 he became involved in the civic government of the city of London, and was appointed in 1644 to be a commissioner for the sale of captured royalist ships. Because of his standing in the mercantile community, Avery became in the same year a treasurer for the Long Parliament's general tax assessment on the nation, and from 1645 to 1649 a customs commissioner. From 1645 to 1646 Avery was master of the London Merchant Taylors' company. As a leading City of London alderman, he was much in demand for other committees: for the redemption of captives, the sale of bishops' lands, the London militia, the relief of the poor in London, settling differences among 'adventurers' (Protestant property speculators) in Ireland. He was an MP for London in the first protectorate parliament, 1654-5, but shortly afterwards he and his son found themselves at the centre of a corruption scandal which ended in their disgrace and Avery senior's being forced to accept a debt burden of over £16,000.

F&R i, 392, 552, 667, 733, 880, 928; ii, 942; Beaven, *Aldermen*, ii, 67; History of Parliament Trust, 'House of Commons 1640-1660', draft biography.

BLACKBORNE, ROBERT

Secretary to the Admiralty commissioners (d. 1701). Possibly a native of Plymouth, Blackborne appears as a clerk for the parliamentary commissioners of the navy in 1643. In 1648 he was a secretary to the parliamentary commissioners negotiating with Charles I at Carisbrooke Castle, and by the early 1650s was solicitor to the customs commissioners, and a secretary to the navy committee of MPs. He became secretary to the customs commissioners in 1652 and from December of that year, to the admiralty and navy commissioners. He was a radical puritan; when the Rump Parliament fell in April 1653, Blackborne called it 'the dawning of the day of redemption'. He lost office at the restoration, but became secretary to the East India Company.

Aylmer *SS,* 266-7; Capp, 125, 128, 131, 157, 301, 363-4, 372.

BULKELEY, THOMAS

Accountant-general to the customs commissioners, 1645-9. His service ended with that of his masters. In February 1656 he was arrested with Dudley Avery, with whom he had closely worked while the latter was receiver, and made to review his accounts before the new auditor.

CSPD 1655-6, 248-9, 578; Aylmer, List.

BYRD, EDWARD

(d.1663), JB's son, killed in a brawl in an inn at Faringdon, Berks. (now Oxon.) during a journey from London to Gloucester assizes. He was articled to an attorney or scrivener.

BYRD, MATTHIAS

(d. 1700), JB's son. Educated in Bristol, he became an officer in the royal navy, serving on warships *Henrietta, Cambridge, Transporter,* and *St David,* consecutively.

He rose to the rank of captain in 1672, and commanded the fireship *Leopard,* burnt in service in the Dutch war in August 1673. Noted as dead in Pepys's list of commissioned officers, Matthias was in fact captured by the Dutch and back in London by October 1673. His will included bequests of silver 'sea plate' and his property was valued at £309 on his death. Married Margaret, daughter of Edward Morgan of Pencrug, in 1674, by whom he had three children.

J.R. Tanner (ed.), *A Descriptive Catalogue of the Naval Manuscripts of the Pepysian Library at Magdalene College, Cambridge Vol. I* (Navy Records Society XXVI, 1903); NLW Llandaff wills, LL 1700/77.

BYRD, SUSANNA

JB's niece, daughter of his brother William. She was living in London in the 1650s, and later moved to Kent, when JB seems to have lost touch with her.

BYRD, WILLIAM, BROTHER

(1592 - ?), JB's eldest brother. Born Bristol (baptised parish of St Werburgh). By 1665 he was certainly living in London, but had very probably been living there for many years before this, JB's letters to him that year perhaps prompted by filial anxiety about the plague raging in the capital. Lived at Skinners' Rents, properties owned by the Skinners' Company, perhaps through the good offices of Thomas Pennant. He is described in a tax list as having one hearth and being 'poor' (PRO E 179/147/617). Byrd was not himself a member of the Skinners' Company. He had at least two children, William and Susanna.

BYRD, WILLIAM, NEPHEW

Son of William B, JB's eldest brother. An attorney, with a post somewhere in government service in London (perhaps the Excise Office) until February 1651, when JB describes him as 'out of employment'. By September 1653 was settled in Dublin, and by 1668 was an attorney in the Exchequer there. He lost touch with JB for eight years from the time of Charles II's return to England as king.

BYRD, WILLIAM, SON

Eldest son of JB. Educated Bristol, admitted to Lincoln's Inn, June 1655. An attorney, by 1661, when his father describes him as of Lincoln's Inn [**246**], he was performing the same intermediary functions for JB as his nephew William had done a decade earlier. By the 1670s was back in Caerleon, presumably practising as an attorney. There is no record of his having married.

CAYSUM, ELIZABETH

A Gloucestershire woman who sought JB's advice on whether to move to Monmouthshire to practise her trade of silk-weaving.

CHARNOCK, GEORGE

A receiver of revenues at the treasury of the London customs house, and probably a relation of Roger Charnock, clerk to Sir Philip Warwick and a treasury official during the 1660s. In 1649 he received a salary of £13 per annum. This may have been the George Charnock one of eighteen waiters in the port of London in 1662, whose post was then worth £70 p.a. Of an office-holding family, Charnock was a sergeant-at-arms from 1660; Roger and John C. were waiters at the London custom house in 1672.

Pepys,*Companion;* PRO E122/236/19; BL Add. 33590 f. 181; *CSPD 1660-1661,* 72; BL Add. 6133 fo. 41.

COMMISSIONERS FOR REVENUE OF THE EARL OF PEMBROKE

Both Philip Herbert, 5th earl of Pembroke (1621-69), and his son and heir, William, 6th earl (1640-74) who succeeded him, were absentees from South Wales, as was the 7th earl, Philip, who held the title from 1674 to 1683. Their family seat was Wilton, near Salisbury in Wiltshire. The family wielded considerable economic and electoral power in Glamorgan and Monmouthshire, nevertheless. In post restoration elections, this power was known as the 'Cardiff Castle interest'.

Glam. Co. Hist.; DNB.

COMMISSIONERS OF THE CUSTOMS

By an ordinance of May 1643, the customs were placed by Parliament under the supervision of eight commissioners, Thomas Andrewes, John Fowke, Richard Chambers, William Barkeley, Maurice Thompson, Francis Allyn, James Russell and Stephen Estwick. All were merchants, known to historians as the 'interlopers', committed to breaking the monopoly of the trading companies, and to promoting free trade. The appointment of the commissioners followed a period under James I and Charles I when the customs were 'farmed', that is, leased to a syndicate of businessmen for a fixed revenue. From 1645 to 1649 the commissioners were Samuel Avery, Richard Bateman, Charles Lloyd, Christopher Pack and Walter Boothby, and from 1649 they were Stephen Eastwick, Robert Tichborne, Mark Hildersey, Daniel Taylor, Edward Parks and Edmund Harvey. At the restoration, the 'old farmers' from before the civil war resumed their administration, but this time as commissioners directly appointed by the government. They were Sir Job Harby, Sir John Jacob, Sir Nicholas Crispe and Sir John Harrison, with new partners Sir John Shaw and Sir John Wolstenholme. From the autumn of 1662 the commissioners became farmers once again, until 1667, when a fresh lease of the customs was granted to a new syndicate.

F&R, i, 163-5, 667-9; *CJ* vi, 193; Chandaman, 21-5.

COMMITTEE FOR THE NAVY

The committee for the navy was one of the earliest committees of the Long Parliament to wield executive power. It was a committee of MPs, and extended its brief to cover customs matters. It was concerned more with appointments and resources than with naval strategy.

CRESWICK, EDWARD

One of a leading Bristol family of merchants. Edward Creswick witnessed the will of Aldworth Elbridge, a prominent merchant in the city, in 1653.

Merchants and Merchandise, 57, 93 n.1.

DENNETT, THOMAS

Auditor to the 6th earl of Pembroke. He or another of his name was an auditor in 1639, and was still occupying the position in 1681.

NLW Bute L 4/3, M 61/30.

DRAPER, HENRY

Clerk to the commissioners for the South Wales estates of the earl of Pembroke, and the landlord of the Angel Inn, Cardiff. He may have been the custodian of Cardiff Castle; his payment of tax on 13 hearths in Cardiff in 1670 testifies to his local importance.

Glamorgan Hearth Tax.

DEYOS, MICHAEL

Water bailiff of Bristol from at least 1645. He was presumably a relation of Walter Deyos, who was sheriff of Bristol in 1639, mayor in 1655 and a prominent member of the merchant venturers' company. The water bailiff controlled civic revenues arising from the water front, and Deyos evidently also assisted the customs officers in Bristol. Michael Deyos was a part-owner of a number of ships and left a soap-house and five ships in his will. In 1670 he owned a house on Welsh Back, near the custom house. He was not a member of the merchant venturers' company of Bristol, but described himself as a merchant in his will.

Latimer; *Deposition Books of Bristol 1643-1647* and *1650-4;* Beaven, *Bristol Lists; Merchants and Merchandise,* 218 n. 2; Leech, *Topography*, 168.

FLETCHER, THOMAS

An associate of Evan Seys, based in Gloucester.

FOXE, EDWARD

A customs officer working with Thomas Shewell at the Bristol customs house, described in **195** of the Letterbook as 'surveyor of customs'. He also held the rank of captain, probably in the Bristol garrison, and was named as a Bristol militia commissioner in March 1660.

F&R ii, 1442.

FOXE, GERRARD

An officer in the London customs house to 1649. He lived in St Helen Bishopsgate parish, in the same area as Thomas Pennant and William Byrd, JB's brother. He married Sarah Armstrong in 1633, and five children were born to them there. He is described in the parish register as a yeoman.

St Helen Bishopsgate PR.

FUTTER, HENRY

(b. 1596) Henry Futter was a London goldsmith and an acquaintance of Thomas Pennant; he may be the 'Mr Futer' who in 1638 had a house and shop at the Talbot, Fish St., in the city. He was of Norfolk parentage, but was settled in London by 1631, when he married. He lived in St Mary Woolnoth parish, where his sons were baptised in 1634 and 1641. Henry Futter was associated with the mint, and before the civil war found himself charged in a Star Chamber case with being part of a ring involved in melting coin for bullion and exporting it. He was fined £500. By 1650 he was in financial difficulties, and after the restoration petitioned Parliament for relief. He had paid customs duty, presumably at a port in JB's charge, on tobacco which had rotted and which in any case had been re-exported. Such cargoes attracted a repayment of half the duty paid. After the restoration he seems to have recovered some of his former status.

W. Chaffers, *Gilda Aurifabrorum* (1899), 59, 64; *Boyd's Inhabitants of London;* Dale, *Inhabitants of London,* 102; Orridge, *Citizens of London,* 237; F&R i, 1041; Aylmer, *List; HMC 7th Report,* 160; J. M. S. Brooke, A. W. C. Hallen, *The Transcript of the Registers ... of St Mary Woolnoth...* (London 1886), 41, 44; HLRO, Main Papers, 21 Feb. 1662.

GRIFFIN, ROGER

(d. 1676). Roger Griffin was a draper, and an alderman of Oxford, occupying a five hearthed house in Queen Street there in 1665. In 1662 he was mayor of the city, and in 1667 Griffin was a commissioner for the poll tax in Oxford. At that time his household consisted of himself, his wife Jane, daughter Ursula and one servant. He married Jane, the daughter of Thomas Pennant, JB's trusted agent in all business affairs. At the time of his death, Griffin held leases of houses in Oxford from Exeter College and All Souls College, and his goods were valued at £206.

H. E. Salter (ed.), *Surveys and Tokens,* Oxford Historical Society lxxv (1923), 185, 239, 344, 351, 434; Clark (ed.), *Wood's City of Oxford,* iii, 38, 40; Oxfordshire RO, MS Wills Oxon 166/2/11.

GUNTER, THOMAS

Agent to Piers Butler, owner of Sôr mills, Caerleon, upon which JB had a lease. Butler was married to Lady Mary Morgan of Llantarnam. Gunter lived at Abergavenny.
Bradney; *Visitations in Wales,* 228.

GWYN, GEORGE

(1623-?), of Llanelwedd, Radnorshire. JP Brecon and Radnor 1653 to mid-1660s. MP for Radnorshire 1654, 1656, 1660. Sheriff of Monmouthshire, the county of his mother's family, in 1663. Landlord of a piece of property held by JB.

DWB, Phillips, *Justices;* Dodd, *Studies.*

HANDS, THOMAS

'Cousin' (actually nephew) of JB. Likely to be the son of John 'Hamme'

and his wife Anne Byrd, JB's sister, who were married in Bristol in 1615. Thomas Hanns or Hands and his wife Margaret occupied 93 or 94 High Street, Oxford, where in 1665 they were taxed on two hearths, and in 1667 had living with them a servant, two apprentices and a lodger. Hands was a shoemaker, who was bailiff of Oxford in 1672.

Bristol St Werburgh PR; *Surveys and Tokens,* 204, 237; Clark (ed.), *Wood's City of Oxford, 39.*

HARRIS, JAMES

Neighbour of John Morgan of Pentrebach, who was a debtor to William Seys, JB's wife's first cousin. Harris was a surety for Morgan's bond.

HARVEY, EDMUND

(c. 1602-73), of Aldermanbury, London and Fulham, Middlesex, customs commissioner from April 1649 until November 1655, when he was arrested on the evidence of his brother-in-law, William Langham, and accused of defrauding the customs of over £30,000. He was released from prison on bail of £20,000, and only ever paid back a fraction of the final sum of £57,000 he was estimated to have stolen. Harvey had first been active in the service of Parliament as a London militia officer, and became MP for Wiltshire in July 1646. He was closely involved with parliamentary sales of bishops' lands, and bought for himself Fulham Palace, formerly the residence of the bishop of London. He was a commissioner of the high court of justice set up to try Charles I, and attended thirteen sittings of the trial, but did not sign the death warrant. Before the scandal of his defrauding the customs broke, he was elected MP for Middlesex in 1654. At the restoration he was tried at the Old Bailey for his part in the trial of Charles I, and was sentenced to life imprisonment. He died in Pendennis castle, Cornwall, in June 1673.

Aylmer, *SS,* 160-2; draft biography, History of Parliament, 'House of Commons 1640-1660'; *DNB.*

HERBERT OF CHERBURY, RICHARD, LORD

(?1600 - 1655). Second baron Herbert of Cherbury, son of Edward Herbert, first baron, the distinguished philosopher and diplomat. Richard Herbert served with Charles I in the civil war, was governor successively of Bridgnorth, Ludlow, Aberystwyth and Newport, and was penalised as a royalist delinquent. He was MP for Montgomeryshire and Montgomery boroughs in the Short and Long parliaments. He was a notorious debtor, even as early as 1639, and by 1649 his debts were assessed at £7000, so JB's loan was a small one among many larger advances. He married Mary, daughter of the earl of Bridgwater. As well as Montgomery castle, Herbert held the estate of St Julians, near Caerleon. With JB, Herbert was a customary tenant in the crown lordships of Liswerry and Lebenith.

DNB; Bradney iv, 286-93; *Herbert Correspondence,* 118, 131; draft biography, 'House of Commons 1640-1660'.

HERBERT, EDWARD

(d. 1667) Of the Grange or Moor Grange, Magor, Monmouthshire. He was a descendant of an illegitimate son of Sir Richard Herbert of Coldbrook, brother of William Herbert, first earl of Pembroke. The family was established at Moor Grange by 1533. EH was a JP from 1649 through the 1650s, and named to various county committees from April 1649 to 1660. A member of the commission for the Propagation of the Gospel in Wales (1650) and the high court of justice (1651) dealing with the 1648 rising in South Wales, he was reported to be an Independent and, later, a staunch Cromwellian. He was a trustee of the estate of Col. Henry Herbert in 1656. He dealt roughly with quakers in Magor. It is a very strong possibility that he married the sister of Morgan Llwyd, the renowned preacher, mystic and writer, who was for a while associated with dissenting congregations in Monmouthshire and Bristol. He was named as a commissioner for the security of the Lord Protector in 1656, and in the same year sat for Monmouthshire in the second protectorate parliament. He acquired leases of sequestered lands of the marquis of Worcester, bought Undy manor from Col. Philip Jones and was an important fellow-tenant with JB in Lebenith lordship, and in Caerleon, where he held tenancies of the earl of Pembroke. As a neighbour of a sitting customs officer, a radical Puritan sympathiser and a tenant of the Pembroke interest he was well-placed to acquire office. Although JB seems to adopt a more deferential tone when writing to the JP than when addressing the customs officer, this may have been conditioned by his respect for the former office, and does not necessarily imply that he was writing to two different people. The only other plausible Edward Herbert who might have been the customs officer would be EH of Cogan, near Penarth (d. 1670), who sat on Glamorgan committees of sequestration and assessment during the late 1640s, but it is difficult to detect any linkages of patronage to support this interpretation. Herbert of the Grange was arrested in November 1662 because of his anti-royalist past. In 1683 William Herbert, presumably Edward's son, was living in Magor.

PRO SP 28/213; SP 29/44/34 (*CSPD 1661-2*, 141); F&R; Phillips, *Justices;* Williams, *Parliamentary History;* Bradney, iv, 286-93; *A Record of Some Persecutions* (1659), 8-9; Gwent RO, MAN/B/15/0007; Abbott, *Writings and Speeches* ii, 479; GRO D/ DF 1978; *Visitations in Wales*, 30-1, 218; Richards, 'Eglwys Llanfaches'; *Gweithiau Morgan Llwyd* i, 57; iii, 201.

HERBERT, ELIZABETH

This could well be the widow of Edward Herbert of the Grange. She appears to have moved to London after her husband's death. To support the idea that she was the sister of Morgan Llwyd's wife is the reference in **428** to her 'sister Anne': the first name of Llwyd's wife. Furthermore, it is known that after Llwyd's death in 1659, his immediate family moved to London. Elizabeth's survival until at least the mid-1670s contradicts Thomas Richards's supposition that she had pre-deceased her husband.

Sources as for Edward Herbert; see also *Gweithiau Morgan Llwyd* ii, 282, 284, 314, 315.

HOBBS, JOHN

Clerk to George Langham, accountant-general for the customs.

HUGHES, THOMAS

Of Moynes Court, Mathern parish, Monmouthshire. Hughes was the eldest son of Thomas Hughes (d. 1624), and became a colonel in the parliamentary army and governor of Chepstow castle in 1647. He was MP for Monmouthshire in the first protectorate parliament of 1654, and was prothonotary of the court of great sessions for Brecon, Glamorgan and Radnor. He was a trustee of the will of Col. Henry Herbert in 1656. He died in August 1664. His younger brother, Charles, was a major in the royalist army.
Bradney iv, 55; Williams, *Parliamentary History.*

HYNDE, CAPTAIN

Providor for the army's horse in Ireland. His task was to secure a supply of oats from the Severnside area to furnish the needs of the army in Ireland. He had formerly been a London militia officer, described by a presbyterian author as one 'that hath done the Parliament very eminent service at the beginning of these troubles as a commissary of horse.... a very discreet, prudent and stout man, and a good souldier, that truly feares God and walkes close with him'.

A Pair of Spectacles for the City (1647), 11.

JENKINS, RICHARD

Of the Glascoed, a township in the parish of Usk, Monmouthshire. There were two of this name, father and son. The father married Margaret, daughter of Nicholas Parker, and after Jenkins senior's death, Margaret Jenkins married Henry Williams of Usk. Jenkins junior married Anne Springett, daughter of Herbert Springett (q.v.).

Bradney, iii, 76, 148, 149.

JONES, PATRICK

JB's deputy in Swansea, an alderman of the town. He was portreeve (mayor) in 1641, but was never important enough to achieve office as a committeeman or JP in the county of Glamorgan.

M. Price (ed.), *The Account Book of the Borough of Swansea, Wales, 1640-1660* (Lampeter, 1990).

JONES, SIMON

A man for whom Byrd acted as mediator between him and the parents of someone whose hand he sought in marriage.

JONES, WALTER

Son of Robert Jones of Magor, who was sheriff of Monmouthshire in 1621. Walter married Cecil, daughter of Sir Nicholas Kemys, baronet, the royalist governor of Chepstow who was killed in the siege there on 25 May 1648.

JONES, WILLIAM

(d.1666). Eldest son of the royalist Sir Philip Jones (1602-1660), and his wife, Elizabeth Morgan of Llantarnam. William Jones's grandmother was Lady Frances Somerset, daughter of the catholic Edward, fourth Earl of Worcester. Of Treowen, which he left to live at Llanarth. J.R.S. Phillips suggests that this William Jones may have been a JP from 1649, but his background makes this unlikely. He was certainly a JP from 1663 to his death in 1666, was on the putative list of 'knights of the Royal Oak', intended by Charles II to reward royalist families, and was considered at least by some to be a Roman Catholic. This WJ should not be confused with Byrd's deputy in Chepstow, of the same name.

Bradney, ii, 303-4, 306; *South Wales and Mon. Rec. Soc.* i, 193; Phillips, *Justices*, 359-63.

LANGHAM, GEORGE

(d. 1683). Colonel George Langham was accountant-general to the customs commissioners, on a salary in 1652-3 of £200 p.a. He was a commissioner of excise from March 1654 to May 1656. In 1649 he was named a trustee for the sale of dean and chapter lands, and in 1650 a member of a high court of justice to try any persons charged with treason, a commission which was renewed in 1653 and 1654. In 1659/60 he was named as a militia and assessment commissioner for Middlesex. He was probably the eldest son of George Langham of Vintry ward, City of London, a merchant and city of London radical who sat on six committees of the city government between 1634 and 1641. George Langham senior was warden of the merchant taylors' company in 1636, and George junior was a member of the same company. Either George Langham the elder or his son was lieutenant-colonel in the London militia. Colonel George Langham married in 1641, and eventually settled in Clapham, Surrey. His sister Judith married Edmund Harvey, and his brother, Captain Henry Langham, cashier-general in the customs treasury, was with Colonel Edmund Harvey accused in 1655 of having defrauded the customs of over £30,000.

F&R; Aylmer, List*;* Aylmer, *SS*, 161-2; *The Visitation of London* ii (Harleian Society, 1883), 45; *Visitation of Surrey 1662*, 71; *Boyd's Inhabitants of London* 9805, 35387; personal communication, Dr G. E. Aylmer; K.J. Lindley, *Popular Politics and Religion in Civil War London* (1997), 189n., 209.

LEWIS, EDMUND

A commissioner for the estates of the earl of Pembroke. He was named a JP for Glamorgan in 1670.

Phillips, *Justices.*

LOCK(E), JOHN

Collector of customs at Bristol to July 1649, and therefore JB's opposite number; and alderman of Bristol. Originally of Bedminster, Somerset, he was apprenticed in Bristol and became a burgess in 1616. He was a member of the corporation of Bristol from 1620-56 and from 1660 to his death in 1666. Locke became a member of the merchant venturers' company in 1639. He was mayor in 1655-6, and was warden of the merchant venturers of Bristol in 1642-3; their treasurer, 1644-5. Locke was a persecutor of quakers in the 1650s. He seems to have attracted opprobrium, at least from his nephew, Richard Locke, who described him in a deposition of the civil war period as 'a monster of nature'. He was certainly politically supple. He has to be distinguished from another JL who was sheriff in 1626-7, treasurer of the merchant venturers 1627-8 and mayor 1641-2. Our John Locke was a cousin of the celebrated philosopher of the same name.

Merchants and Merchandise in Seventeenth Century Bristol, 154 (107 n.4 for the other JL); *Merchant Venturers,* 261; Besse, *Sufferings* i, 40; *Deposition Books of Bristol 1643-1647*, 251-2; Beaven, *Bristol Lists,* 300; PRO E 351/648.

LUCAS, RICHARD

Cousin to JB's wife, Margery Byrd. Margaret Seys, daughter of Richard Seys, Margery's father's brother, married George Lucas of the Hill, Gower. Later generations of the family built Stouthall, Reynoldston, but it seems safe to identify this Richard with the one occupying a two-hearthed house in Llanmadoc in 1670. Like JB, the Lucas family held their property on lease from the earls of Pembroke. William Lucas, presumably Richard's brother, was in London during Edward Byrd's last days, and both Lucases seem to have been servants of their uncle, Evan Seys.

GRO D/DF Manorial box 113; *Limbus Patrum*; *Glamorgan Hearth Tax*, 116; RCAHMW, *An Inventory of the Ancient Monuments in Glamorgan volume iv: Part 1: The Greater Houses* (Cardiff, 1981), 303-4.

MALORY, FRANCIS

Checker (check, cheque) in the customs establishment at Cardiff from 1649 until some time later in the 1650s.

MANSELL, JOHN

Customs collector at Swansea, replacing Griffith Bowen at the restoration. Possibly of a minor offshoot of the Margam family, his name does not figure in their pedigrees.

MORGAN, EDWARD

Of Staple Inn, London, and Caerleon. It seems most likely that this is actually Edmund, rather than Edward, Morgan, son and heir of Andrew Morgan of Michaelston, Mon. He was admitted to the Middle Temple in 1608 and was called to the bar there in 1615. JB himself was admitted to the same inn in 1616 (*Register of Admissions...to the Middle Temple*). He may have been of the Morgan family of Pencrug, brother of Margery Byrd's grandmother, Mary Vaen, *nee* Morgan.

MORGAN, HENRY

Of Risca, Mon. It seems likely that this was one of the Morgans of Llantarnam, perhaps the brother of the second baronet, or possibly one of the Lansôr Morgans, who were themselves a branch of the Llantarnam family. Both these families were royalist in the civil war.

Bradney ii, pt. ii, 231, 255.

MORGAN, ISAAC

An officer in the Bristol customs house from 1660.

MORGAN, LADY MARY

Of Llantarnam, Monmouthshire. JB was her tenant at Sôr Mills, Caerleon. She was the daughter of Sir Francis Englefield of Wootton Basset, Wiltshire. She married firstly Sir Edward Morgan of Llantarnam, secondly Richard Hanbury, and thirdly Piers Butler. She was the mother of Sir Edward Morgan, the second baronet, and with her son was sequestered for royalism during the civil wars. Her first husband, son and grandson (Sir Edward Morgan the third baronet, who was MP for Monmouthshire in 1680) were Roman Catholics.

Bradney iii, pt. ii, 231; *CCC;* PRO SP 28/ 213; *S Wales and Mon. Rec. Soc*. i, 193; *House of Commons 1660-1690* iii, 96-7.

MORGAN, WALTER

An attorney at Barnards Inn, Holborn, London, who acted unsatisfactorily for JB in a lawsuit in 1648. He became the executor of the will of James Parry (q.v.): after the restoration he claimed to have taken this duty with reluctance (PRO E 112/569/1076). Barnard's Inn, like Staple Inn, was one of the lesser inns of court, where many attorneys kept their chambers.

NICHOLLS, CATHERINE

JB's sister-in-law, sister of Margery Byrd and wife of John Nicholls of Llantwit Major. She was the daughter of Alexander Seys of Caerleon and his wife Florence, the daughter of Andrew Vaen. Letter **159** shows that she was alienated from her mother. Catherine was still alive in 1669.

Bradney; *Limbus Patrum.*

PAGET, WILLIAM, FIFTH BARON

(1609-1678), son of William, fourth baron. Initially sympathetic to parliament in the build up to civil war, he sided with Charles I in the conflict, and was sequestered for his royalism. He held a lease from Henry Lucas, Sir Job Harbie and others of the duty of 4s. per chaldron on coals, granted them by Charles I.

DNB.

PARRY, JAMES

Named to Brecon assessment commissions during the 1650s, he was briefly a JP in that county in 1649.

F&R ii 46, 312; Phillips, *Justices,* 272.

PENNANT, THOMAS

(1595-1669), JB's 'brother' and London agent. Born in Halkyn, Flintshire, the son of John Pennant, who had died before Thomas arrived in London as an apprentice in the skinners' company, in 1614. It seems unlikely that he ever traded as a skinner after becoming free of the company, as by 1623 he was settled in St Lawrence Pountney parish in the city, and was described in parish records as a scrivener and notary. He became a member of the parish vestry of St Lawrence in 1626, was an auditor of parish accounts there, a trustee of the parish in leases and held a watching brief on the progress of a legal suit involving another parish: all roles appropriate for a man with his professional background. At least seven children were born to him, but only three were mentioned in his will, and two at least died in childhood. His first wife, Barbara, died in 1629; his second wife, Martha, was eighteen years his junior. In the later 1630s he was churchwarden of St Laurence Pountney for two successive years. In 1640 he was elected clerk of the skinners' company and left St Lawrence to live at skinners' hall. He held the office until 1667. During the 1640s he acquired leases of the company in properties in Bishopsgate and Leadenhall St., and by 1647 he was building himself a house in Acorn Alley, St Botolph Bishopsgate parish. He remained in Acorn Alley until his death, having to leave temporarily because of the Great Fire in 1666, in which he lost property. When he died he had lands in Low Leighton, Essex and Billiter Lane, London. He was buried at St Botolph Bishopsgate, 31 December 1669.

Flintshire RO: Halkyn PR; *Miscellanea Genealogica et Heraldica* 3rd series i (1895), 195; London Guildhall Library, Skinners Company records, court books 3 and 4, receipts and payments book 6; MS 3908/1 (St Lawrence Pountney vestry minutes; Wadmore, *Skinners,* 196; PRO PROB 11/332/60; Hallen, *Registers of St Botolph Bishopsgate,* 180; *Boyd's Inhabitants of London.*

POINTS, JOHN

One of the Poyntz family, an ancient and mainly royalist family, of Uley, Iron Acton and Alderley, Gloucestershire. Perhaps the son of Thomas Poyntz, by Elizabeth Clavile, nee Basset. Certainly his using the military rank and his attachment to one of Charles II's most dedicated supporters identifies his politics. Sir Edward Morgan of Llantarnam was brought up in the household of James Butler, twelfth earl and first duke of Ormonde (1610-1688), who employed Points.

Visitations of Gloucestershire, 128-35, 207; *House of Commons 1660-1690* iii, 97; *DNB* for Ormonde.

POWELL, WILLIAM

Of Boulston, three miles from Haverfordwest, Pembrokeshire. A justice of great sessions in Carmarthenshire and Pembrokeshire from 1647 to 1653, he became a serjeant-at-law in 1648. He was resident in the parish which was the home of the Wogan family for many years. Edmund Wogan was, as customer of Cardiff, JB's colleague in his early years in office. This connection may explain JB's familiarity with him, as may the fact that Powell and Evan Seys were both from Lincoln's Inn. Seys became a serjeant a year after Powell.

Phillips, *Justices*; PRO E 190/274/8, E 190/1275/15, E190/1276/1; J H Baker, *The Order of Serjeants at Law* (1984), 188, 441, 531.

ROBERTS, ARTHUR

(c. 1599-1668), JB's deputy in Cardiff, and an alderman of that town, holding at least four burgages and two houses in 1666. A case involving him was before the court of high commission in 1640, but he did not maintain his radical religious outlook: his will of 1668 contained bequests to the Anglican churches of Cardiff. He was still an alderman there in 1662, and he supported JB in his attempt to retain his office against Richard Dutton.

CSPD 1640, 381, 386; J.H. Mathews (ed.), *Cardiff Records* (Cardiff, 6 vols. 1898-1911), i, 428; NLW Bute M7/61, D263/43.

ROBERTS, HUGH

A schoolmaster in Bristol, he kept school at the house of Bartholomew Allen, grocer, in Wine St., near its intersection with High St. JB's sons William and Mathias were educated there as boarders with their cousin Rees Jones, son of Eleanor Jones, JB's wife's sister. By 1664 Allen's widow was occupying the four-hearthed house.

BRO, corporation records, 'chimney book' f. 35v; Leech, *Topography,* 200.

RUSSELL, JAMES

(c. 1610-1655). One of the regulators of the navy and customs from 1649. A London merchant, with a family background in Hereford. Served on the common council of London from 1642, and held posts in the customs, as commissioner and cheque-general for the outports. An active orthodox puritan, he was a tryer for the seventh London classis, a contractor for the sale of bishops' lands, a commissioner for penal taxation on the estates of royalists and a commissioner for the admiralty and navy (1652-3). As an active opponent of the dissolution of the Rump Parliament by Cromwell, he lost all offices in the spring of 1653, and died intestate in 1655.

Aylmer, *SS*, 216.

SANKEY, WALTER

Solicitor to the customs commissioners from at least 1649 to at least 1663. He was in 1657 also examiner of coast bonds, certificates and returns in the customs exchequer, and registrar of seizures. His combined salary for these posts was £110 a year. A Thomas Sankey, probably a relative, was registrar of customs seizures, 1660-68.

PRO E351/ 658; Aylmer, List.

SANSOM, MICHAEL

Secretary to the customs commissioners and perhaps the excise commissioners, in 1649-50. Sansom was a lawyer of the Middle Temple. He was a freeman of the city of London and an investor in the East India Company. He had five children living in June 1650 when he made his will. Samuel Whittle, another of JB's correspondents, is described at that time as Sansom's servant. Francis Parsons, another London customs official, is described as Sansom's friend in the same source. JB's last letter to Sansom is dated 6 May 1650, and the latter's will was proved on 10 June. Another of Sansom's family, probably his son, was clerk to the secretary of the customs commissioners from 1671-7, a surveyor in the early 1680s and secretary to the commissioners in 1684.

Aylmer, List; PROB 11/ 212 fo. 373.

SEYS, EVAN

(1604 - ?1685). First cousin to Margery Byrd, JB's wife. Second son of Richard Seys of Boverton Place, Glamorgan. He succeeded to his father's property in 1639, his eldest brother having been disinherited. The Seys family had acquired lands at Boverton from the earls of Pembroke, under whom they were still freehold tenants for part of their estates. Evan's grandfather Roger Seys had been steward of the Pembroke manors in Glamorgan. Evan Seys matriculated at Christ Church, Oxford, in 1621, was admitted to Lincoln's Inn in 1624 and was called to the bar there in 1631. Nominated as a member of a royal commission about the Thames, 1636. In 1638 married Margaret, daughter of Robert Bridges of Woodchester, Gloucestershire. Attorney-general for Glamorgan, Brecon and Radnor under Charles I, throughout the interregnum, and until 1668, when he resigned in favour of his son. On Glamorgan county committees throughout the 1650s, and a commissioner for the security of the Lord Protector in 1658. Serjeant-at-law 1649 and retained the title in 1660, although he lost his judgeship. MP for Glamorgan 1658-9, Gloucester 1661-81. JP for Gloucester and Glamorgan until 1680. Recorder of Gloucester from 1660 until 1662, when he resigned in advance of the visit of the commissioners for corporations. Seys's Glamorgan estates included lands in the border Vale of Glamorgan areas of Llantrisant, Llanharan and Newton Nottage, as well as around Cowbridge and Llantwit Major. In his behaviour and pronouncements as an MP after 1660 he at first confined himself to technical legal matters, generally supporting the government, but from 1675 he was identified with the Whig opposition, being regarded as 'worthy' by the exclusionist leader, the earl of Shaftesbury.

RCAHMW, *Glamorgan iv, part 2, Farmhouses and Cottages*, 421; Williams, *Parliamentary History of Wales*, 98; *House of Commons 1660-1690* iii, 424-6 ; *Limbus Patrum;* GRO D/DF Deeds 675, D/DF M/395, D/DF E/34.

SEYS, LEYSHON

Younger brother of Evan Seys, his father's fifth son, and a first cousin of JB's wife. He lived in Swansea, occupying a five-hearthed house in the Market Place there in 1677. A burgess of Swansea from 1645, he quickly became 'common attorney' (a financial officer equivalent to a chamberlain) there in that year, but in 1647 was removed from his place as an alderman because of his royalist sympathies. Troops were billeted at his house in 1649. In 1660 he was active in proclaiming the restoration, and was portreeve or mayor in 1660-61. Seys must have been a leading merchant of Swansea.

Limbus Patrum; *Glam. Hearth Tax*, 104; Price (ed.), *Account Book*; L. W. Dillwyn, *Contributions towards a History of Swansea* (Swansea, 1840), 28, 32.

SEYS, RICHARD

Younger brother of Evan Seys and his father's third son. He was a first cousin of JB's wife, Margery. He lived at Rhydding, in Blaenhonddan, Cadoxton-juxta-Neath (for an account of the farmhouse, see RCAHMW, *Glamorgan iv, part 2, Farmhouses and Cottages*), which he held from Bussy Mansel of Briton Ferry on a 99-year lease. In 1674 he was from Neath the most significant shipper of coal mined on the lands of the earls of Pembroke, operating on a larger scale than Bussy Mansel and Herbert Evans, more substantial gentry figures. Richard Seys's son William married the daughter of William Williams, another relative of JB. Richard was a JP from 1660 until 1677, when he was omitted from, and reinserted in, the lists of magistrates, probably as a result of his brother Evan's association with the opposition cause.

GRO D/DF Deeds 354, 371; NLW Bute A 10/ 242; *Limbus Patrum*; Phillips, *Justices.*

SEYS, WILLIAM

Another brother of Evan, Leyshon and Richard Seys, as Letter **342** makes clear. William does not appear in the pedigree given in *Limbus Patrum.* He must have been the William Seys of Cilan (Killan), Llanrhidian, Glamorgan, with substantial properties there in 1670. He, or more probably his son, held land in Llanrhidian, Wick and Llandow, mentioned in a 1686 inventory of property worth £354 in total.

D/DF Deeds/ 334, 882, 2539.

SHEWELL, THOMAS

Shewell or Showell was a woollen-draper of Bristol, and customs collector there from the summer of 1649, succeeding to the post from John Locke. A navy committee decision that he should not be appointed cheque or check there and that the post should go to Luke Hodges (see 1) instead seems to have been reversed or never implemented. His salary for his customs work, to include remuneration for a clerk, was £170. Just as important as his trading and customs work were his activities as navy agent at Bristol, from late 1652 until the summer of 1659. He became a key agent of the state at the port and in the city, involved in pressing seamen, fitting out ships, reporting on shipping movements and commenting on the suitability of individuals for navy posts. His own mercantile activities expanded: in 1656 he was trading in sugar. By the 1660s he had somehow become related to JB by marriage. In 1665 he occupied a two-hearthed property in St Michael's parish, Bristol, a modest enough address for someone who had been a mainstay of commonwealth and protectorate administration in Bristol.

BRO, Chimney Book f. 36v; PRO E 351/658; Bodl. MS Rawl. A 224 fo. 79v; *Merchants and Merchandise,* 242; *CSPD 1651-52 - CSPD 1658-9* many refs.

SPENCER, ARTHUR

One of a family of merchants that hovered on the edge of the ranks of the Glamorgan gentry. The seafaring Spencer family were the dominant figures in the small port of Aberthaw, Thomas Spencer describing himself in the 1630s as 'one of the chiefest merchants' there. One of the family, William, brought over the moderate royalist John Willoughby from Somerset to visit Oliver St John at Fonmon in August 1645. None of the family became JPs. Arthur was master of the New Thomas, a ship plying between Ireland and South Wales, and 'Captain' Spencer had a small estate in East Aberthaw after the restoration. JB evidently fell foul of the family over customs dues they should have paid.

T. Gray (ed.), *Devon Household Accounts, 1627-59, Part 1* (Devon and Cornwall Record Society, new series xxxviii, 1995), 258; GRO D/DF E/6.

SPENCER, THOMAS

Father of Arthur Spencer and probably of William and Samuel Spencer, of Aberthaw. In the late 1630s he was importing tobacco from the island of St Christopher in the West Indies to Aberthaw, and became so resentful of what he saw as the oppressive behaviour of JB and his colleagues, who detained his cargoes, that he sued them in the exchequer in 1646. Although it was William Spencer who was named to a number of Glamorgan assessment committees in the late 1650s, Thomas Spencer was a more active supporter of Parliament. He was nominated for committees in Glamorgan from June 1647 to November 1650, and was certainly serving on the Glamorgan militia committee in August 1648.

Limbus Patrum, 433; F&R i, 979, 1097, 1137, ii, 47, 314, 483; Bodl. MS Tanner 57, f. 181; PRO E 134/ 22, 23 Charles I/ Hil. 2.

SPRINGNETT, HERBERT

Herbert Springett *(sic)* (1639-1726) of Trostrey, Monmouthshire, had a son, also called Herbert, who predeceased him in 1689. His daughter Anne married Richard Jenkins of Glascoed (q.v.). It is not clear whether the Monmouthshire Springetts were related to the much more distinguished family of that name from Ringmer, Sussex, which provided a Herbert Springett to parliaments in the 1640s and 60s.

Bradney, iii, 122; M.A. Lower, 'Sir William Springett and the Springett Family', Sussex *Archaeological Collections* xx (1868), 34-46; *House of Commons 1660-1690* iii, 469-70.

STILES, RICHARD

The innkeeper of the White Lion, Ratcliff, where JB's son, Matthias lodged, and who corresponded with JB on his son's behalf.

STRADLING, THOMAS

(d. ?1680). The third son of Sir Edward Stradling of St Donats, second baronet, and the younger brother of Sir Edward, the third baronet, who died in the civil war. Thomas was the uncle to Sir Edward, the fourth baronet who inherited St Donats, and who died in 1685. Thomas was a lieutenant colonel of foot, the rank possibly acquired in 1648. He was commissioned initially in his elder brother's regiment, and was involved as an insurgent in the Glamorgan revolt of 1647 and the second civil war of 1648. He fled afterwards to Ireland, and compounded for his royalism during the interregnum. He was active on behalf of the future Charles II in 1658. Styled 'senior' to distinguish him from his nephew, he was a JP from the autumn of 1660 through to his death around 1680. Buried at Merthyr Mawr, Glam.

Limbus Patrum, 438; P. R. Newman, *Royalist Officers in England and Wales, 1642 - 1660* (1981), 360-1.

TANNER, JOHN

JB's deputy, or waiter, at Penarth, from at least 1649. The letter book suggests he died in 1663. *The Glamorgan Hearth Tax Assessment of 1670* indicates that the name was common in the Sully area.

TENCH, GEORGE

Surveyor of customs under JB from at the latest 1649. In the later 1650s he seems to have transferred to work with Griffith Bowen at Swansea, on a salary of £40 a year.

PRO E351/658.

THORNBURY, WILLIAM

Collector of the great customs in the London custom house, from at the latest 1648 to at the earliest 1662. In 1649 he received £12 10s. for a quarter's salary. He survived the restoration by petitioning, and held his office by patent. His post was worth £50 in 1662.

PRO E 122/236/19; *CTB 1660-1667,* 1-2; BL Add. 33590 f. 181.

THURLOWE, EDMUND

Of Laugharne, Carmarthenshire, or more likely Llanfihangel Abercywyn, nearby. Thurlowe, evidently a man of minor gentry standing, was engaged in property transactions in his own locality in the early 1670s.

NLW Llwyngwair 2479, 16952.

TREVOR, SIR JOHN

(d. 1673). Of Trefalun and Plas Teg, Denbighshire, eldest son of Sir John Trevor. Married the daughter of John Hampden. MP Denbighshire 1621, Flint 1624, Great Bedwin 1628, Grampound 1640-53, Arundel 1656, Steyning 1660. Farmer of the tax on coals. A spokesman on North Wales issues, and on important committees such as the Committee of Both Kingdoms (1648) and the Commission for the Propagation of the Gospel in Wales (1650). Reputed to have acquired much of the property of the earl of Worcester, he was pardoned at the restoration. In 1646 he acquired a lease of the lordship of Coldra from Eton College, and became JB's landlord. On many parliamentary tax and militia committees for Middlesex - he lived mostly in London - and Denbigh and Flint throughout the 1640s and 50s. In 1645 he was added to a parliamentary committee for the Admiralty and Cinque Ports, which had the power to appoint all officers in the navy, and by extension, the customs. Philip, earl of Pembroke had already been nominated to this committee. In 1656 with Evan Seys he was named a commissioner for the security of the Lord Protector, and in 1657 he was nominated to a committee to investigate the viability of a possible farm of the customs and excise.

DNB; *DWB*; Williams, *Parliamentary History*; F&R *passim* but esp. i, 669, 783; ii, 343, 1040, 1268.

TURNER, EDMUND

Surveyor of the outports at the London custom house from 1660. His office was thought to be worth £253 p.a. Collector of the excise duty on imported spirits, from March 1661. Customs collectors were to account for their receipts from spirits separately, to Turner, who was on a salary for this post of £100 per annum. By 1667 Turner had been knighted and was one of the syndicate farming the customs.

BL Add. 33590 f. 181; *CTB 1660-1667*, 228, 242; Chandaman, 24.

VAN, CHARLES

(1631-1704). Of Llanwern, Monmouthshire. Son of Lewis Van of Coldra manor, in Christchurch parish (d. 1636), and Cecily, daughter of Rowland Williams of Llangibby. Charles Van began to appear on Monmouthshire county committees from early 1660, was sheriff of the county in 1659 and 1660, and a JP from late 1660 to 1667, and from 1679 to

1682. He married Blanch, the daughter of Thomas Morgan of Tredegar and his second wife Elizabeth, daughter of Francis Windham of Sandhill, Somerset. He was a member of the interest of the earls of Pembroke, being a reeve for the Pembroke estates in 1680.

Bradney, iv, 249; Phillips; F&R; *Visitations in Wales,* 214, 219; NLW Bute M 44/20.

VAUGHAN, HENRY

Of Caldicot. Son of William Vaughan and Cecily his wife, daughter of David Kemys of Cefn Mabli. Henry Vaughan married Mary, the daughter of Henry Herbert of Caldicot, and was sheriff of Monmouthshire in 1649.

Bradney iv, 116,120.

VICKRIS, ROBERT

Son of Richard Vickris, merchant and alderman, Robert Vickris was a leading Bristol merchant, with a house in Chew Magna. He became a freeman of the city and a member of the merchant venturers in 1648, was one of the common council of Bristol from 1650 to 1662, and was sheriff in 1656-7. He was master of the merchant venturers' company in 1669-70. In 1660 he was captain of the trained bands or militia of Bristol. After 1660 he was on a number of important Bristol merchant venturers' committees, including those seeking confirmation of their charter and legislation to secure their privileges. He was one of those merchants who developed King Street there, and was an orthodox puritan who invited Thomas Ewins, pastor of the Llanfaches congregation, to serve in Bristol in 1651. Robert Vickris was a persecutor of quakers, although his son, Richard, became a quaker in 1668.

Merchants and Merchandise, 68-71; *Merchant Venturers,* 16, 26, 29, 245; Richards, *Puritan Movement*, 99; *Records of Church of Christ,* 103; Besse, *Sufferings*, i, 40, where 'Richard' Vickris should read 'Robert', 55.

WHITTELL, SAMUEL

Cashier in the treasury at the London customs house in 1657, paid a salary of £100 a year. He is not mentioned in a list of London customs officers of 1649, but in June 1650 is described as a servant of Michael Sansom, the solicitor to the customs commissioners. He may have been the brother of Ralph Whittell or Whittle, secretary to the customs commissioners in 1664.

CSPD 1663-4, 489; PRO E351/658, E122/236/19; PROB 11/ 212 fo. 373.

WILLIAMS, PHILIP

An associate of JB's - the searcher of customs - in 1649; later holding the office of waiter at the port of Aberthaw. Letter suggests he was from Caerleon; a family of that name with the tradition of Philip as a forename, was prominent there by the 1780s. He had been employed as a searcher from at least as early as 1638.

E 134/ 22, 23 Charles I/ Hil. 2; Bradney iii, 202.

YOUNG, JAMES

Possibly a relative of the Lewis and Roger Young, for whom JB was acting in 1674. Roger Young was a hearth tax payer in Caerleon in 1663, but was not mentioned in the subsidy list for 1661. In 1665 James Young sat with JB on the Monmouthshire assize grand jury and brought to the court's notice a number of roads in disrepair.

PRO E179/148/95; E179/148/91; ASSI 5/2.

GLOSSARY OF WORDS AND PHRASES

The modern forms of spellings have generally been given here. Where the modern form might not be obvious from the text, the original is provided, with the modern version in brackets.

absolute prize: ship wholly forfeit to the state, because it originated from a port held by enemies to the Commonwealth.

accomptant (accountant): one responsible for handling public revenues.

accountant-general: superintending accountant in a government department, here the treasury of the customs.

acquittance: a document proving discharge from a debt.

act for increase of shipping and navigation: the Navigation Act, 1660 (12 Car. II c. 18), which tightened up an act of 1651 to confine trade between England and its colonies to English shipping.

act for the assessment: one of a series of acts and ordinances of the 1640s and 50s which authorised collection of monthly taxes to support the armed forces. One was published on 26 November 1650, and the restored monarchy adopted the same system in the 1660s; there was a 36 months' assessment from 25 December 1664.

act for relief of truly loyal and indigent commissioned officers.

act for doubling money: by an act of 6 February 1651 those who had lent Parliament money were encouraged to advance a further loan equal to the original, and both principals and interest would be secured on confiscated fee farm rents of the Crown remaining unsold.

act for the militia: act of 11 July 1650 authorising commissioners in the counties to maintain a militia.

act for regulating the officers of the navy and customs: act of 16 January 1649 appointing a committee of London merchants and navy commissioners to remove royalists from places in the customs houses and the navy.

admire: to marvel, to be astonished.

advertize: to inform.

advize: to consult with, as well as to offer advice to.

affidavit office: a section of the office of the king's remembrancer of the court of exchequer, in which affidavits, sworn statements voluntarily made, were recorded.

Algier duty: by various ordinances from 1644, a tax of one quarter of one per cent of customs duties payable by the book of rates was levied on commodities. The sums thus raised were used to fund attempts by the navy to retrieve English captives of Turkish and other pirates operating off north Africa: 'redemption of captives'.

aliens: foreign merchants.

All Saints tide: 1 November.

alliesman: kinsman.

answer: a written counter to a charge.

answering the value of: meeting or matching the financial value of.

antient (ancient): long-standing.

aquitaine apple: a variety not recorded in standard lists of the period and unknown to the national apple register of the Brogdale Horticultural Trust.

assignes: assignees, those to whom a right of property is legally transferred.

assizes: common law courts held twice a year in English counties and Monmouthshire, but not in other counties in Wales. There the equivalent courts (which exercised civil as well as criminal jurisdiction) were courts of great sessions.

attempt: to try to move by entreaty or petition.

audit week: here the examination of the accounts of tenants to the earls of Pembroke.

authentical: authentic or proper.

Barbary hides: hides from north Africa.

barke, barque (bark): a ship of a particular rigging.

bayleif: bailiff, equivalent in some towns, including Cardiff, of mayor.

bill of charge and disbursements: document detailing liabilities and expenses.

bill of exchange: a promissory note, by which money could be raised or conveniently transferred.

bill of fees and charges: document detailing money owed by the officer and the fees owed to him.

bill of mortallety: bills of mortality were weekly official reports of burials.

bill of store: a custom house licence for a vessel to carry stores for a voyage custom-free.

bishopps next court: the next consistory court of the bishop of Llandaff, which enforced tithe payments.

bond: an undertaking to pay a certain sum by a certain date, with heavy financial penalties for default.

book of rates: book of fixed official customs valuations on commodities, agreed by parliament. Customs officers charged a percentage of the fixed valuations given in the book, which were then the duties payable. Books of rates were revised periodically.

break the entail: entail was the settlement of property so that it must descend to the owner's heirs in a specified way.

breed a fraccion (fraction): cause dissension.

breiffe (brief): a summary.

British army: parliamentary forces in Ireland, supported by taxes levied on the authority of acts for assessment.

Brittons: Breton ships.

burden: carrying capacity of a ship.

by the way: on the way.

Cambridge frigate: a 3rd rate frigate, 70 guns, built Deptford 1666; wrecked 1694.

carryed (carried): managed or conducted.

causes: cases or business.

certayne (certain): reliable or definite.

certifficatt (certificate): 1. (loosely), a document certifying something.
2. a document issued by a customs officer to show that a shipper had entered into a bond to unload at another port within the realm. Certificates were

issued at one port and returned at the destination port.

chaldron: measure of coal, not standardised, which varied widely between and within coalfields. The 'London chaldron' on which customs duties were paid in South Wales has been described as being two tons in weight, but the most recent authority concludes that it was more likely to be 28 cwt.

chamberlayne (chamberlain): an attendant at an inn, in charge of bed-chambers.

chapman: an itinerant dealer.

charge: expense, financial burden.

chequer office: the office of the king's remembrancer of the exchequer.

chief rents: chief rents arose from freehold property, here lordships belonging to the late Charles I.

circuit: a network of assize courts: Monmouthshire was in the Oxford circuit.

cock boats: small ships' boats.

cockett (cocket): sealed receipt issued by customs officers to a merchant to show that import or export duties had been paid. 'Port cockets' were for goods from or for overseas; a 'coast cocket' was a manifest, issued as a check against smuggling, of a cargo carried between home ports.

collacion (collation): a light meal.

collector: customs officer responsible for issuing cockets and preparing accounts for the treasury of the customs.

commissioners for prize goods: By an ordinance of 17 April 1649 commissioners were appointed by parliament to sell ships whose cargoes and tackle were seized by the state. Among the ships which could be seized were rebel ships, those flying the Stuart colours and those carrying contraband. Throughout the seventeenth century, jurisdiction over prize goods rested with the high court of admiralty.

commissioners for the excise: the first commissioners responsible for ensuring that the new excise tax was levied were appointed by an ordinance of July 1643.

committee for prize goods: see commissioners for prize goods.

committee of sequestrations: in the aftermath of the second civil war of 1648, by an ordinance of 23 February 1649, a committee covering South Wales as a whole was appointed, with powers to fine propertied supporters of Charles I and confiscate the property of those refusing to comply.

common pleas: a court which normally met at Westminster Hall to consider civil litigation between subjects.

composicion: composition took place when a royalist was allowed to 'compound' for his estate, and pay a fine instead of forfeiting his property. More generally, to compound was to pay a fine and then recover property, and in the specific context of customs revenue, it was the procedure by which merchants whose cargoes were for some reason difficult to value were allowed to pay an agreed sum to discharge their customs obligations.

compound: see composicion.

comptroller: controller; a customs officer who made an independent account of transactions, and who controlled the cocket seal jointly with the customer.

conceave: to think, judge or consider.

const[abularius] castr[i]: (Latin) constable of the castle, or warden.

constantly: regularly, consistently, continually recurring.

contrybucion (contribution): taxes levied by the assessment (see Assessment).

coresponds: correspondents.

counter security: security given someone to cover risk of standing surety for a bond.

country: region, area or possibly county.

court for probate of wills: in south-east Wales most wills were proved in the episcopal consistory court of Llandaff. Between 1653 and 1660 all testamentary business was overseen by commissioners operating under identical procedures to the those of the former prerogative court of Canterbury.

courts of sewers: commissioners of sewers were appointed by chancery commissions to consider neglects and repairs of sea-walls, rivers, streams and ditches. Their proceedings were regarded as courts of record.

cozen: loosely, a relative.

cozen jerman: first cousin.

crab stocks: young crab-trees used to graft upon.
credit: authority or reputation.

creek: in customs parlance, a small harbour without its own custom house.

cribbs: frameworks of timber.

cum membris (Latin): with its members.

customer: chief financial customs officer, recording shipments and collecting customs.

customs inwards and outwards: customs on imports and exports.

dampnified: injured or wronged.

debiter: debtor.

decree: a judgment in a court of equity.

demised: sold.

discharge: certificate proving financial liabilities have been met (see acquittance).

disinabled: disabled, prevented.

dispose: (v.) deploy, use.
(n.) disposal.

diurnall: newspaper published at short regular intervals.

Doctors Commons: the college, near St Paul's in London, of the doctors of civil law, specialists in church law.

doubt: (v.) to fear.

doubtful: uncertain, fearful.

drafte: draught, a drink.

ell: a length of 45 inches.

engage: 1. (metaphorically) to lay someone under obligation.
2. to give security for.

engagement: 1. by an act of January 1650 an oath of loyalty to the commonwealth regime was to be taken by officeholders. It was repealed during the protectorate of Oliver Cromwell.
2. a commitment, promise or agreement; the state of being taken on to do something.

enlarge: discuss further.

enlargement: release from custody.

enter the seizure: seized cargoes had to be recorded in the king's remembrancer's office of the exchequer (during the commonwealth the first remembrancer's office).

entered into commons: here, boarded at school together.

entryes: entries of cargoes and duties paid, in port books.

estreat: copy or record of a fine made in order to create a debt to the crown or the state.

exchequer: the court concerned with the receipt and audit of crown (during the 1650s, state) revenues. Customs dues were received and audited in the customs treasury, but had to be accounted for at the exchequer. Process against defaulters was instigated in the exchequer.

excise office: from July 1643 the new tax of excise was administered and received at an office in Broad Street, City of London.

execucion: writ of execution.

express: 1. exact
2. on purpose; hence, by implication, speedy.

either by or self ends: either hidden or personal gains.

either in love or by law: with or without recourse to law.

fairely written: written free from blemishes.

farmers: tax farmers paid the government a fixed sum on the basis of anticipated revenue, then took responsibility for collecting the taxes, which they kept. Both customs and excise were for periods farmed during the seventeenth century.

father in law: stepfather.

first penny: cost price.

fittest: most suitable.

flannen: flannel.

follow his own occasions: pursue his own business.

foraine trade: goods carried in foreign ships.

formerlie: 1. in the past.
2. recently.

formes: types or patterns.

fowl: flesh of birds used for food.

frize cloth: coarse woollen cloth.

fullers earth: a hydrous aluminium silicate, used for absorbing grease in cloth-making.

furnish me with against October: provide me with by October.

fustick: a kind of wood used for dyeing yellow.

gallant: splendid, fine, excellent.

good bills: bills of credit which would prove sound.

grand jury: a jury which considered whether a defendant had a case to answer, or which brought to the attention of justices or judges matters of local concern.

great sessions: in Wales but not Monmouthshire, courts which met twice yearly to consider common-law actions, civil and criminal.

great store: great quantity.

habitt: clothing.

handsome: handy.

Henrietta: 50-62 gun warship, built 1654 as *Langport*, wrecked in 1689.

heriot: feudal due by which a beast was delivered from the estate of a deceased tenant to a manorial lord.

honourable committee at Derby House: the Derby House committee was formed in the winter of 1647-8 as the supreme committee responsible for public affairs in England and Wales. It consisted of members of both houses of parliament, with a balance towards members of the House of Commons.

houseings: house.

husband: 1. a manager
2. a spouse.

hussie apple: the only reference to this variety to be found in the national apple register of the Brogdale Horticultural Trust, or in a survey of the main lists of varieties of the seventeenth century, is to Hussey's Pearmain, extant in the 1880s, but no longer so.

impleadance: law suit against someone.

importing: conveying information.

impost: tax.

in suite: in legal process.

indenture: any legal deed with a serrated edge, showing that it was once attached to an identical copy; (loosely) a document containing an agreement.

infeccion (infection): (usually) plague.

informacions (informations): depositions, sworn statements.

instant: (Latin) of this present month.

institucion: induction of a clergyman into a living.

jennet moyles: Gennet Moyle was a noted variety of cider apple in the seventeenth century and is still extant today.

kilderkin: (lit.) cask of 16-18 gallons capacity, quarter size of a tun.

kyne: cattle.

lade: load.

lay with him: stayed in the same bedchamber as him.

letter of lycence: a licence.

lettpasses: permits.

lord treasurer: a principal minister of state, presiding over the exchequer.

lordship: territory of a lord, a demesne.

marches: marshes, low-lying lands.

margent: margin.

mark: two-thirds of one pound sterling (13s. 8d.).

marvel: to wonder at, or be surprised by.

masters in chancery: officials in the court of chancery who reported to it on matters of practice and who executed orders of the court.

mayle (mail): to bind with cords or wrap up an object before despatch by a carrier.

member: in customs parlance, a landing-place subsidiary to a principal port.

mercer: a dealer in luxury textiles.

miscarry: to go wrong, to get lost.

missing to see: failing to see.

mistaken: 1. in error.
2. missed out.

moarneinge: mourning, black cloth sent to relatives and close friends of the deceased prior to a funeral.

mocion (motion): 1. a move or step.
2. a proposal.

model: a pattern of organisation.

moiety: one half.

monthly assessments: direct taxes on land collected monthly.

moy of herrings: measure used for salt; perhaps a bushel (*OED* gives this as a Scottish word).

move: to entreat.

nayled and mayled: made ready for carriage.

neat: net (weight).

next term: the sittings of law courts took place in three terms.

Norman: a ship from Normandy.

not full to: not quite.

note of engagement: a written undertaking.

oath by you prescribed: after 1660 officeholders were made to take an oath of allegiance to the King.

on the back: The Back (Welsh Back), in the maritime quarter of Bristol.

on the publique: a loan on the public faith, i.e., lent to the government.

ordinances: laws and orders passed by Parliament without the king's consent (to 1649), and afterwards those laws and orders initiated by council of state rather than by Parliament.

packet: package or parcel.

papist in arms: A Roman Catholic who had fought for Charles I.

parcel: a quantity or portion.

patent: a grant or confirmation of a public office.
paynes: trouble, care or effort.

petty customs: duties on cloth additional to the main duties or subsidy.

port: a principal centre for the collection of customs.

port cocketts: see cockett.

portage: postage or carriage.

post house: post office.

predict. [Latin, predictus]: aforesaid.

preferment: advancement.

premisses: the matters or things stated previously.

presentment: the act of laying before an authority a statement of some matter.

pretending: claiming.

Princess: a fourth-rate ship, built Forest of Dean, 1660, burden 602 tons. Could accommodate 240 men in wartime service abroad, with a maximum of 54 guns. Broken up, 1680.

privately: secretly.

prize office: office of the commissioners for prize goods, for whom see above.

provoking: urging, entreating.

process: legal action or a lawsuit.

procure order: get an order.

promisely: promising, fair.

proprietors: owners of property.

providore: provider; officer responsible for provender of horses.

pruens: prunes.

punctually: precisely, in every detail.

put his bond in suit: begin legal action to implement penalty clause in a bond.

quarter book: quarterly returns of imports and exports made separately by customers and collectors of customs and sent to the customs commissioners.

quarters are very high: accommodation is very expensive.

quietus: discharge from a debt.

rate: price.

really: 1. truly.
2. straightforwardly, honestly.

recognizance: legal undertaking to perform some action, with a financial penalty in case of default.

redemption of captives from Algier: see Algier duty.

redound to: (here) bring advantage to.

register: registrar.

requiset: requisite, required.

requite: pay back.

rolls: office in the chancery of the master of the rolls, the second most senior judge and the official custodian of chancery records.

rolls, great and hand: tobacco leaves rolled into cylindrical masses of different sizes.

room: place or stead.

sack: white wine imported from Spain or the Canaries; sherry.

save you harmless: discharge your obligation.

scandalous books: by an 'act against unlicensed and scandalous books and pamphlets' of 20 September 1649, no books were to be imported anywhere except the port of London. The act tightened up censorship and was aimed against sectaries and political opponents of the commonwealth regime.

scrawlings: scions or cuttings for grafting on to root stocks.

searcher: officer superintending customs business on the quays, checking that details of cargoes agreed with cockets shown by the merchants.

serjeant: serjeant-at law; member of a superior order of barristers, originally located in the court of common pleas, but in the seventeenth century in decline.

Serjeants Inn: common rooms of the serjeants-at-law.

seasonably: timely; at the right time.

sequestrator: committee man or his employee responsible for collecting fines from, or administering the property of, royalist 'delinquents'.

sequestered: seized by the state.

sheriff, list for: list of possible names for office of sheriff, one of which would be 'pricked' by the lord chancellor.

silly: simple-minded.

Silly: Scilly Isles.

simple: honest.

skinners hall: hall of the London company of skinners.

skinners rents: houses in London owned by the skinners' company.

St David: a 4th rate ship, built 'Conpill' (?Cogan Pill) 1667, 685 tons burden.

St Matthias his day: 24 February.

St Pauls tyde: 25 January.

staple accion: legal action to enforce a statute staple, a strict form of bond.

Staple Inn: one of the London inns of court.

state: 1. the commonwealth.
2. statement.
3. condition.

stone horse: a stallion.

subpoena: a writ demanding the presence of a defendant or other party in court.

subsidy: 'subsidy of tonnage and poundage': consent given by parliament to the collection of customs duties, usually granted to sovereigns for life, but an issue of contention under Charles I.

suites: legal actions.

surcease: give over; put a stop to.

sureties: in a bond or recognizance, those agreeing to pay fines if the person bound defaulted.

surveyor: customs officer identifying ships and cargoes.

surveyor of the outports: London-based customs officials overseeing collections in ports other than London.

tellinge: accounting.

temper: character.

tenor: meaning.

term: period when law courts were sitting.

token: a sign (of affection, loyalty etc); a present.

Transport: Transporter, a royal navy hoy (small sloop-rigged ship) commissioned sometime after 1660 and still in service in 1688.

treaty: on 21 July 1667 a treaty was signed at Breda between the English and the Dutch, ending the second Dutch war of 1665-7. The terms of the treaty had been discussed between the two sides since May.

trow: boat of shallow draught, around thirty tons burthen, used as long-distance carriers on the Severn. When the boats moved down-river from Gloucester, draught boards were let down over the sides to act as keels, making their navigation in the lower Severn and the Bristol Channel possible.

turned of: turned out.

u[ltimo]: [Latin] the last (day of the month).

unhandsome: unpleasant; unseemly.

unhappily fired: unfortunately driven out by fire.

unprovided: having no money.

uppon his back: back to him; returning to settle the business with him.

ut supra: [Latin] as above.

vacacion: periods when law courts did not sit.

vaynely: unprofitably.
vent: sell; distribute.

vented: sold.

videlicet: [Latin] namely.

want: 1. lack.
2. desire.

wayter: customs officer who boarded ships to examine cargoes; often called a tide-waiter.

wharth: warth; a flat meadow close to a river.

whether it was boundinge: where it was bound for.

withall: with.

woose: ooze; mudflats.

writ at attachment and rebellion: attachment was the process issued from a court, here, the court of chancery, upon an affidavit that a defendant did not appear at a hearing or upon non-performance. A writ or commission of rebellion was directed out of chancery to commissioners to give them authority to apprehend the party in default.

writt of appraisement, writt of apprizement: writ empowering customs officers to value cargoes.

yet the last weeke: only last week.

Spelling of these places mentioned in the text has been modernised where the modern version is obvious. Main sources: R. Hyde, J. Fisher, R. Cline (eds.), *The A to Z of Restoration London (the City of London, 1676)* (London Topographical Society Publication no. 145, 1992); J. Stow, *Survey of London* (2 vols., ed. C.L. Kingsford, Oxford, 1908); Pepys, *Companion*; Bradney; Leech, *Topography*; B. de Gomme's map of Dublin, 1673; C. T. M'Cready, *Dublin Street Names* (reprinted Blackrock, Dublin, 1975).

Acorn Alley right against the Spittle: Acorn Alley was off Bishopsgate St., near Spitalfields, in St Botolph's Bishopsgate parish, London. The skinners' company held property there. The Spittle was Spital Square (see Spittle below).

Avon Lloyd: Afon Llwyd, Caerleon: the river which runs into the Usk there.

Angel: an important inn in Cardiff from the 1660s, situated opposite the castle.

Angel in Lumber Street: Lombard St., in the heart of the City of London, near the Royal Exchange.

Barnard's Inn in Holborn: one of the London inns of court.

Bilboa: Bilbao, northern Spain.

Blackamores head in Bread street: Bread St. ran south from Cheapside to Watling St., east of St Paul's.

Blue Boar and Maiden Head, near Fleet Bridge: Fleet Bridge crossed the River Fleet (later New Canal) between Fleet St. and Ludgate Hill, London.

Boe: Bow, in the seventeenth century a rural hamlet three miles east of the City of London, to which Londoners would resort for fresh air.

Bride Streete, Dublin: St Bride's Street led from St. Bride's church towards the quay, and at Christ Church cathedral became Fishamble Street.

Brittayne: Brittany.

Carter Lane: Carter Lane was south of St. Paul's Churchyard, in the City of London between St Paul's and the Thames.

Chepstoll: Chepstow, Mon.

Colbroke: Coldbrook, near Abergavenny, Mon., seat of the Williams family.

Coldre, Coldrey: Coldra, a manor in Christchurch parish, Mon.

Countess of Devon without Bishopsgate: Devonshire House, off Bishopsgate St., and near St Botolphs Bishopsgate church, was the London house of the earls of Devonshire. It seems to have been split into several apartments, and in the 1660s had 52 hearths.

Croisick: Le Croisic, Brittany.

Cross Keys in White Cross Street: Whitecross St. ran north from St Giles Cripplegate at the north west corner of the City of London.

Crown, Farringdon: see Faringdon.

Dall road at Milford: Dale roads, shipping lane off Milford Haven, Pembs.

Dial, sign of, near the Tolesey in Bristol: The tolzey was a lean-to against another building. In Bristol there were two: one for merchants, adjoining All Saints church, and a civic one adjoining the Council House. Their purpose was to facilitate business. The sign of the dial was presumably at the watchmaker's shop front.

Farringdon: Faringdon, a market town in the Vale of the White Horse, Berkshire (now Oxfordshire).

Fish Shamble Street, Dublin: Fishamble Street was the location of Dublin's fish market, and was a main street leading from Christ Church cathedral to the quay.

Gapton: see Gatehampton.

Gare: Gaer, the house in Caerleon of JB's father-in-law, Alexander Seys.

Gatehampton: hamlet in the parish of Goring, Oxfordshire.

Glacecoed: Glasgoed, in Llanbadoc parish, Monmouthshire.

Goldinge Lane: Golden Lane, Dublin, was named after the Goldsmiths' Hall once there.

Golden Lion at the Savoy in the Strand: This tavern in the Strand is mentioned by Pepys: *Diary* vii, 424. The Savoy at this time was partly an almshouse and partly a varied collection of premises leased by the Crown.

Hoape: The Hope was that part of the lower Thames below Tilbury and Gravesend.

Howick: an extra-parochial liberty, rather than a parish, just over three miles north west of Chepstow, in which Cophill is a principal residence.

Kevan Hylith: Cefn Ila, Llanbadoc parish, Monmouthshire.

Kil lan: Killan Fawr and Killan Fach are farms near Dunvant, Llanrhidian, Glamorgan.

Lanarth: Llanarth parish, Monmouthshire.

Llanelwith: Llanelwedd, Radnorshire.

Llanguby: Llangybi parish, Monmouthshire.

Llyswery and Lebenyth: Liswerry and Lebenith were commotes or manors lying in Christchurch parish, Monmouthshire. They were in the hands of Parliament after the civil war, and were acquired by Henry Rumsey of Sudbrook by 1655.

Lymbrick: Limerick.

Lincoln's Inn: one of the London inns of court.

Northly: North Leigh, Oxfordshire.

Oxenford: Oxford.

Peacefeilde: Piercefield, the estate of the Walter family, in St Arvans parish, Monmouthshire.

Peacock in Cornhill: Cornhill was a major City of London street, on to which the Royal Exchange fronted. The Peacock was evidently an inn or tavern there.

Pell Mell: Pall Mall, an exclusive street near St James's Palace, Westminster.

Pencreek, Pencreeke: Pencrug, Llanhennock parish, Monmouthshire.

Pennalt: Penallt, Trelleck parish, Monmouthshire.

Penarth road: the Bristol Channel off Penarth.

Penrose: Penrhos parish, Monmouthshire.

Porbery: Portbury, Somerset.

Quimbourrough: Queenborough, Isle of Sheppey, Kent, a few miles away from Sheerness, which was beginning to be fortified by the royal navy during the reign of Charles II.

Roochell: La Rochelle, Charente-Maritime, France.

Reddriffe: Rotherhithe, between Bermondsey and Deptford, London. In 1664 there were 400 houses there, dependent on the Thames and associated activities.

Skinners rents, without Algate: these properties let by the Skinners Company were in Northern Folgate, the northern extension of Bishopsgate St. in London. Skinners Rents were a short distance from Acorn Alley.

Skinners Alley in Great St Helens: Further down Bishopsgate St. than Acorn Alley, within the City of London boundaries, Skinners Alley would have lain between Gresham College and Leadenhall St.

St Woollos: parish adjacent to the town of Newport, Monmouthshire, on its western side.

Sore (Sôr) mills: The Sôr brook runs into the Usk at Caerleon.

Spittle: St Mary's hospital, Bishopsgate, had been founded in the twelfth century as a priory. It was demolished after the dissolution of the monasteries, and the churchyard was left as a square, known as the Spittle or Spital. To the east of the Spittle lay Spitalfields.

Swan at Holborn bridge: Holborn bridge crossed the New Canal at the eastern end of this main east-west road in London.

Staple Inn: one of the London inns of court.

Three Cups in Bread Street: see Blackamore's Head.

Tredonock: Tredunnock parish, Monmouthshire.

Trostre: Trostrey parish, Monmouthshire.

Wallnutt tree Yard: very close to Devonshire House, this was used briefly as a *poste restante* address by JB in his correspondence with Pennant, after the latter's house in Acorn Alley was destroyed in the Great Fire of London.

Waterperry: a parish to the east of Oxford.

Weight: Isle of Wight.

Whateley: Wheatley, Oxfordshire, a parish to the east of Oxford.

White Dragon in Holborn/ White Dragon near Grays Inn: probably the same inn is intended, on High Holborn, somewhere between Staple Inn and Chancery Lane.

INDEX OF PERSONAL NAMES AND PLACES

References are to entry numbers of letters in the letter-book, not to pages, except those in romans, which refer to pages of the introduction. References in italics indicate a recipient of a letter. The suffix n indicates material will also be found in the note to that entry number. An asterisk indicates an author of a letter. All other letters are by John Byrd. Variant spellings of surnames are in round brackets; supplied forenames are in square brackets.

—, Margaret 52
—, Edward 52
Abuo, Peter, ship's master 279
accountant general 255
Aberafan, Glam. 66, 86
Abergavenny, Mon. 284, 358
  deanery of xli
  fair at 323, 324
Aberley (Abberley), Thomas 5n
Aberthaw, Glam. xxii, xxiii, xxxii, 49, 66, 71, 76, 85, 86, 100, 131, 143, 146, 157, 158, 210
  ships of xxi
Adams, William, porter 352, 355
Afon Llwyd river, Mon. 409, 444
Allen, — 145, 167, 177
Amberson, Robert *353*
Andrewes, Jonathan 35
  Thomas 35
Arlingham, Glos. 387
Arnold, Jenkin xxxv, 49, 67, 81, 133
Arthur, David 318
Avery, Dudley 3n
  Alderman Samuel xvii, xxxv, 3n, *36,* 54, 63n, 64
Avon river, Hung-Road in xxi
Axtell, Col. Daniel xxxix

Badminton, Glos. xl
Barbados xlii, 25, 125
Barefoote, Ann of North Leigh, Oxon. 436
Barker, Robert 47n, 49, 200n
Barkeley, William 35
Barnstaple, Devon 138
Barry, Glam. 49, 66, 67, 100
Barnes, Mary 312
  Richard 312
Barton, — 290
Bassett, Henry 306
Bateman, Alderman Richard 63n, 64
Baznett (Basnett), Robert 49, 133, 223
Beesurd, Thomas 385
Bennett, David 49
  Col. Robert xxxvii
Bettley, John *301*
Bevan, John 52
Bideford, Devon, ship of 128
Bilbao, Spain 406
Blackborne, Robert xxxiv, xxxvii, 116, 118, 120, 121, 122, 124, *128*, 130, 131, 132, *133*, *164*, 169, *172*, *176*, 184, 187, *188*, *196*, 197, 202, 208
Blake, Humphrey 95n
Boulston, Pembs. 7
Botsford, — , a London lawyer 431
Boverton, Glam. xiii, xvi, xxxi
Bovey, Edward 29
Bowen, Edward 186
  Griffith xxix, 210n, 214, 216, 221, 223, 260, 262n
Bridgwater, Som. 138
Bristol, Glos. xi, xii, 21, 24, 28, 29, 37, 57, 61, 65, 66, 67, 68, 72, 76, 80, 81, 92, 99, 100, 102, 105, 106, 111, 114, 116, 118, 120, 128, 130, 138, 359
  Back, house on 330

collector at 241
College Green xi
custom house xxvii, 252
Dial, nr. Tolzey 267
goods landed in xxiv, 353
money paid in, 131
St Ewen's parish xi
St Werburgh parish xi
shipping from 232
shipping to 234
silkweavers of 387
Wine St. 177
Bristol Channel 91, 233
King-Road in xxi
trade in xxii, xxvii
Briton (Burton) Ferry, Glam. 124
Brookes, William, of Upton-upon-Severn, Worcs. 137
Browne, Thomas, watchmaker 267
Bubb, Daniel 165
Buckridge, Francis 40n, 47
Bulkeley (Bulkely), Thomas, 4, *14*, *22*, 24, 25, *42*, 53, 98, 106, 168, 173, *179*, 180, 185
Bunbury, — 108
Burgen, Henry, haberdasher 355
Burleigh (Burley), Thomas, carrier 259, 418
Burrows, — (maid of Mrs. Sansom) 26
Burry, North (*alias* Llanelli), Carms. 121, 164, 210, 223, 285
Burry Port (*alias* South Bury), Carms. 49, 66, 100, 164, 246
deputies at 131
officers at 169
ships of xxi
Butler, James *see* Ormonde, duke of
Piers 241n, 242, 290n, 395, 398, 413, 444
his wife 241
Bynon, John, merchant 223
Byrd, Andrew (JB's son) xv, 257n, 408, 425
Edward (JB's son) xv, 251, 257n, 259, *281*, 282, *283*, 286, *287*, *288*, *292*, *294*, 295, 305, 307, 309, 315, 405
his master 281, 282, 292
John, sons of 126, 145, 167, 339, 412
unidentified brother of 366
Margery (née Seys, JB's wife) xiii, xv, xxxviii, 10, 24, 55, 60, 117, 122, 159*, 177, 232, 236, 241, 245, 247, 259, 280, 281, 284, 309, 324, 339, 350, 356, 367, 382, 388, 390n, 391, 392, 397, 401, 403, 412, 419, 425, 428, 430, 432, 438
Mary (née Langford, JB's mother) xi, xii
Mathias (JB's son) xiv, xv, xvi, xli, 177, 257n, 280, 301, 309, *322*, *323*, *324*, *332*, *336*, 337, *339*, 341, 342, *345*, *346*, *349*, *350*, 352, *354*, 357, *361*, 366, *367*, 368, 373, 374, 377, *379*, *380*, *381*, 382, *383*, *384*, *385*, *386*, 390n, 391, 393, *394*, *397*, 400, *401*, 402, 403, 405, 406, 407, 408, *415*, *416*, *418*, *420*, 424, 425, *426*, *427*, 428, 430, 438, 446
his daughter 439
his wife 438, 439
Susanna (JB's niece) 55n, 138, 173, 181, 191, 195, *226*, 232, 405
William (JB's brother) 4, 55n, 138, 173, 199, 209, 219, 226, 308, 326, 330, 331, *333*, 334, 338, 339, *340*, *341*, *342*, *373*, 374, 378, 383, 387, *393*, *399*, *403*, *406*, *407*, 412, *424*, 428, 439

William (JB's father) xi, xii
William (JB's grandfather) xi
William (JB's grandson) xv
William (JB's nephew) 34, *43*, *50*, 54, *55*, 58, *60*, *64*, *69*, 74, *75*, *80*, *83*, 87, *88*, *90*, *98*, 106, *107*, 112, 113, 116, *117*, *122*, *130*, *138*, *141*, *148*, *150*, 154, *157*, 168, *169*, *173*, *177*, *178*, 180, *181*, 185, 190, *191*, *193*, 195, *198*, 199, *201*, *204*, *206*, 209, 219, *232*, 386, *405*, 406, *412*, *428*, *438*, *439*, *442*
his wife, 116
William (JB's son) xv, xxv, 167, 177, 195, 234n, 235, 236, 237, 238, 239, 240, 241, 242, 245, 247, 249, 251, 255, 256, 257n, 259, 263, 264, 268, 274, 280n, 284, 363, 390n, 391, 392, 408, 419*, 422, 428, 430, 438

Caerleon, Mon. xiii, xiv, xv, xvi, xxvii, xxxiv, xxxviii, 79, 80, 81,100, 210, 360
Afon Llwyd at 411, 444
constables of 409
Millbrook House xiii
mills of 391, 401, 402 403, 409, 322, 444
poor of 446
postmaster 293
Sôr mills xv, xl, 290, 395, 398
vicar 298
Canary Isles 393
Cardiff, Glam. xxi, xxxiii, 7, 20, 25, 27, 28, 31, 37, 38, 39, 66, 68, 70, 76, 81, 86, 91, 94, 95, 96, 97, 98, 105, 106, 128, 136, 137, 141, 143, 224, 390, 391, 401, 409
Angel at, 411
assizes (great sessions) at 163
castle xvi
custom house 234
duties at xxiv
garrison 233
port of, xix, xxii, xxiii, xxv, 49, 71, 105, 120, 156, 164, 171, 185, 197, 210, 212, 213, 214, 234, 237, 250, 254, 258, 285, 304
alterations to 210, 278
customs officers at *39*, *125*, *135*, *142*, 158, *171*, 273
customs receipts at 202, 266, 275
Carmarthen, garrison at 233
mercer of 335
Caysum, Elizabeth *387*
Charity (?JB's maid) 26
Charleton, Richard, carrier 258
Charnock, George 16, *17*, 21, 24, 27, *28*, *37*
Chepstow, Mon. xxi, xxii, 11, 49, 66, 70, 86, 100, 104, 105, 106, 110, 162, 210, 227, 282, 410
coal landed at 254
customs receipts at 202
customs officers at 291
duties at, 197
garrison 233, 254
Christchurch, Mon. xiv
Clegg, John DD 329n
Colchester, Essex 350
Coldbrook, Mon. 379
Coldra (Coldrey) lordship, Mon. xiv, xxxii, 30
Colt, John Dutton xliii
Commissioners of customs (letters to) *25*, *40*, *49*, *53*, *62*, *66*, *78*, *89*, *91*, *94*, *96*, *100*, *105*, *108*, *114*, *120*, *124*, *131*, *182*, *187*, *210*,

216, *217*, *233*, *237*, *238*, *239*, *243*, *244*, *246*, *250*, *254*, *258*, *266*, *269*, *271*, *275*, *276*, *277*, *278*
Commissioners for relief of indigent officers 293*
Committee for navy (letters to) *56*
Cooke, — 317
William 306, 308
Coolishe, Henry 76
Cooper, John 293, 299, 300
Cophill, Howick, Mon. 295
Cork, Ireland 124
Cornewell, John 309
Corrock, Robert 79n
Couch *alias* Thomas, Elizabeth 415, 416
Cowbridge, Glam. 85, 358
Cradock, —, of Margam 415
Walter 180n
Creed, John, brother of Richard 332n
Richard, brother of John 332n
Creswick, Edward *45*
Crispe, Sir Nicholas xvi, 237, 243, 244
Curson, Sir Thomas, of Waterperry, Oxon. 364n

Dale roads, Pembs. 394
Dancer, Thomas of Dublin 386
Danne, Thomas 85
Davis (Davies), — 130
Humphry 315
Rees 95, 145
Rice, of Cardiff 263
Richard 294
Thomas 415
Dawes, Abraham xvi
John 5n, 234, 235, 253, 280
Sir Thomas 5n
Deamonde, Capt. 124
Deane, Col. Richard 57n
De la Vale, Thomas 305n, 308
Dennett, Thomas *409*
Dennis, James 89, 94, 120, 124, 128, 139
de Ruyter, *see* Ruyter
Deyos (Dayes), Michael 19, 27, *46*, 126, *127*, 138, 330, 361, *362*
Disbrowe, Col. John xli
Ditty, [Edward] 130n, 138
Dobbins, Henry 309
Dover, Kent, duty collected for harbour 279n
Dowell (Dowle), John xii, xiii
Robert xii
Draper, Henry *390*, 391, *411*
Drewe, Elizabeth 269
Dryver, Mary 297
Dublin, Ireland,
Bride St. 386
exchequer at 386
Fish Shamble St., Bell 386
Golding Lane, *Coach and Horses* 405, 412, 428, 438,
Golden Ball 439
St. Patrick's church 386
shipping to 232
Dutton, Richard xxxii, xxxix, xli, xlii, 280n, 283, 284, 286, 293, 304, 308, 319n, 326, 330, 331

Edlogan lordship, Mon. 444
Edwards (Edward), Blanche 432
Ellis 295
Morgan 405, 428
Sarah 297
Walter 414
Ellis, —, drowned in Scotland 337
Ely, river, Glam. 20, 66, 91

Estwick, Stephen 35
Eton College, Berks. xv, xxxii
Evans, Herbert xl, 263n
Joseph 57, 58, 81, 206, 232
Lyson 274
Eyvis, — 317

Fairfax, Sir Thomas, lord general xxxi, 2, 90
Faringdon, Berks. 309, 315n, 405
Crown Inn, 315n
Flatholm, Bristol Channel xxi
Fletcher, Thomas *432*
Forest of Dean, Glos. 9
Foxe, Capt. 124, 131, 144
Capt. Edward *140*, 157, *158*, *161*, *166*, 183, 191, 193, 195, 200
Gerrard 4, *15*, 23, *41*, 59, 60, 64n
France, duty on coal shipped to 176
Franklyn (Francklyn, Franclyn) Mathew 31n, 32
Robert 122
William 116n, 117
his wife, 117
Futter, Henry xix, *3*, 53, *63n*, 64, 75, 98, 107, 112
Robert 3

Gadbury, Oliver 364n
Gatehampton, Oxon. 443
Gaurdon, Denis 108n
Gawler, Major John 91n, 95, 233
Gent, widow 265
George, Thomas 138
Gerard, General Charles xxxii, xxxviii, 284n
Gerard, Ratcliff 295
Gibbon, James 79n
Gibbs, John 263
Glamorgan, excise in 138
Gloucester, Glos. , 283, 292
customs officers at *252*
Goldcliff Pill, Mon. 49
Goring, George lord xvi
Gosport, Hants. 367
Gough, James 428, 438
Gower, Glam. harbours in xxii
Grassingam, Richard 339
Graunte, Thomas 66, 71
Great Yarmouth, Norf. xx
Greene, John 386
Griffin, Jane *nee* Pennant 440
Alderman Roger, of Oxford 421, 423, 430, 433, 434, *436*, 437, *440*, 441n
Griffith, John 49, 81, 86, 133
Morgan 4, 6, 81, 141n
Rees 49, 68, 91, 120
Groat, Thomas, merchant 223
Guernsey, Channel Islands, cargo for 223
Gunter, Thomas 395, 398, 413, 414
Guy, Rice 234n
Gwynn (Gwyn), George *325*
Rees 79, 80, 252n, 353n
his widow 353

Hadson (Hudson), — (messenger at custom house, London) 16, 21, 79
Ham, Hierom xii
Hampton, Captain [Robert] 10n
Handbury (Hanbury), Capel 252n
Hands, Mary 364, 392
Thomas *364*, *392*, 393, *408*, *421*, *423*, *430*, *433*, *434*, *435*, *437*, 440, *441*, *443*
his relatives John, Margaret and her son 408

Harbie (Harby), Sir Job xvi, 237, 238, 243, 244, 247, 285
Harris, James *376*
John 376
Richard 436
Walter 301
Harryson (Harrison), Sir John xvi, 291n
Harrison, Col. Thomas xxiii, 81n, 108, 170
Harvey, Col. Edmund xvii, xix, 62, 116, 118n, *228*
Edmund 415n, 416
Helliar, George 19, 27
Herbert, earls of Pembroke, *see* Pembroke
Herbert, — 4
family of Swansea xxiii
Edward xiv, xxv, xxix, xxxii, *6*, 21, 28, *35*, 49, 55, 59, 66, *110*, *170*, *261n*, *265*, 270, 429n
Elizabeth *429*, *431*
her sister, Anne 429
Col. Henry 30n, 170
John xxxiii, 91n, 95, 228, 233
John 391
Richard, second lord Herbert xiv, *149*
William, of Tintern, Mon. 262
Hereford, Heref. 283
Hill, Richard 35
Hilman, — 76
Hobbs, John, clerk to accountant-general of customs *121*, *129*, *132*, *134*, 138, 148, 150, 199
Hobbs, John, Berkshire coroner 315
Hodges, [Luke] MP xxxi,1n, 2
Holland 428
Hollande, John 35
Hope, River Thames 366
Horse Pill, Mon. 49
Howick, Mon. 295
Huggett, William 49, 66, 70, 86
Hughes, Charles, of Trostrey (Trostre), Mon. 262, 293n, 329
Thomas, of Moyne's Court, Mon. 162
Hulls, — (JB's aunt) 30n
— (JB's uncle) 30n
Huntley, Glos. xi
Hutchinson, Richard 35
Hynde, Capt. 100, 102, 103, *104*

Ireland 56, 100, 101, 102, 103, 108, 124
duty on coal exported to 176
emigration to 177
shipping from 131
shipping to 223, 232
See also Cork, Dublin, Limerick, Munster
Isle of Wight 357

Jacob, John xvi
James, George, carrier 322
Richard 298
William 325
Jeffries, — 439
Jenkin (Jenkins), Elizabeth 339
Morgan 66, 68, 71, 79, 82, 146, 151
Owen 164
Richard, of Glascoed, Mon. *447*
Thomas 173, 177
William 265, 270
Jesse, John 391
John, Meurig (Mirick) 398, 415, 416, 426
Jones, family of Llanarth, Mon. xli
Arthur 292

Eleanor 126n, 159n
Elizabeth 398
Florence 159, 167
Herbert 414
James of Llanfihangel Llantarnam, Mon. 199n, 245, 251, 259, 283, 284, 286, 289, 292, 293, 295, 298, 308, 310, 320, 330, 349, 350, 434, 440
his wife 245
James, rector of St. Brides Netherwent, Mon. 298n
Col. John xxxvii
John Rosser 52
Lewis 263
Morgan 49
Alderman Patrick xxxvi, 27, 49, 133, *186*
Col. Philip xxix, xxxiii, xli, 95n, 170, 210n
Rees (Rice) 126n, 167, 370
Rowland 412, 428
Simon *223*, *231*
Thomas, tailor 363
Walter, of Magor, Mon. 162
William, customs official 49, 86, *207*
of Cardiff 263
of Llanarth, Mon. 293n, 343, 347*, 348, 356, 360, 434
magistrate, of Usk, Mon. *123*
porter of London 322, 323, 324

Kanerley, — , minister 446
Kellam [George] 1, 2n
Kersley, (Kerseley) Henry xix, 147n, 234, 242, 259
Keymes, — 30
Knight, William 12n, 18

La Rochelle, France 91
Lancelot (Launcelott), — 317, 321n
Langham, Captain 131
Col. George xix, 108, 111, 112, *118n*, 121, 132, 134, *139*, *147*, 148, 150, *153*, *160*, 172, *184*, 185, *189*, *194*, *197*, 200, *202*, *203*, *208*, 209, *211*, *212*, *214*, *218*, *222*, 225, 227, 228, 229
Langley, John 35
Laugharne, Rowland xxxix, 319n, 326n
Launder, Francis, of Oxford 363
Layton, — 432
Lawrence, John 323
Le Croisic, France, ship of 238
Lewis, Edmund 411, 422
Rees 384
Sir Thomas xxiv
Thomas xxix, xxxvi, 9n, 11
Limerick, Ireland xxxiii, 91
ship of 232, 233
Lisbon, Portugal, shipping bound for 216
Liswerry and Lebenyth, Mon. xiv, xxxv, 173, 401
Llanelli, Carms. *see* Burry, North
Llanfrechfa, Mon. xiv
Llanhennock, Mon. xiv
Llantwit Major, Glam. xiii, xvi, 12
Llewelyn ap Thomas ap John 442
Lloyd, — 60n, 203
Arthur 263
Hugh 64, 90, 130n, 138
John, brother of Walter 208n, 210n, 218, 223
Thomas 315
Walter, brother of John 208

Llwyd, Ann 429n
Lock(e), John *12*, 14, 17, *18*, *19*, 22, 25, 26, *27*, 28, *29*, *31*, *32*, 40, 46, 47, *48*, 53, 61
London, 10, 17, 21, 405
places in:
Acorn Alley, Spital, 361, 367, 374, 386, 405
All Hallows, Barking xviii
Botolph Bishopsgate 361n, 367, 374, 386, 405
Angel, Lumber Street 169
Barnard's Inn, Holborn 177
Bear Lane 16
Bishopsgate church 355
Blackamore's Head, Bread Street 280
Blue Boar and Maiden Head, Fleet Bridge 301
Bow 232
Child and Coat, Blackfriars 81
Devonshire House 355
Drury Lane 290
Golden Fleece, Watling Street 63, 77
Golden Lion, Savoy, Strand 285
Gray's Inn Lane 431
Lincoln's Inn 419, 437
old post house 92
Peacock, Cornhill 241
Pell Mell 293, 300, 306
post house 106, 351
St Paul's Head, Carter Lane 259, 310
Serjeants' Inn, Chancery Lane 350
Skinners' Alley, Great St. Helen's 428, 439
Skinners' Hall 279
Skinners' Rents, Aldgate 387, 405
Staple Inn 365
Swan, Holborn 385
Three Cups, Bread Street 209, 322, 323, 324
Three Kings, Lees Yard, St. Martin-in-the-Fields, Middx. 268
Tower Hill, 116
Tower of London xviii
Walnut Tree Yard 355
White Cross Street, *Cross Keys* 418
White Dragon, Holborn 353, 368, 379
silkweavers of 387
Longe, Robert 310
Longman, Moses 126n, 131, 140, 158, 161, 166
Love, Richard 124n
Lovelace, Francis 293
Lucas, Richard 292, *309*, *372*, *375*
William 257, 281, 283, 359
Ludlow, Col. Edmund xxxvii
Lyson, Hopkin 49
Watkin 49

Magor, Mon. xxii
Malory (Mallory), Francis xxv, xxxvi, 68, 77, 99, 119, 165, 169, *175*, 186, *190*, 191, 263
Mansel, Sir Anthony xxxviii
Mansell, John, collector at Swansea *321*
Philip, deputy at Swansea xxxix, xl, 242n, 246, 254, 255, 264, 280, 282, 286, 291, 292, 296, 299, 304, 308, 311
Manwareinge, Major Robert 285
Mathern, Mon. 49
Meredith (Merredith), William 28n, 138, 280, 298

Merrick, — 65
Milford Haven, Pembs. xix, xxxiii, 40, 90, 394, 397
port of 121, 164
Mills, John xvi
Minehead, Somerset 66
cargoes landed at 131, 146
Monmouth, Mon. 36, 418
assizes at 241, 409
?school at 259
Monmouthshire, excise in 138
Morgan, Andrew 52
Morgan, — 98, 261, 265
family, of Llantarnam, Mon. xv, xl
family, of Tredegar Park, Mon. xli
Anne, of Pencrug, Mon. 263n
Charles, of Penrhos, Mon. 313, 314, 316, 318n
Christopher 325
Edmund, of Newport, Mon. 262, 329n
Edmund, of Penrhos Fwrdios, Mon. 236
Sir Edward, baronet 247n
Edward 36, 51, *52*, 98, *113*
Edward of Llantarnam 434n
Edward of Pencrug xv, 438
Eleanor 52
Elizabeth, wife of Christopher 325
Florence 159n, 394n, 397n
George 325n
Giles, of Tredunnock, Mon. 359n, 397
Henry, of Cardiff 263
Henry, of Risca, Mon. 162
Isaac 242, 247, *248*, 249, 251, 353
John xxxviii, 8n, 13, 33, 75, 80
John of Pentrebach, Mon. xiv, 8n, 204n, 205, 376
his wife 376
John 342, 347, 355, 357, 359
John of Llantarnam 434n
John, of London 429
Margaret, of Pencrug xv, 438
Lady Mary, of Llantarnam 241n, 247, *290n*, 395, 398, 444
Miles, of Cardiff 263
Robert 358, 360
Robert of Llantarnam 434n
Rowland 429
Thomas, brother-in-law of Sir Edward Morgan 247n
Thomas, of Lansôr, Mon. 293
Thomas of Llantarnam 434
Thomas, of Machen, Mon. xxiv
Thomas, of Penrhos, Mon. 262, 313n, 314, 329n, 356, 360, 409
his servant, Charles 345
Thomas, of Tredegar Park, 262
Walter *8*, *13*, *33*, *51*, 52, 173, 177
William 49, 66, 70, 124, 131, 140, 158, 166, 186, 200, 236, 429
William, of Pencrug, Mon. 173, 177
William, of Pencrug 262, 290
William, of Tredunnock 359n, 370, 371
William of Tredegar Park 329n
Morgans, William 293
Moulton, Capt. Robert 151n, 152, 154, 155, 157, 162, 168
Mountney, — 317
Moyer, Samuel 35

Munster, Ireland 86

Neale, Samuel 169n, 190, 191
Neath, Glam. xxiii, 49, 66, 70, 81, 86, 96, 100, 124, 210, 246
abbey 124
coal shipped from 254
deputies at 131
goods seized at, 131, 158
officers at, 169
ships of xxi
Newbury, Henry xliii
Newent, Glos. xi
Newfoundland 406
Newport, Mon. xiv, 20, 49, 66, 92, 93, 106, 128, 141, 210, 265
cargo seized at 188
customs officers at xxxv, 254, 273
deanery of xli
mayor of 314, ?320
poor of 182, 187, 196
ship at 275
Newton Nottage, Glam. xxiii, xxiv, xxxv, 49, 66, 67, 81, 100
deputies at 131
officers at 169
Nicholas, Sir Edward, Secretary of State xxxix
Moses xxxvi, 254
Nicholls, Catherine *159n*, 397n
Nicholls, Edward 68, 71, 146, 151
Northerne, Thomas 68, 72
Nowell, Francis 238
Nulls, John xvii

Ormonde, James Butler, first duke of 386
Oxford 393, 430
Christ Church 435

Paget, William lord *285*
Palmer, [Thomas] 55n, 60, 64n
Parry, James *30*
Parsons, Francis 10n, 16, 21, 69, 79, 185, 197, 202, 234, 241, 282, 305
Paulett, William xl
Payton, Francis 32, 46, 48
Pearson, — 367
Pembroke, Pembs. 11
Pembroke, earls of xiii, xiv, xvi, xxiii, xxxviii, xl, xli
Pembroke, Philip Herbert, 4th earl of xxxviii, 81n, 91n
Philip Herbert, 5th earl 389, 391
William Herbert, 6th earl xli, 409, 423
commissioners of *444*
mills of 444
Penarth, Glam. xxiv, 20, 56, 57, 66, 76, 81, 100, 128, 155, 210
customs officers at 273
Pencrug, Mon. 223
Pennant, Jane 441n
Martha 122, 199, 249, 251, 259, 310, 334, 355, 378
Thomas xii, xix, xxx, xxi, *2*, *4*, *10*, *16*, 17, *21*, 23, *24*, 26, 34, *44*, 47, *50*, *58*, 60, 64n, *74*, *87*, 88, 90, 98, *106*, 107, 109, 111, *112*, 113, *116*, 117, 122, 130, 138, *154*, 157, *168*, 173, 178, *180*, *185*, 189, 191, *195*, *199*, 201, *204*, *205*, 206, *209n*, *219*, *225*, *229*, *234*, 241, *242*, 247, *249*, *251*, 253, *255*, *259*, *264*, 268, 279, *280*, *282*, 283, *286*, *291*, 292, *294*, *296*, *299*, 300, 301, *304*, *305*, *306*, *308*, *310*, *311*, *326*, *330*, *331*, 333, *334*, *337*, *338*, 339, 341, 350, 351, *352*, *355*, *357*, 361, *366*, 367, 368, *374*, *377*, *378*, 383, 386, 393, 403, 405, 406, 441n

Pennoyer, William 35
Penoyer, Samuel 35
Perkins, Christopher, sheriff of Mon. xli, 365n
Peterston Pill, Mon. 49
Phaer, Dr. Thomas xxii
Phillips (Philipp), Giles 263, 312
Pindar, Paul xvi
Plummer, — 326
Plumley, John of Newport xxxvi, 8n, 49, 66, 123n, 128
Points (Poyntz), John *386*
his wife 386
Stephen, son of John 386
Portbury, Somerset 9
Porter, Endymion xviii
Port Eynon, Glam. 49
Powell, — 145
Charles 167n
Hugh 298
James xxxiii
Thomas 33
William *7*
William of Llangadoc-juxta-Neath, Glam. 405, 428
Price, — , tobacco merchant 127
Captain 319
David 165
George 137
Jeffrey 298
John 49
Pritchard, Roger 439
William 438, 439
Pryddie, Joan, of Newport, Mon. 270
Probert, Sir George, of Penallt, Mon. xl, 262n, 293n, 329n
Pye, Sir Robert 315n
Pynder, Michael, haberdasher 280

Queenborough, Kent 352

Raglan, Mon. xl, xli
Ratcliff, Stepney, Middx., *White Lion* at 366, 380, 388, 393, 397, 400, 403, 406, 407
Raynolds, Thomas 110
Reading, Berks., assizes 315
Redriffe (Rotherhithe), Surr. 157
Redwick Pill, Mon. 49, 68, 72
Rees, Lewis 73, 79, 80
Richard (Richards), Godfrey, stationer 241, 247
William 440
Roberts, — 126n
Alderman Arthur, of Cardiff xxxvi, 49, 70, 133, 136, *156*, 165, 171, 263n
Hugh, *145*, *167*, 177
Roche, Luke *alias* Mark 91, 233
Samuel 72
Rochester, Kent 349, 357
Mermaid inn, 350
Rogers, Christopher xxxi,1, 2,
Roger 305, 349, 371
Phineas 258
Rosser, John 49, 73, 79, 80, 110
Margaret 8
Rousworth, John 443
Rowe, — 333, 334
Rumsey, Edward 283n
Henry 390n, 391, 409, 411
John 390n, 409n, 411
Russell, James xvii, 35, 64, *77*
Ruyter, Admiral Michiel de 428n
Rymbron, Thomas 27, 29, 31, 32

St. Kitts, West Indies xvii, xxi, xxv
St. Pierre, Mon. 9n
St. Woollos, Mon. xiv, 8, 283n
Sankey, Walter 53, 63n, 64, 67, 69, 73, 75, *79*, 80, *82*, 84, 107, 112, *146*, 148, 150, 151, 158, 161, *165*, 166, *183*, 191, 193, 195, *200*, 201, 234, 282, 305
Sansom, Michael xxxi, 2, 4, 10n, 14, 16, *20*, 21, 22, 24, *26*, *47*, *54*, 55, *57*, 58, 60, *61*, 64, *68*, 69, *73*, 75, 79, 80, *81*, *86*, 90, *92*, *95*, *97*, 98, 100, 101, *102*, 103, 106, 107, *109*, *111*, 112
  wife of, 26, 101, 112
Savell, George, shoemaker of Dublin 405, 406, 428, 438, 440
Scilly, Isles of 25, 124
Scurluck, Evan 335
Selinger, — , chaplain to master of rolls 352
Severn river *see also* Bristol Channel xxi, xxiii
Seymour family xl
Seys, Alexander, of Caerleon, Mon. (JB's father-in-law) xiii, xv, xvi, 446n
  Alexander (JB's brother-in-law) xiii
  Andrew 13n
  Evan, serjeant-at-law xiii, xxxi, xxxiv, xxxvii, xli, 30n, 33, *34*, 241, 247, 263, 281, 283, *284*, *289*, 292n, 295, *307*, 309, *327*, *328*, *344*, 350, *351*, *359*, *363*, *365*, 369, *370*, *371*, 372, 373, 374, 375, *382*, *391*, *395*, *396*, 397, *410*, *413*, *414*, *417*, 418, *419*, *425*, 432
    Alexander, his servant 303
    Rogers, his clerk 305, 349, 371
    Vorst (Vosse), his servant 397
  Florence (JB's mother-in-law) 13n, 159n, 178, 180, 195
  Leyshon, of Swansea, Glam. *343*, *348*, *356*, 358
  Margaret, of Cowbridge, Glam. 358n
  Richard, of Boverton, Glam. xiii
  Richard, of Rhydding, Glam. xlii, *445n*
  Roger xiii
  William, of Caerleon, Mon. 339n, 356, 358n, 376
  William, of Cil-lan, Glam. 343, 347, 348, 356, *358n*, *360*, 419, 437
  William his son 419n, 437
Shawe, Sir John 237, 238, 243, 244
Sheere, John 263
  Roger 263
Sheres, Richard 165
Shetland, Scotland, drowning at 337
Shewell (Shuall, Shuell), Thomas xxix, xxxv, 1n, 32n, *65*, *76*, 81, *85*, *99*, 102, 111, 114, *115*, *119*, 124, 131, 140, 146, 158, 161, 200, 202, 203, 210, *215*, 217, *220*, *221*, *224*, *227*, 229, *230*, 313n, *314*, *316*, *318*
Shute, Richard 35
Sicklemore, Samuel 27
Sissell, — 264
Smythier (Smyther, Smither), [John] 283n, 292n, 305, 307
Snowe, John 186
Somerset, marquesses of Worcester, *see* Worcester
Southampton, Thomas Wriothesley, 4th earl of, lord treasurer xxxix
Spencer family, of Aberthaw, Glam xvii, xxii

Spencer, Captain Arthur, of Aberthaw 79n, 131, 136, *144*, 154
Thomas, father of Captain Arthur xxi, xxii, xxv, xxxii, 79n, 136, 151, *152n*, 154, 155*, 157, *163*
their wives, JB's greetings to 136
Springnett, Herbert *320*
his wife 320
his brother 320
Steepholm, Bristol Channel xxi
Stiles (Styles), Richard, of Ratcliff, Middx. 380, 388, 393, *402*, 403, 406, 407
Stradling family of St Donats, Glam. xxiii
Stradling, Sir Edward xxiii
Mansel xl
Col. Thomas xxxix, *319n*, 326
Streater, Benjamin 200n, 203
Streley (Strely, Strelly), - 10, 16, 21, 69n, 79, 106
Stuart, James, duke of York, later James II xliii
Sully, Glam. 49, 66, 67, 100
Swansea, Glam. 1, 12, 27, 29, 38, 39, 49, 53, 62, 66, 70, 81, 86, 90, 96, 100, 124, 164, 246, 280
coal shipped from xxxviii, 254
customs officers at *174*, 270, 273
creation of new port of xliii, 210, 214, 234, 237
customs receipts at 202, 221
duties at 197
ships of xxi
Swynmoue (Swynmour, Swynmoure, Swynmowe, Swynnowe), Thomas 10, 16, 21, 63n, 69, 79, 132, 134, 148, 150
Symms, Thomas 364n, 392n
Symons, Richard 1, 2

Tanner, — 254
John 66, 67, 81, *302*, *303*, 304
Thomas 49
William 85
Tate, Thomas 52, 113
Taynton (Taynter), Thomas 19, 27, 29
Tenby, Pembs., garrison 233
Tench, George 68, 89, 121, *156*, 165, *186*, *192*, 200, *223*
Tewkesbury, Glos. 65
merchant of 252
Thomas, Alice 52
alias Couch, Elizabeth 415, 416
John 49
Mary 52
Morgan 298
Robert, JB's attacker 7
Robert, MP 319n, 326n
Walter 186n, 203n
his wife 223
William 49
Thompson, Maurice 35
Robert 35
Thornebury (Thornbury), Isaac xxiv
William xviii, xxiv, 4, 10, *15*, 16, *23*, 24, 43, 55, 60, 64, 234, *235*, 242, *253*, 255, 259, 282, 305
Thruston, James 316, 318
Thurlowe, Edmund, of Laugharne, Carms. *335*
Tomkins, Mrs. — 429
Isaac 256n, 268, 281n, 288, 292, 295, 334, 352, 355, 357, 363, 365, 377, 378, 393, 399, 407, 413, 414, 418, 424, 431
Toomes, [William] xviii, 15n
Tredunnock, Mon. xiv, 394
Trevor, Sir John xv, xxix, xxxi, xxxvi, *1*, 2, 9, *11*
Tuckey, William 72

Turner, Edmund 5n, 238, *272*, 273, *279*, 280, 330
John, innkeeper 309, 315
Tyson, Col. [Edward] 76n, 118

Usk, Mon. commissioners for pious uses meeting at 446
lordship 391
river 81, 182, 187

Van, Charles of Coldra, Mon. 262, 329, *389*
Vaughan, Henry *162*
Vickers, Francis 252
Vickris, Robert *404*
Virginia 120
Vorst (Vosse), Edward 396n, 397

Walter, Henry xlii, 180n, 283n, 414n
John 186n
John of Piercefield, Mon. 262
Walterworth, Capt. John 380n
Wapping, Middx. 339
Warde, John 66, 180n, 187
Warren, Sir William 339n
Waters, Edmund 283n, 284, 295
John 292
Susanna (Susan) 283, 286, 295
Warwick, Sir Philip 241, 247n, 326, 327, 331
Watkins, James 392
his wife 392
Wells, Nathaniel 263
West, Robert 315
Wharton, — , the Oxford carrier 241, 247, 423
Wheatley, Oxon., JB's relatives at 392, 421, 430, 433, 435, 437, 441, 443
Whip, Robert 75
Whittell (Whittle), John, brother of Samuel 308, *317*, 321
Samuel, brother of John 233, 234, 259, 272, 273, 280, 282, 305, 308, 310, 311, 321, 331
Whittley (Whitley) George 283n, 286, 289, 295
Roger of Aston, Flints. xxxii, xxxviii, 283n, 284, 295
Wickam, Thomas 115
Wight, Isle of 357
Willett, William, of Bristol 115n, 317
Williams (William), family of Caerleon, Mon. xlii
— , JB's cousin 122n, 130
Charles, JB's cousin 236n
Christopher 49
David, of Caerleon, Mon. 265, 270n
Jenkin 49
John, chaplain aboard *Henrietta*, 341
Mathew 27
Philip xxiv, 49, 66, *67*, 68n, 71, 73, 79, 80, 82, 84, 86, *136*, 143, 146, *151*, 158, 165, 180, 187
Philip, of London 354, 368, 379
Rees 180n, 187
Robert 49, 252
Roger 180n, 187
Roger, of Cefn Ila, Mon. 262, 293n, 329n
Rowland 150, 225
Thomas 122n, 123
Thomas, of Caerleon xv, 236n, 262
Thomas xxiv
Sir Trevor of Llangybi, Mon. xli,

xlii, 329n, 365n, 409, 444
Trevor, of Usk, Mon. 262
William, JB's cousin 346, 423, 430, 437, 440, 445n
daughter of 445n
wife of 445
junior, of Caerleon, Mon. 379n
William, waiter at Newport, Mon. 254n, 304
William, of Abergavenny, Mon. 262
Willoughby, William 35
Wogan, Edmund xxxix, xl, 234n, 271n
Wolstenholme, John xvi
Wood, Capt. Walter 323n, 324, 332
Wooddall, [Thomas and Anne] 209n
Woolluyn, John 263
Worcester, Worcs. 260, 262, 263, 283, 284
Worcester, earls of xxiii, xxxviii
Worcester, Henry Somerset, 3rd marquess of xl, xli, 414
Worthen, Richard 315
Wriothesley, Sir Thomas *see* Southampton, earl of
Wye river xxiii

Yeomans, Francis 46n, 48
William 32n
Young (Younge), Ann of North Leigh, Oxon. 436
Christopher of North Leigh 436
James 115, *126n*
Lewis 434, 435, 436, 437
Roger 434, 435, 436, 437, 440
widow of 440
Thomas xxiv, 27n, 204

INDEX OF SUBJECTS

References in roman numerals are to pages of the Introduction; those in arabic are to letter numbers of the text.

acts and ordinances of parliament 64, 66, 80, 177
- for assessment 141, 148, 173
- for foreign coin and bullion 147
- for militia 141, 150, 173
- for regulating officers of navy and customs 34, 35
- for prohibiting imports from France 67
- for prohibiting exportation of wool and fullers' earth 151
- Navigation Act 243, 246, 250, 254, 258, 266
- on customs matters 70, 169, 172, 207
- on excise 60
- on scandalous books 89

advice to son, JB's 281, 283, 292
allegations, against JB xxxii, 68
arms, delivered for Parliament by JB 151, 152, 154, 155, 157, 162, 163, 168
army in Ireland, supplies to 100, 101, 102
arrest, of JB by royalists in civil war 284, 295
assault and manslaughter, JB's son 307, 315
assessments, monthly (taxes), inequities in 110
attorneys 51
auditing
- of customs accounts 42
- of earl of Pembroke's rentals xvi, 136

bills of exchange xix, xxi, xxxvi, 29, 32, 57, 61, 104, 105, 108, 251, 255, 300, 301, 318
books of rates xx, 131, 186
butter, price of 118
cargoes xxii
- butter 67, 68, 91, 99, 118, 233
- calfskins 120, 216
- coal xxvii, xxxviii, 53, 62, 66, 68, 137, 186, 188, 216, 237, 238, 243, 246, 254
- cotton 66
- fullers' earth 125
- fustick wood 66
- ginger 66
- herrings 158, 216

hides 91, 118, 233
horses 131, 186
iron 252
oats 101, 102, 108
pipe clay 125
prunes 128
salt 63, 128
sugar 66, 81
tallow 91, 233
tobacco 20, 25, 53, 66, 68, 72, 75, 79, 80, 82, 90, 99, 127
wine 186
wool 66, 67, 68, 71, 73, 79, 80, 82, 95, 233
Catholicism xli, 74
charity 446
cheese 46
church, lay impropriator of, Caerleon, 298
coal, outcropping in River Usk, Mon. 182, 187, 196
committee for admiralty xxv
Monmouthshire 74, 162
for navy and customs xxv, xxxi, 1, 2, 6, 53, 56, 57, 66, 77, 106, 118, 120, 132, 169, 210
for prize goods xxxiii, 162
for regulating navy and customs xxv, 35
for sequestrations 74, 75
constables 110
council of state, orders of 120, 125
courts
assizes xxxiii, 7, 36, 74, 282, 289
bishop's 290
chancery xii
charitable uses 446
common pleas 283, 286
great sessions xxxi, 7, 74
manorial 30
sewers xxxiv, 409
courtship, JB interceding in 231
customs
accounts, arrears of 302, 304, 308, 310

duplicates of 276, 277
bonds, xxvi, 63, 317
supplies of blank xxix, 67, 80, 118, 140, 158, 176, 185, 186, 187, 241, 247
volume of 86, 133
books xviii, xxvii, 192, 194, 208, 217, 235, 239, 242, 253, 271, 272, 282
cockets and certificates xxiv, xxvi, 35, 65, 66, 78, 86, 99, 133, 147, 153, 223, 252, 254, 353
made by collector not customer 86
possible double-payment on 223
commissioners xvii, xix, xxv, xxviii, 17, 20, 22, 24, 25, 26, 27, 31, 32, 35, 40, 41, 46, 47, 48, 49, 50, 54, 57, 64, 67, 68, 70, 73, 75, 77, 81, 83, 86, 234, 278
changes to 55, 68, 99, 278
farmers xvi, xix, 278, 280, 282, 285, 291, 296, 304, 310, 311, 317
'letpasses' xxvii, 68, 174
officers, allowances of 78, 81, 86, 132
exemption from service on juries 176
frequency of remuneration 133, 134
disputes with soldiery 91, 92, 95
fees xix, xxviii, 35, 49, 64
paper on, by JB's brother 373, 374
patents of xviii, xxiv
salaries xix, 35, 49, 54, 66, 68, 86, 87, 118, 214, 254, 304
shortfall of customs receipts to meet 86
officers, South Wales 39, 66, 70, 273, 304
attempts by JB to increase establishment 169
attempts by JB to recover post 310, 319, 326, 329, 330, 331, 333, 334
check, cheque or chequer xxv, 68, 77, 100, 118, 119
collector xxv, xxvi, xxix, xxxi, 66, 86, 100, 210, 214, 255, 321
comptroller xiii, xxiv, xxv, xxix, xxxii, xxxvi, xxxix, 49, 271, 279, 293, 299, 300, 308, 310
patent for office of 280, 284
rumoured sale of 326
customer xxii, xxiv, xxv, xxvi, xxix, xxxii, xxxix, 4, 6, 15, 21, 23, 24, 28, 35, 41, 49, 64, 66, 86, 271, 273
deputies xxxv, 49, 66, 78, 86, 91, 96, 97, 118, 120, 124, 128,

THE FAMILIES OF BYRD AND SEYS

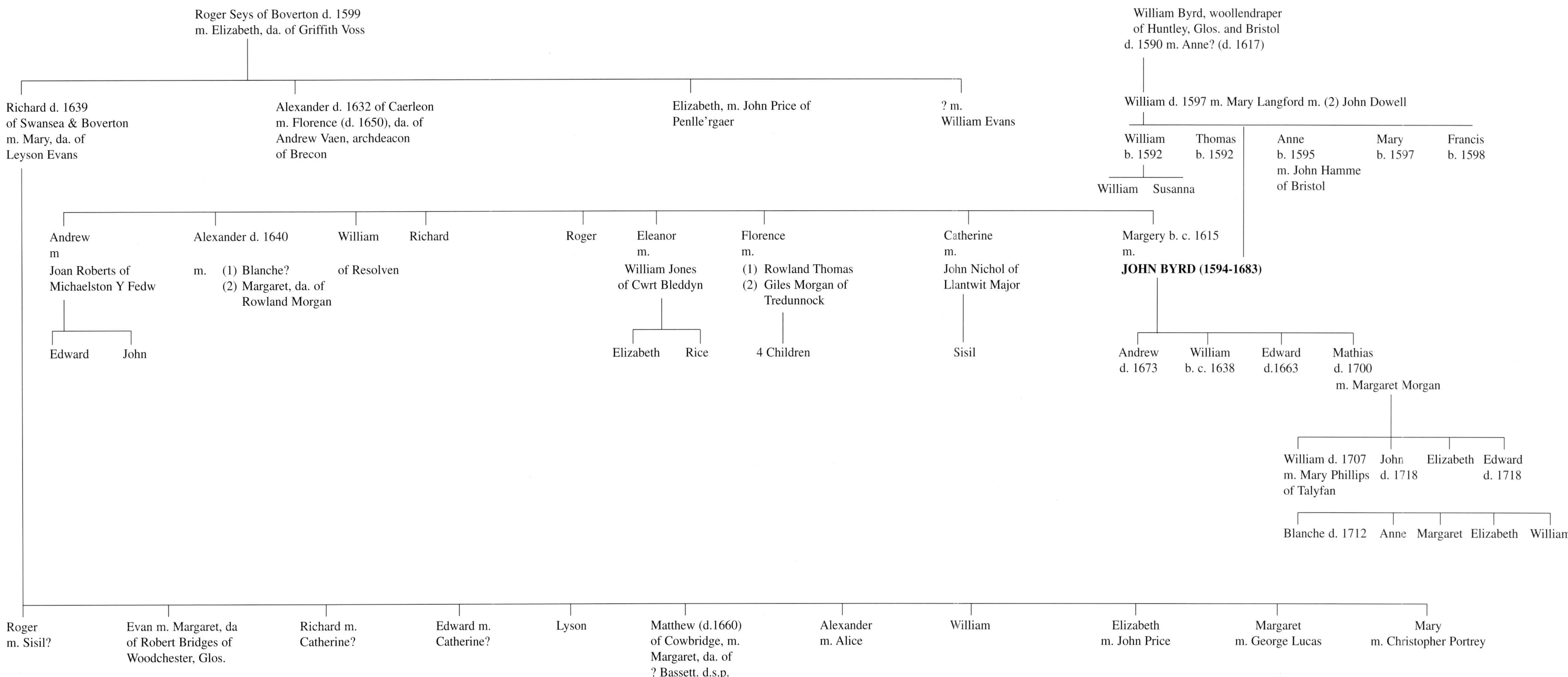

Sources: *Limbus Patrum;* Bradney; PRO PROB 11; NLW Llandaff wills; GRO Fonmon MSS; Byrd Letter-book; BRO FCP/St W/R 1(a)1, 1(a)3; GwRO MAN/b15/0007; PRO C2/Chas I/B136/63.

131, 133
differing allegiances of 234
oath to be taken by 186
postage and riding charges 81, 86
reorganisation 210, 234
searcher xxii, xxiv, xxv, xxvi, xxxix, xl, 49, 56, 66, 68, 71, 89, 94, 100, 120, 310
sale of office 311
surveyor xxv, 49, 68, 89, 101, 129
threats to posts 190, 210
threats to JB's post 262, 263, 264, 278, 280, 284, 291, 296
waiter xxv, 66, 68, 81, 100, 120, 128, 254
recommendations for posts in 164, 254
seizures xxxix, 66, 67, 68, 71, 72, 73, 75, 79, 80, 82, 84, 91, 99, 124, 131, 136, 143, 146, 147, 151, 158, 171, 183, 196, 200
custom houses
Bristol xvii
officers of xxii, xxiii, xxix, xxxv, 124, 131, 140, 146, 158, 161, 200, 202, 203, 210, 215, 217, 218, 220, 221, 224, 227, 229, 230, 241, 253, 353
Cardiff xl, 67, 81, 164
rent on 234
London xiii, xvii, xviii, xxviii, xxxix, 246
accountant-general 111, 112, 131, 255, 305, 321
caretaker of 117
officials xviii, xix, xxiv, xxxi, 4, 5, 10, 14, 15, 16, 21, 23, 25, 42, 43, 55, 58, 63, 64, 67, 69, 79, 106, 116, 121, 122, 132, 134, 147, 148, 150, 185, 197, 202, 234, 242, 255, 259, 282, 305, 317
surveyor-general 305, 308
Milford 164
Swansea xxvi, 81
debts,
collected by JB xxxv, 36
owed by JB 389, 404
owed to JB 149, 178, 246, 280, 304
see loan
Doctors' Commons 138
'doubling' on contributions to Parliament xxxiv, 173, 205

duties xvii, xx
    Algier (redemption of captives) xx, 16, 17, 21, 24, 27, 28, 37, 135, 136, 186, 197, 202
    dangers of transporting 17, 21, 24
    disputes over 154
    local xxiii, xxiv
    on butter 120, 233
    on calfskins 120
    on coal xvii, xx, xxviii, 106, 111, 121, 169, 171, 172, 175, 176, 182, 186, 197, 202, 203, 285
    on currants xvii
    on hides 233
    on horses xxxii, 136, 143, 144
    on oats 101, 102, 103
    on tallow 233
    on tobacco xvii, 25, 142
    on wine xvii
    on wool 233
    petty customs 111
    rebate of 15 per cent 135, 139
    total sums collected 105, 108, 114, 124, 139, 153, 184, 189, 197, 202, 203, 211, 213, 215, 221, 227, 228
    tunnage and poundage xx, 28, 81
election, Monmouthshire, 1667 xlii
exchequer xvii, xxii, 75, 283, 284, 286
    commissioners 73, 165, 166, 187, 200
excise xxviii, xxxiv, 10, 35, 60, 68, 72, 86, 90, 96
    commissioners 10
    farming 138, 141
    sub-commissioners 68, 90, 130, 138, 208
emigration, to Ireland 85
Engagement, subscriptions to 89, 94
exports, restrictions on 40
Fire, Great 350, 351
fraud, by merchants xxviii, xxxv, 76, 100, 124
garrisons xxx, xxxiii
gifts by JB xxxi
    cheese 209

dolphin 209
pies xxxi, 259, 310, 312
grand jury, Monmouth 241
heriot, disputed 30
horse theft, suspected 123
husbandry
apple trees xvi, xxxi, 370, 371, 372, 375
horse xxxi, 289, 359, 363, 365
indigent officers, relief of 293, 300, 306
kinship xxxvii
land holdings by JB xiii - xv
leases on property by JB xiv, 325, 390, 391, 395, 398, 401, 402, 403, 444, 447
legal cases 7, 8, 13, 30, 33, 36, 51, 52
involving customs 63, 68, 73, 79, 80, 82, 84, 107, 161, 186
involving JB's personal property 74, 75, 80, 113, 283, 285, 409, 411, 413, 422, 444
involving JB as intermediary or adviser 123, 265, 270, 314, 320, 343, 347, 348, 356, 358, 359, 360, 363, 364, 376, 392, 414, 429, 432, 434, 435, 436, 437, 440, 445
loan, JB declines to make 433, 435
magistrate 123
manslaughter and assault, JB's son 307, 315
merchants xix, 35, 53, 64, 65, 75, 115, 119
compounding by xxiv, xxviii, 131, 136, 146, 151, 158, 165, 183
foreign 111
haberdasher 280, 301, 355
mercer 335
woollen-draper 313
Monmouthshire, politics in xxxviii - xliii
navigation xxi
navy, commissioners of xxv, 366, 367
conditions in 349, 350, 352, 367, 373, 402
engagement of, at sea 428
JB's pleasure in its successes and best wishes for 324, 339, 379, 388, 425
Navy Office 280
oaths, to be taken by officials 271, 273
Parliament 350
patronage

customs 1, 2
piracy 25, 49, 124
plunder 8, 12, 74
poor, the 68, 182, 187, 196, 446
Popish Plot xliii
poverty of Monmouthshire tenantry 361
prison, Fleet, London 283
prize, ships as 91, 92, 95, 228, 233
rebellion, 1648, in South Wales 11
in the Scilly Isles 25
reparations, for war plundering 75
royalists, compounding by 204, 205
schooling, of JB's sons 145, 167, 257
security, matters of 38, 39, 40, 49, 56
sheriff, office of, JB threatened with xxxiv, xli, 307
JB's anxieties concerning xxxiv, xli, 344, 365, 410
ships and boats
barques xxi
barque of Bideford 128
bound for England 68
bound for Portugal and Spain 216
frigate, pirate 124
from Caribbean 90
investment in, JB's advice on 406
named,
Abraham, of Bristol, 68
Alice, of Bristol 65, 66
Cambridge 352, 354, 368
Charles 56, 57
Eagle, of Limerick xxi, xxx, xxxiii, 91, 228, 233
Elizabeth, of Barnstaple 124
Elizabeth and Anne, of Bristol 68
Elizabeth, of Upton-on-Severn 137
Endeavour, of South Bury 186, 223
Gift, of Caerleon 252
Great Thomas xxi
Henrietta 339, 341, 352
Hunter 56, 57

James, of Swansea 186
Long Thomas xxi
Mary, of Neath 124
Marygold 76
Michael, of Le Croisic 238
New Thomas, of Aberthaw 131
North Star, of Dort 128
Princess 280
Reason 56, 57
Reformation, of Swansea 216
Repulse, of Swansea 186
St. David 380
Thomas, of Aberthaw 71
Thomas and William, of Aberthaw 85
Transporter 388, 393
Trinity, of Le Croisic 279
Truelove, of Kinsale 186
of Brittany 53
of France 62, 275, 279
of Sully/Barry 67
trow, of Tewkesbury 65, 66, 252
trows xxi
Skinners' Hall, custodians of 209
smuggling 67, 68, 72
soldiers 81
taxes 110
tithe 289
trade 10, 20, 62, 66, 387
Cardiff ports, described xxvi - xxviii, 81, 85, 86, 235, 244
foreign xxvi, 62, 66, 68, 81
increase of 78
tradespeople
carpenter 115
carriers 128, 209, 258, 259, 309, 310, 322, 330, 418, 423
innkeeper 309, 315, 380, 388, 393, 402, 403, 406, 407
silk weaver 387
tailor 363, 415
waggoner 385

watchmaker 267
vicar, Caerleon 298
will, terms of and probate of xiv, xvi, xxxii, 159, 180, 185, 195
copy of a 268